SARTRE'S
POLITICAL
THEORY

Studies in Continental Thought
John Sallis, general editor

SARTRE'S POLITICAL THEORY

WILLIAM L. MCBRIDE

INDIANA UNIVERSITY PRESS

Bloomington and Indianapolis

The paper used in this publication meets the minimum requirements of American
National Standard for Information Sciences—Permanence of Paper for Printed
Library Materials, ANSI Z39.48-1984.

Manufactured in the United States of America

Library of Congress Cataloging-in-Publication Data

McBride, William Leon.
   Sartre's political theory / William L. McBride.
      p.   cm. — (Studies in continental thought)
   Includes bibliographical references and index.
   ISBN 0-253-33621-X (alk. paper). — ISBN 0-253-20655-3 (pbk.)
    1. Sartre, Jean Paul, 1905– —Political and social views.
  I. Title. II. Series.
JC261.S372M35 1991
320'.01—dc20   90-25291

1 2 3 4 5 95 94 93 92 91

CONTENTS

SARTRE'S
POLITICAL
THEORY

Introduction

Jean-Paul Sartre died in 1980 in his seventy-fifth year, having spent the better part of the last decade of his life in a painfully debilitated condition, unable to read and often afflicted by other maladies typical of the less fortunate aged.[1] Since then, there has been a revival of interest in him, fueled in part by the posthumous publication of a number of Sartrean manuscripts, as well as by the appearance of the first comprehensive Sartre biography[2] and of a number of other significant studies of aspects of his life, of his thought, or of both considered together; this book itself will, I hope, be a contribution to that revival. As one would anticipate under such circumstances, new images of Sartre have begun to emerge and proliferate.

What constitutes, in a sense, the first "posthumous publication" actually appeared in print approximately one month before Sartre's death, a juxtaposition in time that should probably not be considered purely coincidental. It consists of edited interviews of Sartre conducted by the last of a series of personal secretaries whom he employed, Benny Lévy, whose relationship with the aging and dependent writer had clearly become much closer than the title of "secretary" normally implies. Sartre had frequently spoken with others about his venture with Lévy, which he envisaged as an uniquely dialogic reexamination of fundamental questions about politics and ethics, to be entitled *Pouvoir et Liberté*.[3] The printed fragments, as they should properly be labeled, were first presented to the public in three March issues of *Le Nouvel Observateur*,[4] a newspaper that had frequently carried interviews with and stories about Sartre in the past, under the general title, "L'Espoir maintenant" (Hope, now). Among the features that many found astonishing about these brief pages of transcribed dialogue were the uncustomary tone of intimacy in which Sartre and his much younger secretary addressed one another; Sartre's apparent retreat from positions or at least emphases with which he had been identified in the past, such as the notion of conflict as fundamental to human relations in the world as we have known it up to now; his offhand dismissal of his earlier existentialist concentration on the phenomenon of dread or anguish as having been a useful because then-popular conceptual vehicle but not something that he himself had experienced in a serious way; and his great professed interest in aspects of the Jewish religion, which was then becoming, as it has since become to an even greater extent, the principal focus of Lévy's life.

The range of actual and possible reactions to this unusual publication is wide. At one extreme, one can see in the interviews the basis for an entirely new Sartrean ethical, social, and political philosophy, supplanting many of the ideas that dominated both his literary and his philosophical works

1

throughout his previous life, and achieving this in a positive, constructive way. Even Benny Lévy himself, however enthusiastic he may have been about his dialogues with Sartre, appears not to subscribe to such an extreme view, as his subsequent collation of Sartrean texts from various periods, *Le Nom de l'homme*, makes clear;[5] but there certainly exist serious Sartre scholars who, given their own intellectual agendas, would like to believe that in his last years he had begun to pay more heed to one or more of the cardinal virtues and less attention to the negative aspects of existence. At the other extreme, one can simply dismiss these texts as painful illustrations of the manipulation of an old man by someone in whom he had been forced to trust.[6] It is an open secret that Simone de Beauvoir, to whom, over many years, Sartre had offered his writings for prepublication criticism and correction, as she had hers to him, was strongly opposed to publication of the Sartre-Lévy dialogue.[7] Or one can try simply to bypass much of the controversy generated by this publication by taking the position, as I shall throughout most of this book, that remarks attributed to Sartre in interviews should on the whole not be accorded as much importance, in understanding his thought, as written texts (even posthumously published ones, assuming no serious editorial distortions), on the ground that he at least had greater opportunity, even if he did not always avail himself of it, to correct the latter.

But this position of mine is more of a procedural guideline than a proposition, the validity of which could be demonstrated—if indeed it would even make sense to speak in this way. Therefore, the controversy over the meaning and importance of Sartre's "last words," as contained in this interview, cannot be laid to rest, even though their potential significance for a study of his political thought in particular is considerable. I make this admission with a view to establishing a pattern for my subsequent interpretations: I cannot claim to be furnishing a "definitive" interpretation of Sartre's political thought, not because of a lack of competence on my part, but because of obstacles intrinsic to Sartre interpretation. On the one hand, interpreters may reasonably disagree, as they do in the rather crucial case of the dialogue with Lévy, over the relative importance to be attributed to interviews (or perhaps to *certain* interviews) as opposed to letters, to letters as opposed to published occasional essays, to the latter as opposed to more systematic philosophical and/or literary treatises, and among such treatises to those that were published during Sartre's lifetime as opposed to those that have been or still will be published posthumously. On the other hand, Sartre himself would no doubt have been amused at the very idea of trying to produce a definitive version of any aspect of his thought, for his often highly assertive style of expressing his views went hand in hand with the clear realization on his part that no philosophical formulation, however systematic and comprehensive it may appear to be, ever merits being taken as final.

Texts written and actions taken at the most varied periods of Sartre's life tend to confirm this observation. Writing to Simone de Beauvoir from his military post at the end of 1939, he alludes to the notebooks that he has been composing and that he intends to take to her when he goes to Paris on leave: "You will have four of them at once when I arrive in Paris and a completely new theory concerning *nothingness*. Another concerning *violence*. Another concerning *bad faith*."[8] Note that he is proud of his theories, all of which will of course become key notions in *Being and Nothingness*, but he does not pretend that they are something more than that, namely, worthwhile theories. In the posthumously-published *Cahiers pour une morale*, written during 1947–48, he at one point says the following about the two nineteenth-century philosophies that occupy his attention throughout large parts of that unfinished work: "It is desirable that History have its crisis, like physics, and detach itself from the Hegelian and Marxist absolute."[9] It is this notion of an absolute end of history and the philosophical outlook that points to such an absolute end, attributed by Sartre in different ways to Hegel and to Marx (whether accurately or inaccurately is not my present concern), that he here rejects in favor of a philosophical openness and tentativeness. He continued to reject such absolutist claims even during the period when he felt the greatest affinity with Marxism, the 1950s and 1960s.[10] And it was during those same years (in 1963, to be exact) that his very carefully crafted autobiographical fragment, *Les Mots (The Words)*, was published, in which he concludes his presentation by insisting forcefully on the extent of changes that he has undergone in his intellectual outlook over time.[11] Finally, in his 1974 conversations with de Beauvoir, he reflects calmly, along with her, on the relative merits of his various philosophical pieces and says that he feels little solidarity with his past and hence a readiness to admit "misdeeds or mistakes, since they were committed by someone else."[12]

This strikes me as a rather authentic expression of Sartre's attitude toward all his work, at once serious, ironic, and detached. It serves as a vivid contrast to the intense polemics that have often been waged about it by commentators. And it helps to set the tone of the present study.

The label that I have chosen to focus the object of this study is Sartre's political theory, or political philosophy, or political thought; for present purposes I am not distinguishing among these terms. In fact I could with equal accuracy have denominated this a study in Sartre's "social theory" or "social and political theory," terms for which I myself have a preference. But "political theory" is the older and still more familiar expression, and one of my purposes in examining these aspects of Sartre's thought here is to demonstrate some of the many ways in which, in dealing as he does with questions concerning the nature of society and history in an often unfamiliar, sometimes even eccentric, vocabulary, Sartre is nevertheless reconsidering some of the issues that have dominated Western philosophical thought about political life from the pre-Socratics and Plato onward.

It should be emphasized that Sartre himself seldom, if ever, employs the expressions, "théorie politique" or "philosophie politique," much less "philosophie sociale," in referring to what he is doing. How does he characterize it? The answer is not obvious or univocal. If we regard, as I think we must, the *Critique of Dialectical Reason* as the single most central work for understanding his political theory, we find him frequently referring to what he is doing there in the words of the title itself, and we find him subtitling Volume 1, the only completed volume of the work, with the rather bland and unevocative expression, "Theory of Practical Ensembles." (The subtitle given to the incomplete Volume 2 is "The Intelligibility of History.") We also find him saying that the single central question of *Search for a Method*, the long, separate essay that serves as a preface to the *Critique*, is whether "we have today the means to constitute a structural, historical anthropology,"[13] and we later see him characterizing his lengthy *The Family Idiot* as an exemplification of the method in question.[14] ("Anthropology" is to be understood in the broad European sense of a theory/science of the human species rather than as the narrower, more strictly empirical type of research that it has sometimes, though perhaps less often now, been considered in the United States.) At times he seems eager to distinguish all of his theoretical work in the social and political domains from the domain of *ontology*, "first philosophy," of which he always regarded his *Being and Nothingness* as an instance. Rather, he sometimes implies, the *Critique* and related works are to be considered *sociology*[15]—a quasi identification of sociology with anthropology that might provide food for thought to the members of American university academic departments in which these two disciplines coexist, often very uneasily!

In contrast with this babble of possible labels, however, the listing of which no doubt offers some valuable preliminary insights into Sartre's perceptions at various times of the nature of his theoretical inquiries, there is one garden-variety candidate for an all-encompassing descriptive term that was at one time most clearly favored by Sartre himself: ethics. As every student of Sartre's early philosophy knows, the closing sentence of *Being and Nothingness* contains an unequivocal promissory note for a work to come in ethics.[16] Sartre never published such a work *eo nomine* in his lifetime, although Simone de Beauvoir's well-known *An Ethics of Ambiguity*, heavily influenced by the terminology and thought-structure of *Being and Nothingness* and published in 1947, had always been thought to suggest some of the general lines that such a Sartrean work of ethics would have followed. With the posthumous publication of the *Cahiers pour une morale*, which was being composed at about the same time (and which includes one approving reference to de Beauvoir's discussion of the relationship between subjectivity and objectivity, between individual ambition and commitment to a militant group such as the Communist Party),[17] it has become obvious that Sartre really did try to work hard at fulfilling his promise. That he never did so during his lifetime, just as he failed to complete many other projects at various stages, is no doubt attributable to a variety of reasons, not the least of which is the one cited elsewhere by de Beauvoir herself, on the basis of some unpublished notes of Sartre's, to the effect that in 1949 he abandoned his ethics project because he became persuaded that ethics is an unacceptably idealistic combination of intellectual tricks that facilitate acquiescence in inferior living conditions created by material scarcity and technological backwardness[18]—ethics as ideology, in other words, in the Marxian sense of that term. The abandonment was never, in fact, total, as the existence of several as yet unpublished additional Sartrean manuscripts on ethics, written during the 1960s, attests.[19] The *word* "ethics" *(morale)* sees little use, it is true, in the *Critique* or in some other significant later writings of Sartre's, but a very good case can be made, as I shall show in more detail later on, for maintaining that those later works continue to capture the *spirit* of "ethics" as understood in the very broad sense that it has in the 500-odd pages of the *Cahiers pour une morale:* not only or even primarily ethics in the sense in which it is used in twentieth-century analytic philosophy (both normative ethics and meta-ethics), but also political and social theory, and also philosophy of history. As Sartre says in one especially aphoristic passage in the *Cahiers* (in a late section in which he sketches an outline for what he calls, interestingly enough in light of his later reluctance to call his political theory ontology, "an ontological ethics"): "History ↔ ethics. History implies ethics (without universal conversion, no meaning to evolution or to revolutions). Ethics implies History (no morality possible without systematic action on the situation)."[20]

Thus, it is appropriate to regard the range of topics that will occupy me in this study as including, or perhaps even as being identical with, the *ethics* of the later Sartre, beginning with the time at which his systematic thinking about the normative aspects of human existence began consciously to include a sociopolitical-historical dimension, a more complex range of human interactions than the almost exclusively dyadic ones that dominate the analyses of *Being and Nothingness*. The emphases of this later sociopolitical ethics are on the whole very different from those that have been characteristic of the large literature on Sartrean ethics based upon his earlier work, notably the phenomena of bad faith and authenticity, even though, as I shall show, one can discern a considerable continuity of concerns on Sartre's part. The apparent inconsistency involved in asserting that a study of the political theory of the later Sartre is also to be understood as a study of the later Sartre's ethical thought will begin to disappear if one recalls Aristotle's claim, in his *Nicomachean Ethics*, that ethics is really a subdivision of the more encompassing science of politics,[21] and if one further remembers the community-oriented view of norms and values that lies behind this claim. The resemblance between Aristotle and the later Sartre on this matter is at best a formal one, and the disanalogies are no doubt much greater and more important. Sartre abhors, for example, the naturalistic, essentialist conception of the universe that underlies the Aristotelian claim that the human being is by nature a political animal, and Aristotle expressed contempt for the study of history that Sartre regards as key to his political thought. But it is worthwhile to bear in mind from the outset of this study that Sartre's serious theoretical inquiries into politics owe a great deal, especially in their beginnings, to his reactions, both positive and negative, to the philosophies of Hegel and Marx, and that both of these thinkers (who are both directly indebted, as Sartre is not, in numerous ways to Aristotle) also treat ethical problems, when they treat them at all, within the framework of a broader political philosophy and philosophy of history. It is in light of such considerations that the later Sartre's insistence on solidarity with the oppressed of the world—"in willing freedom, we discover that it depends entirely on the freedom of others, and that the freedom of others depends on our own"[22]—enunciated as early as his famous 1945 lecture on existentialism and humanism, may begin to seem less puzzling and ad hoc to those whose principal image of him as ethical thinker remains that of an advocate of heroic individualism.

While, for those who like labels, there is therefore an important sense in which the present study can be considered a study of Sartre's ethics, I shall devote very little attention here to his early philosophical works, those written prior to the end of the Second World War, notably *Being and Nothingness*. The reason for this is not that Sartre was wont completely to abandon the conceptual frameworks of his earlier years, even though he sometimes speaks and writes as if that were the case; *authenticity*, for example, is a prominent theme in portions of the *Cahiers pour une morale*, and neither Sartre's depiction of Flaubert nor his analysis of the Second Empire social milieu in which Flaubert rose to fame can adequately be understood without some awareness of the meaning of *bad faith*. However, as both de Beauvoir in her biographical sequence and a study of Sartre's letters and notebooks and later reminiscences make abundantly clear, it was only during those war years that politics and history became serious objects of reflective thought on his part. In the next chapter, I shall document a few of the steps in this process of Sartrean self-revelation about the centrality of politics, broadly construed, to human existence. For the moment, let me simply ask those readers who are familiar with *Being and Nothingness*, that major work of Sartre's early thought that was first published right in the middle of the German Occupation period in France, 1943, to try to recall a single passage in it in which anything recognizably political serves as an object of sustained analysis; it cannot be done. That is why I shall not be focusing very much of my attention, proportionately speaking, on any single one of the works of Sartre's earlier years.

Moreover, in the present book, I shall not be devoting a great deal of attention, either, to Sartre's more literary works, even those of his postwar years, nor shall I attempt to be comprehensive in dealing with his works of political journalism that appeared first, for the most part, in the revue that he helped to establish and for many years edited, *Les Temps Modernes,* and later in his essay series, *Situations.* (*Some* of these essays, on the other hand, will be important for my purposes.) These judgments are perhaps more difficult to defend than that concerning his earlier works. For it is true that Sartre was "the complete writer," whose achievements in nearly all recognized genres, with the glaring exception of poetry, were at least noteworthy and, in the eyes of some, outstanding, and that readers have always found it relatively easy to find the same human being with approximately the same set of concerns and world-outlook in Sartrean works of very different genres, at least in those written within the same general time periods. Thus, his early novel, *Nausea,* surely *does* anticipate, in story form, many of the principal themes of *Being and Nothingness,* even though the publication of his letters and diaries has revealed more clearly than before the addition of important new influences, perhaps most notably Sartre's in-depth study of Heidegger, in the brief intervening years. Sartre, then, was apparently not given to strict compartmentalization between his theoretical writings and the rest;[23] should *we* subscribe to such a division?

On the other hand, Sartre himself did not fail to distinguish among his different types of literary production. From at least the time of his letters from his war post, in which he sometimes seems compelled to justify to himself and to others his allotment of a portion of his time to the reading and writing of philosophy, right up to the time of the conversations recorded in *Adieux,* in which he devotes considerable reflection to questions posed by de Beauvoir about the course of his writing career, he seems to have felt that different modes of literature call for different approaches and styles. Thus in *Adieux* he admits to writing philosophy in a less careful or crafted fashion than a novel, making no rough draft in the case of the former but seven or eight drafts for the latter. "A novel I write so that it will be read by someone. In philosophy I'm explaining to someone—I'm doing it with a pen but it might just as well be with my tongue, my mouth—I'm explaining my ideas just as they come to me today."[24] He clearly concurs with the usual identification of the *Critique* as a work of philosophy and *Saint Genet* as something of a cross between philosophy and literature.[25] And earlier in the same dialogue he straightforwardly admits that "The whole of *Situations* is made up of pieces written for the occasion," "committed" writing of the sort that "will no longer have any meaning in twenty years [sic] time."[26]

Thus, ample support from Sartre himself exists for my decision to concentrate the bulk of my attention in this book on more systematic works of political theory. It is to some degree arbitrary, but only to some degree. And, since publishers and readers alike harbor certain expectations about reasonable lengths for single works—expectations that Sartre was able to violate more easily than most writers, it is true—this decision will allow me to enter somewhat more deeply into interesting issues raised by these more systematic works, rather than feeling obliged to disperse my analyses across the entire enormous spectrum of Sartre's literary production, or even of his postwar literary production. My strategy is to concentrate, in chronological succession, on those works that I consider most significant in the evolution of his political theory, beginning with some scattered early passages; next moving to a few short essays of the immediate postwar period and the *Cahiers pour une morale;* then devoting three integrated chapters primarily to work of the 1950s that culminated in the completed first volume and the incomplete second volume of the *Critique of Dialectical Reason* (including the semiautonomous essay *Search for a Method*); and finally discussing texts from Sartre's last twenty years of life, including, notably, what is known about his mostly unedited writings on ethics from the 1960s, relevant portions of *The Family Idiot,* and the dialogue with Lévy.

What are the central themes that the reader may expect to see emerging from this study? Sometimes the most obvious answer to a question of this sort is the wisest. At the time of his return from a German prisoner-of-war camp during the Occupation period, Sartre organized a short-lived Resistance group, devoted primarily to writing activities, that called itself "Socialism and Freedom." These twin notions, both subject to the most diverse interpretations in our world society, are probably the two most important keys to the entire range of Sartre's political thought. If one of the two has a lexical priority, it is freedom.

Sartre's intuition of human freedom must at all times be understood as two-pronged: freedom as a fundamental fact about the human condition, and freedom as an often-suppressed, always-threatened, asymptotic objective of human activity. The story of Sartre's evolution as a social and political theorist is one of an increasing awareness, over the years, of the immense difficulties, often bordering on near impossibility, faced by individuals and then by groups in attempting to exercise freedom: freely to choose projects and sometimes, if but momentarily, even to see those projects succeed. Thus, in his later years, he himself would express amazement at formulas about freedom to be found in his earlier work, formulas suggesting the heroic but ultimately unreal, idealist perception of freedom that is found in the Stoic slave Epictetus or in the English poet's assertion that "Stone walls do not a prison make . . ." In the unfinished second volume of the *Critique of Dialectical Reason,* Sartre constantly returns to the question of whether, given all the historical circumstances, at least the main lines, if not all the gruesome details, of the institutions and practices that we now call Stalinism were in some important senses inevitable, and his answer is, though qualified, affirmative. In *The Family Idiot,* most of the early pages are devoted to an excruciatingly detailed discussion of Flaubert's early life and juvenilia that owes a great deal to the kind of determinism through childhood experiences which we associate with the tradition of Freud—this despite the often very penetrating philosophical critique of Freudian presuppositions, from the perspective of a philosophy of freedom, that Sartre undertook in *Being and Nothingness*. Yet, throughout this entire evolution, Sartre never abandoned his bedrock conviction that free self-determination was both a human possibility and the only basis for a worthwhile human life.

What, then, of socialism? In mainstream American thought, it seems reasonably accurate to say, a widespread conviction has always existed that socialism and freedom are incompatible and that of course the latter is to be preferred. A quite similar conviction has always been held by the *"bien pensants"* members of the French middle classes, though it was not shared by a large segment of France's intellectual leadership throughout most of the life of the individual who was perceived as one of its supreme leaders in the mid-twentieth century, Sartre himself. Even in France, however, as a result of such particularly traumatic events as the massacres carried out in the name of "socialism" in Cambodia and the invasion of Afghanistan by the "Union of Soviet Socialist Republics," there has been a marked, though by no means total, shift in intellectual opinion since roughly the mid-1970s. In his 1974 dialogue with de Beauvoir, Sartre declares: "At twenty I was apolitical—which is perhaps only another kind of political attitude—and I am ending as a Socialist-Communist, envisaging a certain political destiny for mankind."[27] And, while there is abundant evidence—in the controversial interviews with Lévy, in his joint manifestation, together with his old schoolmate and later ideological antagonist, Raymond Aron, in support of French government aid to the Vietnam "boat people," etc.—that Sartre in his very last years shared in the malaise of the French Left, I know of no evidence of his having given up his commitment to socialism as an ideal. The question is, what does this "socialism" mean? (The linkage of this word with "Communism" in the de Beauvoir dialogue is misleading: it clearly is not a reference to the Communist Party, as some American readers might be inclined to think it was.) While, consistent both with his belief in the freedom of individuals and social groupings to construct their own future, and with his anti-essentialism, Sartre never attempts to spell out in detail any allegedly essential components of a socialist society, it is at least clear that for him such a society would be radically different from ours by virtue of being nonhierarchical, nonauthoritarian, and not dependent for its functioning on the economic, political, or even social dominance of some over others. Thus defined at a (necessarily) high level of abstraction, the Sartrean socialist ideal appears as an extension to the social dimension of his other key notion of freedom, something very akin to anarchism as understood in the literal sense; and so it is. The juxtaposition of this frequently unstated, extremely radical ideal with analyses of actually existing societies of the relatively recent past (e.g., capitalist France of the Second Empire period, or Communist Russia under Stalin) is what gives Sartre's texts of political theory both their peculiar sense of directedness, of *engagement*, and many of their peculiar problems and tensions.

To speak of a socialist society immediately implies, of course, some notion of community, of a togetherness of human beings having some objective or objectives in common; and yet so radical was the individualism, the nontogetherness, of Sartre's early ontology in *Being and Nothingness* that he there insists throughout his treatment of "being-for-others," the category under which relationships between individuals are introduced almost halfway through this long book, that the very existence of other human beings is a contingent fact. This observation points to the most basic tension in Sartre's political theory, that between individuals and collectivities, a recurrent theme throughout the history of Western political thought. As Ronald Aronson brings out very well in the introduction to his recent study of the second volume of Sartre's *Critique*, much of Sartre's later work in this area can be viewed as a response to the charge of his distinguished sometime colleague, Maurice Merleau-Ponty, in his book, *The Adventures of the Dialectic*, to the effect that Sartre's philosophy was incapable of dealing with social "mediations," groupings intermediate between the individual and the social totality, however the latter may be defined.[28]

The problem of the individual and the collective is for Sartre, as for all of us, at once not only normative but also, and perhaps even more fundamentally, descriptive; whether one's political ideal is a Kropotkinian anarchism of "mutual aid," a Lockean proto-capitalist utopia of acquisitive property-owners sheltered from illegal depredations by a minimal government and some minimal rules, an organic Platonic Republic, or whatever, one is compelled, if one wishes to try to be rational, to root this ideal in a true account of the actual and/or possible natures of human beings and of their actual and/or possible interrelationships. Sartre, who had the courage never to yield to the ever-popular temptation of simply stipulating certain salient behaviors as constituting the core of an allegedly fixed trans-temporal human nature, realized very early in the politically-conscious phase of his career that he had to approach the question of how individuals and collectives are interrelated (or, to put the same thought in different words, of what human collectivities *are*) from a *historical* point of view. The underlying normative and descriptive concerns of Sartre's entire political theory can then be captured together in the following sort of question: why have human beings throughout their history continued to create and recreate, albeit in novel forms, certain types of social configurations, in particular alienating, hierarchical institutions (e.g., governments), the ultimate elimination of which would seem to be entailed by a consistent commitment to "socialism and freedom"?

The story of Sartre's principal publicly recorded efforts to answer roughly this question, some of them published during his lifetime and some posthumously, constitutes the contents of the succeeding chapters of this book. Many of the details of that story are highly "contingent"—to employ a notion that obsessed Sartre throughout much of his life—dependent in certain respects on readings that particularly impressed him (e.g., Mauss, Hegel, and Marx), in other respects on the great historical events

that dominated his lifetime (the World War, the Soviet-American confrontation, the political emancipation of the countries of the Third World, etc.), in
still other respects on facts about his specific national cultural upbringing
(e.g., the special, though not unique, importance attributed to Flaubert
among the literary figures to whom he was exposed at an early age).
Certain intellectual convictions that were not integral parts of the initial
Sartrean commitment to "socialism and freedom" became increasingly
important as his political theory evolved; among these were the view that
history can only be comprehended dialectically,[29] his perception that Marxism was the dominant philosophy of his era, and his belief that *scarcity* has
played a pivotal role in all of human social interaction up to now. Other
habits of thought that antedated Sartre's coming to political consciousness,
such as his frequent recourse to the phenomenological method, continued
to play important roles in the works that we shall be examining. But in
these convictions and habits there are discernible waxings and wanings; for
example, much of the detailed analysis in *The Family Idiot*, as contrasted
with the *Critique of Dialectical Reason*, is not self-consciously dialectical, and
in his later years Sartre quite deliberately distanced himself from the close
identification with (a variety of) Marxism to which he had firmly committed
himself at the time (1956–57) of writing *Search for a Method*.[30] I wish to urge
that Sartre's fundamental allegiance to "Socialism and Freedom," on the
other hand, perdured.

Finally, what is it about Sartre's political theory, even if it is conceded
that the recent publication of a great deal of new material by and about him
might well eventuate in new interpretations, that makes it worth the
reader's and the writer's efforts to explore? Given both the change in
political climate in France to which I have already alluded and the succession of philosophical and, some critics would say, of postphilosophical
movements that have crossed the European intellectual stage since Sartre's
heyday—structuralism, poststructuralism, post-Marxism, postmodernism—might one not reasonably regard an interest in Sartre's thought,
despite the comparatively recent date of his death, as merely antiquarian?
In a book chapter of a decade ago that was devoted almost exclusively to
considering some of the main currents of the first volume of the *Critique of
Dialectical Reason*, I tried to make a case for Sartre's continued relevance as a
social thinker.[31] In this respect I do not feel that I was very successful,
however accurate or even illuminating my exposition of some of the ideas
may have been. It now occurs to me that my approach to Sartre there was
simply too impersonal, too distanced and purely contemplative, and that a
larger dose of the notion, so important to both Sartre and de Beauvoir
especially in their later years, of "lived experience," "*le vécu*," is appropriate
when one is dealing with questions of "relevance" or "importance."

So I shall write briefly here, by way of concluding this introduction,
about a few of the ways in which Sartre's thought, and especially his
political thought, has affected my own perception of the world over the

years, in the hope and expectation that the narration of some aspects of my experiences will kindle or strengthen readers' own awareness of Sartre's importance. I first became aware of the meaning of "existentialism," as something more specific than a general literary movement to which one occasionally saw vague allusions made in the newspapers, as a college student in the late 1950s. I was at the same time studying traditional Western philosophy, including, as a minor specialization, political theory. The name of Sartre was brought to my attention as a serious but, through his novels, plays, and short stories, accessible philosopher—more systematic than Camus, more accessible than Heidegger—who ranked as one of the leading existentialist challengers of two overwhelming historical realities, one intellectual, the other in the everyday world, that dominated my life as a student: on the one hand, the confident self-assurance, as I read it, of all the forms of mainstream *"philosophia perennis"* from Plato and Aristotle through (at least) Kant, and on the other the smug complacency of the modern middle-class lifestyle that had returned to reign with vengeance in the West, and particularly in the United States, despite the recent cataclysms of Depression, Holocaust, World War II, and the invention of the atom and hydrogen bombs. I read *Nausea* and at least parts (I forget how much) of *Being and Nothingness,* and I found myself in youthful agreement with many of the main lines of Sartre's challenge. In particular, his existentialist message that it was up to us to create values in a universe that had no meaning *en soi* made considerable sense to me then, as it still does today.

What was lacking in me when I graduated from college, however, was a concrete political awareness. This seems at first blush very paradoxical: I had read most of the major works of Western political theory, I had a reasonably good grasp of the main events of our history right up to my own time, and I had attended school in Washington, D.C., the capital of what it pleased those in power there, a number of whom I had the opportunity to see and even, in some instances, to meet, to call "the Free World." Nevertheless, my perceptions of political realities remained above all at the level of institutions and individuals; and the literature of existentialism, including that of Sartre, with which we were familiar then did little or nothing to alter or supplement those perceptions. (The infamous line in *Being and Nothingness,* "Thus it amounts to the same thing whether one gets drunk alone or is a leader of nations,"[32] exemplifies this point.) There was a large time warp: I and most of my classmates who might have cared were only vaguely aware then of the political turn that Sartre's thought had taken more than a dozen years earlier.

It was my enormous good fortune, however, to have the opportunity to spend one year after college studying philosophy in France; it was my first trip overseas. It was my project to study existentialism, and I managed to do so, though not without some difficulty. The official French university syllabus of the time was quite rigid and did not permit the teaching of much in the way of contemporary thought except "at the margins," as it would now be expressed: either in marginal institutions, such as, in my case, the Facultés Catholiques de Lille, or by "marginal" individuals, such as the wonderfully eccentric Jean Grenier, the one-time *lycée* teacher of Camus, who gave a thoroughly syllabus-free afternoon of courses once a week at the state university in the same city. Even then, however, even in France itself in the year 1959–60, it was not my academic studies, such as an excellent but very traditional course on Rousseau, that evoked any deeper awareness of sociopolitical realities on my part; rather, it was the experience of traveling to new places and particularly of living in a still very old-fashioned French industrial city, known equally for its quintessentially bourgeois atmosphere (neither deeply rooted, as are many parts of provincial France, in premodern, feudal traditions, not yet much affected at that time by most of the salient new features of postwar capitalism) *and* as the birthplace of the *"Internationale."* Most of those who attended the university were themselves from the bourgeoisie and studiedly apolitical, but I nevertheless managed somehow to become aware of a world in which "politics" referred to something more than just Presidents and Congresses (or Assemblées), on the one hand, and millions of individual citizens on the other—a world that had always been there, in my own United States as much, in its way, as in France, but that I had not previously *seen*. It was a world of genuine dominance, exercised at base by economic means though by way of political outlets, and subordination, a world in which the Marxist word "proletariat" referred to an existing concrete reality and not just an abstraction borrowed from the literature of Ancient Rome. I actually saw many thousands of proletarians and their sympathizers massed together, in fact, on the occasion of a state visit to Lille by the First Secretary of the Soviet Communist Party of the time, Nikita Khrushchev.

I mention these details because I believe that they point to some remote but surprising similarities, quite unexpected in someone born more than a generation later and in a completely different country, between my own lived experience and Sartre's. In *Search for a Method*, in his autobiographical *The Words*, and in many other writings and interviews, he has recounted the cocoon-like world, intellectually speaking, in which he was raised, went to school (where Marx and the entire Marxist tradition were never treated as intellectually respectable), and lived until a number of experiences around the outbreak of the Second World War awakened him to the political dimension of reality. (It is true that his closest college friend at the Ecole Normale Supérieure, Paul Nizan, had made an early commitment to the Communist Party and had tried to convince Sartre to follow suit; but it is also obvious, particularly from Sartre's portrayal of the dedicated Communist Party militant, Brunet, in his trilogy, *The Roads of Freedom*, that that very commitment brought about a considerable distancing in their friendship. Nizan himself, of course, was killed by the Nazis, and the news of this had a considerable effect on Sartre.)[33] Thus, when I began to become familiar, later on, with the autobiographical side of Sartre's work I found much with which I could identify despite all the enormous differences; above all, I could understand how, without being at all ignorant of political affairs, an intelligent and well-intentioned young bourgeois intellectual could nevertheless live for years with only the most superficial political consciousness. At any rate, soon after I returned to the United States in fall 1960 to begin my more formal graduate work in philosophy and to reflect upon my newly-acquired awarenesses, I was delighted to learn that, earlier in that same year (April), Sartre had published a long, systematic work of political theory, the *Critique of Dialectical Reason*. I anticipated that it would speak to some of my new concerns in a way in which neither the classical political philosophers nor the best of the British and British-influenced contemporary thinkers, worried as they still were then about the Weldonian question of whether the language of political theory was meaningful and consequently whether political theory still truly existed,[34] could. I began reading the *Critique* as soon as I could obtain a copy, and I was not disappointed.

Since a consideration of the *Critique* will occupy a substantial part of this book, I shall not dwell here on either its strong points or its faults. I had never found myself in total agreement with Sartre's texts (or with any other writer's, for that matter), and I was well aware of his tendency to push concepts and ideas to their absolute limits and hence to sin by analytic excess; upon my first reading, therefore, I immediately discounted the most literal interpretation of Sartre's initial statements in the prefatory essay, *Question de méthode*, about Marxism as the sole and dominant philosophy of our epoch. But at the same time I understood the sense in which, as my own recent experience had begun to teach me, this was correct: Marxism in the broadest understanding of the word had opened up, a century before, certain thitherto unarticulated perspectives on reality, and those perspectives, however distorted they had been by the "official" or "orthodox" Marxists and all the political and intellectual apparatus surrounding them, remained indispensable for understanding the world of the mid-twentieth century. Yet the *Critique* proper, written at a much higher level of abstraction than *Search for a Method* while tacitly remaining within its announced presuppositions, brought fascinating new perspectives to bear on this "Marxist," if one chose to call it that, worldview itself. I saw the book as an intellectual breakthrough, of a sort that occurs rarely in a lifetime. It seemed to me to offer major explanatory clues for understanding most or all of the major sociopolitical phenomena of our times: our alienation amid unprecedented affluence, the ascendancy of the capitalist system, the failures of "Marxist-Leninist" state socialism, the occurrence of sporadic and generally unsuccessful radical revolts, local and global racism, and so on. (It is of very little help, I came to realize, for accounting for the phenomenon of sexism; Sartre seemed to feel, not to his great credit, that he could leave that issue for the most part to his colleague, Simone de

Beauvoir.) By comparison, the "breakthrough" work of the Anglo-American tradition with which I eventually decided to contrast the *Critique* in my doctoral dissertation, H. L. A. Hart's *The Concept of Law*, is quite narrow in scope; that of a decade later in the latter tradition, John Rawls's *A Concept of Justice*, is, while less narrow, very blinkered by its unreflective acceptance of a number of assumptions from both liberal ideology and analytic philosophy; and the collective "breakthrough" effected by Jürgen Habermas in a whole series of writings seems to me much more derivative and eclectic and considerably less original.

Sartre's later and posthumously published works of political theory have added much to an understanding of his thought while not detracting from the opinion that I formed when I first read the *Critique*. It is true that the latter has not been the popular success—an unwonted expression to use about a work of philosophy!—that *Being and Nothingness* was, but that is not a persuasive consideration. In certain circles in France and elsewhere, there has been a sharp reaction against the intellectual hegemony enjoyed for so long by the philosophies of Hegel and Marx, the milieu within which the *Critique* itself was written, and hence also against Sartre himself; and I have already reported Sartre's own insistence, before his death, on the observation that the era of Marxism is being left behind. While I do not fully share this latter conviction, I do agree with the implication of his saying this while still obviously regarding his *Critique* as a sound and worthwhile book, namely, that his political theory can be treated on its own, "without Marx or Hegel"—that is, without needing to appeal to either of them in order to make it meaningful. That is the tack that I intend to take.

The post-Sartrean philosophical landscape in France appears to me, despite the best efforts of a number of clever and even brilliant writers, devoid of truly outstanding figures of his stature, and some of the literary expressions of rejection of the recent past are simply shallow and intellectually regressive. But it is not of the current French philosophical "scene" that I intend to write here, except in passing as it may have relevance to Sartre, because the value of his political theory is in an important sense universal even though singular—a paradox that deeply interested Sartre himself in his study of Flaubert and generally throughout his career—and hence only contingently dependent on its place of provenance. This, at least, is one point on which I hope that this critical study will help to promote my readers' eventual agreement.

ONE

Beginnings

It would be magical thinking to suppose that Sartre became a political theorist as a result of any single event in his life, whether that event be a life experience in the more usual sense or an experience of the kind that is often of greatest significance for persons of intelligence, the reading of one or more books. Indeed, this very way of describing Sartre's evolution, the suggestion that at some point in time he reached a stage at which, for better or worse, we (his historical judges) can affix the label "political theorist" to him, is redolent of the tendencies toward reification and objectification of human beings against which he directed so much of his philosophical criticism. Such tendencies, as Sartre saw, are built into our linguistic habits, which lead us to speak of individual and even national "characters" or of an individual or human "nature," and are reinforced by theories—political, psychological, philosophical. But there is no "essence" of Sartre as a political theorist, only the gradually more self-conscious and intensive realization on his part of certain theoretical projects of understanding human society and history. In this chapter I intend to discuss a few of the moments in this gradual realization. Since I am here attempting to identify "beginnings" which cannot, as I have been insisting, be located in a single text or at a single point in time, the analyses of this chapter will be less focused and will contain more by way of narrative than will those of succeeding chapters.

By the time of Sartre's mobilization into the French Army at the beginning of September 1939, the event that issued in a period of intensive writing on his part that includes some of the earliest written evidence of a nascent Sartrean political consciousness, he was already 34 years old. It would be ironic if we were to repeat the mistake that Sartre himself, in *Search for a Method*, rightly attributes to the typical Marxist writer in the "orthodox" (official Communist Party) tradition, that of pretending that individuals had no childhoods, that they suddenly appear in politically interesting forms with their social and psychological conditionings ready-made.[1] The account of his own childhood that Sartre has left us in *The Words* (better translated into English, in order to capture Sartre's meaning more accurately, as *Words, tout court*) is of considerable interest from the standpoint of the evolution of Sartrean political theory, although it is

16

certainly not a theoretical work. Above all, mention must be made of Sartre's stress on the absence in his early life of a "superego," a typically (for that time and milieu) authoritarian father whose dictates and threats might well have led the little "Poulou" (his nickname) to adopt a more conventional bourgeois outlook premised on "law and order." Instead, Sartre's father had died soon after his birth, and the upbringing that he received at his mother's parents' home, where his cultured grandfather exerted a benign sway and encouraged this only child to immerse himself in literature to the point of considering it to be in effect more important than the world "outside," conduced both to a highly developed imagination and to a sense of personal autonomy and freedom tinged with narcissism. Although the period in question was, as we all now know, the eve of the First World War, and although the Alsatian origins of the Schweitzer family might presumably have led to a heightened awareness, within that household, of the historical possibilities of imminent political upheavals of the greatest magnitude, Sartre records little to nothing of the sort: *eudaimonia,* what passes for "happiness" in the objective sense of that word, seems on the whole to have reigned.

Sartre's presentation of the young Poulou raises serious questions. In sharp contrast to the comparative artlessness of his major theoretical writings, especially the *Critique, The Words* is a carefully studied work, painstakingly revised by Sartre in order to convey a more accurate impression of his attitude toward his childhood.[2] Nevertheless, its fundamental ambivalences are striking. At the personal level, there seems something peculiar about Sartre's admitting to having such intensely negative feelings about a childhood which left him, after all, with much encouragement and many advantages; it is obviously these very privileges, obtained at the price of living for many years afterward with deep-seated illusions about the world, that Sartre later came to question and to resent. At the level of more general theoretical implications, which are of greater concern for our present purposes, *The Words* seems to show brilliantly the extent to which the supposedly free career choice of our philosopher of freedom was conditioned by the circumstances of his early upbringing. Sartre would have insisted that the word "conditioned," or something similar, was the precise one in this context, rather than the obvious alternative, "determined"; in other words, there always remained a sense for him in which one's choices are free, so that it was in fact possible for the young Sartre to adopt a radically different career project from the one that he did, although even this possible alternative would also have had to be chosen on the basis of the objective conditions of the childhood that Sartre has described. This same profound ambivalence about freedom and the exigencies of historical circumstances will, as we shall see, color all of Sartre's later work, most of all the second volume of the *Critique of Dialectical Reason,* in its treatment of Stalinism.

Let us be as clear as it is possible to be, at this preliminary stage, about the implications of this Sartrean "ambivalence," as I have called it, concerning freedom and exigency. It is not an outright contradiction, and to note it is not necessarily to condemn Sartre's thinking, for in uncovering it he may simply be conveying a basic truth about the human world. However, noting it will no doubt lead us to abandon as untenable certain formulas concerning the absoluteness of human freedom that we find in writings of the earlier Sartre, especially in *Being and Nothingness*.

As for the *personal* ambivalence in *The Words* that I have also noted, such ambivalence is surely very characteristic of the "love-hate" attitudes of many reflective persons in modern societies, from adolescence onwards, toward their childhoods;[3] it is Sartre's merit to have attempted, with at least a certain measure of success, to offer an honest retrospective appraisal of his, one in which the weight of condemnation is directed primarily against himself, on the assumption that he could have chosen otherwise. To the extent to which *The Words* also contains an implicit condemnation of the responsible adults in Sartre's early life, persons whom our author has nevertheless depicted as more or less well-intentioned, the conventional moralistic reaction that this shows some kind of "ingratitude" on Sartre's part is inappropriate from two perspectives, both theoretical and practical. On the theoretical plane, it will become evident that Sartre's mature thought about ethics, inextricably bound, as I have already argued it to be, with his political theory, constitutes a sustained critique of the morality of good and bad intentions that is associated with traditional mainstream Western ethics, as exemplified in Kant's notion of the Good Will. On the practical plane, the adult Sartre's lifelong concern for the surviving member of the family circle of his childhood, his mother (who died only eleven years before him), is a remarkable if seldom-mentioned feature of Sartre's way of "being-in-the-world," one that cannot be overlooked if we follow seriously and consistently Sartre's message in *The Words*, in the volumes on Flaubert, and elsewhere, that it is ultimately impossible to disjoin the personal from the political.[4]

Alongside (rather than, I would argue, in opposition to) the frankness and commitment to lucidity and authenticity in human relations that were hallmarks of Sartre's entire career, there were aspects of his life about which he maintained a considerable reserve. His relationship with his mother was one salient such aspect. (His love of music, about which he never wrote at length, was another;[5] indeed, it was closely connected with his relationship with his mother, in that the two of them often played piano duets together over a number of decades.) There are significant though passing references to this in Annie Cohen-Solal's recent biography,[6] and there is abundant documentation of it in the *Lettres au Castor*, many of which were written while Sartre was vacationing with his mother and stepfather,[7] others of which concern arrangements to be made—for example, on Sartre's military leaves—so as to permit him to spend some time with the Mancys as well as with de Beauvoir and other contemporaries. Mention of Sartre's stepfather,

Joseph Mancy, reveals another aspect of his life concerning which he published virtually nothing—the period discussed in *The Words* is only Sartre's early childhood, and he decided not to write any autobiographical sequels—but which clearly influenced him profoundly. This is so not only because of the strong hostility—often quite open, one gathers, during the early years, apparently more latent (to judge from references in Sartre's letters) but still very real thereafter—that existed between Sartre and this engineer with whom he had virtually nothing in common except the fact of the man's having married his mother, but also because of the relocation to the provincial city of La Rochelle that the marriage forced on Sartre just at the outset of his adolescence. He had been living in Paris (to which his grandparents had moved when he was six) and attending school there, but from the crucial ages of twelve to fifteen, when he returned to Paris as a boarding student, he lived a very unpleasant existence both at home and at school.

It is Sartre himself who, in his posthumously published conversation with de Beauvoir, directs our attention to a troubling question of the sort that must be raised by anyone who takes seriously the notion that theory, especially any theory about human social relations, will inevitably be rooted somehow in the theorist's lived experience, however aware or unaware of this he or she may be. He is describing his years at La Rochelle: the boys of his school there identified themselves as respectable young secular French bourgeois, whose two sets of enemies were the boys at the Catholic school, on the one hand, and "the hooligans," workingclass boys who often attended no school at all, on the other. There was constant fighting especially with the latter group, and at the same time Sartre felt himself to be the object of much antagonism and nearly friendless among his own schoolmates (whereas this was not the case during his school years at Paris either before or after). De Beauvoir then asks him: "And did that have an influence on your later development?" He replies: "I think so. In the first place it seems to me that I've never forgotten the violence I learned there. It's in that light that I've seen people's relations with one another." Even the majority of his friendships from that time onward, he continues, real though they were, were always tinged with a suspicion of violence, seen as "imperative in the relations between men."[8] The troubling question that this snatch of dialogue raises, of course, is whether this frank admission on Sartre's part does not in fact constitute a concession to his critics on an absolutely central point of Sartrean social and political theory: his assertion, as a theorist, that human relations are fundamentally characterized by conflict. Critics have repeatedly maintained that this assertion is idiosyncratic and one-sided; has not Sartre himself now acknowledged such a bias?

The claim that conflict is fundamental to human relations, made very explicitly by Sartre in *Being and Nothingness*,[9] will need to be reconsidered later, when we examine Volume One of the *Critique of Dialectical Reason*. In the latter work, as we shall see, there is an important modification in Sartre's thought on the subject, in that he there asserts that conflict is rooted in scarcity, and hence is eliminable to the extent to which scarcity may be eliminable. Still later, certain remarks made in Sartre's famous final interview with Lévy will raise further questions about Sartre's ultimate views about conflict. At present, a few clarifications concerning Sartre's recourse to the lived experience of violence as a methodological basis for his political theory are in order. Had Sartre somehow not gone through the awakening to violence that was his adolescent experience in La Rochelle, or through any similar experience, even vicariously—if this is imaginable for anyone in the twentieth century!—then indeed he would probably have paid little or no attention to conflict and violence in his theoretical writings. But then these writings could only have been impoverished, relative to what they are, because they would be lacking a crucial phenomenon in social life that is confirmed by the experiences of so many of the rest of us. In other words, between Sartre, who insists on the pervasiveness of violence, sometimes overt, at other times only latent, in our social world pervaded by scarcity, and those theorists who wish to minimize the significance of violence as an element in political theory, there is an asymmetry. For he is not denying (as some of his critics, mistaking the function of Sartre's descriptions of mostly alienated "concrete relations with others" in *Being and Nothingness* by treating them as if he had intended them to be *comprehensive* of human social relations, have maintained) that such phenomena as love or friendship or social solidarity are real and really possible, but only that they can never be permanent and entirely without the potentiality of violent conflict; whereas those opponents whom we might label, as a shorthand, "harmony theorists" tend to wish to deny the pervasive reality of violence by claiming that there can be such privileged, sheltered relationships of both a dyadic and perhaps even a communal sort, and moreover that it is on such ideal relationships that we ought to concentrate our attention. Sartre would maintain, and on this point I am in thorough agreement with him, that such an approach to social theory is at best self-deceptive, and is sometimes even a deliberate effort to encourage others not to reflect on the conflict-filled reality of the world around them, in the interest of preserving existing social hierarchies that have no rational basis.

True, Sartre's experiences in La Rochelle may well have left him with more of a personal obsession about the possibility that friendships might go awry than he would otherwise have had, as he implies in the conversation with de Beauvoir that I have cited, and this may well have harmed some of his later personal relationships—while perhaps helping others, by making him more sensitive to the chances of failure and hence more careful about causing offense. This same "obsession," if this word is understood in its vague, ordinary sense and not as indicating a clinical pathology, may no doubt have led to a certain greater emphasis, quantitatively speaking, on phenomena of conflict and violence in Sartre's choices of topics about which to write, both earlier and later, in both his literary and his more philosophical works. But none of this, if true, invalidates a priori his systematic theoretical analyses; it only provides us with better insight into his personal path for reaching them, as well as more generally into the ways in which a writer's lived experience can serve as a basis for, while not determining, her or his authorial products.[10]

It is interesting to consider, by way of contrast, the case of Thomas Hobbes, to whose observations on the condition of human beings in his imagined "state of nature" some of Sartre's statements about underlying violence, especially in the *Critique of Dialectical Reason,* may usefully, though with a number of important qualifications, be analogized. Hobbes, too, was by no means unaware of the basis of his political theory in lived experience: *Leviathan* was written during the civil wars in England, and Hobbes is said to have remarked, in reference to the fact that he was born just as word came that the Spanish Armada had been sighted in the Thames Estuary, that his mother had given birth to twins, himself and fear. But Hobbes's systematic political theory, despite the superficial resemblances between some of his lived experiences and some of Sartre's, is of course very different indeed,[11] culminating in a structure of authoritarian sovereignty that Hobbes seems honestly to hope might last forever, in the absence of external attack.[12] Thus, personal circumstances strongly conditioned the thinking of both Hobbes and Sartre, as of all of us; they cannot be demonstrated to have determined it.

That there was nothing very predictable about the direction that Sartre's later theoretical enterprises would take is well illustrated by his first published theoretical work (a few literary fragments had preceded it by a year), written while he was completing his university studies. Entitled "The Theory of the State in Modern French Thought"[13] and published simultaneously in Paris in French, German, and English by the International University Federation, it has survived, ironically, in its English version. The subject matter, as much theories of law as theories of the state, is at least equally ironic, since law is the one complex and pervasive social phenomenon concerning which, as I have always maintained, Sartre's rare remarks and brief analytical references in his later work are very deficient and lacking in depth. An individual can, I think, adhere to a position akin to Sartre's (still to be explored and specified) normative anarchism while nevertheless according an important place to law in the understanding of past and present societies, but Sartre ultimately fails to do so, and I must admit that this is a significant defect in a theoretical enterprise that I wish, by and large, to defend. A reader of "The Theory of the State in Modern French Thought" in 1927 by the young, unknown student Sartre would never have anticipated that such a criticism could plausibly be leveled against him sixty-odd years later.

For the essay in question is a solid, though hardly brilliant or highly original, discussion of three French theorists, Hauriou, Davy, and Duguit, for whom law and the state are of central importance. All three, according to Sartre, claim in some sense to be realists, starting from social "facts," and his conclusion is that their various inadequacies only serve to demonstrate to a skeptical younger, postwar generation, which admires simplicity and solidity, that to begin with facts entails purely factual conclusions. True, all three of them wish to explain and, in one way or another, to preserve the dimension of values in their theories of the state. But their efforts are not very satisfactory. Hauriou is, in Sartre's view, the least successful, for he pretends to reach a conclusion that is blatantly idealistic—the notion that state sovereignty is based on freedom and that this state is a moral subject—from an initial factual assertion that individuals have private interests. These interests are supposed to lead to the creation of a collective "moral personality" through the group's pursuit of a common goal, but Hauriou lapses into mere metaphor, says Sartre, rather than trying to explain how this can actually come about, and in his account he, like the other writers to be considered, says remarkably little about the role of the free wills of individuals in the overall process.

To Davy, author of *Des clans aux empires* and a student of Durkheim's, Sartre devotes the least attention in this short essay. He shows some familiarity with Durkheim's work and applies to both of them a fundamental criticism, namely, that they must in reality make use of a suppressed metaphysical postulate, the operation of "creative synthesis" within societies, in order consistently to account for the value-laden notions, such as (in Davy's case) the moral personality of the state, which they *claim* to elicit strictly from facts. Sartre says that he accepts Davy's explanation of the mechanisms whereby, over long periods of time, individuals have transferred ideas of sovereignty, initially diffused throughout primitive tribes, first to certain individual chieftains and eventually to the state, so that a certain innate belief in right and law is now to be found in our contemporaries. But, Sartre asserts, with our newfound awareness of these social mechanisms we can now no longer retain the same attitude toward right and law as before. And he is frankly skeptical of the inference drawn by Davy, as a solution to the perceived practical problem of how to reduce or eliminate absolute state sovereignty in favor of a Society of Nations in the aftermath of World War I, that individuals can simply learn to transfer to such a society the values that up to now they have attached to particular states.

As for Duguit, Sartre presents him as a pure naturalist, who sees Society as a large organism in which individuals simply fulfill needed *functions*. He has no truck with the concept of the State as a "transcendental ego" that we find in the other writers; no metaphysical notions for him. He sees communal cohesion as being assured merely by the widespread diffusion of feelings of solidarity. If eventually it seems necessary to create a hyperorganism, a superstate, then so be it: this presents no special problem for Duguitian theory. Sartre portrays Duguit as denying the role of individual autonomy, reducing the meaning of individual freedom to the duty of all persons to fulfill their functions, and seeing all individuals and groups as merely wheels within larger wheels. He apologizes for appearing to caricature Duguit's thought, but defends himself by saying that this ideal that he has delineated can easily be read into all of that author's writings.

This youthful publication has a certain fascination for the student of Sartre's political theory that can hardly be attributed to its intrinsic intellectual value. It is the sort of moderately well-crafted student paper which one might, reading it for the first time, be inclined to regard as "possibly publishable," if it were not for the fact that it was published. It makes its expositions and criticisms rather clearly, is reasonably well and straightforwardly organized, and has a general theoretical point to advance—that we should be skeptical of all varieties of self-styled "realist" theories of the State, just as most readers are assumed already to be skeptical of outdated, blatantly "idealist" theories—though it is advanced very cautiously. It is obvious, however, that Sartre has as yet no developed theoretical framework of his own on the basis of which he is making his analysis. Nevertheless, certain themes and concepts to which Sartre will devote considerable attention in his later thought, especially in his political thought of some thirty years later, are already very prominent here. Among these are his expressions of surprise, in his criticism of Hauriou, that individuals' "free will" (a term that Sartre will later eschew, because of its misleading theory-laden connotations, in favor of simply speaking of "freedom") is relegated to an inferior, secondary level of explanation by these writers; his keen sense for suppressed metaphysical premises and other ruses (what he will later call "mystifications") whereby philosophers try piously to pretend that purely ideal constructs, such as "the moral personality of the State," are preeminently real and in fact superior to the phenomena of our lived experience; his acceptance of Davy's belief that sovereignty has its origins in primitive small groups in which each individual is, as it were, sovereign, coupled with his refusal to support Davy's inference that we can now still continue to adhere to conventional modern conceptions of "sovereignty" even after having subscribed to this analysis; and his tendency to regard purely naturalistic causal or functional accounts of moral and social phenomena, of the sort proffered by Duguit, as ridiculous and even slightly amusing. A hint of the early influence of Bergson, no doubt the most original French philosopher of the period, on Sartre may be detected in the claim that some sort of "creative synthesis" must take place within societies in order for the mechanisms depicted by Durkheim and Davy to work, even though they are unwilling to admit this. Finally, it is evident that the student Sartre who wrote this essay was finding it difficult to identify himself with either idealists or realists, words that pervaded the climate of philosophical discussion in that period, although he seems tempted to consider it important to try to do so; this relatively harmless obsession about realism and idealism, a product of his college training, will continue to afflict him, now and again, throughout his career, as evidenced by remarks made in interviews during his declining years.[14]

There is very little in the writings of Sartre over more than a decade after the publication of this little essay to indicate that political theory would ever become a major preoccupation of his. These were his early career years, years of senior high school teaching after having passed his *"agrégation"* examination on his second attempt and having spent his obligatory eighteen months of military service, years of developing and sustaining his close relationship with Simone de Beauvoir, years of writing and rewriting the manuscript "Melancholia" which was eventually published by Gallimard under the title of *Nausea*, after having been rejected on a previous occasion. His scholarship to spend the 1933–34 academic year at the French Institute in Berlin proved to be very profitable for his philosophical development: he concentrated on learning some of the techniques and problems of Husserlian phenomenology, and there he wrote his important essay "The Transcendence of Ego," in which he both indicates his acceptance of Husserl's overall philosophical project and clearly spells out his objections to the idea of a transcendental ego, to which Husserl had come in his later works. For Sartre, this move by Husserl ran the risk of ultimately reifying the self and thus, as he saw it both then and later, of fundamentally misrepresenting the "nature" of human existence and activity, the source of which is in a very crucial sense nonsubstantive (and therefore without a fixed nature) and indeed spontaneous, always capable of transcending the current state of affairs. In other words he feared that the later Husserlian postulate of a transcendental ego would place unnecessary obstacles in the way of our comprehending the radical nature of human transcendence. It is his concluding remarks to this essay, which was published in a journal (*Recherches philosophiques*) in 1936,[15] that are of considerable interest for students of Sartre's political evolution. They read in part as follows:

> The theorists of the extreme Left have sometimes reproached phenomenology for being an idealism and for drowning reality in the stream of ideas. But . . . nothing is more unjust than to call phenomenologists "idealists." On the contrary, for centuries we have not felt in philosophy so realistic a current. Unfortunately, as long as the *I* remains a structure of absolute consciousness, one will still be able to reproach phenomenology for being an escapist doctrine. . . . It seems to us that this reproach no longer has any justification if one makes the *me* an existent, strictly contemporaneous with the world. . . . No more is needed in the way of a philosophical foundation for an ethics and a politics which are absolutely positive.[16]

These comments show that Sartre certainly felt during the mid-1930s that the sociopolitical dimension of existence was important and that philosophy ought to be able to treat of it. They also show a certain mildly Left political orientation on his part. But one must also bear in mind that they are isolated concluding remarks in a work that is otherwise devoid of political references, even to the new European reality that had come about with Hitler's accession to power in Berlin just nine months before Sartre's arrival there. Although the letters that Sartre wrote to de Beauvoir from Berlin have been lost, we know from her autobiographical account and from a few remarks made by Sartre in later years about that period that he did not have a very clear sense of the magnitude of what was taking place in Germany during his sojourn there: he immersed himself in research and writing and in a small circle of mostly French colleagues. Since he was not in personal contact with Husserl, he was probably unaware of the fact that the latter was himself just beginning to turn his attention to issues of society and history at that time: Husserl commenced writing *The Crisis of the European Sciences*, in which he introduced the notion of the *Lebenswelt*, in 1934.[17] And Sartre's first book-length publication in philosophy (indeed, his first published book in any genre), *L'Imagination* (1936),[18] written during the period immediately following his Berlin year, does not contain any political references comparable to the concluding remarks of "The Transcendence of the Ego."

One series of historical events of the mid-1930s did, however, exert a significant influence on Sartre's thinking: the civil war in Spain. It is referred to frequently in de Beauvoir's record of that period of her and his lives, *The Prime of Life*, and serves as the setting for his first important work of fiction to be published, "Le Mur," a short story that was presumably written in 1936 and that appeared in a journal in July 1937. (It is this story that gives its title to the collection of short stories, *The Wall*, which, appearing as it did less than a year after the greatly-acclaimed novel *Nausea*, assured Sartre's literary success, just as the Second World War was becoming imminent.) In fact, John Gerassi, the son of a couple who were friends of Sartre's during these years and who later served as models for fictional characters in *The Roads to Freedom*, argues that it was the outbreak of that war and particularly the dramatic news of Franco's decision to initiate it in July 1936, rather than, as Sartre and most of his students were later to claim, the subsequent experience of mobilization for the *"drôle de guerre"* with Germany, that first awakened his political consciousness.[19] Gerassi hints at a certain embarrassing ambivalence and perhaps even subsequent psychological repression in Sartre's attitudes concerning that conflict, and what he suggests receives confirmation in comments made by Sartre at one point in the long filmed interview with him in the 1970s. Here, he emphatically denies having contemplated (as did his former student and friend, Jacques Bost, whose decision apparently inspired Sartre to imagine the plot of *The Wall*) joining the international brigades that supported the Republican cause against the fascists, but at the same time admits to having had regrets that he "was not needed."[20] Of course, the decision that he was not needed was Sartre's own, reinforced by Simone de Beauvoir and other friends and based in large measure on an evaluation, no doubt fairly realistic, of his relative unsuitability for military combat. I think it significant, however, that in this same portion of the interview Sartre identifies his decision of noncommitment (of an active sort, that is) to the Spanish Republicans with the dramatic refusal of his Sartre-like fictional character Mathieu in the first volume of *The Roads to Freedom (The Age of Reason)*, to accept Brunet's invitation to become a Communist militant on the eve of the outbreak of World War II. Sartre, like Mathieu, saw the Communist Party's view of our complex world, which it insisted that its members accept, as too simple to permit him to join it, however sympathetic he might be with some of its positions. But whereas Sartre left Mathieu in an appallingly desperate situation right after he had at last decided to "commit" himself by engaging in a hopeless rearguard action against advancing German troops—a situation from which, given his creator's decision not to continue *The Roads to Freedom* beyond the third volume, Mathieu was never to be extricated—the war years became for Sartre himself a time of enormous growth in sophistication about both the political dimensions of reality and the possibilities of a political commitment that would imitate neither the Mathieu nor the Brunet pattern. The origins of this growth surely lay in the lived experiences of Sartre and of some of his associates on the occasion of the traumatic events in Spain.

In fact, important events swiftly followed one after another for Sartre during the eight years (1936–44) that followed this first significant ingression of social and political reality into his consciousness. His first major publications in both philosophy and literature appeared in rapid succession, and the literary works, especially *Nausea*, won him considerable public recognition for the first time. In the midst of all this came the mobilization orders, then the period of less than a year during which he played the role of meteorologist with the French Army in various locations near its "Front" with the German troops, and then a roughly equal period of imprisonment following France's surrender. He returned to Paris in the spring of 1941 to face, like so many others, more than three additional years of German occupation: Resistance activities, difficult decisions, deprivations, arrests and even executions of personal acquaintances, and yet a need to continue with one's daily activities, which in Sartre's case included his job as a philosophy professor. The summer of 1944 must be seen as a major new turning point in Sartre's development for several reasons, notably his decision at the beginning of that summer to resign from teaching to devote full time to his writing commitments and the effects on him, along with the rest of the society in which he lived, of the Liberation of Paris by the Allies toward summer's end. Although Sartre's journalistic, eyewitness accounts of the days of the Liberation are not uniformly ecstatic—he notes, for example, the occurrence of sadistic episodes of petty personal vengeance visited on helpless individuals under the pretext, whether correct or not, of their having been collaborators with the Nazis—nevertheless their overall tone of strong, positive solidarity with masses of fellow human beings engaged in a common activity constitutes the crucial experiential background to understanding key aspects of Sartre's later social vision, in particular his conception of the "group in fusion" in the *Critique of Dialectical Reason*. But if the events surrounding the Liberation can now readily be recognized as setting the tone for so much of the later Sartre's social thought, this must not cause us to forget his extraordinary intellectual activities of the years that immediately preceded it, activities that took place simultaneously with all the personal and national upheavals that I have just been enumerating.

Three posthumous publications, the two volumes of Sartre's *Lettres au Castor et à quelques autres* and *Les Carnets de la drôle de guerre, Novembre 1939– Mars 1940*, have brought impressive new evidence to bear in support of his enormous energy during this period. The first volume of letters begins with a few from 1926 and continues chronologically through December 31, 1939, but approximately 250 pages of it, or nearly one-half, were written by Sartre once he had been mobilized at the beginning of September 1939; while the second volume begins with a New Year's Day letter of 1940 and contains only sixty pages written after 1941. What we observe is an individual totally, almost pathologically, dedicated to writing and reading at every free waking moment of his military life. Fortunately for him, his duties as meteorologist were not very burdensome, and he managed quickly to create an atmosphere in which he was mostly left alone by his fellow soldiers to pursue his activities, although his daily interactions with others were still sufficiently full to provide the material for most of what he wrote, particularly in his letters. The latter testify to the voraciousness of his reading: fictional works of all periods and qualities, histories (e.g., a study of Kaiser Wilhelm II which shed light for him on the origins of the two world wars), and philosophical works alike. We see him, for example, pursuing his first serious study of Heidegger, whose influence on him "has in recent times struck me as providential, since it supervened to teach me authenticity and historicity just at the very moment when war was about to make these notions indispensable to me;"[21] this study was indeed of overwhelming importance for his development, and he was even to make immediate use of it during his prisoner-of-war period by giving an informal course on Heidegger to some fellow prisoners. His letters to de Beauvoir contain repeated requests for still more reading material.

But even more astonishing than the volume of Sartre's reading is that of his writing. We have his virtually daily, often lengthy letters to de Beauvoir, but from them we learn that he was regularly corresponding with his mother and with other friends, as well. (For instance, a tangled and compromising affair involving Sartre and two other women was playing itself out, mostly by letter, at this same time; Sartre, typically, kept de Beauvoir *au courant*.) Of the original *Carnets*, which he was composing daily with a view to possible eventual posthumous publication,[22] the 400-odd pages that we have constitute perhaps one third or less; the rest were lost. Meanwhile, Sartre was also completing his novel *The Age of Reason* (in his letters he discusses his rewriting of certain scenes and deciding on an ending); keeping in touch with his publisher and others concerning the reception of his earlier works, plans for future writing, and the publication of his newest philosophical treatise, *L'Imaginaire* (which actually went on sale in February 1940); and writing the first drafts of sections of what was to become his longest and most famous early work, *Being and Nothingness*! (A brief note to de Beauvoir from Sartre in prison in July 1940 concludes: "I have begun to write a treatise of metaphysics: *Being and Nothingness*."[23] But there are also references to some of its eventual contents, though not to that precise title, in earlier letters.) The completed text of *Being and Nothingness* was published in June 1943, as was Sartre's first generally known play, *The Flies*. (He had already written and produced a Christmas play, *Bariona*, for his fellow prisoners in 1940.)

In summary, there are few if any records in the history of letters that are comparable to Sartre's for a similar time period, in terms of quality, quantity, and diversity of genres produced under conditions of considerable stress while the writer was simultaneously employed (though this word may not be quite appropriate for the prison months) in more regular outside occupations. All of this has seemed to me important to mention, especially in light of all of the relatively new evidence that we now have concerning it, both because of its intrinsic interest and because of the light that it sheds on Sartre's lived experience, the experience of an intensely active individual, as the background to his theoretical works. Just what portion of all of the literary products of this period constitutes a serious sustained, direct contribution to political theory? The answer to the question when posed in this way is, as I have already indicated, "Relatively little." Nevertheless, the *Letters*, the *Carnets*, and even *Being and Nothingness* contain at least suggestions of significant perspectives in the areas of social and political philosophy, and I think it useful to discuss a few of them here.

Against the background of the increasingly enveloping war, Sartre was becoming conscious of himself in relation to both social structure and historical time; this stimulated him to begin thinking, though for the most part in a still rather unsophisticated fashion, about possible socioethical worldviews, including his own such views at various stages in his life up to that point and the view that he might wish to adopt henceforth. One of the few cross-references from his letters to an extant notebook deals with his place in the social structure. On March 6, 1940, he writes with pride to de Beauvoir about a passage that he has just written in his notebook, in which he has depicted himself as "the monstrous product of capitalism, parliamentarianism, centralization, and bureaucracy [le fonctionnarisme]."[24] He had good reason to be proud of this passage, in my opinion, because it is a small masterpiece of self-analysis. In it he explains that, by virtue of capitalism, he is cut off from the working class and yet not part of the ruling milieux; that from the parliamentary tradition he has inherited his passion for civil rights and for freedom itself; that as an effect of France's historical tendency toward centralization he finds himself totally unfamiliar with farm life and a hopelessly citified, chauvinistic Parisian; and that the fact of his having been born into a family of state employees has given him his strong sense of universalism and rationality as well as his total incompetence in handling money. It is "to all these abstractions taken together," he says, that the fact of his being "an abstract and rootless person" is attributable. He also happens to be relatively cold rather than sensual, and the net result is a personality that obviously displeases him and that he wishes to change. "Je ne suis solidaire de rien, pas même de moi-même," he reflects; "je n'ai besoin de personne ni de rien."[25] (He has solidarity with nothing, not even with himself, and he has need of no one and of nothing.) He now sees, he continues, that true freedom is not the Stoic ideal of total detachment from the world, but rather presupposes a rootedness, a being-in-the-world, contrary to the extreme individualism which had characterized his earlier years.

There is no question that this remarkably straightforward and perceptive passage, stimulated in part by his experiences of association and working together with other members of his army company, most of them less economically privileged and more burdened by family and other social responsibilities than he, points to crucial elements in Sartre's later development. It anticipates his later movement toward social theory and toward a more nuanced and less purely individualistic view of the nature of freedom; it foreshadows some of the self-criticism that one will later read in his autobiography; and for the less distant future it can be seen as somewhat prophetic, paradoxically enough, of some of the harshest criticisms that were to be directed against the philosophical reasoning of *Being and Nothingness*. In other words, it was to be some time before Sartre would be able more fully to integrate into his own published theoretical writings the recognition of deficiencies within his thought-framework, rooted in his social environment, that this notebook entry contains!

The slow but, in retrospect (though certainly not in Sartre's own perception during the early stages), relentless onslaught of the war itself understandably evokes a series of Sartrean reflections on his own and his generation's place in history, reflections that reinforce his growing conviction of the importance, for philosophical understanding, of history itself. He comes to recognize that in addition to all the other "irrational" contingent elements of facticity (to use his later, more precise terminology), such as birth and death and social class, with which he and de Beauvoir and others of their generation had been surrounded, there had always been the menace of the war to come: "I disguised it and what I did not see was that our era (18–39) drew its meaning from nothing other (in its entirety as well as in its smallest details) than a being-for-the-war."[26] He goes on to say that this had rendered his thinking radically inauthentic, since he had not paid attention to his insertion within history. Is Sartre suggesting here that World War II was inevitable? In a sense, yes, given a great many facts about the world at the time of the armistice of 1918; and this attitude of his anticipates some of his attitudes about the Stalinist regime during the latter part of the same period that will preoccupy him in the second volume of the *Critique of Dialectical Reason*.

But this nascent sense, so new to Sartre in late 1939, of an overarching historical fatalism must be balanced against reflections on history, inspired by his reading of the history of Kaiser Wilhelm II, that we find him making a few months later. What intrigues Sartre in these reflections is the apparent incompatibility among different types of historical explanation—those based on individual personality, those based on economic factors in the manner of Lenin's book, *Imperialism . . .*, etc.—and the obvious philosophical need to reconcile these types. He begins the conclusion of this passage, quite consistently with his thinking elsewhere about freedom and determinism in history, by insisting that explanations dependent upon alleged causal mechanisms, even of the psychoanalytic sort that account for events on the basis of historical actors' alleged neuroses or similar entities, are fundamentally ahistorical, and that explanation must rather be an attempt to comprehend the free projects of the actors in question, seen as human projects and not as pure determinants of impersonal forces. He thus anticipates central themes of his much later works of social theory, including even his study of Flaubert (although he here imagines undertaking such a study with respect to Wilhelm II), when he writes: "So I shall outline another type of historical description, which reverses the explanation [by comparison with the biography of Wilhelm by Ludwig that he has been reading] and goes from the man to the situation, rather than from the situation to the man."[27] He then goes on to suggest, very much in the spirit in which he was to write *The Family Idiot*, that what would matter would be less the accuracy of every detail of his interpretation of the individual in question than the process of generating plausible hypotheses about the latter's projects that would permit the writer, Sartre, to *illustrate* this method of historical explanation; and, moreover, that even the importance of this methodology for the historical enterprise would be subordinate to the philosophical purpose "of showing how historical man historicalizes himself within the framework of certain situations." He ends in a humorous vein by remarking that of course he will begin taking up this task the next day.

It was in fact to take Sartre many years and many apparent turns in his personal and intellectual life before he was to carry out the project outlined here in early 1940, but when he did so his fidelity to its original formulation was to prove quite considerable. What may be said eventually to have changed, to have become somewhat more prominent in Sartre's thinking about historical explanation (which must be seen as one aspect of his social theory), is the role of collectivities; by the time of the writing of the *Critique of Dialectical Reason*, for example, he would not find it strange to use the terminology of common or group projects, though always with the understanding that their basis lies in the individuals who constitute them, whereas such terminology was still not a part of his vocabulary in 1940. But even this change can be regarded as more of a clarification and a development of greater theoretical sophistication and depth than as a rejection of his earlier views. In these 1939–40 writings, for instance, we do find Sartre exhibiting, at least at times, a very strong sense of identity with *certain* sorts of collectivities, particularly with the human beings who make up his own historical generation in France and whose very temporal location vis-à-vis the two world wars gives them a certain common definition, and even more particularly with his army comrades. (For example, in reflecting on news of the surrender of the Belgian army just a few days before the French capitulation, he remarks: "It's a funny condition; moreover, I don't think it would be possible for me to push the sense of the collective any further.")[28] Only in a short section of the unfinished second volume of the *Critique of Dialectical Reason*, which was intended to deal with social groupings across time, will we find any systematic Sartrean analysis of this notion of the collective identity of a historical generation. Much of his later writing, on the other hand, was to be pervaded with the terminology of social *class* identity, always understood as a very complex phenomenon. At the earlier time that we are considering here, Sartre certainly shows a sympathy for "the weak against the strong"[29] and an awareness of class differences—he realizes, for instance, how his ability to eat at local restaurants rather than in the mess hall must appear to one of his fellow soldiers who cannot afford it and who therefore regards Sartre as one of the "jeunesse dorée" (gilded youth)[30]—but he cannot be said to have anything approaching a theory about them.

However, these same writings contain, if anything, an overabundance of Sartrean theories about ethics and corresponding sociopolitical worldviews—most of them expressed, as I have already indicated, in a rather unsophisticated fashion. At one point in the *Carnets,* Sartre reminisces about the evolution of his personal ethical attitudes, distinguishing among three periods: first, "a period of optimism, the time when," he says, "I was 'a thousand Socrateses,'" a time at which he saw salvation as coming through art; second, the period between 1929 and roughly 1937, when he still saw salvation as coming through art but was much more somber and pessimistic about life, being constrained now to work for a living as "a single Socrates," a solitary philosophy teacher in a high school in the provinces, even more impressed than before by the unjustifiability of human existence; and finally an emerging new era that began with Gallimard's acceptance of *Nausea* for publication and Sartre's almost simultaneous appointment to a position in Paris and recovery from an unhappy love affair.[31] As autobiography, this is undoubtedly important, and Annie Cohen-Solal has made the contrast between "1000 Socrateses" and "a single

Socrates" the basis of an important division in her chronology of Sartre's life; but of course it is very superficial if viewed as ethical theory,[32] and it serves to reinforce the impression that Sartre's ethical views prior to the late 1930s were quite lacking as far as the social dimension was concerned.

To counterbalance this impression, however, one can find several passages in which he sketches alternative worldviews within which, even if they are still comparatively superficial, this dimension figures very prominently. He draws up a taxonomy, for instance, of three types of synthetic "conceptions of man"—narrowly conservative, narrowly conservative but with novel (theoretical) underpinnings (racism and Marxism are the two examples he gives), and broad, namely humanitarianism—that are contrasted with a fourth, an "analytic conception: anarchic individualism."[33] But none of these, he says, really focuses on the human condition, with individual human reality as its starting-point. Again, in a letter written to de Beauvoir just a few days after this entry in the *Carnets*, he begins with the assertion that ethics must be a system of ends and goes on to reject three possible responses to the question of what the ultimate end should be taken to be: (a) the individual as an end in him/herself, (b) social utility, and (c) humanity as a species, the ethical *telos* of humanism.[34] Here, too, he argues for an ethical conception of the human situation based on a notion of human reality as at once freedom and facticity—an anticipation of some of the principal themes of *Being and Nothingness*. Whereas the latter work was to contain only a concluding promise of a future work on ethics to be based upon its ontology, here we see, albeit in very sketchy form, a reverse movement: ethical reflections, motivated by the need to choose among alternative sociopolitical worldviews, leading to considerations of ontology.

We thus find, in these writings from the time of the war's outbreak, the germs of a number of later Sartrean themes concerning ethics and politics in addition to those that I have already discussed concerning conditioning by social structures and historical explanation. We find an eagerness on his part to write a systematic work on ethics, one which will avoid both the simplistic positions, such as humanism[35] and "anarchic individualism," to which he might naturally have been tempted, and certain other positions, such as Marxism as he then understood it and various conservatisms,[36] to which he was not tempted at all at the time, together with a concomitant tendency constantly to rethink just what ethics or morality *is*. These tendencies are always accompanied by the feeling, on Sartre's part, that he is just on the verge of "getting it straight" concerning this most central of philosophical issues. One passage in the *Carnets* epitomizes this Sartrean combination of eagerness, self-confidence, and doubt about the nature of ethics, or at any rate of *his* ethics, so well that I can do no better than to cite it at length:

> I think I understand, and can now *feel*, what true morality is. I see how metaphysics and values are connected; humanism and contempt; our absolute

freedom and our condition in a single life bounded by our death; our inconsistency, as beings without a God yet not authors of ourselves, and our dignity; our autarkic independence as individuals and our historicity. I shall explain about this tomorrow or some other day; I want to think some more about it. But at least this time it will be a morality I've felt and applied before having thought it.[37]

Throughout the vicissitudes of Sartre's subsequent thinking about ethics, including those years when he did not believe it possible to construct one, right through his last few published remarks, in interviews, on the subject, much of the same spirit would continue to prevail, informed by the same view of the ambivalent character of the human condition.

Before leaving these writings of Sartre's earliest politically conscious years behind completely, I wish to call attention to two other relatively minor themes in them that will appear again in his subsequent thought: seriousness and property. Seriousness would not be at all serious as an issue in Sartre's social theory were it not for the fact that he was to identify the "spirit of seriousness" as a major target of criticism in the three or four pages anticipatory of a future Sartrean ethics with which *Being and Nothingness* ends, and that soon thereafter, in his essay "Materialism and Revolution" he was to accuse (orthodox) Marxism of being pervaded by this spirit. True, Sartre's more frequent model for the serious individual is the smug bourgeois who acts as if all values were already given in our world, rather than freely chosen, and as if he, the bourgeois man (*not* woman), were the fullest embodiment of these values. In Simone de Beauvoir's essay in existentialist ethics, *Pour une morale de l'ambiguïté (The Ethics of Ambiguity),* this notion of "the serious man" (interestingly enough, she seems to favor this more concrete formula over Sartre's more abstract *"esprit de sérieux"*)[38] plays a much larger role than in any of Sartre's writings, and her principal examples are also reactionaries and conservatives of various types; but she, too, gives as one example of such a person "a member of the Communist Party."[39] We find an early Sartrean reference to this idea of the spirit of seriousness near the end of the extant portions of his *Carnets;* this reference reveals an interesting juxtaposition of reflections on his lack of religious faith, which has permitted him to be "frivolous" in the sense of not thinking of the world as an imposed, given reality, with observations about the seriousness of "materialism": "For revolutionaries are serious . . . I hate seriousness."[40] But this is the same Sartre who, in a letter to de Beauvoir some two months earlier, envisaged writing a "literary fantasy" soon as a relief from his serious work on his novel *(The Age of Reason)* and on his notebooks, remarking: "There is no more serious writer than I; an American has even reproached me for it."[41] He then suggested that the war would provide him with an excuse (!) for his more frivolous writing project. Of course, it is easy enough to absolve Sartre of any conceptual contradiction between these two sets of remarks by noting that in the second he is using the words "serious" and "fantasy" in very ordinary senses, whereas in the first he is beginning to employ the notion of "the spirit of seriousness" as a technical term of criticism. However, I am inclined to believe that these two passages reveal a more fundamental tension, not only in Sartre's personality—that is exceedingly obvious!—but also in his developing thought about politics and society. As an old man many years later, he was, for example, to assume the directorship of a relatively obscure, bombastic newspaper of the extreme Left, *La Cause du Peuple*, and even to distribute copies of it on the streets, all in the name of serious revolutionary commitment, while simultaneously working hard to complete his lengthy, complex study of Flaubert. Yet he always retained a certain playfulness and distance, a certain elusiveness, with regard to his writings, his acquaintances, and himself.[42] I am further inclined to believe that this was a relatively fruitful tension in Sartre, and one that was reflective of the genuinely ambiguous character of human social existence in general, rather than a destructive one; but it was one about which Sartre himself was not always entirely clear.

Finally, with regard to property, the *Carnets* contain an isolated but very interesting passage. In it, Sartre begins by expressing surprise that, given the controversial and central nature of the question of property, it has not been the object of phenomenological description.[43] He then proceeds to analyze the act of appropriation as "an essential structure of man. This, moreover, irrespective of any political theory, since one can just as well thereafter be a socialist or a communist."[44] His analysis contains the germ of his much longer discussion of possession, of "Having" as distinguished from "Doing" and "Being," in *Being and Nothingness*. The core idea is that, in possessing some thing (or in *attempting*, impossibly, to possess some person), one is endeavoring to give oneself a proxy substantiality, or a fixed and definite hold on reality, through that thing. (In the technical terminology that Sartre was already beginning to employ here, *"To appropriate something for oneself is to exist in this thing in the mode of the in-itself."*)[45] The human individual is, for Sartre, fundamentally free and not a fixed substance, and so appropriation is one basic means for the individual to make up for this sensed *lack* of substantiality. What renders this passage in the *Carnets* so distinctive is that here, after having outlined his theoretical views, he proceeds to analyze his own personal relationships to property ownership, comparing his typical behaviors with those of some of his close friends. From the distance from it that is ours today, the passage can be seen, especially in light of the subsequent publication of *Being and Nothingness*, as a case study in the intricate connection between an individual's philosophical outlook and his or her lived experience.

One of Sartre's best-known and most curious idiosyncrasies throughout his life was his tendency to be extremely generous with money. His royalties brought him a great deal of it in later life, but he managed to spend most of it, supporting a number of other people at various times, and tipping very lavishly whenever he went to a restaurant or a cafe. He would normally, in later years, carry very large sums of cash with him, amounts equivalent to many hundreds of U.S. dollars.[46] At the same time he lived rather simply, in the sense that he never owned a home of his own and had very few personal possessions; even his sense of proprietorship over his personal writings was at best extremely attenuated, as demonstrated by his very casual, careless attitude toward his unpublished manuscripts. The *Carnets* reveal that these habits and attitudes were of long standing—yet more threads of continuity in the life of a man who was constantly exploring the possibilities of radical change. In the passage in question, he first attempts to trace the roots of these personal traits to his family background, suggesting that the type of work, pedagogy, in which his grandfather and he had both engaged was conducive to disassociating one's daily activities from the idea of earning money, and moreover that the tradition of being a government employee encouraged a disinterest in private property, particularly landed private property. So, he says, he could adapt more easily than anyone else to the collectivization of property, "since I'd lose nothing by it save the pleasure of giving—and I could still give in a thousand other ways."[47] This lack of dismay at the prospect of collectivization and Sartre's feeling of already being collectivized to a considerable degree by virtue of his background actually serves, he adds two pages later, to reinforce his individualism and his taste for freedom.

However, he immediately adds, such autobiographical or genetic explanation of his behavior patterns with respect to property is inadequate, because, after all, many, even most, of those who come from backgrounds similar to his tend to exhibit a love of private property. To find an adequate explanation, he says, entails considering the individual's own being-in-the-world, which, "chez moi comme chez tout homme" [in me as in every man], lies in the area of his or her own solitude, beyond the common historical situation. Sartre attributes to himself, above all, a "metaphysical pride," a desire, rooted in his own nothingness, to possess everything altogether, which of course makes the institutionally-sanctioned personal possession of a few items appear symbolic and comparatively unimportant. "This [metaphysical] possession consists, essentially, in capturing the world's meaning by sentences."[48]

This unique passage, so powerful as an exercise in self-analysis, is highly significant for several other reasons as well. It anticipates better than almost any other extant passage in the *Carnets* the central themes and even the language of *Being and Nothingness:* the *pour-soi* (for-itself) as *néant* (nothingness) which is lack and also desire—desire to "fill itself up" by possession, or *having*—and the unsatisfiability, in principle, of this cosmic desire. It deals with one of the perennial central issues in political theory, the concept of private property, showing by the structure of its analysis, which is in part phenomenological description, that the usual dispute over whether or not "property" as such can be abolished—the terms in which some liberal, anarchist, and Marxian discussions of the issue, and perhaps even some passages in Marx's own early manuscripts, are couched—is extremely shallow; to be human, Sartre contends, is quite clearly to desire to appropriate, but that does not mean, as the personal experience of Sartre himself proves, that human appropriation *must* take the specific form of the appropriation of landed property, or ownership of a portion of the means of production, or any other particular institutional form. Finally, by blatantly connecting together Sartre's fascination with philosophy, some of his most idiosyncratic personal behavior, the ontological theory-to-come of *Being and Nothingness*, and the socialist ideal to which Sartre was soon to become consciously committed, this passage raises once again the question, to which I referred earlier, as to whether an awareness of the biographical roots of a theorist's thought-framework should be considered to invalidate that framework.

I repeat that, to me, the answer to this question is decidedly negative. The knowledge of a certain number of facts about *any* given thinker's life would enable us to undertake a plausible reconstruction of the configuration of his or her individual being-in-the-world similar to the one in which Sartre has briefly but with such brutal honesty engaged here with respect to himself. If such a reconstruction were equivalent to an invalidation of the thinker's theories, then no theory would be exempt from invalidation—a highly undesirable consequence, tantamount to an invitation to intellectual chaos. But to account for the genesis of ideas is not to make a judgment about their comparative worth or veraciousness, and there is no reason in principle why experiences of an unusual or even unique sort might not lead to greater, more profound insights into reality than do the more commonplace experiences of most of us most of the time. Indeed, there is good reason to expect that greater insight would be a very possible outcome of such experiences. Thus, Sartre's acknowledgement of his "metaphysical pride"[49] and his reconstruction of the connections between that pride and his theories are likely to appear destructive of those theories only to philosophers who still wish to separate systematic thought from the lived experiences of thinkers. It is important to reflect on these questions about the nature of philosophy as we turn to a brief consideration of *Being and Nothingness* itself.

In my introduction, I asked rhetorically whether anything recognizably political serves as the object of any sustained analysis in *Being and Nothingness*, and I answered in the negative. If this characterization is indeed accurate, the situation is rather puzzling, because, as we have now seen in light of the *Letters* and the *Carnets*, the periods of Sartre's political awakening and of his remarkably rapid composition of his long *magnum opus* in fact coincide. The puzzle is somewhat resolved when one realizes that Sartre himself was still subject to a considerable extent, at this time, to the hierarchized compartmentalization of mainstream Western thought, according to which serious philosophy, which deals with transcendent structures, is separable from and of superior importance to reflections on history and politics, which deal with what is ephemeral. If Sartre's 1940s philosophical radicalism consisted in part in the brilliant reversal of the meanings and values of central concepts and categories of the *philosophia perennis*—for example, the use of an "ontological proof" in the Introduction to *Being and Nothingness* to demonstrate, not the existence of a God, but rather the independent existence of *being* which is in itself and not reducible to the sum total of appearances, followed by the obvious downgrading of the positive connotations of the word "being" that even Heidegger had retained from the tradition—nevertheless he continued to think in terms of those general concepts and categories.[50] Thus, *Being and Nothingness* is a monument to Sartre's passion for doing metaphysics or ontology[51] in something like the grand style even while it undermines all the intellectual pretensions that accompanied that style in writers like Descartes and Leibniz, and one of the style's rules that it implicitly respects is that reflections on politics and history are at best very incidental to the central issues. The antipolitical prejudices of his college years, which he discusses in *Search for a Method*,[52] were continuing to affect his work as a professional philosopher.

This artificial compartmentalization between philosophy and political theory may even have been abetted, rather than mitigated, by the circumstance that Sartre was immediately impelled into political activism upon his return from prison camp in Germany by the formation of the group "Socialisme et Liberté." The preparation and distribution of clandestine political writings, some of them by Sartre, were among the group's major activities. The pressure to produce relevant political analyses of the constantly changing situation of the Occupation while he was simultaneously writing his first major work of systematic philosophy may be supposed to have intensified the contrast between the philosophical and the political, both as modes of theorizing and (although even by that time he would not have accepted this formula if pressed) as distinct spheres of reality, in Sartre's mind. It is a pity that no copies of these early political writings, which included a 100-page model constitution drawn up by Sartre for postwar France, appear to have survived; the recent recollections of several others, generally more sympathetic to the Communist Party than Sartre at the time, who belonged to his group are recounted by Annie Cohen-Solal but shed very little light on the writings' contents.[53] One of those who read Sartre's constitution, for example, Simone Debout, remembered his ideas as having been heavily influenced by Proudhon, but it is by no means obvious just what this is supposed to mean.

This assertion of Sartre's alleged Proudhonianism during the years of Occupation is somewhat ironic in view of the fact that Proudhon is one of the few political theorists to whom Sartre refers by name in *Being and Nothingness*, and the reference is negatively critical. It occurs in the analysis of appropriation and possession, anticipated in the *Carnets*, that constitutes one of the very last extended discussions within the book.[54] Sartre makes the point, here as in the *Carnets*, that appropriation has an ontological basis in the structure of human reality in relationship to the world. As fundamentally free and not predefined as any certain, fixed substance or nature, I am bound to seek to give myself substance through action on "being-in-itself," the undifferentiated world of objects, and this means that in one way or another I must constantly appropriate this world, attempt to make it a part of myself. To define possession in the traditional way as "ability to use," says Sartre, is unsatisfactory; there are too many counterexamples. Similarly, possession is not definable in terms of "ability to destroy," although indeed destruction is one salient way in which human beings attempt to express their urge to appropriate. As for the legal concept of property or ownership, it must itself stem from something more basic about human beings, namely, this ontological need to appropriate that Sartre is attempting to explicate; the notion of the "sacredness" of private property is only a later construct. In light of the intellectual requirement that we first understand the ontological basis of appropriation, Proudhon's famous dictum that "property is theft" is superficial and explains nothing.

Although the name of Rousseau receives no mention throughout this fairly extended discussion, it seems to me reasonable to invoke it as a background to what Sartre is saying here. Proudhon himself is known to have admired the early Rousseau, that is, the Rousseau who wrote the *Discourse on the Origins of Inequality* rather than the Rousseau of *The Social Contract*, because the argument of the former work is more conducive to a political theory of anarchy. In that work, Rousseau undertakes an imaginative reconstruction of human history that begins with a primitive state of equality and takes the invention of the institution of private property, a usurpation concocted by those who have, in the course of time, acquired more possessions than others and now seek to secure this inequality by persuading their fellows to join in placing the full force of the entire community behind this new idea of property as a sacred *right*, as the decisive turning point. In his discussion of appropriation in *Being and Nothingness*, Sartre writes in sympathy with the socially critical, ultimately somewhat anarchistic spirit of the early Rousseau with respect to private property and the notion of a legal right thereto, even while (rightly) criticizing the superficial formula to which Proudhon later reduced it. In his later, more evidently political writings, in particular the first volume of the *Critique of Dialectical Reason*, Sartre will remain sympathetic to this spirit. But in another respect the present discussion in *Being and Nothingness* runs counter to the Rousseauean spirit as well as to that of the later Sartre inasmuch as it includes virtually no reference to the importance of historical conditions and historical change in understanding the stances that specific societies and individuals take toward property ownership. Rather, Sartre's principal thrust here is ultimately to use his often interesting and valuable analysis of various forms of appropriation in order to reinforce his ontology of being-in-itself. His conclusion is that, just as "doing" can ultimately be seen as a form of "being," so, in the final analysis, can "having."

This somewhat skews his description, in my opinion. The analysis incorporates much more of what is already to be found in the Sartrean passage on appropriation in the *Carnets*, including his insistence that possession of a finite number of objects is merely *symbolic* of the underlying metaphysical passion to possess and hence (in a way that is never to be satisfied) to *be* everything, and his exploration of some of the ways in which appropriation involves elements of *magic*. But here the connection with Sartre's lived experience is not made explicit (except for a brief and only mildly interesting reference to the possessiveness that Sartre once exhibited towards smoking, a habit that he later abandoned), whereas the ontological doctrine looms very large, to the point of becoming Procrustean—even in the otherwise useful comments that Sartre makes about generosity and gift-giving, comments that anticipate central themes of the *Cahiers pour une morale*. Here, near the end of *Being and Nothingness*, generous giving is said not to be "irreducible," but rather "to give is to appropriate by destruction while utilizing this destruction to enslave another."[55] It is clear that Sartre's temptation to engage in ontological reductionism, always present in his thought but most often counterbalanced by more generous tendencies, has here gotten the better of him at the price of viewing all generosity and gift-giving in the most negative possible light, and hence falsely. Sartre will attempt to redress this one-sided account in his *Cahiers*.

It is not entirely true to say that historicity is never mentioned in *Being and Nothingness*; it is, but in a way that only reinforces my previous observation about the absence of a feeling for historical conditions and historical change in that book. There is a brief reference or two to historicity in Sartre's discussion of temporality, where he in effect equates the two concepts: "Reflection therefore apprehends temporality . . . as historicity."[56] But it is important to realize that this key concept, for the "discovery" of which, in the course of his wartime reading, Sartre appears to have been most beholden to Heidegger and, to a lesser extent, to his former classmate Raymond Aron, who had by then published his first book on the philosophy of history, remains at this point only an abstract concept for him. For a closer study of this and following passages, in which Sartre is employing a new, difficult, and somewhat obscure distinction, the subject of considerable subsequent scholarly literature,[57] between "pure" and "impure" types of reflection, reveals that he wishes to confine the recognition of historicity, as distinguished from the "psychic" sense of temporality that we have in our day-to-day activities when we are not trying to be metaphysicians, to the *pure* type; and he wishes to avoid discussing the latter in any detail:

> But how can reflection constitute [psychic temporality] if reflection is the pure and simple discovery of the historicity which it is?

> Here we must distinguish between pure reflection and impure or constitu-
> ent reflection, for it is impure reflection which constitutes the succession of
> psychic facts or *psyche* . . . Pure reflection can be attained only as the result of a
> modification which it effects on itself and which is in the form of a katharsis.
> This is not the place to describe the motivation and the structure of this
> katharsis.[58]

The idea of a "katharsis" mentioned here seems to correspond to that of a
"radical conversion," which is to loom especially large in the *Cahiers pour
une morale*. In the latter one will find hints, undeveloped though they are,
of a Sartrean vision of a possible, though unlikely, society-wide conversion
to an ethical life of a "kingdom of ends" which would in some sense take us
beyond the patterns of history as we know it. One will find much that is
utopian and idealistic, in the most negative senses of those words, in the
Cahiers, and this will help in an important way to explain Sartre's subsequent decision to abandon them. But at least by the time of writing the
Cahiers, roughly five years after the writing of *Being and Nothingness*, Sartre
will have *begun* to integrate a sense of the actual flow of real historical
events into his philosophical framework; at this earlier point, on the other
hand, "historicity" remains merely a concept, attainable only by the rather
mysterious process of "pure" reflection.

One genre of historical event is, however, used by Sartre in *Being and
Nothingness* for the purpose of illustrating his extreme conception of freedom: war. All those who have read the book will certainly remember the
brief subsection, one of the briefest in the entire volume, entitled "Freedom
and Responsibility." Some find it incongruous, different in tone from the
rest—more personal, perhaps more emotional. Others regard the notion of
responsibility defended here by Sartre, whereby I must be said to have
"chosen" a war through which I live (the indefinite article, "a," is employed
throughout, but no reader can escape the realization that Sartre's then-
ongoing World War II experience is the basis of his entire analysis), as
impermissibly broad, a distortion of the language and concept of "responsibility"; I do not. What Sartre is claiming in this subsection is that it is I,
every individual, who ultimately chooses the stance that he or she is taking
and will take toward all the "givens"—the elements of "facticity," in Sartre's
technical language—within his or her personal situation. Thus it is true but
naive and in an ultimate sense irrelevant to whine, "I did not choose to be
born," for one is always confronted with a range of possibilities for dealing
with one's life. In the section in question, Sartre applies this general idea to
the individual's responsibility for a war that is occurring in his or her
lifetime, showing that whatever behavior one adopts with respect to it
(fighting, deserting, committing suicide rather than having to live through
it, psychological denial, etc.), and however limited one is by physical and
other circumstances, as long as one is conscious the war is in a sense one's
own, and hence one's own responsibility. Paradoxically enough, even

though Sartre would later be inclined to wince at some of the extreme formulas that he employs in this passage in order to highlight his insistence on the unavoidability of our need freely to choose (e.g., "Thus in a certain sense I *choose* being born"[59]), instead placing much greater emphasis on the force of circumstances and less on the absoluteness of individual freedom than in *Being and Nothingness*, nevertheless the concreteness of Sartre's phenomenological description here foreshadows his later political theory much better than does almost any other part of his earlier work. True, there are a number of other fine concrete descriptions throughout *Being and Nothingness*, beginning with those involving "patterns of bad faith"—the "perfect," perfectly insincere cafe waiter or the young girl who is the object of a male escort's attentions but pretends not to be—early on, but most of these concern either single individuals or dyadic relationships; very few others deal explicitly with those more complex sorts of interpersonal relationships which directly involve sociopolitical structures and history.

Of other passages that may be said to do so, by far the most important for our purposes is Sartre's two-part analysis entitled " 'Being-With' *(Mitsein)* and the 'We,' " subdivided into successive treatments of "The Us-Object" and "The We-Subject." (Hazel Barnes is responsible, in her classic translation of *Being and Nothingness*, for better bringing out, through her choices of "us" and "we," respectively, the crucial conceptual distinction that Sartre is attempting to make here but cannot express in his French subtitles, in both of which the pronoun is *"nous."* This is one of those relatively rare instances, I think, in which a philosopher's meaning can legitimately be better clarified in translation.) The first part in effect lays out, in some detail and within the language and parameters of the framework of *Being and Nothingness*, some of the concerns that will be central to Sartre in the first volume of his *Critique*. Suppose, he suggests, that two individuals are in conflict, as has been the case in all the previous "Concrete Relations with Another [*Autrui*]"[60] that he has been investigating, but that now the two individuals are observed, looked at, by a third person. What may ensue, depending on the circumstances, is an experience of *solidarity* between the first two; this experience makes us aware of the phenomenon of the "Us-Object," which for the Sartre of *Being and Nothingness* has a peculiar ontological status.[61] This "Us-Object" is not an object of knowledge in the ordinary sense, nor is it like the concrete object of some specific feeling, nor is it even *experienced* directly: what is experienced is the sentiment of solidarity that is a symptom of its presence. Rather, one is somehow aware of this "Us-Object" prereflectively, and "Reflective consciousness can not apprehend this 'Us'. Its appearance coincides on the contrary with the collapse of the 'Us'; the For-itself disengages itself and posits its selfness against *Others*."[62] Certain situations, Sartre says, notably common work on a material object, tend to evoke these experiences of solidarity with others, but in fact any situation of human interaction may take the form of an "Us-Object" as soon as a third person

appears. Sartre then goes on to introduce the phenomenon of class consciousness as pointing to a particular kind of "Us-Object," born, though
often only very slowly, of conditions of oppression by one or more "third
persons," and sometimes leading to a deliverance by means of a "We-
Subject" rather than simply by individual self-awareness. His treatment of
the "Us" ends with some remarks about the assumptions of humanism,
with which, as usual, he finds fault, as involving (impossibly, hence the
notion must be considered empty) an "Us" conception of humanity as a
whole, which would have to presuppose as its complement a God who
contemplated this human totality.

It is in the succeeding discussion of the "We-Subject" that the limitations
of the early Sartre's philosophy for political theory are most clearly revealed.[63] A somewhat simplistic but not altogether incorrect way of indicating the later direction of his sociopolitical thought is to see it as a massive
effort to overcome some of the limitations that are revealed in these pages—
to cope with the "problem of mediations," all of those forms and structures
of human interaction, such as institutions of all kinds, that lie somewhere
in between human individuals, including their one-on-one conflictual relationships, and the whole of reality, the two polar topics to which the early
Sartre, in his "metaphysical pride," has devoted most of his attention.
However, a careful rereading of this early Sartrean treatment of the "We-
Subject" reveals some important insights of which Sartre will later make
considerable use—for instance, the idea, no doubt borrowed (whether
consciously or unconsciously) from Marx, that work is alienating whenever
it does not benefit the worker's own goals, and the conclusion that an
oppressor class, such as the bourgeoisie, is in principle incapable of experi-
encing the sort of solidarity that an oppressed class, as the collective object
of the oppressors' "look," sometimes can. This same passage also reiterates
and places in clear perspective a criticism leveled by Sartre earlier in the
book[64] against Heidegger's assertion that *"das Mitsein,"* "being-with" or
"togetherness," is an essential and fundamental relationship among
human beings: this is an unproven, stipulative assertion on Heidegger's
part, Sartre contends, and in any case cannot solve the concrete problems
of recognizing and dealing with other human beings, where the possibility
of conflict is always present. Nevertheless, Sartre's overall tone with regard
to the phenomenon of the "We-Subject" is highly negative, seemingly
designed to demonstrate that the experience of it is something very close to
an illusion—"of the psychological order and not ontological,"[65] "a pure
psychological, subjective event in a single consciousness,"[66] having

no value as a metaphysical revelation; it depends strictly on the various forms
of the for-others and is only an empirical enrichment of these forms. It is to this
fact evidently that we should attribute the extreme instability of this experience.[67]

A few remarks are in order concerning this one sequence of passages in *Being and Nothingness* that might qualify for consideration as a fragment of political theory, were it not for the fact that it treats everything political as somewhat incidental and in a significant sense unreal. First, it is important to note its brevity: approximately 25 pages in a work that is over 750 pages in length. Second, one should view it as a good-faith effort on Sartre's part (while recognizing, along with him, that attempts at good faith have a way of sliding into instances of bad faith)[68] to come to terms philosophically with some of his personal experiences of army service and imprisonment that I have recounted. Third, on the positive side these analyses of the "Us" and the "We" do include some valuable early efforts by Sartre to deal with such quintessentially *social* phenomena as triadic relations, solidarity, and oppression. Fourth, certain fundamental features of these analyses, such as Sartre's suspicion of all attempts to view human collectivities and even all of humanity as if they were completed totalities, in the way in which God (or, in the terms of the science fictional imagination to which Sartre will occasionally resort in the two volumes of his *Critique*, visitors from another planet) might, and his concomitant insistence on the impermanence, the comparative instability, of all human interrelational configurations, will remain valid for him throughout his subsequent career. But fifth, the highly negative manner in which Sartre at times discusses even the "Us-Object," as when he reduces our awareness of it to something prereflexive and not knowable in any genuine sense of "knowledge," to say nothing of his wordy but ultimately rather decisive dismissal of the "We-Subject" experience as a purely psychological phenomenon, shows that he was still not ready at this point to treat sociopolitical phenomena with full philosophical seriousness.

Seriousness, in fact, is the trait that Sartre attributes once again, in an important reference here in *Being and Nothingness* as earlier in the *Carnets*, to his opponents on both the Right and the Left (although he does not use these words of political shorthand in the context), who abjure his more playful view of life. He remarks that this false seriousness is the one respect in which both "revolutionaries" and "their ancient adversaries, the possessors," concur: both see the world in terms of ineluctable givens to which human beings must conform, rather than in terms of freedom. They are both in bad faith. But Sartre appears to be more concerned in this passage with the bad-faith seriousness of his "revolutionaries" than with that of the bourgeoisie, with which he had already come to grips years before in such works of fiction as "Childhood of a Leader." And so he completes his discussion here of the spirit of seriousness, regarded as the starkest contrast to the activity of play that he is about to go on to consider, by making a specific reference, very rare for him at that time, to Marx: "Marx proposed the original dogma of the serious when he asserted the priority of object over subject. Man is serious when he takes himself for an object."[69]

The combination of misunderstanding and impasse suggested by this passage is a good point at which to end this discussion both of *Being and Nothingness* and indeed of the entire history of Sartre's "beginnings" as a political theorist. The peremptory judgment about Marx and Marxism that he has rendered here, though when properly interpreted it may not be so very far from his final recorded views about the Marxian worldview, is insupportably superficial, as is the crude dichotomizing of subject and object, and the dismissal of both Right and Left as equally "serious" and therefore equally indefensible *implies*, logically, at least an abstention from taking any political stance within a real-world context, if not an apoliticism or even an aestheticism. This attitude, as we have by now seen in some detail, is by no means reflective of all of Sartre's nascent philosophical thinking about politics; and, although it may to some extent be understood in light of the virtually insurmountable barriers to political expression that had been imposed by the German Occupation, Sartre's participation in some Resistance activities and in particular his success in getting his play, *The Flies*, which was clearly intended as a mythologically veiled statement of protest against the Occupation,[70] performed on the Paris stage during that same epoch argues against reading the philosophical passage in question as a simple case of Sartre's "playing it safe," politically speaking. Rather, the passage should be seen as a particularly clear demonstration of the fact that he was still only beginning to feel his way as a political thinker.

Four published essays and one very long unfinished and until recently unpublished effort of the next several years, the years immediately following the Liberation of Paris, will take up the challenge of attempting to develop a political theory at a level at which the writer of *Being and Nothingness* was as yet unable to. *Anti-Semite and Jew*, written immediately after the Liberation but published many months later, will deal with the most salient contemporary example of oppressive, reactionary "seriousness"; "Materialism and Revolution" will repeat some of the same Sartrean animus against Marxism as philosophy that we have found in *Being and Nothingness* and in the *Carnets*, but now with a view to preserving what Sartre has come to regard as the very positive value of revolutionary change in society by placing it on a more solid theoretical footing; and *What Is Literature?* will develop an aesthetics of commitment which will be at the same time a political theory of commitment, an idea already proposed in the earlier "Presentation" of the new journal, *Les Temps Modernes*. Finally, in the *Cahiers pour une morale*, Sartre's lengthiest and in the end least successful writing effort of the immediate postwar years, we shall find his most direct effort at fulfilling the promise with which *Being and Nothingness* terminates, of developing an ethic on the basis of its ontology, an effort that becomes at the same time a first version of a systematic Sartrean philosophy of history and social and political theory.

TWO

First Ethics

Since the posthumous publication of his *Cahiers pour une morale*, a great deal of the earlier confusion in the scholarly literature about Sartre's attitudes concerning his 1943 promise to write an ethic based on the ontology of *Being and Nothingness* has been dissipated. The *Cahiers* are, in fact, his failed effort at fulfilling that promise—failed inasmuch as Sartre left them unpublished and incomplete, failed inasmuch as he became dissatisfied with their tone and orientation, but still interesting and philosophically valuable in many respects. Even Sartre himself, toward the end of his life, apparently refused to regard the *Cahiers* as a complete failure: when Simone de Beauvoir, in her published conversations with him, characterizes this early Sartrean ethics as having been "abandoned," he corrects her, saying, "I didn't abandon it. These notes were made to be treated at greater length."[1] It is important to realize that ethical/political themes to which Sartre was to pay detailed attention both in the *Cahiers* and later were already surfacing in some of his shorter, published essays before and during his roughly two-year labor (1947–48) on the manuscript(s) that we now know as the *Cahiers*. It is equally important to realize that, somewhat in contrast to his best-known short essay of this period of the mid-1940s, *Existentialism Is a Humanism*, which is not of great interest for our present purpose of presenting Sartre's political theory,[2] these other essays are already very successful—more than the *Cahiers* themselves—at manifesting the inextricable interconnection between the ethical and the political.

Of the essays of this genre upon which I wish briefly to focus here before turning to the *Cahiers*, the first in order of composition, though not of publication, is the richest and most stimulating. Entitled *Réflexions sur la question juive*, translated into English under the obviously inaccurate but not entirely misleading title of *Anti-Semite and Jew*, it was written, according to a Sartrean footnote right in the middle explaining what he meant by "today,"[3] in October 1944, a matter of weeks after the Liberation of Paris. The first two sections of it, less than half, were then printed just over a year later (December 1945) in the third issue of the important new journal with which Sartre was to be associated for the remainder of his life, *Les Temps Modernes*. Finally the entire essay, including the long set of descriptions, phenomenological in orientation, of inauthentic Jewish behaviors that had been deliberately omitted from the *Temps Modernes* version, was published in book form one year after that.

In recently rereading this essay with a view to situating it within the context of Sartre's evolution as a political theorist, I could not help being struck by the contrast in tone between it and all of the Sartrean writings that I have discussed in the previous chapter. The text of *Anti-Semite and Jew* implies that its philosopher-author has thought deeply about other fundamental political issues in addition to those which directly pertain to anti-Semitism, and indeed has developed some systematic perspectives and principles concerning them. In other words, the essay cannot be considered merely an *"article de circonstance,"* even if the circumstances in question are those murderous social attitudes of supposedly "civilized" people that gave rise to one of the most disgraceful episodes of human history. It is evident from the text, from what is not said in it, that the vastness of scope of the Holocaust was as yet not fully understood by Sartre at the time at which he wrote *Anti-Semite and Jew,* and it is equally evident from the *Cahiers pour une morale,* written several years later, that Sartre had in fact not yet reached the level of clarity about political theory that he may *appear* to have attained in this essay. Nevertheless, it remains a significant work, sometimes brilliant and moving.

The essay begins with a "portrait of the Anti-Semite," the apt title that Sartre gave to the original published version of this first portion of it. Here, Sartre attempts to delineate the set of attitudes of such a person: passionate, irrational, inhumane, Manichean, traditionalist, seeking a perverse kind of "distinction," and ultimately murderous, afraid of the human condition. This portrait is followed by a very brief discussion of a theme already mentioned at the outset, namely, the inadequacy of the "analytic spirit" of the sort of individual whom Sartre denominates "the democrat"—the rational, well-intentioned liberal, who insists that there really is no Jewish question and that the solution to whatever problems may be posed by anti-Semitism is the full, enforced assimilation of Jews into the mainstream of society. Sartre then undertakes the series of descriptions of inauthentic Jewish behaviors that I have mentioned, behaviors that include certain kinds of emphatic gestures, masochism, lack of tact, a tendency toward abstract calculation, and a concomitant love of money and of other forms of intangible property, such as stocks. Sartre's contention throughout this series of descriptions is that, to the extent to which such conduct merits condemnation, which it often receives in the form of anti-Semitic caricatures, it simply reflects the fact that it is the anti-Semites who have created and who sustain this caricatural and ultimately illusory object that they call "the Jew," trapping many real individuals into conforming to these inauthentic Jewish stereotypes. He admits that authentic conduct is always very difficult to achieve, but he urges Jews to choose themselves authentically, as Jews, rather than to try to adapt the unrealistic liberal democratic route of immediate, enforced assimilation. He concludes, after having admitted, at the end of this longest section of his essay, that such authentic conduct may succeed at an ethical level and still not resolve social and political issues that have become even clearer as a result of the movement to establish a Jewish state, by pleading, in a brief conclusion, for a "concrete liberalism" based on a frank recognition of the realities of anti-Semitism and its consequences. In the long run, he claims, assimilation would come about as a matter of course, rather than by being artificially forced, if French Jews and non-Jews alike were to raise their consciousnesses in the direction of such a "concrete liberalism" and abandon optimistic, abstract rationalism.

The essay is a bold one, treading on very delicate and unstable ground, by no means always successful in avoiding missteps, somewhat limited by the time and place of its authorship, and yet prescient in a number of respects. Sartre himself admits that "in such delicate matters we must protect ourselves with all sorts of reservations."[4] He is particularly concerned in this passage with the fact that his phenomenological descriptions of "inauthentic" Jewish behaviors do not hold universally, but that they are simply broad generalizations. But equally delicate and subject to serious reservations and qualifications is the very strategy that Sartre employs here, that of explaining certain types of actions that anti-Semites deem offensive and regard as "typically Jewish," in light of his thesis that Jewishness is a social construct for which primary responsibility is attributable to the anti-Semite. Although Sartre's blending of facts and arguments in this section is often cogent and illuminating—his discussion of the claim that there is a typical, universal "Jewish physiognomy," for instance, decisively demonstrates to a narrowly provincial French reader the vast differences in what is regarded as physiognomically typical in different countries—his very emphasis on characteristics often utilized in racist caricatures could be regarded as furnishing more potential ammunition to the anti-Semitic enemy; it was just this fear, on the part of some of Sartre's Jewish friends who had read the manuscript, that led to his initial decision, later reversed, to publish only the first portions of the essay. Moreover, the claim that any particular behaviors, "defense mechanisms" (to borrow the terminology, unacceptable to the anti-mechanistic Sartre, of another tradition in psychology) developed in partial acceptance of the demeaning objectification of oneself by others, must depend to some degree on the intentions, the (Sartrean) "choices of oneself," of the individual(s) engaging in these behaviors; but just what these are can certainly not be known by observing a few isolated gestures, and in fact it seems to me that some of the same isolated gestures that reflect one individual's inauthenticity might very well be integral expressions of authentic Jewishness on the part of another individual. Sartre's text occasionally compounds the confusion by reading "the Jew" in contexts in which these words are clearly intended as shorthand for "the inauthentic Jew," or so it seems to me. (*Search for a Method*, written years later, is notorious for exhibiting the similar defect of reading

"Marxists" in certain passages in which Sartre is clearly referring to the rigid, "orthodox" Marxists who are the objects of his criticism, and not to *all* Marxists of whatever stripe, among the more "authentic" and flexible of whom he even counted himself at the time of that writing.)

In addition, one must consider the ultimate "indelicacy" of writing intimately and frankly about "the Jewish question" when one is not oneself Jewish. Particularly revealing in this respect is a passage in which Sartre asserts that it would be a mistake to equate the Jew's very understandable uneasiness *(inquiétude)* concerning his or her property, power, and even life itself with "the anxiety [*angoisse*] that the consideration of the human condition provokes in us . . . Metaphysics is the special privilege [*apanage*] of the Aryan ruling classes."[5] If one sets aside the obvious hyperbole of this passage (in the course of the essay, Sartre himself has evoked the names of many great philosophers who were Jewish) and focuses on the point of the distinction that Sartre is making here, one will be better prepared to understand the special relationship, itself uneasy rather than anguished, that he always had throughout the rest of his life to Jews and to Jewish concerns—e.g., his defense of the State of Israel, though of course not always of its policies, against some of the strongly anti-Zionist and some-times anti-Semitic currents within the French Left, and his personal attach-ments to certain Jewish people *as Jews* (to use his own expression from *Anti-Semite and Jew*), notably to his adopted daughter, Arlette Elkaïm, and to that close confidant of his last years, Benny Lévy. This passage sheds some prospective light on his otherwise astonishing claim, in his famous published interview with Lévy, that he had never personally experienced anguish, although the notion, developed by Heidegger, had been much in the air in the 1930s, and he had therefore utilized it.[6] When Sartre was writing *Anti-Semite and Jew*, the memory of Heidegger's collaboration with the Nazis was still very fresh, as was the Nazi language of "the Aryan." Sartre's often remarkable personal sensitivity to others' situations, which is so evident in his treatment of "the Jewish question" despite whatever blunders he may have made in discussing it, includes a recognition on his part, consistent with all of his philosophy, that one can never fully identify oneself with, or become, another: the institution of the law might make a Jewish person his daughter by adoption, but he knew he could never become a Jew by adoption.

And of course there is an important sense in which, as Sartre wishes to emphasize throughout the essay, there is no such thing as essential Jew-ishness, and there is no such human being as a Jew by birth, or a thief or a homosexual or a "leader" by birth, or even, if one abstracts from considera-tions of biological sex and focuses on all the constructs of social con-ditioning that are usually connoted when we use this word, a *woman* by birth. (This was, of course, the point of Simone de Beauvoir's famous assertion, in *The Second Sex*, that "One is not born, but rather becomes, a woman.")[7] But if this is so, as I am inclined to think it is, then the *history* of one's "becoming" a Jew takes on an extremely significant role, one which cannot possibly be completely explained by the activities and attitudes of anti-Semites. Being, or rather becoming, Jewish clearly has a great deal to do with the rich and complex history of the Jewish religion and culture, a point about which Sartre reveals only a very deficient awareness in *Anti-Semite and Jew*: he dismisses Jewish history as one of dispersal, which has left Jews with only an *abstract*, rather than concrete, national community, and he points out that one can be the object of anti-Semites and either an inauthentic or an authentic Jew without having any religious beliefs. This is true but by no means the whole story, and Sartre himself in later years readily admitted the essay's deficiencies from the historical and economic points of view.[8] In his last published interview with Lévy, he expressed great satisfaction in having been able to begin to learn more about Judaica from the latter; to some, this has seemed irrelevant to the main concerns of Sartre's life as a philosopher and hence one more evidence of Lévy's having led a helpless old man along paths that he would not have wished to follow.[9] But in fact, as we have seen in reviewing this essay—one of Sartre's earliest pieces of sustained social theory, in which he has arrived at a partial but still not a robust grasp of the importance of *history* for such a theory—the truth about this serious interest of Sartre's last months of life is both more interesting and more complex.

To conclude this brief discussion of *Anti-Semite and Jew*, it will be useful to consider some of its most salient values from the point of view of Sartre's evolution as a theorist. Probably the foremost of these is its unequivocal advocacy of a certain type of authenticity, a topic upon which Sartre had touched in *Being and Nothingness* only in a famous footnote in which he had said that, while authentic existence was possible, that was not the place to discuss it. His insistence on confining himself there to the description only of inauthentic modes of conduct has given rise to rather wild claims, on the parts of some hostile critics, to the effect that Sartre never really considered it possible to live authentically. While a reading of the posthumously published *Cahiers pour une morale*, to which we shall be turning shortly, makes such a thesis quite untenable now, it would already have been untenable to anyone who seriously considered *Anti-Semite and Jew*. On the other hand, the friendly critic of Sartre's thought must acknowledge the fact that Sartre's vivid descriptions of both the anti-Semite and the inauthentic Jew leave more of an impression on most readers than does his plea for authentic Jewish modes of conduct. There is a good reason for this, which is deeply rooted in Sartre's entire thought about positive modes of conduct, as it must be in the thought of anyone who emphasizes the free and creative possibilities of human behavior: whereas the fixed, often caricatural gestures of the inauthentic Jew can be captured in phenomenological descriptions such as his, Sartre points out, the Jew who has become authentic by that very fact *eludes* description, "like every authentic man."[10] In other words, authentic conduct, because it constitutes a free and creative response to a given human situation, cannot be completely captured and predictively described in advance. So it is much more difficult to talk about authenticity than about inauthenticity.

This observation points to two other important Sartrean ideas that find significant formulations in *Anti-Semite and Jew*: that of being "in situation" and that of distrusting universal concepts. The notion that a human being is above all always "in situation" was already utilized by Sartre in *Being and Nothingness* as one of his principal systematic bulwarks against traditional idealist and Cartesian (dualist) assertions that what is essential to every human individual is his or her immaterial psyche, conceivable in abstraction from every element of what Sartre calls facticity: one's body and one's physical and social environment. At the beginning of his discussion of inauthentic and authentic Jewishness, Sartre explains with exceptional clarity what he means by this notion:

> that [man] forms a synthetic whole with his situation—biological, economic, political, cultural, etc. He cannot be distinguished from his situation, for it forms him and decides his possibilities; but, inversely, it is he who gives it meaning by making his choices within it and by it. . . . What men have in common is not a "nature" but a condition, that is, an ensemble of limits and restrictions: the inevitability of death, the necessity of working for a living, of living in a world already inhabited by other men.[11]

It is for this very reason, Sartre says, that the abstractly universal way of conceiving of "the Jewish question" that characterizes the liberal democrat is unacceptable; indeed, Sartre says, he is going to limit himself to a description of the situation of the *French* Jew, for that is his present concern. This notion of "situations" was of course to be the inspiration for the title of the very important series of collected essays that was published in book form by Sartre over many years, most of them after having first been published in *Les Temps Modernes*. Although his opposition to universal concepts as being inevitably abstract and incapable of reflecting concrete situations, an opposition that is closely linked in this passage with the notion of being "in situation," is somewhat less frequently mentioned in the secondary literature and in any event was not always, in my opinion, consistently adhered to by Sartre himself, it too was to remain a *leitmotif* in his thought and to find perhaps its best expression in the second volume of the *Critique of Dialectical Reason*.

Closely linked, in Sartre's thinking at the time, with the abstract universal reasoning of traditional liberalism was an attitude that he labels at the outset of this essay *"l'esprit analytique."* The liberal cuts up the objects of his or her reflections into small pieces, thus hopelessly distorting them. To this mainstream approach of modern Western philosophy and science Sartre opposes, of course, a spirit of synthesis, but he is well aware that the anti-Semite too has a synthetic, wholistic outlook on the world: "It is the spirit of synthesis which permits him to conceive of himself as forming an indissoluble unity with all France. It is in the name of this spirit that he denounces the purely analytic and critical intelligence of the Jews."[12] So we must distinguish between syntheses of the Right and those of the Left. But just how does one go about this? When he wrote this essay, Sartre was as yet relatively unfamiliar with the Hegelian-Marxian tradition (already strongly influenced by it, yes, but still not prepared to make an active and fully conscious use of its principal intellectual tools)[13] and so apparently unable to say very much about the differences between the two opposed types of synthetic worldviews. Like his approach to the opposition between seriousness and playfulness upon which I have already commented with reference to earlier works,[14] Sartre's treatment of the opposition between synthesis and analysis remains somewhat ambiguous throughout *Anti-Semite and Jew,* even while he emphasizes its capital importance for the argument of that work.

It is in an essay that appears to have been composed only a few months later (and that found its way into print somewhat earlier), the "Presentation," or inaugural editorial statement, of *Les Temps Modernes,* that Sartre begins to make progress in resolving, or at least in explicating, this ambiguity. The original editorial advisory board of the journal included a number of important figures from whom Sartre was later, at various times, to take his intellectual distance and separate; Aron, Camus, and Merleau-Ponty are among the best-known of these. We have no evidence that this Sartrean essay evoked outrage or strong opposition in any of them, and yet it is above all a clear, if brief, statement of important themes in Sartre's nascent political theory, as well as serving at the same time as a practical indicator of the sort of articles that the editors were seeking to publish and of the somewhat vague political line, non-Communist Left, that they espoused in common. In the process of furnishing these indications, the "Presentation" proclaims the ideal, upon which Sartre was soon to elaborate in much greater detail in *What Is Literature?*, of a literature of commitment *(engagement)*—politically responsible, but still *literature,* as Sartre emphasizes in his concluding remarks.[15]

It is interesting to find, in the very opening paragraph of this "Presentation," the name of Flaubert invoked as an instance of the type of writer to whom Sartre and his journal stand opposed. As Sartre points out, Flaubert is considered as at one and the same time an advocate of the notion of art for art's sake—pure, disengaged formalism—and a proponent of naturalism, an admirer of the dominant philosophical viewpoint of early modern science; Sartre's point is that, while this combination may appear contradictory to some, it in fact makes sense as an epitomization of the bourgeois spirit that he finds so false and unacceptable. The core message of Sartre's enormous late work, *The Family Idiot,* is thus already announced in 1945. Even at the time, Sartre's nearly lifelong love-hate relationship with

Flaubert was already of long standing, and the context makes it evident just why this relationship was so intense: Flaubert was a great and (eventually) highly regarded writer of a still not very distant earlier time, and Sartre at once aspired to the fame and influence that Flaubert enjoyed and yet was repelled both by many aspects of Flaubert's personality and by the ultimately conservative or even reactionary nature of his influence.

Sartre's clarification, in this "Presentation," of what he understands to be implied by the opposed "spirits" of analysis and synthesis is helpful in making much more intelligible what had remained rather vague in *Anti-Semite and Jew*. He suggests that he would like to term what he is advocating a "totalitarian" conception of human beings, were it not for all the pejorative connotations, extraneous to his own meaning, that have come to be attached to that word.[16] He goes on to explain what he means by this through an analysis of the notions, so dear to the French bourgeois tradition, of equality, fraternity, and liberty, showing that the analytic spirit interprets "equality" in an essentialist way, asserting that there is a common, abstract human nature; treats "fraternity" as some sort of passive bond that unites these essentially equal entities without serving as a motivation for them to act in solidarity to change their world; and cannot assign any purpose or direction to human "freedom" at a social level except to say that we are free to be the human beings that we presumably already are. Although Sartre does not return in this essay to his preferred but admittedly misleading notion of the spirit of synthesis as entailing a "totalitarian" conception of human beings, it is obvious from the ensuing discussion that he already has in mind the idea of "totalization" which will become so central in the *Critique of Dialectical Reason*. The universal concept "man" (in the generic sense of the word) is a myth and does not really exist, Sartre contends: there is no human nature, only a human condition, and therefore we must together forge what we are going to become, rather than finding a human nature ready-made, as the spirit of analysis would have us believe we can do. But what we must continually create is not to be conceived of as fixed and final, an end-state, either: it is only those who are totalitarians in the pejorative sense who think in such ultimately illusory terms. This ongoing synthetic process of striving both theoretically and practically to bring about a working human solidarity rather than merely postulating it or attempting to enforce it through coercion is what Sartre will capture in later years with the neologism of "totalization" and its corresponding verb forms, meant to connote activity and open-endedness.

Some of Sartre's other contentions in this brief "Presentation" are less precise, of interest primarily for the light that they now shed on the evolution of his thought. For example, he proclaims that the new journal will be devoted to "defending the autonomy and the rights of the person,"[17] an assertion of unaccustomed banality and vagueness. He mentions the need for a *dialectical* conception of the passions (as opposed to the analytic approach which treats them singly and mechanically),[18] but he says little about what this means. He deplores the oppositional character that modern thought so often assigns to the relationship between individual freedom and socialism,[19] a clear and significant reassertion of his commitment to *"socialisme et liberté"*; but it is evident that he is still only in the early stages of thinking through to a theoretical position underlying his socialism that would be comparable to and compatible with the support given to the notion of individual freedom in *Being and Nothingness*. Finally, and perhaps most importantly from the standpoint of his future philosophical allegiances, in this "Presentation" Sartre explicitly denies that he is a materialist[20] and criticizes contemporary Marxism for adhering to an outmoded conception of human psychology;[21] but at the same time he makes it abundantly clear that he finds common ground with Marxists in insisting that fundamental social change is needed and that he admires their advocacy of it.

"Materialism and Revolution," published only a few months later (June and July 1946) in *Les Temps Modernes*, is valuable for its more extended articulation of this ambivalence on Sartre's part concerning Marxist revolutionary thought as he understood it at the time; it is in fact his first really significant published statement on the subject of Marxist theory. It shows that Sartre had by this time begun to familiarize himself with some of the writings of Marx, Engels, Lenin, and even Stalin, and that he was becoming conversant with the thinking of the principal French Marxists of the day: Hervé, Naville, Lefebvre, and, above all, Roger Garaudy, with whom he reports having had extended discussions. Much of this essay consists of reasoned refutations of various aspects of their "orthodox" Marxism: the infamous "reflection theory of cognition" (knowledge as a mirror-like or photographic representation of objective reality) first enunciated by Lenin,[22] the idea that a society's "superstructure" is determined by its "base" of productive forces, Engels's conception of a dialectics of nature, and other salient components of what came to be called, contemptuously, "diamat"—the canned philosophy, made canonical by Stalinist decree, of dialectical materialism. What Sartre attempts to show is that the underlying strong causal determinism of this worldview undermines itself by implying, against the evidence, that there is only one possible outcome of history and that human freedom and subjectivity are illusions. To me, this attempt still seems highly successful, more than forty years later.

A footnote to the title line of the essay's reprinted version, in *Situations*, 3, shows that Sartre was already in the late 1940s being forced to deal with the troublesome question of just what is and what is not Marxism. It is a peculiar question, from one point of view purely a matter of terminological convention and hence without great interest or importance, but from another point of view enormously weighty because it bears on both the validity and the integrity of the most important new political movement of the past century. In the footnote Sartre says that he has been reproached by some for not citing Marx himself in the essay (a charge that is not entirely correct, by the way) and responds by saying that "my criticisms are not addressed to [Marx], but to the Marxist scholasticism of 1949. Or, if one wishes, to Marx *through* Stalinist neo-Marxism."[23] The issues implicit in this footnote—for instance, whether the so-called Marxism of theorists belonging to the French Communist Party, with its undeniably close ties to Stalin and the CPSU, was at all faithful to the Marxism of Marx, or whether, even if this doctrine constitutes a *neo*-Marxism rather than the pure philosophy of its originator, Marx may not still bear considerable ultimate responsibility for it (the point of Sartre's last sentence in the footnote)—are very much alive and of concern to us today, as they concerned Sartre, along with his contemporaries, throughout the remainder of his life. To summarize quickly, by way of anticipation, later developments in Sartre's attitude toward Marxism, it can be said that he came eventually to identify Marxism less closely with the "Stalinist neo-Marxism" with which he was most familiar in the late 1940s, but that his substantive philosophical views about determinism and freedom underwent only modifications, not sea changes; and that, finally, offhand remarks that he made in the last years of his life suggest that at that time he came back again to a closer identification of "Marxism" with its "orthodox," strongly deterministic version(s). Thus, what may seem from a superficial reading of texts and transcripts of interviews to have been a considerable wavering in Sartre's attitudes toward Marxism over the years will turn out to be due in large measure to this question of the *labeling* of a body of theory, which is only in part a philosophical question. To a considerable extent, it depends on what a writer or speaker expects her or his audience to understand by a given label, such as Marxism.

The essay's title, at any rate, refers to "materialism" rather than to "Marxism"; but this word also poses somewhat similar problems. There is no doubt that Sartre was later to express a willingness at one point in the *Critique of Dialectical Reason*[24] to accept the materialist label to which he reacts so negatively in the essay under consideration here, where he takes it to refer to the unacceptably strong determinist doctrines that are the focal point of his criticism, while at the same time showing the vague and even self-contradictory nature of the concept of "matter" employed by his opponents.[25] But it is arguable, once again, that the later, qualified acceptance of this label on Sartre's part has as much or more to do with his changed understanding of what "materialism" might be taken to mean, than with a major modification of his philosophical perspectives. At any rate, in "Materialism and Revolution" the "orthodox" Marxist materialism that Sartre has in mind there is vigorously attacked as a myth, a dogma, an unsupported faith. However vociferously, according to Sartre, the self-styled dialectical materialists may claim to be propounding the only viable philosophical alternative to idealism, which of course he also rejects, and to be relying on the findings of science rather than on metaphysical postulates, the fact is

that their doctrines constitute an a priori metaphysics that does not correspond to the ways in which contemporary scientists regard their own
fundamental conceptions, including causal phenomena themselves. The
Communists' dogmatic notion of truth, which as a matter of fact is highly
ambiguous, frequently taking the merest opinion for absolute objectivity
(as in the commonly heard allegation, "The Trotskyite is a police in-
former"—objectively speaking, that is, regardless of whether Trotskyites
themselves realize it),[26] requires the thinker to abandon reasoning and to
fall to his or her knees, as Pascal once demanded in the name of Catholic
Christianity.[27]

It is important to notice the occasional identification in this essay of both
"Marxism" and "materialism" with yet a third referent, the Communist
Party, as is evident in the passage of the text upon which I have just
reported. This identification is of course quite untenable, as the Trotskyites
of the time would themselves have pointed out and as the fact that both
Henri Lefebvre and the prolific even if not intellectually distinguished
Garaudy[28] were later forced, at different times, to leave the Party because of
deep disagreements with Soviet policies was to make abundantly clear. On
the other hand, the identification in question held good for the writers and
theorists whom Sartre knew best at the time, and it helps to explain the
otherwise somewhat curious direction that is taken in the portion of "Materialism and Revolution," roughly the second half of it, in which the solid
philosophical criticism of the concept of materialism is no longer his principal concern. Although this portion is not nearly so clear-cut as the first, it
seems to me to have two major purposes: first, to account for the success of
the materialist myth despite its obvious theoretical weaknesses, and second, to suggest the possibility of a revolutionary alternative.

Throughout this second half of his essay, Sartre speaks of "the revolutionary." This employment of the definite article turns out to be somewhat
confusing, because Sartre is contending, at one and the same time, both
that the revolutionaries of the day quite understandably accept materialism
and yet that revolutionary practice is ultimately incompatible with materialist thought, so that, presumably, the *lucid* revolutionary will be anti-
materialist. The adoption of materialism by the vast majority of
revolutionary workers and by the party that represents them is readily
explicable, he argues, when one realizes that revolutionary workers have
issued from the ranks of the oppressed, the class whose members are
treated like things by the ruling classes. The latter have claimed at different
times various special rights and privileges on the grounds that they, by
contract, are better than mere things. But the revolutionary has seen
through such claims. He or she sees that every human being is equally a
part of the natural world and that no one has a special divine or other
supernatural right. Moreover, the revolutionary is well aware that the
oppressors try to support their bogus claims to superiority by an appeal to
their own allegedly more refined reasoning and to the primacy of reasoning

over physical labor. These valid observations about the role of intellectual elitism in the ideological trickery that helps sustain oppression lead the revolutionary, understandably but nevertheless fallaciously, to an attitude of ambivalence toward thinking itself and to the conclusion that we are all, oppressors and oppressed alike, natural "things," first and foremost, and like all other things are completely subject to a deterministic causality; this is the basis of the materialist myth. That myth has been enormously successful in organizing revolutionary action.

But the crude pragmatist criterion of truth ("truth is what works") is itself idealistic and untenable, Sartre agrees, and the *success* of the materialist myth does not make it true. Even while "the revolutionary" adheres to materialism, revolutionary philosophy must by definition be a philosophy of *transcendence*[29]—i.e., one which is committed to the historical possibility of human beings' freely going beyond their existing states of affairs, their conditions of oppression, toward a novel and open future. It is I who have added the words, "by definition," to the Sartrean passage that I have just cited; Sartre only says, *"doit être"* (must be). Therein lies the ambiguity of his position: the ideology of the actual revolutionaries with whom he is familiar is the materialist myth, according to which freely chosen "transcendence" of this sort is in principle impossible. But his own ambiguity, he might well reply, only mirrors theirs: since socialism is only the means to attaining "the reign of freedom," and since, as he has already argued, there is no room for a notion of genuine human freedom in the materialism that he has been criticizing, "a materialist socialism is therefore contradictory because socialism proposes as its goal a humanism which materialism renders inconceivable."[30] And so those individuals, with few if any exceptions (Sartre himself, perhaps, and those whom he might be able to persuade through his writing), who are most strongly committed to the socialist goal, namely, the revolutionaries of the day, remain committed to an antisocialist myth or faith: "What will happen some day," Sartre concludes his essay by asking, "if materialism stifles the revolutionary project?"[31]

With this essay in defense of a philosophy of freedom against "orthodox" Marxist determinism, it may ironically be observed, *"les jeux sont faits"*[32]—the chips are down—for Sartre as far as his future political theory is concerned. In it, he has succeeded in articulating both his own concrete commitment to fundamental social change and most of his major differences with those who share that commitment but rally to the banner of dialectical materialism as the means of promoting it. As anticipated, the reaction of the French Communist Party theoreticians was quite negative, but Sartre had now opened a dialogue even though they did not especially welcome it. As we shall soon see, the sophistication of this essay is actually greater, with respect to Marxism, than is that of the *Cahiers pour une morale*, composed over the ensuing two years, and some of its arguments against Engels's idea of a dialectics of nature, for instance, will only be rehearsed and elaborated upon, rather than changed, when a Sartre with more positive attitudinal ties to Marxism takes up the same topic more than a decade later as he writes the first volume of his *Critique*. If there are important notions touched upon in "Materialism and Revolution" about which Sartre will later come to believe that his previous understanding has been deficient, such as "Marxism," "materialism," and "humanism,"[33] the essay itself is characterized by a confident tone[34] that is not to be found in most of his early excursions into political theory, notably those discussed in the previous chapter. It is slightly glib but not inaccurate to say that in "Materialism and Revolution," by contrast even with *Anti-Semite and Jew* and the "Presentation" of *Les Temps Modernes*, Sartre shows that his class consciousness, along with other aspects of his social awareness, has been decisively raised.

Sartre's principal work of relevance to political theory written during the following year, *What Is Literature?*, is the last upon which I shall touch before discussing the *Cahiers pour une morale*. *What Is Literature?* is, by widespread consensus,[35] one of the most interesting, provocative essays of his entire career. First published serially in early to mid-1947, hence at the time at which he had presumably begun the *Cahiers*, it is introduced with a certain tone of exasperation. Citing some of the criticisms that he considers particularly outrageous among the many that have been raised concerning his advocacy in essays[36] and in the editorial policy of *Les Temps Modernes* of a "committed" literature, Sartre complains that people have apparently not read carefully what has been said, so he shall have to begin all over again: "This amuses no one, neither you nor me. But the nail must be driven in."[37] Thus the reader is prepared for a careful and detailed exposition of the notion of a literature of commitment, organized around the questions of what writing is, why and for whom one writes, and what the situation of the French writer in 1947 actually is. It is obviously as much an essay in literary history and in aesthetics as in political theory, but it certainly qualifies as the latter by virtue of its focus on political commitment.

In retrospect, the Sartre of *What Is Literature?* can be faulted, or at least seriously questioned, for the enormous seriousness with which he takes the writer's vocation, in the belief that, at least as it still existed at that time in his country (though not, for example, in the United States, with which he shows considerable familiarity as a result of his readings of American literature and his extensive travels there in 1945), the writer may still be capable of changing the world.[38] By the time he wrote *The Words*, Sartre was far less sanguine about this and somewhat embarrassed by his earlier illusions. But the tone of *What Is Literature?*, especially when one reads the concluding section, is itself far from optimistic. Sartre notes that the committed writer of his time, unlike those in some of the earlier epochs that he has depicted, notably the eighteenth century, has no natural audience, no "public": the bourgeoisie, which was the oppressed class two centuries ago and is now the dominant class, furnishes the writer's only actual readers, but of course the writer committed to fundamental social change must write *against* this declining bourgeoisie rather than *for* it. As for the working class, the one for which the committed writer writes, it is, as Sartre has already stressed in "Materialism and Revolution," by and large under the discipline of the Communist Party and hence approachable only from within that group, with its thoroughly unacceptable, degraded Marxist ideology. Moreover, one of the most salient features of our time, to be found in Naziism, in Communism, and in American anti-Communism alike, is the rise to prominence of propaganda, the concomitant degradation of the meaning of words (e.g., "revolution," "fascism," "democracy," "communism," etc.), and the widespread reliance on mystification; the writer's Herculean task is to try to be honest, to call a spade a spade, to restore words to their real meanings. Finally, Sartre takes note of the climate of the Cold War, in which there is widespread insistence that one must join the camp of one or the other Superpower, the USSR or the USA. Against the overwhelming odds suggested by these observations, Sartre concludes his essay by holding out a faint hope for a democratic socialist Europe.

The case that Sartre makes in earlier sections for the central theme of his essay, namely, the necessity that prose literature be *committed* if it is to count for anything at all, is very strong. It is bolstered by historical analyses—the function of the Medieval clerk in reinforcing the existing order, the role of the *philosophes* in helping to undermine it—, by a carefully drawn distinction between prose literature and other art forms such as poetry (the function of which Sartre claims to be radically different, while denying that he is a Philistine with respect to poetry or music or other arts), and by appeals to his critics to produce counterexamples (for instance, to furnish a single instance of an anti-Semitic or anti-Negro novel that is good literature). The historical period that he seems once again to regard, as he already did in his "Presentation" essay, as the most challenging to deal with from the perspective of his theories of committed literature is the late nineteenth century, the period of Flaubert and of art for art's sake. In an extended analysis he tries to show that the extreme negativity and inwardness of the dominant literature of that era actually served bourgeois purposes and values by its withdrawal from sociopolitical commitment and its view of itself as being in essence what Sartre calls a "literature of consumption"—to be devoured by a bourgeois public that knew that its typical writer posed no threat: "He wishes to preserve the social order in order to feel himself an outsider at home there; in short, he is a rebel, not a revolutionary."[39] Such analyses are always subject to criticism, as Sartre is aware, for drawing lines too sharply between periods and between different literary attitudes and for overgeneralizing; perhaps his late, very extended study of a single writer, Flaubert, can be seen as an effort to deflect such a criticism. But here, the very scope of Sartre's claims and of his evidence in support of them is part of what renders the essay so valuable.

What Is Literature? contains a number of other signposts in addition to the treatment of Flaubert and his epoch that point toward important future developments in Sartre's social thought. Among them is his first published use, to the best of my knowledge, of the more or less Aristotelian distinction between *exis*, or what is habitual and given, and *praxis*, or "action in history and on history" ("we must abandon the literature of exis to inaugurate that of praxis"),[40] a distinction which is to play a major role in the *Critique of Dialectical Reason*. There is also a remarkably clear announcement of his intention some day to undertake the latter work:

> I shall try some day to describe that strange reality, History, which is neither objective, nor ever completely subjective, where the dialectic is contested, penetrated, corroded by a sort of antidialectic but still dialectical.[41]

The essay also relies heavily, especially in addressing the question "Why write?", on the notion of human creation, in this case literary creation, as being at once an *appeal* (by the creative author) and an act of *generosity* (ultimately on the part of both parties, writer and reader, when the act of creation is successful); these notions are to be, as we shall see, very central in the *Cahiers*, though not in Sartre's later works of political theory.

In addition Sartre makes several references to the social ideal which will serve as regulative for so much of his later thought, though he will seldom discuss it explicitly and never at length, that of a classless society. Here in *What Is Literature?* Sartre also alludes to certain implications of this ideal, which at one point he admits to be utopian—conceivable, but unrealizable under present conditions[42]—for literature. For one thing, in such a society, the internal structure of which, he points out, would be "permanent revolution," the writer would serve as a "mediator *for all*,"[43] not just for a certain class. For another thing, Sartre says, the type of literature characteristic of such a society would be a combination or synthesis of the two contrasting types of literature that he has described: the "literature of production," activist, practical, that is required today, with the "literature of consumption" which he has attributed to the nineteenth century.[44] While his insistence that the ideal future society would be one of "permanent revolution" rather than an end-state strikes me as being, however one may feel about the shopworn Trotskyite terminology, an important and useful point, I find the last-mentioned characterization of the literature of this society as a *"total literature,"* a synthesis of production and consumption, of exis and praxis, just too facile to be taken very seriously. It is a superficial use of dialectical thinking to bring about, in effect, a purely verbal "happy ending," and it should make us thankful that Sartre devoted so little of his writing to the construction of social utopias.

Finally, *What Is Literature?* contains passages in which the reader feels above all Sartre's strong *moral* commitment and his ongoing desire to write an ethics. It was during this same year, 1947, that Sartre also wrote a Preface in high praise of what still remains an excellent book, Francis Jeanson's *Sartre and the Problem of Morality*, written by a young man who drew ethical implications from *Being and Nothingness* and other works that in some respects went beyond what Sartre himself, as he acknowledges, had as yet realized to be present there.[45] (Jeanson later became a close associate of Sartre, an important supporter of the Algerian War of Independence against France, and a prominent member of the *Les Temps Modernes* editorial board.) Sartre was coming increasingly to see himself as a moralist. In "Materialism and Revolution" he had commented on the incapacity of "official" Marxism, with its adherence to a strong determinism, to admit that it was a value-laden philosophy, even though Communist Party publications were always redolent of strong moral indignation; now, in *What Is Literature?* he refers to this and makes the point even more forcefully: "the materialist dialectic has as its effect, I have shown elsewhere, to make Good and Evil vanish together; there remains only the historical process."[46] But the experiences of World War II—the mass executions, the concentration camps, etc.—have shown, he says, that Evil is not a mere appearance and have made the writers of his generation rediscover the "absolute within the relative."[47] Thus, the "commitment" of the committed writer is ultimately a moral one: "although literature is one thing and morality a quite different one, at the heart of the aesthetic imperative we discover the moral imperative."[48] But despite all the fervor of his sense of moral commitment and his enormously heightened awareness of the centrality of politics, Sartre is left with many unanswered questions, prominent among which is the following: "What is the relation of ethics to politics?" In this passage in *What Is Literature?* he goes on to say that, while one could deal with such questions abstractly through philosophical reflection, he and his fellow writers wish to deal with them more concretely, through works of fiction, even though the old, prewar techniques for doing so no longer work.[49] But presumably, even as he was writing these words, he had either just begun or was about to begin his first major effort to deal with these issues through abstract, rigorous, philosophical reflection: the *Cahiers*.

Of all of Sartre's book-length unfinished manuscripts that have been published posthumously thus far, the *Cahiers pour une morale* are at once the most important, philosophically speaking, and the least well developed in terms of organization. Thus any attempt to provide a comprehensive summary of them is bound to be extremely frustrating and unsatisfactory. The edition of them that has been prepared by Arlette Elkaïm-Sartre (whose only personal interventions in the text consist of a one-page introduction and very occasional and brief annotations to identify a book referred to by Sartre or to correct a grammatical error) includes the contents of two notebooks of unequal length, the first consisting of more than 400 pages and hence constituting the majority of the book, and two very short manuscripts that appear as appendices.

The first of these appendices was composed over two days in December, 1945, and is perhaps most noteworthy for the very traditional, un-Sartrean tone of its opening sentence: *"Le Bien doit être fait"* (The Good must be done).[50] The fact that Sartre frequently refers here to "the Good," a term that is only rarely found in any of his other more systematic writings, including the *Cahiers* proper (although he was to continue to use its opposite, *"le Mal,"* evil, often enough in many different contexts), is an interesting indication of the extremely undeveloped and inchoate nature of certain aspects of his thought about ethics at the end of 1945. The essay also contains, it is true, some more characteristically Sartrean themes—e.g., the necessary role of human subjectivity, the impossibility of an absolutely universal doing of "good" by all of humanity at once (in which case the very idea of "doing good" would lose all meaning), a critique of self-interest theories of ethics, and an observation to the effect that religion's ploy of asserting the existence of a preestablished good is inauthentic.

As for the second appendix, entitled "Revolutionary Violence" and subtitled "Oppression," it more obviously belongs to the period of the *Cahiers* themselves and takes up some of their themes. What we have here deals, as is the case with the *Cahiers* proper, with only a part of a subtopic of the general issue announced in the title—in this case, a discussion, phenomenological in part, of the oppression involved in Negro slavery in nineteenth-century United States. (There was to be a complementary discussion of the oppression of workers under capitalism, but it was apparently not written.) Sartre argues in this manuscript that there is something of a difference between violence, which implies the *violation* of some putative law, and oppression, which the oppressors in cases like that of slavery regard as legitimate and backed by the authority of the State; within the *Cahiers* proper, as we shall see, he sees this distinction as collapsing and has a good deal to say about the violence of law itself. He shows a considerable subtlety of thought in analyzing certain typical behaviors and attitudes on both sides, slaves and masters—e.g., the importance of laughter and humor in the slaves' sustaining themselves under these conditions; the felt need for slaves not just to work for their masters but also to *please* them, an aspect of the relationship that he chides Hegel for not taking into account in his famous Master/Slave dialectic; and the various types of actions taken by those masters who attempted to play the role of "good," "generous" masters, condemned in the long run to be met with less than complete gratitude and hence to see themselves as "unjustly" treated by their slaves. This manuscript breaks off very abruptly.

The first portion of the principal Cahier, 1, is extremely aphoristic, very reminiscent in style, as readers have commonly noted, of Pascal's *Pensées*. These early aphorisms are numbered; #50, for instance, reads, simply, *"Faire la morale des suspects"* (Compose the ethics of suspects, or of those who are suspect),[51] which leaves considerable leeway to the imagination. Soon, however, the aphorisms give way to longer remarks bearing on diverse though related topics: ethics, history, dialectic, right and law, the philosophy of Hegel (his phenomenology,[52] philosophy of history, and philosophy of law). There are occasional references back to the ideas of *Being and Nothingness*. Toward the middle of the first Cahier, there is a fairly extended discussion of violence. This is followed, by way of illustrating and unearthing the existence of violence in certain typical human interactions, by a still rough but relatively self-contained phenomenological analysis of sixty pages entitled *"Prière et Exigence"* (Prayer and Requirement, although no single English word quite captures the breadth of meaning implicit in Sartre's use of *"exigence"* here). The last few lines of this section, in which Sartre is summarizing the effects of living in the alienated social world of requirements and duties where I recognize that I and the Other are exactly the same by virtue of having freely internalized these requirements and duties, well capture the flavor—morally passionate, socially and politically aware, and yet somehow lacking a broader context to give clear direction and purpose to the analyses that are being offered—both of this segment and of the *Cahiers* as a whole:

> Duty in [the Other], duty in myself, his right, my right, my requirement [i.e., what I am obligated to do] are one and the same thing. I am thus no longer *opposed* to him; requirement is apparent truce, deep-down violence. It is thus at once violence and trick. Total alienation. Suppression of the world of the human, absolute subordination of man to his own ends presented as transcendent and to a will which is that of no one but of which I make use as if it were mine, treatment of man as a means under the guise of treating him as an end.[53]

There next follows a much more fragmentary phenomenology of "Appeal, Acceptance, Refusal"; the first two are treated as more positive modes of conduct, the analysis of which (although there is actually very little about acceptance) occasions some of Sartre's most eloquent formulations of the notion of generosity, regarded as the supreme human value throughout most of the *Cahiers,* while refusal is of course considered very negative but is at any rate only briefly discussed. "Ignorance and Failure" are the next topics; Sartre's analysis of ignorance and stupidity is one of the most original, especially for the time at which it was written, and interesting parts of the *Cahiers*. The remainder of the first Cahier and much of the second wander over a great diversity of topics, including many of those treated previously; there are, inter alia, extended discussions of oppression, of Engels's hidden values and the ideas, of so-called primitive thought, of resignation and humility as attitudes, of the notion of historical progress, and of the use of universal concepts. In the middle of Cahier 2, the reader comes upon a rigorously schematized, though intellectually very puzzling, *"Plan d'une morale ontologique"* (outline of an ontological ethics),[54] which is soon followed by a discussion of *conversion* to moral authenticity (including brief elucidations of the notions of joy and of authentic love).[55] Finally, Cahier 2 returns to an extended discussion of *creation* from a number of viewpoints, terminating with analyses of two polar sorts of creative activity, that of the engineer and that of the artist.

The *Cahiers* are, in short, a goldmine for scholars and other readers with any number of interests in various aspects both of Sartre's philosophy and of the philosophical issues themselves. But this mine is of less than bonanza quality, and so often much digging is required to unearth the most valuable nuggets. If, in a certain sense, all of Sartre's writings can be seen as provisional and transitional, rather than as having been intended by their author as definitive philosophical statements for all time, the *Cahiers* are the most provisional and transitional of all. My first concern, now that I have attempted to furnish something of an overview of them, will be to indicate some of the notions developed here whereby Sartre begins at once to fulfill the promise of an existentialist ethic made in *Being and Nothingness* and to realize that in doing so he is going beyond his earlier, more individualistic conceptions of ethics and toward the sociopolitical dimension. I shall then go on to discuss some of the more salient ideas typically associated with this dimension that Sartre takes up in the *Cahiers*: violence, law and right, sovereignty and the State, and oppression. These topics will naturally lead to a consideration of Sartre's evolving attitudes toward Marxism and toward its principal concerns—e.g., alienation, the class struggle, dialectics, and above all history and historical progress—at the time at which he was writing the *Cahiers*. Finally, in considering some of the passages of the *Cahiers* in which Sartre alludes to such utopian ideas as those of a kingdom of ends and an end of history, we shall perhaps obtain a better insight into just why the *Cahiers* must be considered something much less than a complete success, as Sartre himself readily conceded by abandoning them.

Authenticity is an obvious notion with which to begin this somewhat more detailed account of the *Cahiers*. One section of the *Cahiers* in particular[56] is devoted to authenticity, the topic mentioned by Sartre in *Being and Nothingness* as needing to be treated at some other time. To those who have already considered the ethical implications of that earlier work, there is initially nothing about Sartre's discussion of authenticity here that should occasion enormous surprise. Authenticity, says Sartre, involves at once recognizing the ultimate gratuitousness of all human projects and yet devoting oneself to one's freely-chosen project with full reflectiveness. It is inauthentic to seek to *be* a certain sort of character, a certain sort of person, because human existence always involves "perpetual questioning and perpetual going beyond." Consequently, reflection on one's projects can never be contemplative (for one contemplates only what is fixed), but can be of only two opposite sorts: complicitous, that is, accepting of the *status quo* and hence of the values and fixed beliefs of one's social environment, or what Sartre calls "purifying"; only the latter type of reflection, of course, is authentic and autonomous and results in authentic choices of conduct.[57] To achieve authenticity through purifying reflection requires that the individual undergo a *conversion*, as a result of which one no longer either identifies oneself with what already exists, being, or attempts to appropriate other persons in order to try (impossibly) to possess them as a part of oneself. The outcome of this conversion of purifying reflection whereby one renounces such appropriation, Sartre says, is "to introduce into the internal structure [*rapport*] of the Person the relation of *solidarity*, which will later be modified into solidarity with others."[58]

It is in references such as this final clause, I think, that Sartre signals a decisive departure from (or, if one prefers, transcendence of) the much more individualistic intellectual and ethical climate of *Being and Nothingness*, despite his continuing, heavy use of the terminology of that work (in-itself and for-itself, nothingness, etc.) in the larger passage from which this citation is taken. Only a few pages later, following his discussion of *joy*, Sartre makes what is perhaps his most explicit formulation of that departure in the entire *Cahiers*:

> One of the structures of the *Mitsein* is to reveal the Other in the world. In the Hell of the passions (described in *B.N.*) this revelation of the other is conceived as pure going beyond. And the other, in effect grasped as transcended transcendence, as a fragile body in the universe, is immediately disarmed: I go beyond his or her ends by my own, therefore they are no longer anything more than data; I transform his or her freedom into a given quantity; I can do violence to him or her. Later we shall see how all of this can be transformed by conversion. But what I wish to note here is that already in this hell there was generosity and creation.[59]

In the *Cahiers*, the central themes of generosity and creation are intimately linked. Creation, or at least creativity, was already a prominent subtheme in *Being and Nothingness*, since the emphasis on free activity as the very definition of the human being is all-pervasive there. But certain kinds of creativity, such as that of the artist, have often been associated in Western thought with an extreme individualism, and it is easy to put such a gloss on the notion of creativity in the earlier Sartrean work. Here in the *Cahiers*, however, while strongly proclaiming that "Every action is creation. Creation of the world, of myself, and of man,"[60] Sartre emphasizes even more strongly, in a number of passages, that creation always involves a *gift*, hence other individuals and the social dimension. He goes so far as to say that, since the series of choices whereby I forge my character involves an element of creation, "Even egoism is an aberrant gift."[61] But the more paradigmatic form of creative gift-giving, of which continuing, ongoing *generosity* represents the most complete and full expression and hence can be seen as constituting the supreme human value,[62] is the accomplishment of a concrete task, or work, and this always involves a communal dimension:

In a word, the object restores to me a concrete *We* wherein my I arranges itself and loses itself. I restore to myself at once my justification and my non-existence as an isolated individual [*personne singulière*.] Thus what is impossible at the level of the For-Itself and of the Project (the ontological organization of a We) becomes real at the anthropological level of the common work.[63]

In both of the longer passages just cited, the references to *Being and Nothingness*, though explicit only in the first, are unmistakable. In neither case does Sartre flatly repudiate his earlier views; he simply says, quite characteristically for him, that he is now operating at a different level or in a different though related domain. And he is not altogether unjustified in saying this: for instance, even in his earliest writings on aesthetics one finds a strong awareness of the fact that an artist does not create simply for him- or herself, that artistic creativity is incomprehensible on a purely solipsistic model. But at the same time the change of focus from that of *individual* ethics to social and political theory is blatant, even if Sartre himself may not fully recognize this. A large measure of the credit for this shift of focus, in addition to or in conjunction with the various new sociopolitical interests of Sartre's immediate postwar years that I have already chronicled, must be given to his renewed, intensive reading of Hegel: in particular, at the conclusion of the paragraph in which the last-cited passage occurs, he mentions Hegel's key but somewhat enigmatic notion, the subject of quite diverse interpretations and even translations, of *die Sache selbst* (the thing itself),[64] as a source of his reflections on the idea of a common task and of the dialectic of personality and impersonality (the role of the impersonal pronoun, *"on"*) that it involves. In addition, there was the stimulus provided by Marcel Mauss's widely influential and groundbreaking work in anthropology, *Le Don (The Gift)*, which analyzes the complex, often alienating and malign, role of gift-giving in so-called primitive societies.[65] Thus, world events, philosophy, and social science were combining to encourage Sartre to become a political theorist.

My reference to the "primitive" giving of gifts with very long strings attached, to which Sartre devotes considerable attention,[66] should reassure us that the Sartre of the *Cahiers* period is not suddenly losing his critical sense in a carnival of joy, love, and self-satisfaction over the common human condition. In all of his stress on creation, generosity, and gift-giving, he is by no means turning a blind eye to the reality of conflict and the constant possibility of violence that had been omnipresent in his treatment of being-for-another in *Being and Nothingness*. Now, however, he begins to see a great need to comprehend such phenomena as work at a common task that had been left relatively incomprehensible by his dismissive discussion of the "We-Subject" and by his purely negative criticism of Heidegger's notion of the *Mitsein* in that book. As can be observed in one of the passages that I have cited, Sartre seemingly finds no difficulty in writing in the *Cahiers* about the domain of the *Mitsein* as an established human reality; but this should not be taken to imply that he is now repudiating *en masse* his earlier criticisms of *Heidegger's* account of it or taking the phenomenon of community as a given, an unanalyzable starting point for philosophical reflection. Above all, it should always be remembered that the *Cahiers* consist in large measure of unredeemed promissory notes, on this set of issues as on so many others, as the following passages (the second of which occurs less than fifteen pages from the end of the second and last Cahier) illustrate:

> Elsewhere we shall study that essential structure which is transcendent unification through the common result of the operation and creation of the We. In particular we shall have to see what it means to operate on the operation of another, thus to transcend his or her freedom at the highest point of its achievement but in the very direction that it wants. The torch in the torch race.[67]

> It is here that the *Mitsein* intervenes. Further on, we shall develop the essential relationship of creation to the *Mitsein*, here we are only pointing out this structure and its influence [*incidence*] on the original project.[68]

The anticommunitarian structures of violence and force are studied at some length in the *Cahiers*, and they are seen to be closely connected, here as in Sartre's later sociopolitical writings, to right and law. In the *Cahiers*, he attempts to draw a certain distinction between force and violence, treating the former as the more originary phenomenon, the latter as more derivative and reactive. Thus, he begins his explicit treatment "Of violence" with the following remarks: "Originally derived from the concept of force *(vis)*. Force obtains positive effects by acting in conformity with the nature of things."[69] But the relationship of the two is very close, as a parenthetical comment at the beginning of a brief paragraph in which Sartre attempts to outline some of the elements of an *"ethics of force"* makes clear: such principles are, he says, "quite simply an ethics of violence justifying itself to itself."[70] Such an ethic, of course, is abhorrent to him; it includes such ideas as the rightness of conquest, hardness, love of struggle, aristocracy, hierarchy, and pessimism. It is important, for purposes of understanding the strong streak of anarchism that pervades so much of Sartre's social thought, to see that both violence and force have an equally close connection with *droit*.

I have used the French word advisedly. We "Anglo-Saxons," as we are known in France and elsewhere on the European continent, experience considerable surprise when we reflect on the implications of the fact that the word for "right" and the word for "law" in its broader sense are identical in most Continental languages, including French. The effects of this identification are two-sided: on the one hand, it sometimes facilitates the recognition of connections, for example, between one's right and what it is lawful to claim that may be less readily recognizable for speakers of English; but on the other hand it often provokes confusion. In translating Sartre, like most other French writers (such as the philosophers of law whose ideas he analyzed in his 1927 essay) on the subject, one is some-times uncertain as to just when to render *"droit"* as "law" and when as "right," and it often makes a considerable difference in English.

Droit in the sense of legality is closely connected with force, according to Sartre; we speak of "the force of law" (my example), and this reinforces [*sic*] his previously-cited definition of "force" as "acting in conformity with the nature of things," whereas by comparison violence implies a breaking with this nature, illegality, which suggests a kind of weakness. "In order to accept this idea, however," he says, "we must originally postulate that there is a theoretical supremacy of action accomplished in conformity with the laws over that which is accomplished against the laws." But of course, he continues, I may just as well prefer nonlegality, destruction, as the means of attaining my goal.[71] The stronger individual appeals to his "right," the right of the stronger, as the basis of the claimed obligation of the weak to treat him as a person; this appeal is a means for him to ratify the *status quo:*

> In other words, the conqueror does not confine himself to preventing, by force, the conquered from having recourse to violence: he requires of him, as abstract freedom, the moral commitment not to have recourse to it. The trick is turned: the oppressed has as many rights as the conqueror, therefore they are equal as moral persons.[72]

So *"droit"* as law and *"droit"* as right turn out here to coimply one another and to reinforce force. Viewed in this way, both the conceptual relationship and the identity in French of the two English words appear unproblematic; but in fact this appearance rests on a trick that has been and remains pervasive in human society. By contrast, "on the hypothesis of an harmo-nious and egalitarian society," in which there is no exercise of force, *"le droit"* [right, law, both?] disappears."[73]

It must always be remembered, after all, that the violent person (a category that includes, although Sartre does not explicitly say so in these passages, the conqueror himself in the early, uncertain stages of his process of conquest) also appeals to *droit* in his or her effort to shatter the legal *status quo.* In fact, Sartre concludes during a particularly lively discussion of violence (in which he reproduces an imaginary dialogue between a sick old lady who has sat down in someone else's seat and that person, who insists that she had no right to do so):

> *There have never been violences on the earth which did not correspond to the affirmation of a right,* and even if, in its original evolution, a[n act of] violence might at first not have been right it would constitute itself as right in its very evolution.[74]

In this passage, especially in light of the imagined dialogue in which the offended person has insisted that the old lady "had no right" to his seat, it is clear enough that *"droit"* needs to be translated into English as "right," as is probably more frequently the case in Sartre's writings. The difficulty with pursuing the phenomenological analysis of the world of claims and counterclaims of *"droits"* as *rights* very far is that one soon begins to recognize that the world viewed from this perspective is more or less coextensive with the human world as such. For example, when, in his very illuminating discussion of *"prière et exigence"* Sartre reaches the point of showing how a prayer or plea to someone else may become an appeal to his or her *pity,* he observes that "Pity is [a] requirement [or obligation: *exigence*]: it is the right of him who has no right."[75] To my way of thinking, this makes perfectly good sense as a phenomenological analysis, or description, for it captures very well the spirit of someone who has moved from a stance of pleading to one of demanding pity. But it brings out all too well the universal applicability of the notion of *"droit,"* when it is understood in its broadest sense, that is perhaps best expressed in a passage that occurs some thirty pages further on in Sartre's text:

> At base, the Evil in violence comes precisely, not from the fact that it destroys Right but from the fact that it creates it. It places the conquered individual in a situation such that he must either *accept* it (at least provisionally) or die. . . . It is precisely because every situation, even one created through violence, is human because it is lived by men that every state of fact creates a state of right.[76]

If this is so, as in an important sense it surely is, then Sartre's phenomenological approach to *droit,* violence, and force has shed considerable light (although of course he himself lacked some of the intellectual background necessary to discuss this) on the inherent limitations of the large "Anglo-Saxon" philosophical literature about the "concept of rights," in which efforts—themselves often laudable and illuminating, undoubtedly—are made to specify and delimit the exact meaning and extent of rights, both "legal" and "moral."[77] He has shown, in effect, that all such efforts are bound to retain some measure of arbitrariness (at least to the extent to which they depart even to the slightest degree from "rights" that are named and specified in particular legal texts, and thus begin to deal with the philosophical dimensions of the question) and to reflect certain social practices (e.g., certain property institutions, or certain conceptions of privacy, etc.) that are preferred by a given writer. On the other hand, however, he has also seriously undermined his own implied hope, in an earlier passage to which I have referred, for the eventual coming-to-pass of "an harmonious and egalitarian society" in which *"le droit* disappears."

Of course, as I have been suggesting all along, there are at least two and no doubt more senses of the word *"droit,"* and it might have been possible for Sartre to defend the conceivability of its disappearance in one or more of these senses while continuing to contend that a state of *droit* in its broadest sense arises with the occurrence of every new state of fact. But he does not do so. As I have also been suggesting, the vagaries of language have facilitated both this failure on his part to make some crucial distinctions and his concomitant failure, throughout his career as a social theorist, to pay sufficient attention to law, to legal institutions. On the other hand, the ultimately suspicious, negative reaction which the word *"droit"* in all its usages seems to elicit from Sartre (as it did in the nineteenth century from Marx)[78] has the great positive value of facilitating his ability to see through the enormous amount of cant and mystification which so often surrounds claims made on some by others on grounds that it is the right of the latter and the concomitant duty or obligation of the former to act in such-and-such ways. *Droit,* as law, and violence have always been closely intertwined in human affairs, however fervently some advocates of "reverence for the law"[79] may wish to conceal or deny this, and *droit,* as right, has unfortunately been claimed repeatedly throughout human history by victimizers as well as by those victimized.

The supreme embodiment of *droit* in the modern world, it is commonly agreed, is the State. Sartre has relatively little to say about the State, the focal concept of traditional political theory, in the *Cahiers* or, for that matter, even in the *Critique,* but what he does have to say about it clearly expresses the extremely suspicious and jaundiced view that he takes of it. One of his most aphoristic early passages in the *Cahiers* "says it all," so to speak:

> Perpetual slippage through annihilation. The collectivity constitutes itself as a State in order to recover itself as a subject. But immediately the State is posited alongside the collectivity. Alienation. For example in democracy itself, the citizen-voter has only the right to choose between *given wholes* (exactly like the Christian between vice and virtue), whereas the government disposes of the *freedom of intervention.* By means of this slippage the State, while enduring, pursues its own interest. The devotion of the citizen to the State has as its counterpart the State's egoism: the citizen's morality presupposes national immorality. Devotion of morality to immorality. Questioning of all morality.[80]

The crucial notion here is that of the *separation* between the individual citizens and the State that they themselves have constituted. This is elaborated upon in a lengthier and more complex passage further on in the manuscript, in which Sartre begins by considering the evolution of the notion of *duty* from the more personal sense that it had under feudalism (duty toward one's liege lord) to its modern sense, duty toward the State, in which it "inhabits my soul as phlogiston inhabits fire: it is the pure abstract presence of the Other."[81] Here, he goes on to say that, although he has previously described the relationships of the self (the I) to the Other, what he has hitherto omitted to describe is "a third element: *the* others." I am not, he says, in any case alone vis-à-vis my sovereign. He asserts that Hegel himself had neglected to consider how the sovereign, along with his peers or subordinates, creates a new entity under my very eyes as subject;[82] it is an entity of "unconditioned freedom," from an internal point of view, based on their mutual recognition and interaction, and always exists in "a society based on oppression."[83] But Sartre says, characteristically, that he will not further describe this phenomenon at this time.

At least two further aspects of this extended passage, which actually occurs at the end of Sartre's phenomenology of *"prière et exigence"* (a consideration of *exigence*, requirement or obligation, in general has naturally led him to a consideration of obligation based on *droit* and finally to its paradigmatic form, in the modern State), are noteworthy from the perspective of political theory. First, there is a particularly insightful discussion of revolution, emphasizing the difficulties that revolutionaries encounter at first because they are always challenging not just a state of fact, but also an existing *Droit*;[84] this gives them a bad conscience at the beginning. In this context, Sartre alludes to the experiences of the World War II French Resistance fighters, who did not have the active support of the majority of the population. Secondly, there is a very powerful and straightforward statement of Sartre's critical attitude toward the modern democratic State, based as it is on "the contract of submission."[85] The "beauty part" of it, so to speak, according to Sartre, is that I confer omnipotence on the sovereign through my own actions (e.g., through an election), and then the further activities carried out in the name of the State are said to be based on my will. But it is my will totally depersonalized and made wholly Other:

> Of course everything would be perfect if, as democratic doctrine pretends, *my* will were truly returned to me intact by the sovereign. But in fact it is inverted and alienated by the passage from one consciousness to the other and finally it is no longer the will of anyone: it is oppression for all.[86]

In this important discussion, Sartre has laid the groundwork for some of the most central notions of his political theory as it will come to fruition especially in the two volumes of the *Critique of Dialectical Reason*. He has acknowledged, at least obliquely, the failure of his earlier thought to deal with the social dimension in its genuine complexity (it cannot be seen as a simple series of self-Other relationships). He has put his finger on the paradox of the State, whether democratic or nondemocratic, supposed to represent the will of its citizens in some sense or other, and yet neither preserving their individual free choices intact, as it would, he says, if it were dissolved or "detotalized" into *x* individual sovereigns, nor yet ever succeeding in becoming a true organic whole, a "totality"; humanity is, he says, whatever the forms of the collective entities into which segments of it manage to constitute themselves, inherently a "detotalized totality."[87] He has touched on the problem of fundamental social change through revolutionary movements. And he has begun to confront the peculiar notion of sovereignty, etymologically derived from the word for a feudal or even prefeudal personal ruler, but applied, since the beginning of the modern world,[88] to an impersonal concept of total control over free individuals, frequently made the object of their more or less passive or active acceptances.

Sartre returns to the notion of sovereignty at one later point in the *Cahiers*, a passage that is a rich and very confusing (if one is looking for a single thread of discussion leading to some one definitive conclusion!) blend of reflections on *oppression* in light of findings from both contemporary societies (as discussed, for example, by Jacques Lacan)[89] and so-called primitive ones. At this particular point the principal background reading to his reflections is the book *L'Afrique fantôme*, by Leiris; Sartre's text is replete with terms taken from the African cultures that Leiris has studied. He remarks that oppression is transmitted through human societies, in the sense that "An oppressor is a man who transmits to others the oppression that he undergoes. The prime and most striking case is the *sovereign*. The sovereign is the incarnation of the Other."[90] He then immediately brings his discussion back from this high level of generality to certain features of the sovereign, or chief, that are peculiar to "primitive" societies. But the point has been made that the sovereign is at once an oppressor and the *incarnation* of something fundamental in those over whom he is sovereign. This idea will serve as the underlying inspiration for much of what Sartre projected as the second volume of the *Critique of Dialectical Reason*, both in the long, more or less completed discussion of Stalin as the sovereign incarnation of the Soviet collectivity as it had evolved a decade or two after the Revolution, and in the proposed but never written portion of that book that would have dealt with the even more complex reality of the incarnation of "popular sovereignty" in a liberal democracy.

I have noted that the larger context within which this final reference to sovereignty occurs is an extended analysis of oppression. The *Cahiers* are filled with references to oppression, from an early passage in which Sartre links it with oppressors' "spirit of seriousness" and insistence on the "duty" and "obligation" of the oppressed ("Wherever there is *duty*, oppression is not far off"; here the capitalist-worker relationship is the principal model that he has in mind),[91] to the previously mentioned Appendix on slavery in the nineteenth-century United States. Sartre asserts that it is the ontological condition of *alienation*, to which we shall return later, that makes oppression possible, though not necessary,[92] and elsewhere he lists five other, related ontological considerations, notably the facts that oppression only comes about through human freedom and that it entails some complicity on the part of the oppressed, which he thinks must be taken into account prior to the analysis of "economic and social oppression."[93] But in the manuscript just above this last-mentioned set of remarks (which themselves are intended as an outline introducing more detailed, numbered reflections that, quite typically for the *Cahiers*, begin in an orderly fashion but soon trail off and remain unfinished), Sartre does list four specific, concrete "types of current oppressions[:] childhood, ignorance, stupidity, femininity." This very odd list, obviously not intended to be in any sense definitive, is revelatory of some important additional aspects of Sartre's social thought.

It is of some interest, first of all, to note the *range* of phenomena included in this brief list: it shows Sartre's sensitivity to very disparate phenomena of oppression, as well as, by implication, his recognition of how very remote the possibility of entirely eliminating oppressions really is. It is a very imaginative list, forward-looking in the sense that it raises issues which were hardly ever made the subjects of serious academic discussion at the time, and which only emerged much later in such forms as the women's rights movement, the still-fledgling movement for children's rights, and complaints about the uses of (biased) "intelligence" tests in perpetuating elitism. Moreover, while the fact that the list does not include class oppression by name should not mislead anyone into thinking that Sartre was still uncertain at this point concerning the central importance of class division for understanding contemporary society—indeed, in the immediately preceding paragraph he has just concluded, as we shall see, that class division is the basic explanation of the oppression of stupidity—still it does demonstrate how far he was, then as later, from treating "class" as the simplistic, magical, pan-explanatory concept that it has become for so-called orthodox Marxists.

With respect to the content of the *Cahiers,* the list can be divided into two pairs: childhood and femininity, to which only very brief but suggestive references are made elsewhere, and ignorance and stupidity, which go together in an extended phenomenological description. The oppressive relationship between children and parents is the subject of a brief but fascinating analysis, for which Sartre is obviously much indebted to his own very mixed lived experience (in particular his relationship with his stepfather), earlier in the manuscript. It is introduced as a prime example of "violence in daily life."[94] In it, he shows how parents present an appearance of *stone* to their children and, by treating them with the extreme contradictoriness that so typically characterizes parent/child relationships (e.g., beating them while insisting that they behave decorously, ordering them to be respectful toward domestic servants while themselves acting patronizingly toward them), in effect teach them to mistrust reason and to endorse the very notions of fundamental hierarchy among human beings that perpetuate oppression. He distinguishes between parents who simply insist that the child submit to the existing order and those, more "liberal," whose idea of education is to prepare the child for a future time at which he or she will be "allowed" to make free choices. He concludes that nonoppressive childrearing entails treating children as free here and now rather than suppressing their present freedom in the name of such a future time, erected into an absolute end; but he admits that the mere fact that nonoppressive parents are "allowing" their children to act freely and must always be prepared to intervene in order, for example, to prevent an inexperienced young child from harming him- or herself shows that there is always some element of lying and ruse involved in such relationships even at their best.

As for the oppression of women, Sartre in effect demonstrates in the *Cahiers*, a product of the same era as the composition of *The Second Sex* by Simone de Beauvoir (whose work he regularly read and discussed when it was still in manuscript form), as he will elsewhere, that this is one topic of social theory to which he is not really equal. He says nothing of a sustained nature about it, and to select a few isolated references (the "perpetual violence" involved in women's behavior in dressing themselves so as to arouse the Other's sexual desire and thus to make that male Other into an "object" in the process;[95] the recourse to "women's intuition" as a mildly violent defense mechanism employed by one who is weaker in discussion;[96] babbling as a behavior of stupidity that is "still more frequent among women precisely because the woman is regarded a priori as ineffective";[97] woman as the embodiment of Otherness in some primitive societies)[98] is to show at once his interest in the topic, his capacity for occasional genuinely valuable insights, his awareness of the predominance of oppressive stereotypes, and yet his own confusion and ongoing subjection to some of those same stereotypes.

Sartre's treatment of the related oppressions of ignorance and stupidity is quite another matter. Here, he breaks new ground in an area to which, unfortunately, he will not devote a comparable degree of attention in any of his later writings of which we are thus far aware, with the exception of his analysis of the role of stupidity in Flaubert's personality and art in *The Family Idiot*. He begins by showing the essentially interpersonal nature of ignorance: I am ignorant in the eyes of someone else by virtue of something that I do not know (e.g., the German language, a scientific theory) that he or she considers very important. This can be an isolated phenomenon without dire consequences for my social position (e.g., I am medically ignorant, but my doctor is ignorant in philosophy), but "The case is very different when ignorance is lived as definitive and unreciprocal, as happens in a society of oppression."[99] Here, the worker's ignorance serves to perpetuate the oppression to which he or she is subject. Further reflection on such oppression soon leads Sartre to a consideration of the related phenomenon of stupidity, which is said by some to be congenital, inborn. But he shows that such claims are vague and indefensible in the form in which they are usually made. He does not deny that there are objective facts that are measured by "aptitude tests"—one person has performed certain requested tasks much better than another, etc.—but he does reject the simplistic, primitive inference that there are such things as natural "aptitudes," similar to the Aristotelian idea of *exis*, and that there is consequently some natural characteristic known as stupidity, applicable to those who lack a certain minimum quantity of such "aptitudes" as thus defined.[100] He then goes on to show how so much of what is called "stupidity" is a function of an individual's lack of needed instruments, including, often enough, instrumentalities connected with one's body (e.g., properly working sense organs), and how stupidity eventually comes to be internalized by the person who has been labeled "stupid." In conclusion, he compares the problem of stupid people with the so-called Jewish problem or Black problem: it is the oppressors, those who regard themselves as intelligent, who have created it. Repeating with approval Descartes's famous dictum that good sense is the best distributed thing in the world, Sartre adds that we must "act in sympathy with what is true good sense, that is, with the effort on the part of the supposedly stupid person to understand and to go beyond his or her *Umwelt* by using the means available."[101] And finally, claiming that much can be achieved along these lines by individual initiative but also recognizing that the problem is ultimately a social one, Sartre briefly but clearly outlines a set of social policies that would eliminate the "problem of stupidity." These include the abolition of incentives for choosing stupidity as a strategy, the realization of *"full employment"* (he uses the English words) of everyone's capacities, a cessation of the practice of perpetuating class differences by means of inheritance (which often results in placing unworthy children of the bourgeoisie in managerial positions), encouraging the free choice of educational possibilities geared to career development, and lastly "creating a certain type of solidarity in freedom, that is, a solidarity lacking any connection with oppression and classes."[102]

Thus, by means of this stimulating but, to those familiar with his previously published writings, perhaps unexpected topic of analysis, ignorance and stupidity, Sartre has arrived, as clearly and certainly in as concrete a fashion as anywhere in the *Cahiers,* at the espousal of some fundamental principles of a social theory reflecting the twin ideals of "socialism and freedom." But exactly what *sort* of socialism was this libertarian socialism of Sartre's as it began to take shape in the *Cahiers?* To ask this question is in effect, in the context of the times, to inquire first and foremost about the complex relationship between his own thought and the most widely known and thoroughly elaborated socialist philosophy, Marxist theory, a relationship that he had begun to work out in the essays considered earlier in this chapter and that he continues, albeit sporadically, to address in the *Cahiers.*

On the basis of sheer content analysis of specific texts, one would have to concede that Sartre's stance toward Marxism in the *Cahiers* is more hostile than supportive. Consider the following:

> Dialectic. Considering things dispassionately, Hegel represents a high point of philosophy. Moving away from him, *regression.* Marx brings in what he had not entirely provided (development concerning labor). But he lacks many great Hegelian ideas. Inferior. Marxist degeneration next. German post-Hegelian degeneration. Heidegger and Husserl little philosophers. French philosophy non-existent.[103]

. . . The future outlined by Marx with revolution at the end is, precisely, invalidated by the "atomic" revolution. First, revolution has become impossible and is replaced by war. Next, there is bureaucratic and technological dictatorship replacing, little by little, capitalist oppression. . . . In the very name of Marxism, the most important event of the past fifty years is not the Russian Revolution, it is the atom bomb.[104]

If we admit a materialist monism, in the manner of Marxism where there is unity [of history] because the superstructures are inessential by comparison with the economic substructure, we can still preserve unity, but at the price of limiting ourselves to saying that the economic produces the economic.[105]

Man creates himself through the intermediary of his action on the world. That is what one can concede to the Marxists. But at the same time, humanity being a detotalized totality, there is an internal theft of [one's] work, thus the image that man has of himself is perpetually alienated.[106]

Class "struggle" does not determine any of the great phenomena of ancient history: neither the struggle for the Mediterranean, nor the constitution of the Empires. Nor the appearance of Christianity, either. . . . Nor the fall of the empire, either. . . .[107]

To all the evidence of these texts we may add the fact that Sartre mentions Marxism as one of the many traditional Western movements of thought that have adopted an indefensible "ontico-ontological" point of view, which tends toward infinite universalization as opposed to "what is in reality: a singular and limited adventure in which nothing is susceptible of being generalized."[108] While this reference is very brief, most of Sartre's text at this point focusing rather on Kantianism as the epitome of the universalizing tendency, it is probably as portentous as any for Sartre's future attitudes both about Marxism and about social theory. Finally, it is very important to note that the *Cahiers* contain some of Sartre's very finest extended criticisms of the ideas of Marx's colleague, Friedrich Engels, whom Sartre was always to take as a convenient target. Sartre's talent for careful philosophical criticism, which is so often subordinated in his writings to his much rarer and more unique capacity for creating bold, original theories, somehow seems to show to best advantage against Engels; here in the *Cahiers*, for example, he clearly demonstrates that Engels wavers among three sets of thoroughly incompatible norms: a pure preference for technological progress, which leads Engels at times to call the Iroquois, whom he basically admires, "barbarians," and logically eliminates the need for any appeal to class struggle; an ethic centering around community as its highest value, supporting Engels's admiration for the Iroquois, but having no rational basis within his ultra-"scientific" materialism; and an old-fashioned, simplistic eighteenth-century moralism, which leads him often to speak in black-and-white terms (Iroquois good, White settlers bad; workers good, capitalists bad).[109] Of course, this is Engels and not Marx, a difference between individual writers that Sartre, like many others writing in and about Western Marxism during the following three or four decades would with considerable justification erect into a significant difference in philosophical perspectives; nevertheless, this critique of Engels constitutes one major additional element in Sartre's distancing of himself in the *Cahiers* from Marxism as it was commonly understood.

On the other side of the balance sheet, there are few if any comparable texts to be cited. One that may pass muster, although Marx and Marxism are not mentioned by name in it, is the following, which occurs in the second Cahier:

> We go along part way together with the dialecticians because the dialectic is the only method conceived for explaining freedom, for rendering it intelligible, and for preserving for it at the same time its creative character.[110]

On the whole, however, the *Cahiers* exhibit the same Sartrean antipathy, based primarily on philosophical, rational considerations, toward Marxist theory that we have already observed in "Materialism and Revolution," in particular, and in other texts from the same period. Moreover, since most of the remarks that I have just cited, with the exception of Sartre's extended criticism of Engels, are brief and rather allusive and hence fail to come to grips with details of Marxian and/or Marxist theory[111] even to the extent to which some passages in "Materialism and Revolution" do, it may reasonably be concluded that the *Cahiers* show no increase, and in some respects perhaps even a decrease, in sophistication with respect to Marxism on Sartre's part.[112] But I would like to urge, nonetheless, that the *Cahiers*, taken as a whole and in terms of the intentions that appear to have governed Sartre's writing of them, can and should be seen as a part of the evolution of Sartre's thought toward a form of Marxism—*his* form of Marxism, about which, as I have already indicated, one may follow Sartre in having second thoughts concerning the appropriateness of the Marxist label—rather than as a deviation from that evolution.[113] This becomes especially obvious, I think, if we consider some of his reflections in the *Cahiers* on history and historical progress. Before we do this, however, I would like to return to the texts that I have just cited in order, by way of anticipation, to juxtapose them against some of Sartre's later attitudes and pronouncements on the same subjects.

As for Sartre's judgment that Hegel's philosophy is qualitatively superior to Marx's, even though the latter introduces certain essential considerations concerning labor, that is a somewhat superficial matter of taste, based on traditional academic standards (as Sartre interpreted them), about which he developed much more ambivalence in his later life than he seemed to have in the 1940s. On the basis of his knowledge of Marx's thought at the time, which he seems to have acquired more through some of Marx's epigones with whom he was acquainted than through a careful reading of Marxian texts, this judgment would have been an entirely reasonable one; later, his more strongly-developed sense of historical development would lead him to see that it would be quite impossible to resurrect Hegelianism as a living philosophy for the present era, and so any judgment as to Hegel's superiority or inferiority to Marx as a philosopher is simply irrelevant as a guide for contemporary practice *or* theory.

Sartre's assertion that the development of the atom bomb was a more important event than the Russian Revolution does not seem to have been sustained by the bulk of his own later writing, much of which concerned some of the short- and long-term consequences of that revolution; but it is interesting by virtue of its showing a new outlook on his part concerning the relative importance of material, particularly technological, change for human society and history. This outlook is to find its fullest expression, in Sartre's writings, in the era of *Search for a Method* (and the *Critique*), where he says that he accepts the following formula of Marx's "materialism": "The mode of production of material life generally dominates the development of social, political, and intellectual life."[114] It is at the end of the very same paragraph in which this statement appears, however, the conclusion to the first portion of *Search for a Method*, that Sartre also makes his frequently cited claim that Marxism will have ceased to be valid and will be replaced by a new, unforeseeable philosophy of freedom once technological change has allowed the human race as a whole to overcome the condition of scarcity. Thus, one can discern a continuity between his proclamation in the *Cahiers* that the Bomb has rendered Marxism invalid and his later theoretical orientation, more friendly toward Marxism but still anticipating its eventual demise: only the time-frame will change.

Since the Sartrean rejection of "materialist monism," in the third of my longer citations from the *Cahiers* concerning Marxism, adds nothing new to what was said in much greater detail in "Materialism and Revolution," we may immediately proceed to the fourth citation, which is an especially interesting one. Its crucial point, repeated at least by implication in numerous passages in the *Cahiers* and representing a clear continuity with the philosophy of *Being and Nothingness*, is that *alienation* is a fundamental and uneliminable feature of human reality, contrary to what Marxism seems to be claiming. Sartre will never really abandon this point of view, although in the *Critique*, as we shall see, he will attempt to distinguish between this ontological level of alienation and those more concrete, historically relative levels with which Marxism is generally concerned, and he will apparently acknowledge that alienation at these latter levels is superable.[115] The beginning of this same brief textual passage that I have cited is additionally interesting because of Sartre's use of the word "concede" in it. What he says that he is "conceding" to "the Marxists" is the notion that man's self-creation takes place through action on the world. While at first glance this may not seem to be a startling concession, it is in fact evidence that Sartre himself regarded his earlier philosophy as having been insufficiently attentive to the role of matter, of material objects ("the world"), in the perpetual, ongoing activity whereby human beings "make themselves." It also shows, obliquely, that Marxist ways of thought were playing an important role, despite Sartre's reluctance to have them do so, in the evolution of the ethical theory centered around creativity and creation that dominates the *Cahiers*. In other words, the increasing influence of Marxist thought at a deep level goes hand in hand with its superficial rejection. This becomes quite apparent in the passage that I have cited from very late in the *Cahiers*, in which Sartre sees the dialectical method as being *uniquely* suited both for explaining human freedom and for preserving "its creative character."

Finally, the citation in which Sartre disputes claims that class struggle has any explanatory value for understanding ancient and other premodern history must be seen in the context of his increasing preoccupation both with class struggle and with history. It is certainly not the case that Sartre regarded class struggle as irrelevant to *contemporary* society; on the contrary, the frequency of his references to it in the *Cahiers* stands in stark contrast to the rarity of such mentions in his writings of only a few years before. But he recognizes, as he will always continue to recognize—for example, in the latter portion of the first volume of the *Critique*, where he begins to discuss the concept of class in the context of late nineteenth-century France—that class struggle and class itself are very complex ideas:

> It would therefore be completely mistaken to see in class struggle the combat of two dogs insistent on disputing the same bone between them. It is rather a game of hide-and-seek in which one is always fighting against an invisible and imagined opponent, who is never in the place where one looks for him.[116]

As for the role of class struggle in past history, I doubt that Sartre ever completely abandoned his skepticism concerning its explanatory value, but the *Critique of Dialectical Reason* will contain detailed analyses of events of earlier times (e.g., the paradoxical impoverishment of Spain as a result of its importation of hordes of silver from the New World) that will depend heavily on broadly "Marxist," materialist insights, if not specifically on categories of class.

The problem for anyone who wishes to come to grips with the nature and role of class conflict in a cultural setting that has been as heavily influenced, both positively and negatively, as Sartre's and ours have by Marxist theory is epitomized in *The Communist Manifesto*. Written by Marx and Engels jointly and prepared as a popular pamphlet for mass distribution, it begins by proclaiming, in no uncertain terms and with specific historical examples immediately following, that the history of all hitherto existing society is the history of class struggles. Alas, this is an enormous oversimplification, as the next few paragraphs and footnote comments in the text of the *Manifesto* are themselves at pains to indicate; the strongest claim that remains after all the qualifications have been made is the dubious one that *modern* society is *tending* toward increased polarization between two principal classes, the bourgeoisie and the proletariat. Moreover, it is well known that Marx himself was struggling to define and refine the notion of social classes when he died; this is the topic on which the third and final volume of *Capital* breaks off, after one page. But the initial sentence of the first full section of the *Manifesto* has done its damage, at once bringing the notion of "class" inescapably to everyone's attention and rendering it extremely suspect as historical *explanans*.

The larger problem, of which the question of the role of class is only a part, is the problem of the nature and driving forces of history itself. In the *Cahiers* it is obvious that this set of issues has begun to preoccupy Sartre, and it will continue to do so throughout the remainder of his life. The claim about the central role of class struggle in the *Manifesto* makes it sound as if history were propelled forward by vast, impersonal forces that were describable in purely objective terms and that, through their interactions, generated "progress," whereby everything in the world gradually but inevitably became better. The *Cahiers'* early pages in particular are dominated by Sartrean reflections on history, in which he repeatedly upholds the role of human freedom in it and questions the "myth" of progress, but in which at the same time he remains fascinated by the notion that history has a discernible configuration. It is this ongoing fascination, so lacking in his earlier writings, that seems to me the most striking feature of the *Cahiers* in terms of Sartre's eventual evolution toward a kind of Marxism. (Although Hegel's philosophy of history preoccupies him as much as Marx's does in many passages, it seems evident even in these passages that Sartre is not at all tempted to wish for a revival of even a greatly modified Hegelianism.) But to speak of such a "fascination" on Sartre's part, which will lead him, for example in the second volume of the *Critique*, to ponder at enormous length the phenomenon of Stalinism as the outcome of the supposedly "progressive" Russian Revolution, is not to assert that he was ever really to share the calm assurance, comfortable even if ultimately unjustifiable in terms of their own theoretical framework,[117] concerning a happy outcome of history that we can discern in the writings of Marx and Engels. Although there are several passages in which he expresses this sentiment at greater length and with more elaboration, there is an aphorism early in the *Cahiers* which summarizes Sartre's reluctance to accept any account of a necessary historical progress: "Existentialism against History through an affirmation of the irreducible individuality of the person."[118]

Certainly the Sartre of the *Cahiers* has in no sense abandoned the critique of determinism, even when determinism is used to advance the cause of those who are oppressed, that he offered in "Materialism and Revolution"; indeed, he at one point explicitly refers to that treatment.[119] When, in a single paragraph (near the end of the first Cahier), he makes a brief effort at distinguishing four elements in History, they all turn out to be atemporally ontological rather than material factors on the model of the

Marxist class struggle: tragedy (in accordance with Hegel's view of it), otherness (there is always alienation in historical action, so that "the dice are loaded"), "mediocrity" (emphasis on *means* rather than on a final goal on the part of all historical actors), and the continual resurrection of the self, despite all efforts at deceit, as the "true motor (Christianity, Protestantism, ideology of the Revolution, Marxism)."[120] It is this "eternal return of the (human) self," so to speak, that Sartre identifies in this passage as the optimistic element in history. And in a remarkable paragraph, only a few printed pages later, which begins the second Cahier and sheds considerable light on all of his thinking about history, he in effect anticipates the entire overall schema of the first volume of the *Critique of Dialectical Reason*—a schema that, by virtue of its applicability to actual historical events and its very explanatory power, puts seriously into question any thought of a unidirectional historical progress:

> All History must be understood as a function of this primitive alienation from which man cannot get out. Alienation is not in fact oppression. It is the predominance of the Other in the pair, Other and Same, the priority of what is objective and consequently the necessity for all action and all ideology to be projected into the element of the Other and to return alienated and alienating to those who advance them. . . . But on the other hand the alienated individual is also entirely outside of alienation, he recovers himself in his pure subjectivity. . . . So freedom perpetually makes ideology, mythology, and prior rituals burst asunder: it realizes liberation through action and the new idea. It is the moment of Apocalypse (it is also the moment of holiday). Only, Apocalypse immediately gives way to order. In effect, it projects itself of its own accord into the element of Otherness. The Christian idea alienates itself and becomes the *Catholic*. It is the idea become Other. Become the idea of the Other and Other than the idea. The Protestant idea alienates itself into Puritanism. The Marxist idea alienates itself into State socialism. . . . Such is the real historical dialectic. Its three terms are: the given Alienation, Apocalypse, and alienation of the Apocalypse.[121]

He goes on to say that the (any) Apocalypse is both the ethical moment of history and usually also, paradoxically enough, the moment of violence. As we shall see, Sartre's conception of sociopolitical structures as they unfold and regroup through history will never deviate very far from this general schema.

What, then, of "progress"? In a long early passage in the *Cahiers* Sartre analyzes this idea at some length and shows that, while it is basically a myth when applied to history as a whole, it has come to play a real and important historical role as an idea, at least for the past several centuries. We are neither happier, in terms of absolute numbers for example, than the Romans, nor more just as a society, although it may be true that we are in a better position than they "to realize a happy and just society," even if at a given present moment we may be more unfortunate. Moreover, he says, there is the special problem of science and technology, which, though by no means absolutes within history as a whole, are absolute within their own limited domain and may indeed be said to have achieved progress within that domain. But progress in technological or scientific knowledge is by no means equivalent to progress as such, and in some instances, of course (e.g., progress in weaponry), it may reverse apparent progress in other domains. In conclusion, according to Sartre the most that can be said of a particular, seemingly progressive historical event is that it constitutes "real but indeterminate progress." And the most that can be said of "progress" itself is that it is not a Law of History but rather "a secondary structure of History which wants to be a total structure."[122] These assertions, too, will remain central to Sartre's outlook on history, one that is connected both with the ethical vision of the "pre"-political Sartre of *Being and Nothingness* and with the socialist ideal of the political Sartre of later years, a perspective that, by projecting a hopelessly utopian leap of immeasurable progress, in my view goes further toward accounting for Sartre's abandonment of the *Cahiers* than any other element that one could single out. It is with a few reflections on this idea of a "radical conversion," as Sartre sees it in the *Cahiers*, and on the book's underlying problems as epitomized in this idea, that I shall conclude this chapter.

The theme of a radical conversion was already present in *Being and Nothingness*.[123] In the *Cahiers*, however, it has become more prominent, although it would be inaccurate to say that it is pervasive, and it has clearly assumed a more sociopolitical character. The idea of it is roughly a movement toward self-reflection of a "noncomplicitous" sort, that is, a type of thought, leading to action, in which one fully understands one's situation, including our radical freedom, and refuses any longer to accept as mere givens the labels and values that the rest of society is constantly endeavoring to impose. There is a close connection, in Sartre's thought of this period, between radical conversion and generosity, in that the one leads directly to the other. But of course, given Sartre's heightened awareness of the interdependence of individuals in society, he now realizes that an isolated conversion here and there would be quite insufficient to bring about radical social change, socialist revolution. There is no doubt in his mind, although clear and detailed definitions of what it would mean may continue to elude him, that "Ethics *today* must be revolutionary socialist;"[124] this assertion is made in the very earliest pages of the *Cahiers*. On the other hand, given the realities of alienation, mystification, and bad faith everywhere in our world, the possibility of a simultaneous radical conversion is infinitely remote:

> The end of History would be the coming of Ethics. But this coming cannot be brought about from the heart of History. It is a fortuitous combination because it would be necessary that *all* be ethical at the same time, which presupposes an infinite chance, relative to each individual consciousness.[125]

What then is the worth of the socialist goal? Sartre's answer to this question is obvious, all *too* obvious; he reverts to some fundamental notions of Kantian ethics:

> It is the *directive maxim of Action*, it is *the regulative idea*. This idea is Socialism (which, however, must be defined—see further on—beginning with [one's] work and freedom—hence, with movement—and not beginning with happiness—that is, with rest and death).[126]

Much later in the manuscript, at the conclusion of the paragraph, previously cited, in which he enumerates four prominent features of History as we know it, he repeats the same theme and connects it directly with the notion of radical conversion, in the context of imagining a human society of a totally different sort:

> By contrast, at least by way of a category, of an ideal direction, one can conceive of an absolute conversion to intersubjectivity. This conversion is *ethical*. It presupposes a political and social conjuncture (elimination of classes and of the State) as necessary condition, but this elimination is not sufficient.[127]

Not only is this notion of a simultaneous, anarchistic ("elimination of the State"), radical conversion "hopelessly utopian," as I have already characterized it, but Sartre has deep doubts, based on his skepticism concerning historical progress, as to whether in fact it would be desirable. In remarks written only some three pages after his assertion that "The end of History would be the coming of Ethics," he reflects on each great philosophy's implied, but in fact rather sad, intention of "stopping" History by virtue of having finally discovered what is and is not possible in the world. "Deep within himself," Sartre says, "every man is repelled by the end of History. He wants to make himself and to make the world in a creative ignorance. . . . Existentialism does not present itself as end of History or even as a progress."[128] (It goes without saying that he is, in this passage, identifying himself as an existentialist.)

The philosophical difficulties, the "aporias" (to use a gentle, charitable word for them), inherent in this combination of perspectives leap out at us. Sartre, the philosopher of action, the sworn opponent of idealism, has committed himself to a regulative ideal that seems not only to be never completely realizable, as is the case with all regulative ideals, but to be thoroughly unapproachable: no asymptotes here! Moreover, this ideal is endowed with some of the attributes and even, in certain passages (although in others Sartre exhibits skepticism about this notion), with the name of the Kantian "kingdom of ends," which is admitted to be outside of History (at least, to use my qualification, of "History as we know it"). Many of these conflicting tendencies appear plainly in the very interesting three-page first section of Sartre's "Outline of an Ontological Ethics," which mixes references to alienation and other more sociopolitical categories with "values of *subjectivity*" in a somewhat unclear "hierarchy" (Sartre's own word), and terminates with a subsection of which the opening line reads "Meaning of the kingdom of ethics" and the closing line reads "Recovery of the absolute. Apocalypse."[129] The entire outline, in short, is a mess—an interesting, suggestive, never elaborated or resolved mess.

One is tempted to say the same about the *Cahiers pour une morale* as a whole, except that it would be odd to characterize a 600-page text as "unelaborated." Sartre's own late explanation to de Beauvoir, mentioned earlier in this book, of his reason for having, if not "abandoned" them (the word to which, it will be recalled, he objected), at least set them aside, was that some of the phenomenological descriptions that they contained were too idealist in orientation. This is no doubt true, as the longest and most complete of these descriptions, that concerning "Prière et Exigence," illustrates by its frequent lack of concrete referents and its excessive reliance on high-level abstractions about certain types of human behavior. Simone de Beauvoir herself explained Sartre's decision to set aside the *Cahiers*, in a book written years earlier, on the basis of a note written by him in 1949 in which she reports him as saying that ethics is "a combination of idealistic tricks" that helps one to live through the deprivation imposed by material and technological scarcity and that will presumably be replaced by "positive ways of conduct" in a society of abundance.[130] This remark, obviously influenced by Marxian thinking about ethics as a component of ideology, also seems to me to represent a truth, albeit a partial one, especially if it is taken to refer primarily to many of the traditional Western ethical systems, of which the Aristotelian and the Kantian are two of the foremost examples, to which Sartre was clearly looking for a model in many passages of the *Cahiers*. On the other hand, we now know very well that Sartre was to return to the task of writing about ethics, now very much more securely wedded to his concerns both as a political theorist and as an observer of politics, in the 1960s, so that Sartre's 1949 note can hardly be taken as the end of the story as far as ethics as a whole is concerned.

In the *Cahiers*, on the other hand, the union of ethics and politics, which for the Sartre of that period as later also means the union of ethics and history, has still not been satisfactorily effected. Against the passage cited earlier in which Sartre asserts that History and Ethics coimply one another (a passage that occurs on the same page as his culminating reference to the recovery of the absolute and to Apocalypse at the end of the first section of his "Outline") may be juxtaposed passages in which he seems to be maintaining that ethics is somehow beyond or outside of history, as so many writers in the history of philosophy have maintained before him. In short, Sartre was still strongly influenced by his traditional education in ethics and torn between the traditional quest for a definition of what is Good and more radical philosophical impulses. The very idea of devising a "hierarchy" of ethical-cum-sociohistorical values is somewhat surprising and uncharacteristic even of the earlier, to say nothing of the later, Sartre, whose innate egalitarianism usually caused him to be strongly suspicious of hierarchies of all kinds (especially, to be sure, *human* hierarchies), and whose fundamental insight that values are human creations seems to militate against the implied neo-Platonism of any scheme of "ontological ethics"; but here again we see, I think, the influence of earlier traditions still at work.

In their overall aims and scheme, then, the *Cahiers* constitute a rather confused text. I am confident that Sartre must gradually have come to sense this confusion of purposes and orientations and have decided that the entire project was not worth pursuing any further, in light of his many other writing projects and the tremendous further demands on his time brought about by his now enormous celebrity. It was, I think, a correct editorial decision on his part. But I am also pleased that the manuscripts were not discarded and have now been published, because they contain both a great deal of evidence about the evolution of Sartre's political theory and many extended discussions that are, as I have tried to show, of considerable intrinsic interest and value.

THREE

The Masterful Though Unfinished *Critique*

Background and Introduction

The two volumes of the *Critique of Dialectical Reason,* the first published during Sartre's lifetime when he was still regarded as an important intellectual force, the second published only very recently (1986) and, though still longer than most books, bearing mute witness to Sartre's failure to have come close to fulfilling his original intentions in conceiving this project, constitute, together, the culmination of his political theory. That anything resembling a Volume 2 of the *Critique* existed was once considered either unlikely or simply untrue by much of Sartre's public, in light of dismissive statements that Sartre himself had made in interviews concerning it. And it is fair to say that on the whole the terrain of Volume 2—the principal issues, the range (much narrower) of major topics, even some of the language (most notably, the idea of *incarnation*)—differs considerably from that of Volume 1. Nevertheless, they obviously formed a whole in Sartre's mind and were written during the same comparatively brief period of time, the late 1950s.[1] In fact, in their tone and in their level of abstractness, the two volumes of the *Critique* resemble each other more closely than either resembles *Search for a Method,* which is published as an introductory essay in both the original and the later French editions of Volume 1 of the *Critique.* And so all three of these works should be viewed together as a whole.

Throughout this book up to the present, I have been attempting to reconstruct some of the main moments in the evolution of Sartre's political theory. As I suggested in the introduction, that evolution did not come to a halt in the *Critique* or indeed at any particular point before Sartre's death. The *Critique,* however, is by far the most extensive, comprehensive, and philosophically probing expression of Sartrean political thought. As such it deserves, in the spirit of that thought itself and like all his other works, to be placed "in situation," in its historical setting. This will require us to consider briefly the significance for his political theory of a few of Sartre's writings of the period immediately prior to the late 1950s, namely the first half of that decade—a time during which, primarily by virtue of those writings themselves combined with his enormous standing as a celebrity, Sartre was becoming something of a political actor in his own right.

The beginning of the period in question was a time of heightening tensions and hardening attitudes in the international political arena. The creation of NATO, the French Army's brutal colonial war in Vietnam, the rise of virulent anti-Communism particularly in the United States (as manifested, e.g., by the Alger Hiss trial and the beginnings of the McCarthy investigations), and the corresponding maintenance of "hard" political lines and policies by the Soviet Communist Party and its affiliated parties under the aging Stalin all occurred during the same epoch. The single military event that most dramatically intensified this climate of conflict and the related fear of an all-out war between the Superpowers was the outbreak of the Korean War in mid-1950. The first of the Sartrean essays to which I shall wish to refer in this chapter, his preface to a book by Louis Dalmas, *Le Communisme yougoslave*, was published at exactly this time, although the precipitating event for both the book and its preface, Marshal Tito's break with Stalin, had actually taken place two years earlier.

In the spring of 1950, just prior to the events in Korea and the appearance of Dalmas's book, a young French sailor named Henri Martin was arrested by the authorities and charged with distributing tracts that opposed the French government's Vietnam policy and that were consequently said to be detrimental to military morale, a serious offense. When it was decided, in the fall, to make an example of Martin and to turn his trial into a major one—a decision that is primarily explicable, Sartre will argue, in light of the military developments in Korea and the related intensification of global animosities[2]—the machinery was set in motion for one of Sartre's oddest and least known works, but one that sheds much light on the development of his thinking during these years, *L'Affaire Henri Martin*. The bibliographical ledger for the early 1950s is comparatively sparse by Sartrean standards, if we set aside his political essays, with one very outstanding exception: his massive quasi biography, filled as it is with reflections on ethics and psychology, of Jean Genet. (This book, *Saint Genet*, was planned as a simple introduction to a collection of Genet's works and announced for the summer of 1950; it was actually published two years later. Two historical dramas, *The Devil and the Good Lord*, situated in the period of the Thirty Years' War, and *Kean*, an adaptation and rewriting of Alexandre Dumas's play about a famous English actor of the early nineteenth century—a work with virtually no contemporary political implications—were published and produced in 1951 and 1954, respectively. *Nekrassov*, a Sartrean drama with a strong political message of opposition to anti-Communist hysteria, was mounted on the Parisian stage in 1955 and there died a quick death.) But Sartre's political activities, of which his "occasional" (as the expression goes) political writings are the most salient instances, were by contrast very extensive during this time.

It should be recalled, for the sake of the historical record, that Sartre had been involved in a political movement with pretensions to becoming a viable political party during a brief time immediately preceding the period that we are now considering, namely, the better part of 1948 and, though with Sartre showing ever-diminishing enthusiasm for the enterprise, 1949. The Rassemblement Démocratique Révolutionnaire, or R.D.R., was an attempted grouping of elements of the non-Communist Left. It resulted in a thin volume of political discussions, among Sartre and four other leaders of the movement, entitled *Entretiens sur la politique* (1949), which, as Contat and Rybalka rightly note, has very little interest today.[3] A sense of disenchantment on the part of Sartre and many others had followed the revelation of the fact that the most prominent of these other leaders, David Rousset, had (successfully) solicited the assistance of the American labor unions, the AFL and the CIO, as well as of the ex-Marxist, neoconservative philosopher Sidney Hook.[4] Now, in the early 1950s, Sartre was moved by his judgment of the historical circumstances to approach more closely than at any other time in his life to the Communist Party, in both its French and Soviet manifestations. This, then, was the period, not only of his involvement with the Henri Martin Affair, but also of his attendance at important peace conferences, most notably that of December 1952 in Vienna, in which there was a prominent Communist presence; of his series of articles, *The Communists and Peace*, and his related polemic with Claude Lefort; of his break with his former friend, the writer Albert Camus, over the latter's rejection of the possibility of successful revolution in his famous book *The Rebel*; of several brief contributions by Sartre to the journal *France—URSS*; and of his first trip to the Soviet Union, in 1954, during the course of and immediately after which his eagerness to please and his physical fatigue allowed him to make some foolishly fulsome remarks, which he later regretted, to interviewers about the condition of Soviet society.

In contrast with this period, with a few of the intellectual issues with which we shall next want to deal because of their importance for Sartre's political theory, the years 1955–56 represent a turning-point both in the decade itself and in Sartre's positions. In 1955 Maurice Merleau-Ponty, with whom Sartre had worked so closely and toward whom he had contracted such a large debt of learning, especially in the domain of political thought, during the war years and immediately thereafter, published his important work, *Les Aventures de la dialectique (The Adventures of the Dialectic)*; the final and longest chapter of this work is devoted to an attack on what Merleau-Ponty calls Sartre's "ultra-Bolshevism," as distilled and interpreted particularly on the basis of *Being and Nothingness* and of *The Communists and Peace*. Little matter, for present purposes, if, as I believe, some of Merleau-Ponty's criticisms there are exaggerated and unfair; Merleau-Ponty obviously still claimed Sartre's respect, despite the rupture of their personal friendship, in a way in which Claude Lefort or even Albert Camus never had. And so, although Sartre never replied directly to this long chapter-essay by Merleau-Ponty, there is good reason to think of the *Critique of*

Dialectical Reason as being in part an attempt constructively to respond to Merleau-Ponty's charge in it that Sartre's philosophy is incapable of dealing with "mediations," that kind of entity that is intermediate between individual human beings and inanimate things, which make up the world of society and history.[5]

Then, in early 1956, Nikita Khrushchev, the First Secretary of the Soviet Communist Party, pronounced his accusations, soon circulated in the West, against the regime of his predecessor, Stalin. There followed the turbulent year of "Thaw" in international relations and in internal discipline within the countries under Soviet influence, of mass protest in Poland and its near-invasion by Soviet troops, when the spirit of the Thaw was taken more seriously than Khrushchev had intended, and finally of the actual invasion of Hungary under the direction of, as Sartre was to put it, "Stalin's ghost." *Search for a Method* was solicited for publication by an editor of a Polish journal, *Twórczość*, in late 1956 and written and published under the title "Marksizm i Egzystencjalism" within a few months. It was at this point that Sartre apparently made the decision to begin composing the *Critique*,[6] with a revised version of his Polish essay serving as the introductory piece to the first volume.

Thus an entire series of events, some globally political, some specific to domestic French affairs, some resulting from Sartre's position as editor of *Les Temps Modernes* and his consequent ease of access to a rapid dissemination of his ideas in essay form virtually whenever he wished, and finally at least one event that amounted to nothing more than a successful personal initiative by an enterprising Polish intellectual, all combined to motivate Sartre to undertake his *magnum opus* in political theory. The whole sequence of events is an excellent example—at once commonplace and typical, almost to the point of banality, and yet unique in its outcome and its importance—of the interplay of the contingent and the "necessary" or "required" that Sartre discovered at the heart of human history and that so fascinated him throughout his later career.

As I have indicated in the introduction to this book, it would be a mistake to situate the occasional essays that were (for the most part) published in *Les Temps Modernes* and later in *Situations* on the same level of philosophical seriousness as the more systematic works, notably the two volumes of the *Critique*, and accordingly I shall not treat any of them at great length. Nevertheless, some of them do contain some very significant theoretical claims and arguments; moreover it is impossible for any political theorist who regards the historical and the ethico-political as coimplicative, as Sartre did and I do, entirely to separate the transient historical strands from those with more long-lasting theoretical implications in essays of this sort. It is in light of these "on the one hand . . . on the other hand" considerations that I am undertaking the analyses that follow.

"False Scientists or False Rabbits" ("Faux Savants ou Faux Lièvres")[7] is the bizarre but apt title of the first of these, the preface to Dalmas's study of the Yugoslav phenomenon. The title's reference, as Sartre explains, is to a song about some scientists who experimented on a group of rabbits with a view to reconfirming certain preordained conclusions; unfortunately for the scientists, the rabbits knew in advance what the results were supposed to be and consequently falsified them. And so the scientists declared that the rabbits were false rabbits. The "scientists" in Sartre's analogy are the rigid Soviet theoreticians and politicians, moved by the initial success of Tito's break with the Eastern Bloc and Yugoslavia's forging of a different "socialist" path to declare that that path is objectively impossible under present historical circumstances and therefore that "Tito is a false rabbit, Yugoslavia a false Yugoslavia."[8] But this means that in any case, Sartre points out, those ideologues with their repeated insistence on historical objectivity were false scientists, since they had originally considered Tito a *real* "rabbit." It should be remembered that the Titoist break had occurred only two years before and hence was still a matter of quite recent history.

The principal theme of the essay, which has the form of a long, appreciative open letter to Dalmas, is a critique of the "objectivism" (a term that Sartre employs as a shorthand but with some regret, because of its ambiguity and its use in an equally pejorative but very different sense, referring to bourgeois thought, by Stalinist writers themselves) into which Soviet Marxism has degenerated; Titoism, Sartre asserts, has restored a healthy element of subjectivity.[9] "In the countries of the Soviet sphere of influence," Sartre asks, "what bureaucrat still knows what subjectivity is?"[10] He takes the opportunity to apply the key notion of reification *(Verdinglichung)*, developed by Georg Lukács (whose heavy-handed attack on Sartre, Camus, and others, *Existentialisme ou marxisme?*,[11] had appeared in late 1948, as a characterization of bourgeois thinking) to the Stalinist treatment of the Soviet masses. Sartre charges Stalinism with having abandoned human choice, will, failure, and even chance and probability as explanatory factors in history. In Titoism as it is evolving, he sees, by contrast, a willingness to admit mistakes, fallibility, on the part of the leaders. At the same time, although he detects occasional tendencies among those leaders[12] to sound like Rosa Luxemburg in speaking of taking their policy directions from the popular base rather than from bureaucrats, he exhibits considerable skepticism concerning her general notion of "spontaneity," direction from "below," at least when it is applied to a situation in which the proletariat has seized power after a successful revolution. Rather, he believes that leadership must be provided in order to persuade the populace to make the sacrifices that will be needed to build the society of the future, and he seems to think that the Yugoslav regime is on the whole providing such leadership. This theme of opposition to the advocacy of sheer political spontaneity, applied to the case of a French proletariat which has certainly not yet seized power, will become an important one in his series of essays entitled "The Communists and Peace."

This, then, is the substantive theme of "Faux savants ou faux lièvres," developed within a context of acknowledged sympathy for the Tito regime[13]—perhaps even slightly greater sympathy than that of Dalmas himself, whom Sartre portrays as somewhat admiring but also, in contrast to himself, as doubtful whether it should be called "democratic"—and of a consequent lack of sympathy for its harsh critics and would-be suppressors within the Soviet sphere. The critique of "Stalinism" (a word that, like the Yugoslavs themselves, he feels free to employ)[14] and of the sclerosed form of Marxism that it represents continues lines of thought that had already begun to be developed in "Marxism and Revolution" and before, and that will never be entirely suppressed, even during the ensuing years when Sartre will be least critical of the Soviet regime. Lenin, too, comes in for Sartre's criticism here, as proponent of "factory discipline" and of the time-study methods of the American behavioralist, Taylor, seen as reflecting the spirit of *Verdinglichung*.[15] Finally in addition to the central theme or themes of the essay, some note should be taken of its *tone*, which at the beginning is almost apologetic, and which expresses throughout a great tentativeness and openness that is said to reflect the lessons of the Yugoslav experience. The apologetic element consists of Sartre's remarking, in two places, that Merleau-Ponty should probably have written this preface rather than Sartre himself, because Merleau-Ponty has written so masterfully about the problem of political failure and related issues in his book *Humanism and Terror*.[16] As for the spirit of openness, Sartre praises Dalmas for letting the facts that he recounts modify his Marxist methodology as he goes along, a procedure that Sartre obviously intends to make his own within the limits of his still very qualified acceptance of Marxist categories and ways of thinking. As he remarks, very close to the end of the piece, "We must rethink Marxism, we must rethink man."[17]

Between this interesting but scarcely very profound essay of mid-1950 and the period of probably the greatest and most important outpouring of Sartrean occasional essays on politics, 1952–54, there exists, for reasons to be discussed shortly, only one five-page publication that merits special attention, primarily because of the uniqueness of its circumstances. It is an invited contribution to the American magazine *The Nation* concerning "The Chances of Peace." The Korean War had begun, and the international atmosphere was extremely charged; there was deep foreboding everywhere. In his response to the editor's query as to what he judged the chances of peace to be, Sartre takes an unsurprising, moderate line, presciently urging, in one of his few forays ever into the field of United States foreign policy recommendations, that the U.S. government consider a rapprochement with the Chinese regime of Mao Tse-Tung, however much it may dislike him. His principal warning to the American audience, however, made at the outset of the essay and repeated throughout, is against the spirit of virulent anti-Communism. He shows that he understands the difference of circumstances between the American and French political climates when he remarks: "Now your anti-communism is much more dangerous than ours—for a strange reason: that you have no Communists."[18]

It was Sartre's awareness of the dangers, both for the future possibilities of world peace and for the human spirit, of the widespread rabid anti-Communism of the early 1950s that plunged him into his period of most intense political essay-writing. The most important of these essays, *The Communists and Peace*, was written for the most part in 1952, although its third and final "installment" was not published until April 1954. Between the publication of the first (July 1952) and second (October–November 1952) parts there appeared (in the August issue of *Les Temps Modernes*) the Sartrean "Reply to Albert Camus," which marked the end of the friendship between them. Meanwhile, as I have already indicated, *L'Affaire Henri Martin*, a much more complicated undertaking because it was to be book-length and involved an editor's task of collecting testimonials, statements, and even some court records as well as the writing of its principal text, was in preparation. In April 1953 the "Reply to Claude Lefort" appeared. Lefort had written a criticism, printed in the same issue, of the two completed portions of *The Communists and Peace*. Behind the scenes, as it were, of all this furious essay-writing, with all its obvious connections to the political situation of the time, a personal drama, intimately connected with the public ones, was playing itself out: the gradual dissolution of the friendship and collaboration between Sartre and Merleau-Ponty.

Sartre has recounted this movingly and in great detail in a eulogy that he wrote on the occasion of Merleau-Ponty's premature death, in 1961. The essay is a rather remarkable one which I found, upon recently rereading it carefully after having read it many years ago and then referred back to it in only a summary fashion upon occasion in the intervening years, more penetratingly and brilliantly evocative of both the issues and the personalities involved than it had seemed from the perspective of a much shorter time span, when the emotions surrounding them were still too fresh. At the risk of a schematization of the entire rather complex sequence of events, a type of distortion that Sartre himself tried to avoid by recounting the details at such length, I shall summarize them very briefly. (Of course, this account is based on that of Sartre, so that a certain bias is inevitable, but it seems that he tried to be as truthful as he could be about what happened and that, by contrast with those against whom Sartre's fierce polemics of the 1950s were directed, Merleau-Ponty was a person whom he always held in the highest esteem, even after their quarrel.) Sartre had always regarded Merleau-Ponty as politically the wiser of the two of them. Together, they had dreamed of founding a journal of the nature of *Les Temps Modernes* since the middle of the war years, and, after the initial editorial board had proved to be too diverse in political orientation to stay together, it was Merleau-Ponty who in reality served as editor-in-chief while insisting that Sartre's name, rather than his own, appear on the masthead as director. And so they shared their tasks over the several ensuing years—along with other collaborators, of course—their basic agreement on an overall political direction guaranteeing the success of this rather strange arrangement. Once, when Sartre, having completed writing *What Is Literature?*, was on vacation in Italy, Merleau-Ponty read the galley proofs of the article "and thought he found there a sentence equating, as was the fashion, fascism and 'Stalinism' under the common name of 'totalitarian regimes.' "[19] Merleau-Ponty immediately wrote to him, submitting his resignation on the spot if Sartre insisted on putting Naziism and Communism on the same plane. In fact, there was no problem, since the sentence in question had been the result of a typographical error, but Sartre uses this example both to illustrate Merleau-Ponty's extreme sensitivity to the very issues of anti-Communism that were to dominate Sartre's writing five years later, and to cast some light on the puzzle, which he never resolved to his own satisfaction, as to why Merleau-Ponty would not allow his own name to be printed above or at least next to Sartre's on the masthead of the journal. (Whenever he asked him about it, Sartre claims, Merleau-Ponty would offer different, always somewhat evasive, reasons.)

Merleau-Ponty had had closer personal relationships with members of the Communist Party, according to Sartre, than he had. Moreover, even at the time of publication in 1949 of *Humanism and Terror*, Sartre, despite the great admiration in which he held the book and which he was to emphasize in "Faux savants ou faux lièvres," was still less comfortable than his colleague about the effort to make common cause, while still maintaining a distance, both with the Communists and even with Marxist thought. The years 1949–50 were the turning points for Merleau-Ponty: first, the reception in France of detailed documentation, to which he gained access before Sartre did, concerning the existence of massive slave-labor camps in the Soviet Union, a subject on which he published (with Sartre's approval) a scathing editorial in January 1950; then the outbreak of the Korean War, which Merleau-Ponty saw as irrefutable evidence of a Soviet effort to extend its sphere of control in preparation for an all-out war with the United States, in the summer. His reactions to these developments, as Sartre describes them, amounted to a deep and lasting, though not incapacitating, depression. While he never indulged in simple anti-Communist rhetoric, his disillusionment with the USSR was total, and his former friendships with some French Communist Party members came to an end. There followed a period of nearly two years, reflected in the sparsity of political writings even by Sartre himself, during which there was an agreement, initiated by Merleau-Ponty, not to publish articles on political topics in *Les Temps Modernes*—at least not to publish articles by members of the "team." A few outside contributors' pieces were published in time to avoid major dissatisfaction on the part of the readership, and of course essays of a nonpolitical nature continued to appear. The single most decisive turning-point for Sartre, in a direction nearly opposite to that taken by Merleau-Ponty, occurred in spring 1952 while he was again in Italy, working on the

Henri Martin volume. Sartre's own description of the precipitating event and its immediate aftermath deserves to be cited at length:

> The Italian newspapers informed me of the arrest of Duclos [French Communist Party leader], the theft of his notebooks, the farce about the carrier pigeons.[20] These sordid bits of childishness touched me to the core: there were more ignoble ones, but none more revealing. The final bonds were broken, my vision was transformed: an anti-Communist is a dog, I do not abandon that position, I shall never abandon it henceforth. I shall be thought very naive, and, in fact, I had witnessed other such things without being moved. But after ten years of ruminations I had reached the breaking-point, and I only need a little nudge. In Church language, it was a conversion. Merleau, too, had been converted: in 1950. We were both conditioned, but in opposite directions. Our feelings of disgust, slowly accumulated, in an instant made one of us discover the horror of Stalinism, the other that of his own class. In the name of the principles that it had inculcated in me, in the name of its humanism and of its "humanities," in the name of liberty, equality, and fraternity, I swore towards the bourgeoisie a hatred which will terminate only when I do. When I returned to Paris, in haste, I had to write or suffocate. I wrote, day and night, the first part of *The Communists and Peace*.[21]

The tone of that essay itself is not nearly so dramatic as is that of the above passage, written nine years later. Nor, as Sartre goes on to report, was the definitive break with Merleau-Ponty an immediate result of this "conversion" of his. In fact, he says, Merleau-Ponty encouraged him to write the essay, originally intended to be only a single long article, and did not make an issue of Sartre's claim in it that the Soviet Union wanted peace and that the danger of war came from the West; Sartre, on the other hand, refrained from discussing the Korean War itself in the article out of deference to Merleau-Ponty's views about it. But Merleau-Ponty clearly expected Part 2, as the idea of writing a Part 2 gradually emerged, to contain some balancing critique of the Communist side, whereas Sartre had no intention of gearing it in this way. There followed long discussions which included other members of the editorial team and which came to very little, and then Lefort, who had been an acquaintance of both men but closer to Merleau-Ponty, began to plan his critique. The outcome of the rather bitter verbal arguments between Sartre and Lefort was that Sartre and Merleau-Ponty began openly to dispute about a wide range of differences. The latter finally resigned from the journal when, in spring 1953, Sartre removed from the head of a contributor's piece about the contradictions of capitalism an "explanatory" paragraph written by Merleau-Ponty in which the latter had apologized and suggested that there should be a forthcoming essay on the contradictions of socialism. Sartre had accepted the article, though without much enthusiasm. Thus it was a rather petty matter—each was able, with some justification, to charge the other with abuse of editorial power—that actually brought the two philosophers' long-term collaboration to an end, but of course, as Sartre points out, the growing differences in their political perceptions had for some time made the *dénouement* inevitable. (They eventually began a process of personal reconciliation after three years of not seeing each other, which was, at least in Sartre's estimation, progressing slowly but fairly successfully at the time of Merleau-Ponty's death.)

Considered in itself, the personal history that I have just recounted is certainly not a piece of political theory. As Sartre himself suggests at numerous points throughout his eulogy, some differences between him and his colleague in family backgrounds and upbringing, in personal temperament, and many other such phenomena must be brought to bear in order fully to explain what happened. Of at least equal importance was the peculiar nature of the institution, the journal, which they had co-directed: well regarded by its loyal subscribers but not at all mass-circulation, endeavoring to steer its own course while under fire from both the Communist Party (the membership of which, as Sartre pointed out in his contribution to *The Nation*, was quite numerous at the time among the French population and even, though perhaps proportionately to a lesser extent, among intellectuals) and the Right. But in pointing to these factors I have already begun to touch on matters that are *obviously* of relevance to political theory: the nature of small groups within a large modern society, public opinion, ideology, etc. The personal and the political are deeply, inextricably intertwined. However, as we move back up, so to speak, to the less purely personal level of issues dealt with in *The Communists and Peace*, the "Reply to Lefort," and *L'Affaire Henri Martin*, we may again be tempted to ask whether reflections prompted by the temporary arrest of a French Communist Party official and by one or two unsuccessful calls for mass demonstrations by that Party in 1952, much less those surrounding the trial of an obscure French sailor in the same year, have any significant relation whatever to the larger questions of political theory. I want to insist that they do, at least as soon as it is admitted that political theory is a reflection on actual human history and not just a parade of possible abstract forms of association. Even so, as we shall see, the question of whether such forms exist and, if so, what they are is never far from Sartre's mind in the elaboration of his arguments in these essays.

I shall take the first two parts of *The Communists and Peace* together, since they were written in close succession. Sartre's own perception of his orientation in the essay, in light of the preceding reflections, is well expressed in the following remark:

> First of all, I am not concerned with what would be desirable nor with ideal relationships that the Party-in-itself maintains with the Eternal Proletariat; I am trying to understand what is happening in France, today, under our eyes.[22]

A few pages later, he openly acknowledges that critics may find his reasoning "Byzantine."[23] For what he is trying to urge here is that there is reason for the non-Communist Left, of which he is an adherent, to feel regret and concern at the failure of the Communist Party to mobilize very many workers in either a rally in late May (which Sartre regards as relatively unimportant) or a general strike called for one week later to protest Duclos's arrest and other aspects of the French government's domestic and foreign policy. He insists—with greater clarity, to be sure, in the second installment of the essay, written after he had begun to hear from his critics, than in the first—that he is writing from the standpoint of his own principles rather than of those of the Communists, with whom he is in limited agreement in certain areas. And he points out that he and his ideas have been under constant attack in Communist Party publications and will no doubt continue to be so, so that it is hardly a matter of warm personal feelings that might motivate him to take the stance that he does. Why then does he fail to share in the glee expressed by many on the Left as well as the Right at the Communist Party's embarrassing failures?

His answer, to encapsulate it irreverently and with considerable over-simplification but not incorrectly, is that the Party is, for the time being, "the only game in town," the only viable force capable of carrying on the ethically mandated class struggle of French workers to overthrow the politico-economic structures which, reinforced by the class in power, continue to oppress them. The "ethical mandate" (my term, not Sartre's) comes from the commonplace humanistic values which Sartre was to enumerate years later in the dramatic passage about his "conversion" that I have cited from his essay on Merleau-Ponty, as having been inculcated in himself and in all French children from infancy, but as being denied in actual practice to members of France's working class. (This will continue to be an important theme in L'Affaire Henri Martin, in those passages in which Sartre supplies some biographical information about Martin's childhood.) But the proletariat is not, in France or elsewhere, a metaphysical entity, the collective reality of which can be taken for granted. There are millions of workers, to be sure, and their working and other socioeconomic conditions can be described: in the 1950s in France, for example, the relative decline in numbers of both the old syndicalist (craft union) elite and the lowest-paid manual workers had resulted in a predominant configuration of a large mass of industrial workers with more or less interchangeable jobs. They form a class in a meaningful sense, Sartre argues, only when they participate in large numbers in a movement whereby they define their collective objectives. To the extent to which they may remain purely passive, they cannot be said to have any class unity. But neither, he urges, reverting to but modifying a theme that we have already uncovered in "Faux savants ou faux lièvres," can they be expected under current circumstances in France to engage in any unified class activity through sheer collective spontaneity. That is the point at which the Communist Party, because it is at the moment the only organization in existence to furnish the required leadership to the working class, merits support (qualified and limited, to be sure) from both members and nonmembers who, like Sartre, favor the overturning of structures of class oppression.

The modification of Sartre's anti-"spontaneity"[24] stance consists in his extension of its applicability beyond already existing regimes, such as the Soviet and Yugoslav, which consider themselves socialist, to proletarian movements that have not seized power, such as, precisely, the French proletarian movement. Sartre clearly does not expect this movement to seize power in the near future, either, and in fact he devotes considerable space to enumerating facts and statistics (including the arrangement of the French electoral system of the time, "rigged"as it was to ensure a Communist Party representation in the Assembly that was disproportionately much smaller than the percentage of Communist voters) supporting this attitude of pessimism. Nor does he by any means speak in glowing terms of the past history of Communism as a political movement: early in the first installment of the essay, he traces some of the lines of development of the USSR in its early years, showing how its propaganda toward the international working class was soon being enunciated "unfortunately in the form of the Kantian imperative and of military duty."[25] This history is part of the heritage, in 1952, of the French workers and of the French Communist Party, vacillating as it does between parliamentarianism and commitment to revolution, and between French nationalism and allegiance to the Soviet Communist Party and its objectives. This entire complex situation obviously involves many difficulties and contradictions; but this observation only reinforces Sartre's conviction that neither a reliance on the spontaneity of the unorganized mass of workers nor an attempt to replace the French Communist Party with a new party of the Left has any chance, at least at the historical juncture of the time, of achieving the humanistic goals to which Sartre and presumably, at least in theory, the rest of the political Left are committed.

Claude Lefort, whose political orientation at the time was Leftist and influenced by followers of Trotsky, was an adherent of many of the notions, highly unfavorable to maintaining any support for the Communist Party, that Sartre is here opposing. In his critical essay, "Marxism and Sartre," he laid out some of the lines of criticism that Merleau-Ponty was to develop several years later in his attack on Sartre's "Ultra-Bolshevism" in *The Adventures of the Dialectic*. Lefort castigated Sartre for still retaining an extreme individualism while at the same time refusing any role to working-class spontaneity and elevating the Party to a primary role above that of the working class itself.[26] Sartre's simultaneously published reply, much longer than Lefort's critique and heavily overladen with some of the most polemical rhetoric in all of his published work,[27] is more successful in raising serious questions about Lefort's political philosophy (Sartre cites other writings of his in addition to "Marxism and Sartre") and even his character than in advancing Sartre's own "Byzantine" arguments in favor of supporting the Communist Party. Paradoxically, however, this very circumstance

allows the reader a clearer perception of some of the theoretical underpinnings of Sartre's extremely controversial strategic recommendations than is
obtainable from *The Communists and Peace* by itself.

Already in the latter, Sartre had briefly discussed a certain Trotskyite[28]
position that is based in a deeply rooted historical determinism but also
allows "that historical circumstances are arranged sometimes but *very rarely*
in such a way as to permit a human action which is effective and decisive
with respect to the orientation of history."[29] This combination of a rigid
determinism with a certain historical probabilism, Sartre speculates, permits the Trotskyite, an adherent of a workers' party that is out of favor with
the majority of workers, to indulge in its idealistic hope that the right
historical conjuncture just *might* occur that would restore to him or her the
leadership of the working-class movement; it is an idealism of possibilities.
Against such an attitude, Sartre lays stress on the historical situation as it
exists in France at the moment: in light of that situation, he believes, such
hopes are unrealistic. Moreover, he continues as always to reject determinism on the grounds that it is philosophically untenable. In his "Reply to
Lefort" Sartre accuses his critic of the same curious combination of "econo-
mism"—that is, believing that a successful outcome of history is guaran-
teed in advance by the balance of forces and the inevitability of dialectical
progress—and reliance on a very impractical, idealistic hope that somehow
the French workers will in large numbers abandon the Communist Party
and join a new party in the near future. In some of his related accusations,
notably that Lefort is a "secret" adherent of an organicist view of the
proletarian class, according to which that class exists in itself whatever may
occur in historical time,[30] and that he constantly blurs together, like Rousseau in *The Social Contract*, a description of what is with an account of what
he thinks ought to be,[31] Sartre reveals a great deal about what he himself is
coming to regard as the principal pitfalls and the principal *desiderata* of an
accurate, viable social theory. His most fundamental complaint against his
antagonist, Sartre says at more than one point, is that Lefort really lacks a
sense of class *struggle*, that he thinks in terms of interacting social forces
rather than in terms of complex, active human groups unified around
common but conflicting and mutually incompatible projects and hence
clashing with one another.[32] Whatever may be the degree of accuracy or
inaccuracy of Sartre's depiction of Lefort's theoretical position at the time,
we can see in Sartre's half of the debate a serious effort—often half-hidden,
unfortunately, behind an excessively polemical smokescreen—at escaping
the Procrustean beds of both orthodox Marxism (including its Trotskyite
variant) with all its ready-made, dogmatic assumptions about the meanings
of "class" and of history itself, and earlier existentialism with its extreme
emphasis on the freedom of action of the individual and its consequent
dismissal of the significance of either passive distinctions among collective
entities or active group movements. In short, in *The Communists and Peace*
and "Reply to Lefort," occasioned as they were by the ephemeral circum-

stances of the French political scene in 1952, one sees the beginnings of the conflictual dialectic of "series" and "groups" which will serve as the dominant theoretical theme of the *Critique of Dialectical Reason*.

Echoes of other past and future philosophical themes of Sartre's are to be found in these essays as well. There is, for instance, a brief allusion to "generosity" made in the context of a discussion of the type of bourgeois ideology which separates politics from economics to the detriment of the former and insists on letting market mechanisms play themselves out, whatever the consequences for the poor. According to this ideology, any politically motivated act of generosity toward the underprivileged is a *false* generosity. "That means," Sartre comments, "that every attempt to substitute a human order for the mechanical order is doomed to failure."[33] Another theme that is resurrected here from the *Cahiers pour une morale* is that of *conversion*. Unfortunately, it occurs in a passage in which Sartre is trying to be brutally realistic and descriptive of the current situation and hence leaves himself open to the accusation, the inverse of his own comment about Lefort, that he confounds a description of what is with what ought *not* to be. Is the worker passive? No, he says, in France today the worker finds his freedom of action through the Communist Party: "the worker, transformed by the organization into a subject, finds his practical reality on the basis of his metamorphosis; whatever he thinks or does, it is on the basis of his *conversion;* and the latter, in turn, takes place within the present framework of the Party's policy. . . . In a word, one can say that the Party is his freedom."[34] Naturally, Sartre is not intending to laud this state of affairs; on the contrary. This "conversion" of the worker who is a Party member is in an obvious sense a caricature of the "radical conversion" to freedom within a socialist world to which Sartre had pointed as a theoretical possibility in the *Cahiers*. And yet, if one accepts the outlines of Sartre's analysis of the then-current historical conjuncture in France, this caricatural but nevertheless real freedom might be all that made sense and the best that was possible for such an individual at this point in history. In this somewhat desperate, pessimistic turn of thinking, we can see anticipations both of Sartre's historical analysis of the Soviet Union under Stalin and of his more sophisticated theoretical notion of the expression of human freedom through group *praxis* that were to dominate so many pages, respectively, of Volumes 2 and 1 of the *Critique of Dialectical Reason* a few years later.

The times *were* particularly desperate. I do not share the attitudes of many critics today who look back at Sartre's analyses in *The Communists and Peace* and discern in it both an overreaction to passing circumstances and unacceptably broad tolerance of the pretentions and claims of a Communist Party that was already morally and intellectually bankrupt. I shall be considering these criticisms as I bring to a close this brief discussion of some of the theoretical implications of this period of Sartrean political essay-writing immediately preceding his writing of *Search for a Method* and

the *Critique*. It was in part due, I would contend, to the forceful voice of
radical criticism that was Sartre's, together with a few other voices of
prominent writers who joined with him, that eventually the historical
situation in France, as well as in the entire geopolitical situation of which it
was a part, did undergo *some* amelioration in the direction of both political
and economic liberation. But the situation as it stood in 1953–54 was grim
indeed, as a careful rereading of two Sartrean literary enterprises published in that year, *L'Affaire Henri Martin* and the third and final part of *The
Communists and Peace*, should immediately remind us.

What is especially appalling about the Henri Martin affair is the use to
which French law was put to try to suppress dissent from the government's
Indochina policy; if Sartre always felt extreme suspicion towards the law,
his detailed analysis of the language of the laws, particularly that concerning "demoralization" (of troops), the offense for which Martin was
convicted, in *L'Affaire Henri Martin* shows that this suspicion was founded
in a genuine knowledge of just how the law could be made to serve forces
of violence claiming to be forces of order. The French government of the
time, Sartre further shows, borrowed a term from one of the United States's
first postwar neo-Conservatives, James Burnham, the definition of Communism as a "conspiracy," and used it widely in a very odd French translation, *"entreprise,"* to intimidate Communist Party members (especially those
who were subject to military law, at a time of universal male conscription)
from undertaking activities on the Party's behalf that should have been
perfectly legal under the French constitution.[35] The account that Sartre,
citing at length from some of the sailor's letters home, and also some of the
other contributors to the volume give of the atmosphere within the French
military, replete as it still was at the officer level with former Petainists who
retrospectively viewed the World War II Resistance to the Nazi occupation
with contempt and who treated the native Indochinese as subhuman,
makes for very chilling reading indeed, particularly to an American at forty
years' distance from the period in question; after all, history *did* repeat itself
in many ways, one realizes, when the United States began to carry on its
war enterprise in the same place a dozen years later. Sartre concludes the
volume, unnecessary as its publication turned out to have been in light of
Martin's release, by emphasizing the independence both of himself and of
other contributors from the Communist Party; some, he says, are fairly
sympathetic to it, but others are "entirely cut off from it."[36] At any rate,
they were in a position to ask for "pardon" (*grâce*, official pardon), whereas
for the Party to have made an official request for pardon (*pardon*) would
have been to admit that Martin had been guilty of some genuine crime,
which in fact he had not.[37]

The third part of *The Communists and Peace*, published one and three-
quarters years after the first (a period during which, it must be remembered, Sartre's rifts with Camus, Lefort, and Merleau-Ponty had all taken
place), is somewhat different in tone from the other two, concentrating as it

does on a theoretically based analysis of French economic history of, roughly, the previous century. But at the same time, it is like the preceding essays in the series by virtue of its rootedness in the contemporary situation—not so much particular episodes as the general state of affairs; it is Sartre's perception of that situation that I find it particularly worthwhile to recall for present purposes. In an exceedingly dramatic passage, of which I shall reproduce only a few lines here, he says:

> We live badly, very badly: for half of the French people, the salary is no higher than the minimum needed to live; young people suffocate or leave the country, saying that there is nothing more to do in France. And the Government? Does it govern? Maintaining divisiveness through lies, cheating on the election law, imprisoning opponents, refusing their sons admission to the elite schools, setting over our divisions the sly and hypocritical dictatorship of weakness, putting off the vote on social laws, making promises to state workers and bureaucrats then refusing to keep them, crushing the country under the weight of an absurd tax structure—does that amount to a domestic policy?

He goes on to enumerate atrocities committed against colonial opposition leaders in Madagascar, Vietnam, and North Africa, asking whether this amounts to a colonial policy. Then, with respect to foreign policy, he points to the stubborn, hopeless continuation of "a war that we know is lost," the trifling with French sovereignty, and the acceptance of "the domination of the United States over half the world and German hegemony in Europe."[38] All of this, together with much more that was equally deplorable, constituted the experiential basis of Sartre's political thought during these decisive years. I wish strongly to contend that the description that I have reproduced here was not exaggerated or one-sided, but rather fundamentally accurate. After having spent only a few months in France for the first time in 1959–60, and without at the time having read these or similar analyses of Sartre's or even sharing much of his evolving sociopolitical worldview, I came to many of the same perceptions of the national situation; only the identity of the hopeless war had changed by then, the Battle of Dienbienphu in May of 1954 (one month after the publication date of the third part of *The Communists and Peace*) having finally precipitated France's retreat from the war in Indochina, and the Algerian conflict having replaced it.

This is the background to Sartre's discussion, in this essay, not only of the unique and peculiarly bloody and "Malthusian" evolution of French capitalism during the late nineteenth and early twentieth centuries (the massacres of the Communards, the great emphasis on population control resulting in an actual numerical decline in population over a certain number of years, etc.), but also of future possibilities. Sartre clearly expresses himself in favor of increasing production—a position that places him at odds with the fashionable anticapitalist and anti-Marxist critiques of the ideology of productivity offered by Baudrillard and others in the relatively affluent 1980s, but that would have seemed the soul of good sense to a very broad spectrum of French political opinion thirty years earlier. On a more abstract plane, Sartre bids farewell to what he calls the "humanism of labor"—the idea, promoted by the formerly dominant syndicalist unions, that their work was to be regarded as ennobling and as entitling this elite of the working class to be treated with special dignity. In its place, Sartre maintains, one would hope to find a much more radical "humanism of need," no longer based on a working class elite's alleged special *merits,* and answering to the more mass-oriented character of modern industry.[39] The actual current situation, he says, is a confused one, in which these two views vie with one another within the workers' movement. The American reader today will recall the somewhat parallel development of the American labor movement, from the Knights of Labor to the eventual merger of the more craft-oriented AFL with the CIO. The principal impression with which one leaves off reading the third section of *The Communists and Peace,* however, is that it is itself almost as much a matter of now rather distant history—of use in explaining the genesis of certain present states of affairs but no longer vitally relevant for understanding possible future developments—as are certain long-outmoded practices of nineteenth-century industry to which Sartre alludes here. The brief reference to *need,* on the other hand, anticipates philosophical themes that fully retain their resonance; they are to be of central importance in the *Critique of Dialectical Reason* as well as in Sartre's still-unpublished ethico-political writings of 1964.

From the shorter Sartrean essays dating from the same period of the early-to-mid-1950s, I wish only to note a few remarks that may shed additional light on his evolving attitudes toward Marxism and toward social and political theory and historical explanation before finally turning to his most significant effort at coming to grips with all of these things, *Search for a Method* and the two volumes of the *Critique.* In a footnote in his reply to Camus (1952), he rejects Camus's proposed dilemma concerning Marx, to the effect that either Marx's so-called prophecies are true or else Marxism is nothing but a method, by contending that those alternatives neglect "all of Marxist *philosophy* and all that constitutes for me (who am not a Marxist) its profound truth."[40] He ends this polemical piece by focusing, as Camus himself had in his letter condemning the review of *The Rebel* that Francis Jeanson had written for *Les Temps Modernes,* on the question of the meaning of history: Camus's very question as to whether history has a meaning is itself meaningless, according to Sartre, as is the idea, which Camus had ascribed to Marx, that history has a specifiable end or goal. What must be done, Sartre says, since we cannot choose whether or not to be a part of history, is "to try to give it the meaning which seems the best to us . . ."[41]

In "Opération 'Kanapa,' " a commentary on an article about the Communist Party and intellectuals, Sartre takes up Kanapa's tripartite division among intellectuals who belong to the Party, those who dream of belonging, and those who don't and remarks: "For we ourselves belong to the third group and no more dream of entering the C.P. than you dream of accepting us."[42] In "Le réformisme et les fétiches," (February 1956), a commentary on a book, *La Révolution et les Fétiches,* critical of the Communist Party by Pierre Hervé, a member who was clearly risking expulsion by publishing it, Sartre decries the enormous gulf that he sees existing between "Marxism such as it should be" and "Marxism such as it is," as manifested by the Communist Party.[43] Finally, in his "Réponse à Pierre Naville" (March 1956), an indirect by-product of the essay on Hervé's book, he points out the obviously greater embarrassment shown by leaders of the French Communist Party, upon learning of Khrushchev's famous denunciation of Stalin during the previous month, than by their Italian counterparts, admits to having been further removed from Marxist thinking at the time of publication of *Entretiens sur la politique* (1949) than he would later be, and then makes the following clarificatory remarks in answer to Naville's published attack: "The truth is that I wish neither to give up my ideas nor to impose them on others. Marxism is the cultural milieu from which they have emerged, the movement which carries them along, the horizon which reveals them. Does this mean that they are Marxist in the strict sense of the word? To believe that, one would have to be ignorant of what culture is."[44]

In light of these rather fragmentary but consistent remarks, the message of *Search for a Method* should have come as no great surprise to those readers who had carefully followed Sartre's published texts. The invitation to write the essay that was originally entitled (in Polish) "Marxism and Existentialism" seems to have been extended[45] precisely during the turbulent and tense time that immediately followed the Soviet intervention in Hungary (and the abortive simultaneous Anglo-French expedition to destroy the Nasser regime in Egypt) in fall 1956. At any rate, work on what we know as *Search for a Method* and on the long denunciation of the Soviet action and of Communist Party support for it that was published in *Les Temps Modernes* under the title "Stalin's Ghost" ("Le fantôme de Staline"), was undertaken by Sartre within the same brief period of late fall and winter 1956–57: both were published in early 1957 (in April and January, respectively). The contrast between the two genres of writing is plain: "Stalin's Ghost"[46] is clearly a long commentary on current events, albeit events that were of the utmost importance for the evolution of mid-century political thought, whereas *Search for a Method* is a philosophical essay, though one that is more immediately accessible to the educated general reader than is the *Critique of Dialectical Reason* proper. But there is an important sense in which *Search for a Method* is also time-bound, even if its span of time is more extended. Sartre makes this point very well by beginning it with a review of large epochs in the history of philosophy, in order to situate his own work within the present one, that of Marx.

There have, he says, been only three creative epochs in philosophy since the seventeenth century, and they may be labeled according to their most famous thinkers, to wit, Descartes and Locke, Kant and Hegel, and

Marx. By contrast, there have also been a number of marginal parasitic thought systems which he proposes to call "ideologies";[47] existentialism, he says, is one of those. I used to be quite critical of this opening gambit of *Search for a Method* on several relatively obvious grounds: the distinction between philosophies and ideologies is too sharply drawn, the term "ideology" is used in a way that is inconsistent with Marx's own usage in *The German Ideology,* and the periodization appears arbitrary and not fully justifiable. However, these criticisms now seem to me less relevant than they once did. For one of Sartre's announced purposes here is precisely to contest or challenge standard essentialist conceptions of what "philosophy" means. The fact that Marx and Engels were among the first (though not the very first) to make systematic use of the word "ideology" should not consecrate that usage forever, unless one is a dogmatic Marxist of the very sort against whom many passages in *Search for a Method* are going to be directed. As for the use of the great names, Sartre himself makes it clear that he is only invoking them because of their familiarity and not by virtue of the precise contents of the texts written by each of these famous individuals.

Sartre's principal purpose in these opening pages is to make creative use of an idea inspired by Marx, perhaps best identified as the idea of "ideology" in Marx's own sense of there existing a correspondence and even to some degree a dependency relationship between intellectual productions and the social and material conditions of the place and time at which they have been produced, in order to argue that Marxism must be regarded as the dominant philosophy of our epoch. Although the wording is very different, the claim is quite similar to the one that I cited above from Sartre's "Réponse à Pierre Naville." In the way in which he makes this claim, he is anticipating in interesting respects several of the most important developments of French philosophy subsequent to his: Foucault's "archaeological" effort to uncover a level of shared but unarticulated meanings, more basic than the explicit texts themselves, among writers of a given period and culture; Derrida's insistence on thinking on the "margins" of standard interpretations and understandings; and the tendency on the part of a number of thinkers, such as Althusser, to reconceive and reconstruct the meaning of "ideology." To the common trans-epochal phenomenon of a dominant, somewhat vague but certainly discernible and distinguishable set of ideas about the nature of the world, corresponding in a general sense to the rising class of a given time period, Sartre gives the deliberately open-ended name *"Savoir,"* or "wisdom." He does not mean at this point to furnish a precise account of the nature of social classes, nor does he enter into details concerning the contours of the two pre-Marxian *"Savoirs"* that he has identified, except to refer briefly to the historical transition from a bourgeoisie dominated by lawyers, bankers, and merchants to one dominated by industrialists. What the great philosophical world-visions effect, Sartre says, is a "totalization" of the specific *Savoirs* of their epochs.

Thus, as early as the third paragraph of *Search for a Method,* Sartre invokes this neologism, *"totalisation,"* that is destined to play such an important role throughout the two volumes of the *Critique*. It seems doubtful to me that he was yet fully aware, when he first wrote this paragraph, of all of the major implications that he would draw from it. It was, however, to be a very important conceptual breakthrough for him (although, as we shall see, Sartre would not wish to regard "totalization" as a *concept* in the strict sense, and I am in agreement with him on this), an important explanatory tool for exploring both the nature of human societies and the meaning of history. Totalizations, in the Sartrean universe, can range from small- to very large-scale. They are undertaken both by historical actors and, at a remove, by historians or by social theorists seeking to comprehend a segment of human history or society. They amount, in short, to the social counterpart of what, on an individual level, Sartre and other existentialists called "projects"—a term that he attempts to explicate once again near the end of *Search for a Method*.[48] But the word "project" is simply inadequate to characterize, for example, the terribly complex, painful, contradiction-filled effort at "building socialism" that was supposed to be what the Stalinist regime and millions of ordinary Soviet citizens were undertaking in the 1930s: this was the historical totalization, one of a comprehensive and all-consuming sort to which Sartre was to give the name "enveloping totalization" *(totalisation d'enveloppement)*, that was to occupy virtually one-half of the unfinished second volume of the *Critique*. Like individual human projects, historical totalizations often turn out to be great failures.

As the text of the *Critique* evolves, it becomes evident that the contrast-term to "totalization" for Sartre is "totality."[49] (Critics belonging to, or influenced by, the "New Right" who attempt to smear Sartre with the broad brush of "totalistic" or even "totalitarian" thinking must conveniently overlook the fact that this is an absolutely fundamental distinction for his mature social theory.) The theorist or historian who treats a given society or fragment of history as if it were a fixed totality is taking a positivistic and purely external view, a way of thinking that Sartre will also identify as "analytic reason."[50] Of course, it is always *possible* to do this and indeed to formulate the relationships and interactions of the human individuals in that segment of place and time in mechanistic language like that of classical physics. But to do so is, for Sartre, to distort historical and social reality, for human societies are totalizations rather than totalities, which means that they always include an element of open-endedness, of activity and not just passivity—in short, of freedom. This is true to a degree even of those remote societies, especially those called "primitive," which it is easiest for us to regard as mere "totalities."[51] But the perspective of totalization is most eminently applicable to those societies that have a strong sense of human history and of their place within it. This remark suggests the ultimate question, the question with which Sartre had wrestled so much in the *Cahiers*, the issue around which he had focused his final rebuke to Camus:

does history as a whole have an ultimate meaning—that is, can it, as Hegel claimed and the more millenarian versions of Marxism insist, be regarded as one vast movement of totalization? In *Search for a Method,* Sartre strongly suggests that it can: "Our historical task . . . is to bring closer the moment when History will have *only one meaning* . . ."[52] Later, from time to time throughout the *Critique,* he will revert to this question, considered as a question, but he will never answer it explicitly and finally. As a matter of fact if he is correct in rejecting views of history that regard it as closed and fixed in trajectory, then in principle he is unable to answer the question with certitude: only a "Totalizer," some sort of God contemplating history from a standpoint outside of time, could do so.[53]

Sartre's initial application of this notion of "totalization" in *Search for a Method,* it will be recalled, is to the function played by great, epochal philosophies in totalizing the collective conventional wisdom, *Savoir,* of their societies, or at least of those elements in their societies that are in the ascendancy. It is Marxism, he asserts, that plays that role today. Thus perspectives that are apparent alternatives to it must ultimately be seen as ideologies parasitic on the epochal philosophy, as existentialism is, or as reactions against that philosophy. He proceeds to assert that the self-styled mainstream contemporary bearers of the Marxist tradition, to whom he often refers simply as "the Marxists," have brought about a stoppage or sclerosis in a philosophical worldview that is, or should be, quintessentially fluid and heuristic[54] rather than dogmatic. Such Marxists think Platonistically, in rigid formal categories, so that they lazily disregard facts in their eagerness to impose prefabricated interpretations on events. (Here, Sartre alludes to official Communist Party accounts of the events in Budapest.)[55] But, he maintains, "Marxism is still very young, almost in its infancy; it has scarcely begun to develop."[56] With some assistance from existentialist thought, with its emphasis on the importance of individuals and not merely of classes and other collectives, and from other thought currents such as Freudianism, the epochal philosophy of Marxism can overcome the sclerosis of contemporary Marxism and forge ahead. Its core insight into the dominance of a particular material mode of production over the politics and culture of the society associated with that mode will remain true as long as human beings have not been freed from "the yoke of scarcity." Once that happens at some far-distant time, then Marxism will be superseded as epochal philosophy by a "philosophy of freedom," which is as yet unimaginable to us at our point in history.[57]

These claims about the dominance of Marxism for our epoch, probably the best-known feature of *Search for a Method,* once seemed to me to be among the least exceptionable in the book. In many or even most parts of the world except for the United States during the period in which *Search for a Method* was written, and indeed for at least a half-generation thereafter, it was taken for granted that Marxism as a general worldview was on the agenda and to be reckoned with, despite enormous deformations in regimes claiming to be its adherents. Today, however, the situation is less clear-cut. While there is no single rival worldview with the same scope and comprehensiveness as Marxism, and while indeed much of the "post-Marxist" Western intellectual scene is dominated by a profound skepticism concerning any and all comprehensive worldviews, nevertheless deeply conservative and even reactionary ideologies of various, ultimately incompatible kinds—for example, religious fundamentalist and "free market" libertarian—now enjoy renewed respectability in many places, including some of the former "orthodox Marxist" heartlands. In such places the "sclerosis" of which Sartre wrote has proven more irreversible than he had hoped. Moreover, if there is anything resembling a rising social class worldwide, it does not at any rate bear a close resemblance to the European proletariats of the mid-nineteenth to mid-twentieth centuries, around which much of the imagery of traditional Marxism was constructed. Do these observations, apparently so counter to one of Sartre's core claims in *Search for a Method*, perhaps put into question the justifiability of the entire social and political theory of the *Critique*, to which *Search* serves as the introduction?

To put this important issue more clearly into focus, the circumstances of the essay's composition must be recalled in somewhat greater detail. It was commissioned for and first published in Poland, one of these countries in which "orthodox Marxism" was the official ideology, at the time of the first thawing of its intellectual and political climate. Poland had come very close to suffering Hungary's fate during the previous year, when Soviet troops and naval vessels had been on the alert for a possible invasion of the country, and difficult negotiations between the two national Communist Party leaderships had finally succeeded in restraining Premier Khrushchev's hand. Despite the obvious dangers, then, many Polish intellectuals were eager to renew their traditional special cultural ties with France, and the issue of *Twórczósc* in which Sartre's essay appeared, dealing in general with the state of French culture in 1957, was seen as one slightly but not highly provocative way of doing this. Sartre, of course, was the chief potential provocation, since, as we have seen in discussing his political writings of the preceding years, he was always distrusted and frequently attacked by the very conservative keepers of Marxist "orthodoxy" in his own country. His essay "Marxism and Existentialism" (its original title) itself, even while making the perhaps extravagant claims that I have recorded concerning the dominance of the Marxist worldview, was in fact a very substantial contribution from a historical point of view to the discrediting and deconstruction of Marxist "orthodoxy" as a thought-system. It was brutally honest in expressing Sartre's judgment about the sclerosis of that system and in denying, as we shall see, some of its core tenets, notably its strong insistence on historical determinism and on the overwhelmingly greater importance of social over individual factors in explaining human action and history. It was also the first step for Sartre in laying out a defensible social theory to express the liberating, postindustrial-capitalist *"vision du monde"* with which, as he quite rightly pointed out, the name of Marx was conventionally associated at the time.

That conventional association still seems to me to make *intellectual* ("in principle") sense today for many reasons having to do with the nature of Marx's own philosophy: his descriptive critique of the dominance of socio-economic factors in the structuring of so many aspects of capitalist society, his understanding and use of dialectical rather than purely analytic methodology in social explanation, his implicit critique of all interpersonal or group relationships of dominance and subordination as unjustifiable, his awareness of the real possibility of an advanced, complex society rendered better than the present one by virtue of the prevalence of cooperative social arrangements over competitive, antagonistic ones, and so on.[58] But the continued adherence to views and practices often the polar opposites of these (e.g., emphasis on primarily political rather than socioeconomic descriptions and solutions, positivist methodologies, and highly authoritarian, elitist, "New Class" social structures) on the part of so many self-styled "orthodox" Marxists risen to power has by now severely eroded the conventional association between Marxism and the vision that Sartre was attempting to express in 1957. As Sartre makes very clear in *Search for a Method*, he there characterizes the current age as that of Marx by virtue of the dominance of Marx's *name*, i.e., as a convenience or shorthand; there was therefore no fundamental inconsistency, much less dishonesty, involved in Sartre's later abandoning the "Marxist" label. But Sartre himself did not, to the best of my knowledge, ever explain his reasons for doing so in quite the way in which I have here—a way that both demonstrates, with respect to one of Sartre's own philosophical essays, the inherent time-boundedness even of philosophical writing that lays claim to transcending the ephemerality necessarily characteristic of the political essay genre, and that yet defends the validity of the insight behind the claim about Marxism that Sartre makes there.

Sartre's own rather offhand, casual explanation in one late interview of some of his reasons for no longer affiliating his thought with Marxism is somewhat more purely conceptual in nature; here are excerpts:

> The analysis of national and international capitalism in 1848 has little to do with the capitalism of today. A multinational company cannot be explained in the Marxist terms of 1848. . . . [The philosophy of freedom that is being born today] is a philosophy that would be on the same level . . . as Marxism—a philosophy in which theory serves practice, but which takes as its starting point the freedom that seems to me to be missing in Marxist thought. . . . [Scarcity] is not Marxist thought. . . . This notion has been introduced into philosophy by others besides me, and I do not owe it to Marx. I consider that scarcity is the phenomenon in which we live.[59]

The first of these three remarks, concerning Marxism's supposed inability to deal with contemporary multinationals, is made in the context of Sartre's broader claim that Marxism has grown old, almost moribund—a complete reversal of his claim in *Search for a Method* that Marxism was then still young; it is one of comparatively few such explicit reversals of belief that can indisputably be attributed to Sartre, although even in this case it is tempered by his insistence that many terms and ideas will be retained from Marxism. As far as the need to analyze multinationals is concerned, this will remain a real but unmet need within both *Search for a Method* and the two volumes of the *Critique*. On the other two points cited by Sartre in this 1975 interview as points of divergence between himself and Marxism, however, namely, freedom and scarcity, *Search for a Method* introduces important new perspectives for Sartre's political theory. Let us consider them in turn before discussing the "question of method" itself.

If Marxist thought indeed lacks the element of freedom, as Sartre indicates in his interview that he has come to believe it does, he was never at any time tempted to question that element's primacy. Evidence for the view that freedom is lacking in Marxism is to be found not only, of course(!), in the writings and attitudes of the "orthodox" Marxists with whom Sartre was so thoroughly familiar in France, but also in some of Marx's own texts, such as his famous Introduction to *A Contribution to the Critique of Political Economy*.[60] But this evidence is ambiguous, and I myself, for example, am not persuaded by it. At any rate, among writers within the Marxian tradition who do not wish to accept the later Sartre's negative judgment about this, certain of Marx's writings of 1844 and 1845 are seen to contain the core of counterevidence, and a single term that Marx employed primarily in these writings serves as a rallying-point for their position: *praxis*. This is the term that Sartre begins to employ, without special fanfare, in *Search for a Method* as a way of designating human action in "the project,"[61] and it will become central to the entire theoretical structure of the *Critique*. For Sartre, *praxis is* freedom, but freedom now construed far more as action in and on a material world that is full of resistances than it was in *Being and Nothingness*. (It is not the case that the model of freedom in *Being and Nothingness*, as expressed above all in the notion of being for itself or the *pour soi*, is totally different—purely cerebral, for example: that work contains lengthy treatments, in particular, of human action conceived as "doing" *(faire)*, as I have noted earlier in this book. But there is a clear change of *emphasis* in the *Critique*, and this change is well encapsulated in the change of language from *pour soi* to *praxis*.)[62] Human activity can of course be merely individual and isolated, but it can also be undertaken collectively, as *common praxis*. Common *praxis*, to however great an extent it may and often does tie itself up in knots, so to speak, and produce results entirely opposite to those aimed at in the original project, remains an expression of human freedom. These ideas, first broached or hinted at in *Search for a Method*, constitute the key insight of Sartre's entire mature political and social theory in terms of at once defending the reality of human freedom against certain Marxist and other (e.g., behavioralist) methodological denials of it, and endeavoring to explain the complexities of various forms of human social interaction.

Of equal and complementary importance for explaining human activity in this world (the world with which the human race has been familiar up to now, though not in every conceivable world) for the Sartre of the *Critique* is the phenomenon of *scarcity.* Although complementary as *explanans*, scarcity is freedom's contrary from a normative point of view: if freedom is both fundamental fact and ultimate positive goal of human conduct, scarcity is an equally fundamental, albeit contingent, fact and also the source or motivating cause of evil. He introduces it in *Search for a Method* in the following words:

> Certainly, whatever men and events may be, until now they appear within the framework of *scarcity,* in other words in a society still incapable of liberating itself from its needs, hence from Nature, and which by that very fact is defined according to its level of technology and its tools; the tearing apart of a collectivity crushed by its needs and dominated by a mode of production arouses antagonisms among the individuals who make it up; the abstract relationships of things with one another, of commodity and money, etc., hide and condition the direct relationships of men with one another; thus machinery, the circulation of commodities, etc., determine the economic and social development. Without these principles, no historical rationality.[63]

This passage invites a number of comments. To begin with, it is obviously inspired in large measure by Marxian ways of thinking, even if Sartre in his later interview was correct in maintaining that "scarcity" was not an important notion for Marx. It is true in fact that the word seldom occurs in *Capital*, for example, by comparison with the frequency of its occurrences in the *Critique,* and indeed that the notion played a more systematically obvious role in the thought of some of the bourgeois political economist predecessors of Marx, such as Adam Smith. However, Sartre's own employment of the phenomenon of scarcity to explain so much within a framework of thought that is heavily influenced by Marx strongly suggests, from a logical point of view, that the notion is consistent with and even integral to Marxism, even if Marx seldom mentions it explicitly. Indeed, Sartre himself says just this in Volume 1 of the *Critique:* "Marx speaks very little of scarcity, and, I believe, that is because it is a commonplace of classical economy. . . . He takes the thing for granted."[64]

Next, it is important to notice the words "until now," which were most unfortunately omitted from the standard English translation of *Search for a Method:* here already, Sartre is laying the groundwork both for his occasional later speculations in both volumes of the *Critique* about possible worlds with creatures resembling human beings in certain ways but not dominated by scarcity, and for his utopian (my word, not his) aspirations toward a possible future human world in which scarcity would have been overcome. Another important element in the passage is the reference to *needs*, which are cast in a negative light as something from which to be liberated, and which are equated with Nature, which is therefore equally cast in a negative light; this latter equation is, as I have already suggested apropos of earlier Sartrean works, one of the less attractive or defensible aspects of his thought from beginning to end—an unfortunate inheritance from the Hegelian tradition. Finally, the terse sentence at the conclusion of the citation makes it eminently clear just how indispensable Sartre considers scarcity and the basic realities that follow from its existence (the creation of ever-new technologies to meet needs, the conflicts generated by the successive socioeconomic orders formed to produce the tools required by these technologies, the fetishism of commodities—in short, the core concepts of historical materialism) to be for his own central project here, that of comprehending, explaining, history.

Many commentators, including myself,[65] have complained about this central role assigned by Sartre to scarcity, especially, in terms of two related problems: the vagueness of the notion, and the consequent difficulty of envisioning its overcoming, i.e., of understanding what it would mean for such an event to take place. In the further remarks that he made pursuant to the reference to Marxism and scarcity to which I have already alluded in his late interview, Sartre only contributes further to uneasiness on this point when he insists more strongly than ever on the all-pervasiveness of scarcity in human existence, including "a scarcity in our conversation: scarcity of ideas, scarcity of understanding."[66] The overcoming of scarcities of *this* sort seems utterly utopian, in the most pejorative sense of the word, and no more conceivable than classical Western theology's definition of heaven as "the Beatific Vision." However, the conclusion of this portion of the interview in question brings us back to earth with Sartre's conceding that the coming of socialism "would not lead to the disappearance of scarcity. However, it is obvious that at that point ways of dealing with scarcity could be sought and found."[67]

It would seem, then, that the idea of a potential overcoming of scarcity might prove useful as a sort of limiting-concept, an asymptotically approachable goal against which genuinely possible historical change for the better could be measured; considered in this way, it makes greater sense to follow Sartre in not restricting the notion to mere scarcities of material goods, as students of political economy might be inclined to do. Scarcity thus broadly construed could very plausibly be seen as explanatory of some of the deep discontents and antagonisms to be found in comparatively affluent societies today, while scarcity of the traditional garden variety would continue to account, or at least to help to account, for much of past social antagonisms, large and small, and indeed still for much of what takes place in "Third World" societies. However, while this broadened notion of scarcity may be very suggestive for future social and political theory, the term continues to be disappointingly vague throughout *Search for a Method* and the *Critique* despite the frequency of its use, and the fact that we have needed to turn to somewhat offhand remarks made by Sartre in an interview in order to shed needed light on it shows how far from being a fully refined or fully mined idea it remains.

Human freedom as *praxis* acting upon matter in a regime of (somewhat indefinite) scarcity is, then, the central vision of Sartre's mature social philosophy as first enunciated explicitly in *Search for a Method*. One important question still requires exploration before we turn from *Search* to a discussion of the *Critique* proper: what is this *method* for which Sartre suggests that we need to search? In fact, however, to express it in this way is to misstate the question, for *Search for a Method*, it will be recalled, is only the title of the English translation and not Sartre's own. To the French (as distinguished from the Polish) published versions of the essay, both in *Les Temps Modernes* and later as the prelude to Volume 1 of the *Critique*, Sartre gave the title, "Questions de méthode" (Questions of method), a highly general but accurate enough descriptor. As he says in the remarkably brief preface that he added to the *Critique* version, these "questions" are ultimately reducible to a single one: "Do we today have the means to constitute a structural and historical anthropology?"[68] What he means by this is something like a general framework for social theory that would be both synchronic and diachronic, to employ the useful terminology from the structuralism of Lévi-Strauss and others with which Sartre was by then becoming familiar. (He explicitly employs this synchronic/diachronic distinction on the very last page of Volume 1 of the *Critique* as a means of marking the fundamental division, as he sees it, between the subject matters of Volumes 1 and 2.)[69]

Sartre's answer to this question, beyond a simple "Yes," begins with the exploration of the role of Marxism in contemporary intellectual culture that we have already examined. It lays heavy stress, as I have also noted, on the parasitic but needed function of existentialism, with its insistence on the singularity of the human individual, as complementary to an excessively collectivist, essentialist Marxism that is suffering from premature sclerosis. It pays positive attention, far more than anything written previously by Sartre, to Freud's central insight that one must regress to episodes of an individual's early childhood in order fully to comprehend her or his life project; it is in this context that Sartre makes his often-cited quip to the effect that "orthodox" Marxists forget their own childhoods and write as if one were born at the point at which one first earns a salary.[70] (It is also in this context, it is very important to observe, that Sartre makes extensive use of his lifelong obsession, Gustave Flaubert, as an example of the inadequacies of both "orthodox" Marxism, with its neglect of the circumstances of childhood, parents, etc., and classical Freudianism, which pays no serious attention to the political, historical, and cultural circumstances of the individual's life.[71] This anticipates, of course, *The Family Idiot*, the first sentence of which will proclaim that the whole work should be seen as an exemplification of the method first delineated in *Search for a Method*.[72]) It pays attention of a primarily but by no means entirely negative sort to the behavioral approaches of American sociologists, notably the "human engineering" movement, and to the diverse sociological-anthropological theories of Lewin, Kardiner, and Lévi-Strauss himself. In short, the first Sartrean answer to his own question about whether we have the means to construct a structural, historical *Sozialwissenschaft* in our time is to suggest a method that makes use, as he expresses it early in the *Critique*, of all available material ("nous ferons feu de tout bois")[73]—any and every methodology seriously proposed within our culture—but with special emphasis on the intersection of Marxism, existentialism, and Freudianism, and using a vocabulary influenced by structuralism.

Finally, there is also a second, more specific answer to the "question of method" raised at the outset of the essay. While not inconsistent with the first and probably not nearly as important as the first or as some commentators have tried to make it, it merits mention because it furnishes the title of the final and longest subsection of *Search for a Method:* "The Progressive-Regressive Method." Sartre takes the idea from a then-recent article by his contemporary, Henri Lefebvre, a Marxist sociologist-philosopher whose own work, in my opinion, is surpassed in significance only by Sartre's among French political theorists of that generation and who was about to undergo the process of expulsion from the Communist Party, of which he had been a member for some three decades, as a result in part of critical ideas expressed in a companion essay to Sartre's in the special 1957 issue of *Twórczość*. In the article from which Sartre cites,[74] Lefebvre proposes three steps toward a full comprehension of whatever particular segment of culture may be under investigation; the culture of rural communities—so different in type between Europe and the United States, for instance, in part because of the differences in the historical circumstances of their original establishment—is the sort of study with which he happens to be concerned here. Sartre characterizes these three Lefebvrean steps as phenomenological description, followed first by a regressive, and then by a progressive, movement. The regressive movement, according to Lefebvre's own words, has an analytic component, involving both the probing of underlying social structures and the effort to *date* the segment under investigation with exactitude. Finally, the progressive component is an "effort to rediscover the present, but elucidated, understood, explained."[75]

It would be a mistake to try rigidly to impose this tripartite schematism on various portions of Sartre's *Critique*, despite the extremely high praise that he bestows on Lefebvre's text in the passage from which I have derived this summary.[76] It is true, however, that extended descriptions of a broadly phenomenological sort will be scattered throughout the *Critique* and provide some of its most memorable pages (the taking of the Bastille; the queue waiting for the bus on the Boulevard St. Germain; the writer observing two workers, a road worker and a gardener, on opposite sides of a stone wall from his rural hotel window; and so on), while Sartre himself will make a connection between the synchronic-regressive studies of which Volume 1 is composed and the diachronic-progressive ones that are supposed to dominate Volume 2. Of greater interest, I think, is the use to which Sartre puts Lefebvre's methodological proposal, which he says he wishes other Marxist intellectuals would follow, in at once reinforcing his dire warnings of Marxism's sclerosis ("The Marxist method is progressive because it is the result, in Marx, of long analyses; today synthetic progression is dangerous: lazy Marxists make use of it to constitute the real *a priori*")[77] and providing an underlying rationale for all that he is to undertake in what follows in the *Critique* proper. The *Critique*, in other words, is to be a sustained effort at investigating a more basic level of social reality than we find even in the writings of Marx himself, for example in *Capital*,[78] much less in most of the current writers who claim to speak in Marx's name.

The composition of the *Critique* proper, particularly the completed Volume 1, was, as has by now frequently been observed, a work undertaken by Sartre in considerable haste and under conditions of great emotional and physical strain. Begun some time in late 1957, Volume 1 was published, nearly 400,000 words in length, in early 1960. In the meantime, Sartre was undertaking, among other enterprises, the writing and production of his forceful theatrical allegory about Nazi war criminals and the bloody criminality of our whole twentieth-century culture, *The Condemned of Altona;* the publication of a number of short essays, chiefly about the Algerian War (e.g., "We Are All Assassins")[79] and about General De Gaulle's accession to power in France (e.g., "The Frogs Who Demand a King")[80]—both in *Les Temps Modernes*, of which he was also continuing to serve as editor, and elsewhere as prefaces to other authors' books;[81] the unsuccessful collaboration with John Huston on a screenplay about Freud, which involved a rather hilarious sojourn on Huston's farm in Ireland in which mutual incomprehension appears to have been the dominant tone and which has resulted in another long (500 pages), fascinating (although not very revealing from the standpoint of political theory), posthumously published manuscript;[82] and, of course the composition of the unfinished 400-odd pages that we now know as the second volume of the *Critique!* During this same period, Sartre's over-consumption of then-legal but deleterious drugs contributed to his first very serious health crisis, and his feelings of depression about the current political situation that was the subject of his shorter essays reached new heights. The year 1960, as we can see in retrospect, would include several very important marker-events, signaling the beginning of a new period (in fact, the final two decades) of Sartre's life: the death of Camus in January (to be followed by Merleau-Ponty's death the following year), the beginning (in the summer) of negotiations between De Gaulle's government and the Algerian forces that would eventually result (after much additional bloodshed and violence, including the bombing of Sartre's apartment two years later) in Algerian independence, a February-March visit to Cuba resulting in long newspaper articles and essays, a trip to Brazil in the fall,[83] and of course, on April 6, the actual first publication of *Critique de la raison dialectique*, Volume 1: "Théorie des ensembles pratiques."

Volume 1 of the *Critique* has been the object of at least two or three,[84] and Volume 2 already of one,[85] book-length English-language summaries, not to mention numerous less extensive work along the same lines.[86] What I shall be presenting in the following two chapters, while it will include all of what I regard as the main points, will not, I hope, be reducible to a similar undertaking expressed in different words. I wish, of course, to continue the sketch of Sartre's political theory that I have gradually been filling in throughout the earlier parts of this book by indicating how it can be augmented through an examination of the single major Sartrean work that is most exclusively devoted to sociopolitical and historical issues, presenting Sartre's answer to old questions, such as the nature of political authority, and some of the many new questions about and new approaches to these issues that he introduces. As it happens, however (not by mere chance), a good way to group some of the major sets of issues in this entire area is to follow the major sequence of topics as developed by Sartre from Volume 1 through Volume 2. Volume 1 contains an Introduction and two "books"; Volume 2 has alternatively been designated (by the editor, Arlette Elkaïm-Sartre) as Book 3. As I shall be considering them, the topics fall under four headings: (1) methodology, which includes issues of ontology and is the primary concern of the 60-page Introduction to Volume 1 as well as of certain passages toward the end of Volume 2; (2) the relationship between the human individual and the material world, a relationship that immediately involves other human beings, that is the subject matter of Book 1 of Volume 1 ("From Individual *Praxis* to the Practico-Inert"); (3) the domains of what might be called quasi-political and political organization proper, which are the concern of subsection A of Book 2 ("Of the Group"), 300 pages in length; and (4) the philosophy of history, the preoccupation of the comparatively briefer, concluding subsection B of Book 2 ("Of Dialectical Investigation [*Expérience*][87] as Totalization: The Level of the Concrete, the Place of History") as well as of the majority of Volume 2 (i.e., Book 3), "The Intelligibility of History." It is interesting and very much in keeping with Sartre's sense of the circularity of dialectical investigation that he returned near the end of Volume 2, in however sketchy a fashion, to some of the methodological issues with which the book had begun. For convenience of organization, the first two sets of issues will be dealt with in the following chapter, and the last two in chapter 5.

FOUR

The *Critique*

Methodology, Ontology, and the Individual–World Relationship

In the introductory chapter of the *Critique* proper, Sartre continues to deal with methodological issues that were raised in *Search for a Method*, but he now does so at a more profound, more complex level. At stake here are the most fundamental philosophical questions concerning, to express it in our standard, cliché-pervaded shorthand, "the nature of reality"—particularly as these affect sociohistorical and political explanation, to be sure, but inevitably extending to all of human existence and even existence beyond the human sphere. Scattered explicit references back to these questions abound throughout the entire two volumes, but they return to the fore in certain passages late in Volume 2. In the middle of one of the most illuminating of these, more than 1000 printed pages beyond the end of the Introduction, Sartre characteristically reminds his readers of having "discussed these positions, at the beginning of the present essay [sic]."[1]

The outcome of his introductory chapter, as Sartre now summarizes it, is to have shown that the dialectic—that is, the object of his entire two-volume investigation—must be at once the activity, the knowledge, and "the law of the knowledge" (that is, in a paraphrase that only slightly distorts his meaning here, the metatheory) of a given milieu of human *praxis*. What takes place in the sociohistorical world, in other words, takes place dialectically; equally dialectical, at least if they are to have any real value, must be both the actors' contemporaneous and the historians' retrospective comprehensions of what is taking and has taken place, and the philosophical comprehension of this entire "scene" that is attempted in works such as Sartre's own. But what does the adverb "dialectically" *mean* here? Sartre, like any dialectical thinker, would of course wish first to insist that the full meaning of the term can only be understood through detailed examinations of sequences of events regarded by hypothesis as being dialectical: the proof is in the eating, or whichever earthy metaphor pointing to the circularity of the world of human action, the absolute impossibility of taking a stance outside of it, one prefers. However, it is also the case that the broadly dialectical approach to reality has a long and well-known philosophical tradition behind it, the names of Hegel and even more, as far as Sartre is concerned, of Marx being the most illustrious to be identified with it in modern times. Thus, in the first paragraph of his introduction, Sartre points out that everything that is said in *Search for a Method* presupposes an in principle agreement on his part with historical materialism, which is of course a standard name for Marx's worldview, and immediately goes on to name several characteristic features generally associated with the dialectical approach. These include the beliefs (although the list is not intended to be exhaustive) "that a negation of negation can be an affirmation, that conflicts . . . are the motor of History, that each moment of a series must *be understood* in light of the initial moment and that it is *irreducible* to the latter, that History at each instant generates totalizations of totalizations, etc."[2] The validation of these beliefs, it cannot be insisted too strongly, can only be accomplished through detailed, reflective examination of the sort of which the *Critique* consists.

This undogmatic locution, "of the sort," is not mine alone: Sartre also subscribes to it quite explicitly, making such remarks as that he will be happy if this discussion provisionally begun by him "is carried on collectively in some working groups,"[3] that "the critical investigation can and must be the reflective investigation of anyone at all,"[4] and again, on the following page, that anyone at all can carry out this investigation. In the last-mentioned passage, he adds an extremely significant qualification: to wit, that he means "anyone at all" to refer, not to anyone at any time in history, but rather to anyone today, "in this *one World* that is ours, the post-Stalinist period." Here, then, very early in Volume 1, he indicates a basic rationale for the enormous amount of attention that he will pay to the phenomenon of Stalinism in Volume 2, as he in effect characterizes our whole present era of "one World" (an expression that he writes, I think very appropriately, in English) in the following way:

> Consequently, in every life . . . totalization effects the divorce of blind, unprincipled *praxis* from sclerosed thought, or, in other words, the obfuscation of the dialectic is a moment of totalizing activity and of the world. By this contradiction, lived in discomfort and sometimes shatteringly, it dictates to everyone, as his or her own individual future, the thorough re-evaluation [*la remise en question*] of his or her intellectual tools.[5]

"Stalinism," then, is a name for the complex sequence of events whereby history as understood within the increasingly dominant dialectical tradition became (to use a word that will occur frequently in Volume 2) *deviated* in a radical way from the general direction that that tradition had thought of it as taking; this deviation affects all of us today in our own individual lives; what is needed is a thoroughgoing reevaluation of that tradition and of its fundamental methodological and ontological premises. In other words dialectical reason itself must be subjected to radical criticism and self-criticism.

Why not, then, consider simply abandoning it altogether? Because, Sartre is utterly convinced, it is the only theoretical perspective that holds out the promise of ultimately rendering *intelligible* the social world. If we have nothing else, perhaps not even a great deal of *hope* after the repeated and shattering disappointments of the twentieth century, he is saying, we can at least comprehend it all. A poignant passage at the end of the first main subsection of Volume 2 makes this point very forcefully:

> We have just shown that the practico-inert tearings, the conflicts and the disharmonies, far from breaking the unity of the praxis-process, in a society of which the sovereign is a dictator, are at once the consequences of this unification and the means that it chooses to close back upon itself still more. Thus the enormous historical upheaval which produced from 1917 to 1958 Soviet Society as we know it *must be able* to be comprehended dialectically by the historian, in the very unity of a sovereign praxis and of the process which ceaselessly moves beyond the reach of that praxis and which, ceaselessly, the latter reintegrates within itself. These conclusions are in themselves neither optimistic nor pessimistic: we do not pretend that the struggle was not atrocious, that (innumerable) individual disasters do not irremediably condemn certain practices (we shall return to the issue of individual failure at the heart of a common praxis); at the level of dialectical exploration that we have attained, we do not have the right to say that it was impossible to proceed otherwise (nor, on the other hand, the contrary right: we simply know nothing as yet about the possibilities). We have simply discovered that the sovereign praxis, whatever it was, always appeared under the form of totalization; and in its very nature as praxis-process, we have established—this is our only optimism—that it was intelligible as *constituted dialectic*.[6]

This passage also constitutes, incidentally, one of the clearest statements of Sartre's summary judgment of Stalinism in all of the second volume.

What are some of the principal *alternatives* to Sartre's dialectical approach? The discussion of these alternatives constitutes probably the most central task of the introductory chapter. First of all, of course, there is a vast range of social scientific methodologies that Sartre sometimes designates as "analytic reason," even though strictly speaking, as we have seen, he includes an "analytico-regressive" movement within the tripartite method that he borrows from Lefebvre and advocates in *Search for a Method,* and indeed most of the text of the *Critique* as we have it is intended to exemplify this analytic-regressive type of dialectical investigation. "Analytic reason" as understood invidiously by Sartre is premised on the assumption that no overall explanation, however provisional, of the larger movements of history (or even, to be consistent, of very small segments thereof) can be scientifically legitimate—in other words, the assumption that "history is just one damn thing after another." At a few points in the *Critique,* Sartre seems to identify a version of this view with the structural anthropology of his personal acquaintance, Claude Lévi-Strauss; Lévi-Strauss was later to accept this identification and rather eloquently to defend the view, by way of an extended criticism of Sartre, that the study of human societies *ought* to be approached in much the same general way as one would approach the study of the complex structures of an ant colony, and that "history" as Sartre wishes to understand it is itself a culturally relative notion characteristic of our modern Western societies but by no means of all human cultures.[7]

Superficially similar in outcome to, but in fact quite different from, the positivistic approaches to society and history, inspired by natural science methodology, that Sartre designates by the term "analytic reason" when he is using it pejoratively are the various deconstructive techniques that are sometimes said now to characterize our "postmodern" era. At the time of writing the *Critique,* Sartre could not, of course, anticipate these developments in detail although, as I have already indicated, in his repeated insistence on the fundamentally "detotalized" quality of all alleged human "totalities" and consequently on the unfinished "in-course" character of any and all historical totalizations he already conveys to his readers what I regard as the most fruitful aspect of the postmodernist spirit when it is applied to the study of society, history, and politics. To the extent, however, to which proponents of deconstruction, however this is understood, may regard themselves as denying the possibility of any general sociohistorical explanation, they are either reducing their own position to that of a new form of positivism or else, as when they themselves propose to offer a general sketch of, let us say, "the postmodern era," being self-contradictory and inconsistent.

Other principal alternatives to Sartre's approach, alternatives to which he himself devotes the bulk of his critical attention in the Introduction to the *Critique,* arise from within the dialectical tradition. One of these, of course, is Hegel's idealism. Sartre mentions it and discusses it directly in a paragraph or two, but he obviously does not regard it as a serious option today; as he puts it, its very superiority as a method lies "precisely in that which we reject of it today: in its idealism,"[8] a dogmatic position that would permit anyone who were to accept it to dispense with proofs. One may cavil about Sartre's somewhat high-handed "we" in this sentence, but in fact virtually no one does accept Hegel's conception of history in an unqualified way today, and so it would be rather pointless to devote extensive efforts to disproving it. It is, however, interesting to note the changes in Sartre's comparative estimations of Hegel and Marx in the *Critique* by comparison with the *Cahiers:* much lower in the case of the former, much higher for the latter.

Another version of dialectical thinking that Sartre regards as a more serious alternative to his own, and one that it is somewhat more difficult to distinguish from his than the Hegelian view of history as God's self-development through time, is what he denominates "dialectical hyper-empiricism," adopting a label invented by the sociologist Georges Gurvitch.[9] According to this approach, we should adopt a dialectical methodology to explain a given sequence of events if initial empirical inquiry into them suggests that it would be appropriate in this case, but we must refrain from any a priori commitment to dialectical method: sometimes it may work, and sometimes not. Sartre, on the contrary, believes that the theorist's commitment to dialectical reason as the vehicle of intelligibility in the social world must be a priori, apodictic, and it is for this reason that the paraphrase of Kantian language in his book's title is not mere parody. But the *kind* of a priori thinking and apodicticity that is possible for a dialectician who rejects all dogmatic versions of dialectical method and insists on an ongoing, self-referential process to demonstrate the correctness of his or her method must be quite different from what these notions meant to Kant (or, for that matter, to Husserl):

> *A priori* here does not refer to I don't know what constitutive principles prior to experience, but to a universality and a necessity contained in every experience and going beyond each experience . . . [By contrast with Husserl, who] restricted himself to the terrain of pure, formal consciousness . . . we must find our apodictic experience in the concrete world of History.[10]

In short, the critical dialectic that Sartre is advocating is to be accepted from the outset of one's sociopolitical inquiry, but only in a heuristic spirit.

The type of rival, dogmatic dialectic to which Sartre devotes the most attention in the *Critique*, however, is, as might have been anticipated, the "dialectics of nature" approach developed by Friedrich Engels, which served for decades as the basis of the catechetical "diamat" (dialectical materialism) worldview promulgated by "orthodox" Marxists in the Soviet Union and later in Eastern Europe. This approach amounts precisely to the "dogmatic dialectic" to which Sartre contrasts his own "critical dialectic," as he expresses it in the Introduction's first subtitle. Sartre's principal point here is that the formulation of Engels's allegedly fundamental dialectical laws, allegedly applicable across the domains of both natural history and human history, imposes a distortive rigidity on our attempts to understand the latter, human history. He himself does not propose to reject unequivocally the very possibility of a dialectics of nature, but rather holds that the idea is just a metaphysical hypothesis that is not knowable with certitude and moreover that would be irrelevant to the comprehension of human history even if, *per impossibile*, it could be known. Late in Volume 2, he returns to this point in discussing the difference between occurrences that affect human history from the outside—such as, at the limit, a cooling off of the sun which would bring about a cessation of all human life—and those brought about internally, by human activity—for example, again at the limit, the elimination of the human race through global nuclear war. In a footnote to this, he says:

> Were there a "dialectic of Nature," nothing would be changed in the conditions that we have just described. On the other hand, it is not doubtful that pro-

gressive scientific and technological accomplishments have as their effect the enlarging of the practical field and in fact will later, perhaps, permit the staving off of certain disasters. But that is not the question: even if, contained in embryo in human science, there were the practical possibility for man to perpetuate himself . . . across galactic catastrophes, still nothing would prove that these catastrophes will delay their occurrence for us to have the means of staving them off. Nothing would prove it because nothing *can* prove it: we're dealing with two different series.[11]

Sartre's principled opposition to the Engelsian dialectics of nature, already anticipated in certain respects in the *Cahiers*, together with his insistence here on "two different series," might lead one to believe that the Sartre of the *Critique* was still bent on defending the sharp opposition between nature and history upon which Hegel had insisted so strongly and which both Marx and Engels devoted some of their most intensive philosophical efforts to overcoming. But this would be an oversimplification of the later Sartre's position. By contrast with an explicit pronouncement in the *Cahiers* that I have cited, where he categorically rejected materialist monism, Sartre now insists that he is a monist whose monism is materialist rather than idealist in character, and that the duality between merely natural and historical occurrences expressed in the notion of "two series," which he considers more faithful to basic Marxian dialectical thinking than the Engelsian model, *stems from* this monistic view that there are no entities other than material ones.[12] In both the activity and the comprehension of human history, reflective thought plays a role, which is not the case in purely physical sequences of occurrences; the positivistic, Engelsian type of dialectic that tries to impose certain a priori "natural" laws on sociohistorical events, as distinguished from Sartre's heuristic dialectic, guarantees that such events will ultimately elude it.

In both volumes of the *Critique*, Sartre frequently insists on an old, familiar term that does not appear very often in his earlier work and that in effect serves as an intermediary between the polar contrast terms of *praxis* and inert matter and explains his new willingness to be considered a materialist: *organism*. The inorganic—*physis* in its pure form for Sartre—is worked on by the *praxis* of human organisms, and that is what makes history. But organisms, too, are of course material. It is above all through this new emphasis of his on a very traditional notion that Sartre finally makes peace with materialism.

The question arises, however, as to how nonhuman organisms might fit into this scheme—both animal organisms and possible living things inhabiting other worlds. Sartre, in effect, "finesses" this issue, which had always concerned me and some other readers of his works,[13] when, almost at the very end of Volume 2, he says that he has been concerned most centrally with the one type of organism (or what he frequently calls "practical multiplicity") with which we ourselves have experience, namely, "that of men." In a revealing footnote to this remark, he adds:

One may call action or activity the entirety of behaviors of certain insects, of certain mammals; one may even remark that activity begins on earth with unicellular beings themselves. In any case, the questions that this activity raises are without common measure with those that the existence of practical multiplicities whose technical development was equal or superior to ours, but differently oriented by virtue of the difference in the organisms and in the practical problems, would raise.[14]

The fact that in this same closing section of Volume 2 Sartre is concerned to show the importance of an untranscendable, ultimate goal characteristic of organisms in general, "the safeguarding of life,"[15] for rendering history intelligible, shows just how much Sartre has modified the starkly dualistic worldview of *en-soi/pour-soi* in the course of coming to grips with questions about the nature of society and history.

Throughout the relatively brief introductory chapter of the *Critique,* the part of the work in which he concerns himself most directly and uninterruptedly with methodological issues, then, Sartre's principal strategy is to distinguish dialectical reasoning, of the sort that he wishes to defend as being most appropriate for the historian and for the social philosopher because characteristic of social interactions and of history itself, from alternative conceptions, both openly antidialectical and supposedly (but not fully) dialectical ones. This undertaking, like all methodologically oriented introductions, is necessarily quite abstract, as Sartre himself fully recognizes. At the same time, as we have had occasion to observe, it contains important anticipations of the more concrete analyses of social structures and of history that are to follow, as well as of Sartre's attitudes toward fundamental questions of ontology. There is one crucial aspect of the latter that informs the entire work in a decisive way: it is what Sartre calls his "dialectical nominalism".[16] This must now be considered.

That abstract essences do not exist was always a basic Sartrean belief. It accounts for his very well-known claim, to which I have already referred earlier in this book, that "there is no human nature." In a very significant allusion to this claim in the Introduction, Sartre remarks that

> a friendship, in the time of Socrates, does not have the same meaning nor the same functions as a contemporary friendship; but by this very differentiation, which rigorously rules out every belief in a "human nature," we only illuminate more clearly the synthetic bond of *reciprocity* . . . which is a singularized universal and the very basis of all human relations.[17]

Abstract concepts such as "human nature," "friendship," "class," "nation," etc. have no univocal transhistorical meanings for Sartre. The contemplative, intellectualist reduction of human experience to abstract concepts, however commonplace a move it may be both for mainstream philosophical thinking from Plato and Aristotle onward and for the thinking of ordinary people, is the great barrier to social change and to the exercise of freedom. It is this move that undergirds what Sartre throughout the *Critique* calls *exis* (more correctly transliterated from the Greek, *hexis*), habit, which Aristotle lauded as a desirable goal of education but which Sartre frequently opposes to *praxis* as understood in its most normatively positive sense. It is once again a passage late in Volume 2 of the *Critique*, where so many of Sartre's mature ontological insights receive clear if only fragmentary formulations, that perhaps best expresses his virulent anticonceptualism:

> The origin of alienation is there, as we have said: anti-human matter—insofar as it is exiled from the pure domain of exteriority without ever attaining life—returns, in the name of unity . . . , the anti-humanity of man to all men as their true human reality. It is at this level that *essences* . . . and contemplative thought exist. This captive thought is also, very simply, conceptual thought. Analysis dissolves it into external relationships, dialectic makes it burst apart through its temporalizing power; but it is unceasingly reborn as the "natural" thought of man or rather as thoughts that are produced by things, in totalizing circularity, through their reconditioning of men.[18]

This passage well expresses Sartre's central vision of dialectical circularity: the reimposition by human beings, struggling as material organisms to transcend the inhumanity of mere matter, of the thing-like qualities of such matter upon themselves. Here, however, unlike numerous otherwise similar passages in Volume 2 in which physical activity is emphasized, Sartre points to the occurrence of such infernal dialectical movement within language and thought themselves, and goes so far as to identify this site as "the origin of alienation." The always alleged rationale for this kind of move is unity—unity of thinking, unity of action, sometimes even unity of history—but this unity is achieved at the cost of a fundamental distortion of a reality. A more radical rejection of the dominant essentialist and (to use a term more recently in vogue in the United States) foundationalist traditions of Western philosophy is scarcely conceivable.

But what then remains that can legitimately be said of a general nature? Are we not back in the hopeless realm of "hyper-empiricism," whether of a dialectical or nondialectical variety, where it is impossible consistently to make any philosophical utterances about society, politics, history? Sartre's attempt at escaping this trap, articulated without fanfare in the passage from the Introduction that I cited above and soon to become a central theme in his book on Flaubert, is the notion of the "singular[ized] universal." Flaubert himself, a human individual, will be taken as an interesting, complex example of this in *The Family Idiot*, but the example chosen by Sartre in the present text, reciprocity, furnishes a clear clue to the later Sartre's fundamental ontological commitments and hence to the underlying rationale of the entire series of analyses that constitute the *Critique*. Relationships of reciprocity, human interaction, exist throughout the world of human beings, as we know both from personal experience and from the

reading of history. The standard error is to attempt to find some charac-
teristic(s) common to all instances of reciprocity, some essence of human
interaction (perhaps to go along with a putative human essence or nature).
But the type or types of reciprocity characteristic of Greek masters with
their slaves, for instance, will differ significantly from those characteristic
of nineteenth-century factory owners with their workers or even of nineteenth-century plantation owners with their Negro slaves.[19] The highly
abstract universal, reciprocity, must be singularized, by being located in
specific places and times, in order to be understood. There is no transhistorical essence of reciprocity.

What applies to "reciprocity" must apply, pari passu, to those terms,
which commentators are often tempted to designate "concepts," that Sartre
employs prominently in a somewhat technical way throughout the *Critique:*
for instance, *praxis,* series, groups, and (an interesting though less consistently prominent case) alienation itself. There can be no essential qualities
of any of them; this fact does not prevent us from using the terms as
universal descriptors for certain discernible and distinguishable types of
phenomena, just as long as we remember always to "singularize" them, to
render them specific to the *situations* in which they are experienced or
found. An excellent illustration of this point that Sartre himself provides
has to do with *violence,* which the *Critique* well demonstrates to be a deeply
pervasive feature of our world and of human history.[20] In the course of his
very lengthy phenomenological description of the boxing match, the focal
point of the first 75 pages of Volume 2, Sartre comments:

> This match is all of violence and, at the same time, it is *other,* it can only exist as
> its particular determination. Must we understand that it has, with *the* funda-
> mental violence, the relationship of individual to concept? No.[21]

In effect, fundamental, universal violence as such does not exist. Sartre
goes on to explain that the "concept," which he here identifies as a favorite
device of analytic thinking understood in its pejorative sense, ends up
being accorded a transcendent position vis-à-vis the individual instance,
being considered as "an ontological and logical relationship which can only
be given to contemplative reason," and being expressed in abstract determinations of the form $y = (f)x$, which are exhausted in language. But the
position of the individual boxing match in relation to global violence is not
at all like this, and the violence of that match itself is not a mere concept,
much less a metaphor. Violence is there, present, Sartre says, in the boxing
public and in the public at large. The *reality* of this violence is exhausted in
its singularized, concrete instances. The same applies, for Sartre, to all
other similar "concepts."

That Sartre's thinking throughout the *Critique* remains thoroughly informed by this ontological perspective can be conclusively documented by
some incomplete but clear references near the end of Volume 2. These same

passages also reinforce the impression that Sartre's "ontology," already so far removed from the traditional Leibnizean model in *Being and Nothingness*, became even more radicalized through his imaginative though (as I shall explain) somewhat guilty thinking about other possible worlds at the time of the writing of the *Critique*, conducing to a further relativization of the ontological categories of the earlier work and to a reinforcement of his dialectical nominalism. Nevertheless, it is still ontology in some recognizable sense. To see this will at once enable us to cast doubt on claims, however variously motivated, that the *Critique* proper is "merely" sociology,[22] and to put into clearer perspective the social, and political, and historical theories of this book that I shall be examining in subsequent subsections.

Immediately following some interesting observations concerning the notion of "One World" (this expression always appearing in English, as in the passage that I cited earlier from the Introduction of Volume 1) as a guiding theme of contemporary historians who seek to give *meaning*, from their future-based point of view, to past societies without thereby, as idealism would have it, defining or determining the *being* of those societies, Sartre writes:

> These *ontological* remarks allow us to confront the principal question, the one that must, precisely, distinguish the situated dialectic from every idealism (whether it be materialist dogmatism or historical relativism): we must in effect ask ourselves, starting from what we have established concerning the *being of meaning*—that form-in-the-past of the enveloping totalization—what is, as unfolding praxis-process, the *real-being* of this totalization.[23]

He goes on to explain that what he is calling the "real-being" has to do with very large ontological issues—with the relationship between being and knowledge in the domain of human history, with the relationship between situation and totalization, and in short with whether one opts for a positivist nominalism or, as he does, for the "dialectical nominalism" that Sartre here labels "radicalizing realism." He also suggests in the same paragraph that in addition to "being of meaning" and "real-being" inquiries there is yet a third type of ontological enterprise involved, namely, the examination of the complex structures (such as the relationships between the organic and the physico-chemical domains) which *constitute* the "real-being" of historical totalization; it is this last type of examination, he says, that should properly be denominated "ontology of History" as distinguished from the critique of dialectical reason. Such ontology in the strictest sense, he implies, is not his present concern, although in fact he will go on to touch on it in the passages concerning "organism" that I have mentioned. But it is very clear from his language here that he regards both the discussion of "real-being" issues and the analysis of the "being of meaning" that the historian discerns as also being ontological in a wider sense.

The expression "real-being" which appears perhaps nowhere else in the two volumes of the *Critique*, strikes me as awkward and unfortunate, because for the most part the connotations of the word "Being" are increasingly pejorative for him in this work, suggesting passivity, inertness, and the assumption of an attitude of distance from human concerns.[24] But the idea behind the expression becomes very revealing for Sartre's social and political theory and philosophy of history, especially in those passages in which he reflects on possible worlds other than our own—worlds, for example, without scarcity, as this world itself might some day be (assuming a reasonably satisfactory resolution of the problem of the *meaning* of scarcity that was broached in *Search for a Method*). In the course of a thought-experiment involving the visit of a Martian or a Venutian to earth—science fiction fantasy for the self-indulgent and somewhat idealist or even bourgeois character of which Sartre feels compelled to apologize a little, defending it on the ground that it may aid intelligibility[25]—he in effect insists on the human-centeredness of any meaningful ontological claims, including his own:

> It is false that the human adventure is, from this point of view, an adventure of Nature (or of the Universe), as people are too often inclined to repeat: in fact this is to confuse the sector of our action and its interiorization (practical field) with that infinite external dispersion that we falsely (as far as signification is concerned) unify under the word, 'Universe'; we must confine ourselves to saying—as every realism requires—that the being-in-itself of human activity, even when set within the dust of worlds, is, *in its own sector, in its own place*, absolute; whether there are or are not other practical multiplicities, the history of man resists being determined from the outside, it remains as an absolute center of an infinity of new relations among things.[26]

In this and following remarks, Sartre clearly concedes the possibility that any such other acting multiple entities in other worlds might not be characterizable by the *en-soi/pour-soi* duality that he still regards, despite his adoption of the new terminology of *praxis*/inert matter (with all of its new connotations) and consequent abandonment of the old terminology throughout most of the *Critique*, as characterizing *our* world. But for Sartre this would not matter, since the only "real-being" with which he is concerned is ours, not the Martians'. This lends support, it is worth noting in passing, to Joseph Catalano's portrayal of Sartre's philosophy as a consistent and principled "anthropocentrism"[27]—a diagnosis that is based only on Volume 1 of the *Critique*, without the benefit of the important textual passages near the end of Volume 2, from which I have drawn such persuasive evidence to the same effect.

By comparison with the rest of the *Critique*, the more strictly methodological and ontological discussions at the beginning and at the end that we have been considering are brief, although of course they must be taken, as I have indicated, in conjunction with what was already said about these issues in *Search for a Method*. They do, however, provide needed background for the social (not just "sociological") theory, the theory about the relationship between the human individual and the material world, that Sartre proceeds to lay out in Book 1 of Volume 1, "From Individual *Praxis* to the Practico-Inert," and that we now need to consider.

Sunniness is not a salient quality of Book 1. In it, Sartre begins with the simple, intentionally very abstract image of the individual human being viewed as free *praxis*, and yet within a few pages he has plunged his reader into what he calls the "practico-inert field." Three citations, one or two of them by now rather familar in the literature concerning the *Critique*, will suffice to set the tone of Sartre's account at this level of analysis, a tone that is most reminiscent of Hobbes's depiction of his "state of nature":

> History, taken at this level, presents a terrible and hopeless meaning; it appears, in effect, that men are united by this inert and demoniacal negation which takes their substance (that is to say their labor) away from them in order to return it against all of them in the form of *active inertness* and of totalization through extermination.[28]

> In fact nothing—neither great wild beasts nor microbes—can be more terrible for man than an intelligent, carnivorous, cruel species which could understand and outwit human intelligence and whose goal would be precisely the destruction of man. That species is obviously our own as grasped by every man in Others within the milieu of scarcity.[29]

> We have crossed and recrossed the practico-inert field, and our intention was to discover whether this site of violences, of darkness, and of witchcraft did *in fact* possess its own dialectical intelligibility or, in other words, whether the strange appearances of this universe might be covering over a rigorous rationality.[30]

It should be pointed out immediately that the last of these citations occurs much later than the first two, at the beginning of the subsection in which Sartre initiates the transition, crucial to the entire structure of his work, to Book 2, the analysis of "group *praxis*," and moreover that of course he goes on in this passage to claim that the sought-for intelligibility of the malign domain of the practico-inert has in fact been uncovered. Nevertheless, there are obvious parallels here not only with Hobbes, but also with Rousseau's opening gambit, "L'homme est né libre, et partout il est dans les fers,"[31] and with Marx's contrast of "Robinson [Crusoe]'s island bathed in light to the European middle ages shrouded in darkness."[32]

In *Du Contrat Social*, however, as it has not often enough been remarked, Rousseau immediately goes on to say that his aim will be to show what can render this condition of "born free, yet everywhere in chains," which is *roughly* similar to Sartre's view of the human condition in the domain of the practico-inert,[33] *legitimate*;[34] Sartre totally rejects any such legitimizing enterprise, the traditional gambit of every political theory seeking to justify either an existing or an ideal institutional order. Marx's contrast, in his section "The Fetishism of Commodities" in *Capital*, between the simple and apparently perspicuous economic conditions prevailing on Robinson Crusoe's island, a favorite image of his predecessors in economic theory, and the supposed "darkness" of the Middle Ages was intended ironically: there was in fact an openness and straightforwardness about feudal economic relationships, where customary status rules dictated just what portion of the serfs' labor, for instance, was to be undertaken for the benefit of the lord in a way that all could see, in contrast with the concealment of the harsh exploitation and of the elevation of commodities and of the economic order above human needs under the guise of free exchange that Marx discerned in capitalism and that the bourgeois political economists sought to legitimate through their Robinson Crusoe stories. Sartre's treatment of the practico-inert field in Book 1 of the *Critique* is quite compatible with this vivid metaphor of commodity fetishism, but generalizes its applicability (as Marx also does at least implicitly—after all, feudal economic relations were kept in place by many "fetishes" of a religious and philosophical sort) beyond just capitalism, as he makes clear right at the outset in commenting on Marx's reference to feudalism.[35] Later, near the end of Volume 1, anticipating future criticisms (particularly by "orthodox" Marxists) of his choice to begin his theoretical account with what he freely admits to have been a mere abstraction, the human individual considered in isolation, Sartre makes the following significant remarks:

> This concrete moment of the investigation reintegrates all the abstract moments that we have reached and gone beyond one after the other: it puts them back at the heart of the concrete in their concrete function. And, first of all, the free *praxis* of the isolated individual loses its suspect character of a Robinsonade: *there is no* isolated individual. . . . Thus we now know that the concrete dialectic is the one that unveils itself through the common *praxis* of a group; but we also know that the untranscendability . . . of organic action as strictly individual model is the fundamental condition for historical rationality. . . . Without this rigorous and permanent limitation which refers back from the group to its foundation, the community *is no less abstract* than the isolated individual: there are revolutionary pastorales about the group which are the exact counterpart of Robinsonades.[36]

The common *praxis* of a "group," which is a technical term in Sartre's *Critique*, will be his analytic vehicle in Book 2 for pointing to the possibility of collective salvation from the demoniacal realm of the practico-inert featured in Book 1. But, nota bene, Sartre is here, as always, warning against the tendency of many Marxists and perhaps even of Marx himself at times to lapse into a kind of neo-organicist language about the proletariat or some segment thereof, as if it could ever be a real entity in its own right apart from the individuals who make it up at any given time and place. Marx and his followers were right to regard the Robinson Crusoe paradigm as false and misleading. For one thing, if one takes the story literally, Crusoe and Friday were themselves the adult products of a long and complex upbringing within what passed for civilization, who then found themselves in a bizarre situation through force of circumstances; one cannot validly draw inferences from their conduct on the island in abstraction from this background. On the other hand, however, it would be equally invalid to believe that socioeconomic theory can ever for a moment dispense with referring back to the human individual as the foundational unit.

What must be kept in mind about the human individual, for purposes of Sartre's analysis of the practico-inert field, are a few brute, given, and initially rather uncontroversial facts that have already been mentioned in reference to Sartre's ontological underpinnings: the individual is an organism, hence an entity with needs, and the essentially inert, nonagential material objects that are able to satisfy those needs are scarce. The individual is also *praxis:* an agent, necessitated to make free choices about the means to need-satisfaction and, hence, to survival. The perpetual action of *praxis* on inert matter creates the field that Sartre designates as "the practico-inert." An equally brute given for every individual is the existence of others. And this fact combined with those previously mentioned leads, *pace* certain extreme but influential interpretations of liberal individualism, to the conclusion that *reciprocity* is a fundamental phenomenon of our world—though, to be sure, as Sartre's selection of this term to illustrate his opposition to traditional conceptual thinking and his counterepistemology of the "singularized universal" makes clear, there are many different reciprocal relationships and there exists no condition of reciprocity as such. A world characterized by both scarcity and reciprocity is *eo ipso* a world in which there will be struggles, conflict. It is also a world in which, since the prevalence of scarcity entails that there is not enough for everyone, different individuals at different times, and potentially any and every individual, will be identified as being superfluous *(excédentaire).*[37] These few observations already place us within the gloomy world-picture of the domain of the practico-inert that is drawn in the texts that I cited initially.

Several aspects of this picture are highly reminiscent, as one would expect, of elements of Sartre's earlier thought, but with significant differences in every case. For example, the notion of the pervasiveness of superfluousness reminds us at once of Roquentin's stunning insight derived from his encounter with a chestnut tree root in *Nausea:* "[Les Salauds] sont entièrement gratuits, comme les autres hommes, ils n'arrivent pas à ne pas se sentir de trop. Et en eux-mêmes, sécrètement, ils *sont trop* . . . ;"[38] but now the condition of being *de trop* is seen as having a fundamentally material and social explanation. The emphasis on *need* as a basic human reality is redolent of the long analysis of *lack* as a characteristically negative feature of being-for-itself in *Being and Nothingness;* indeed, in the *Critique* Sartre immediately asserts this connection, though without making explicit reference to the earlier work, but then draws the following historically oriented conclusion, using the new language of the *Critique:*

In a word, the intelligibility of the negative as structure of Being can only be seen in connection with a process of totalization in course; negation is defined . . . in relation to the future totality as destiny or as goal of the totalizing movement.[39]

Perhaps most importantly, the existence of the Other, or of Others, of course remains a primary concern of Sartre's, but now the metaphor of the Look has been replaced by the more concrete, complex, and extensive descriptions of reciprocal relationships that constitute the bulk of the new work. Its very first noteworthy phenomenological analysis, that of an intellectual on vacation at a country inn who from his window sees two workingmen, one a gardener and the other a roadworker, separated by a high wall that prevents them from seeing one another,[40] already marks Sartre's new emphasis on the Third Party (*le Tiers*) as a unifying force, positive or negative as the case may be, in the most diverse situations and hence his departure from the primarily dyadic model of interrelationships that effectively dominated his earlier thinking.

Of course, the single most important difference between the intellectual outlooks, as far as the relationship between the human being and her or his world is concerned, of *Being and Nothingness* and of the *Critique* lies in Sartre's gradual assimilation of Marxian ideas that I have been documenting throughout the present work. But the diabolical social world with which Sartre presents us in Book 1 of the *Critique* may seem far removed from the projections toward an unqualifiedly bright future that Marx, with his fundamentally optimistic nineteenth-century belief in "progress," manages to insinuate in so much of his writing, even when he is describing enormous contemporary abuses. Is the *Critique* still in some way faithful to Marx, or was Sartre simply misusing Marx's name and prestige for ulterior purposes of his own? Sartre compares his own theoretical approach with Marx's early in Book 1 of the *Critique*, returning to one of the principal themes of *Search for a Method*, and it is worthwhile to note a few of his claims in this regard. As I have already mentioned in discussing *Search for a Method*, Sartre acknowledges that Marx did not say very much explicitly about *scarcity*, but observes that the notion had been a commonplace among his predecessors in the tradition of political economy and hence could in large measure be taken for granted by him. At the same time, though, Sartre is critical of "the interpretations of Engels—and often of Marx as well"[41] for their ambiguity concerning the role of scarcity; they make it seem, Sartre complains, as if historical societies always have enough in principle to satisfy needs, but that their modes of production create scarcity. He takes strong issue with this view, asserting that "this scarcity [of the product in relation to man] exists as fundamental determination of man: we know that the socialization of production does not eliminate it, unless in the course of a long dialectical process of which we do not yet know the outcome."[42] Later, as part of his criticism of Engels and Marx on this point, he specifically notes the continuation of conditions of undernourishment in socialist societies.

But scarcity is not the only point on which Sartre explicitly takes issue with Marx, or at least with the implications of what Marx wrote about the human social condition: of equal or greater importance is his disagreement in the matter of alienation and the resulting reification of human beings. For Marx, in those early writings in which he was most concerned with the phenomenon, it is reasonable to conclude, alienation (*Entfremdung*) characterizes the capitalist mode of production more than any previous historical mode, and at any rate can be abolished with the coming of the future socialist society.[43] The related phenomenon of reification, rendered central to later Western Marxism by Georg Lukács as an expansion of Marx's analysis of the fetishism of commodities in *Capital*,[44] seems for Marx to amount to a generalized process whereby existing material conditions in a given society are understandably but incorrectly reflected in the brains of most of its members, a process that will therefore automatically give way to enlightenment—in other words, be corrected—with the coming of fetish-free socialist material conditions. Sartre is not so sanguine. He takes alienation in its primordial sense to be basic to the human condition—the ineliminable otherness of free individual human *praxeis*[45] that can never become *totally* fused no matter how high a degree of commonality there may be in their projects of the moment. Yes, he later acknowledges, there may well be a narrower sense of the word "alienation" that applies to certain varieties associated only with capitalism, and in that sense Marx's vision of the eventual possible overcoming of alienation is admissible.[46] But alienation in the more basic sense indicated is by definition ineliminable. (This could perhaps be taken as a return from Marx to Hegel on this point, but without the idealistic philosophical baggage of *Geist* as universal agent that Hegel brought to his treatment of it.)[47] As for reification, Sartre expresses concern that Marx treats this phenomenon too superficially, as if it were the mere epiphenomenon that his famous metaphor of "superstructures" misleadingly suggests,[48] whereas it is in fact a pervasive feature of the practico-inert field: human beings' internalization and incorporation, within their own *praxis*, of aspects of the material world upon which, under specific historical conditions, they work.[49] Only under the unimaginable hypothesis of a permanent dissolution of the entire practico-inert field could reification be ended entirely.

In an important footnote, Sartre summarizes his differences with Marx on the questions of scarcity, reification, and violence (making the important distinction between the claim that everything happens *through* violence, which he denies, and the assertion that the practico-inert is pervaded by an atmosphere of violence, which accounts for the diabolism that he identifies therein), but he opens it with a disclaimer: "It must be well understood here that the rediscovery of scarcity in the investigation makes absolutely no claim either to be opposed to Marxist theory or to complete it. It is of another order."[50] What are we to make of this? The disclaimer is bound to displease those who insist either on a fundamentalist fidelity to Marx's text or on the untranscendable truth of Marx's philosophy as interpreted in one of any number of (specifiable) ways. Equally displeased will be those who are either anti-Marxist or somewhat indifferent to Marx but convinced that the Sartre of the *Critique* is flying under Marx's banner only because this was fashionable at the time. Personally, I am inclined to agree with Sartre's contention that he is writing the *Critique* at a different level—to wit, an ontological level in any or all of the senses enumerated in the previous subsection of this chapter—from that at which Marx wrote, at least in the latter's later works. If this is so and if, as I believe, there are large elements of truth in Sartre's account of this more fundamental level of the relationships between and among human beings and their material world, then a reading of the *Critique* might cause one to modify or to see in a new light Marx's analysis of the workings of the capitalist system without thereby jettisoning that analysis; indeed, it could even increase one's respect for Marx's achievement. When all is said and done, as I have already shown and will continue to show in dealing with the remainder of the *Critique*, it contains many important elements that are attributable above all to Marx and Marxism, so that, for whatever this is worth, one is not at all unjustified in identifying it as a work within the Marxian tradition, just as Sartre proclaimed in *Search for a Method*. But this very identification may, as I have argued, be of considerably less importance now than it was in 1960, and in any case, if the *Critique* is to be said to be Marxist at all, its Marxism is of a profoundly *suspicious* sort. What matters far more for Sartre than the question of his relationship with Marx's ideas is his continued commitment both to freedom, about Marx's own commitment to which he was to entertain grave doubts late in his life, and to socialism, despite all the obstacles to it that he uncovers in the *Critique* and despite his principled rejection of all utopian, totalistic expectations for it.

Among the other topics to which Sartre devotes special attention in Book 1 that I would like to highlight in concluding my discussion of it are the following: the counterfinalities and dialectical necessities experienced by human beings in their ongoing engagement with nature; interest; value; and, finally, collective entities, or instances of seriality, of some examples of which Sartre paints memorable descriptions. With respect to all of these topics, his views, consistent with his overall theoretical framework, constitute interesting challenges to "mainstream" classical liberal philosophy as well as to contemporary Marxism, if not also to the Marxism of Marx. Let us consider each in turn.

Nature. It would be a gross exaggeration to pretend that Sartre was ecology-minded in the contemporary sense. On a personal level, as I have noted, he found the countryside rather unappealing and even repellent by comparison with cities—although these feelings cannot have been unambiguous, since he obviously enjoyed a number of nonurban vacation trips in the course of his lifetime, particularly in younger years. At the level of theory, he remained heavily influenced by the opposition between nature and history that is central to Hegel's thought and that has continued to have philosophical weight right up to the present. He casts very strong doubt, as we have seen, on the Engelsian idea of a dialectics of nature, contending that it would be irrelevant to his philosophical concerns even if it could somehow be shown to be true, and he speaks of matter as the antidialectical moment within the dialectic of human history and, conversely, of *praxis* as antiphysis. Nevertheless, there is an important sense in which, in the *Critique*, Sartre introduces an ecological consciousness that neither classical Marxism nor classical liberalism, unquestioningly accepting as both were of the desirability of human civilization's subduing and dominating nonhuman nature, developed.

The more general point that Sartre wishes to illustrate is the pervasiveness of "counterfinalities" within the practico-inert field, given the numerous sorts of necessities that matter, simply by virtue of what it is, imposes on free human beings who are compelled to work on it in order to satisfy their needs. The choice of means to achieve this satisfaction may be open, but Sartre discerns as inevitable, at least under existing conditions of scarcity, the "change of places" that will take place between human beings and inert matter in an unlimited variety of ways: producers becoming their own products. In a manner reminiscent of Hegel's "cunning of reason" whereby the personal ambitions of world-historical individuals at once serve as the motor of historical change and yet are ultimately frustrated and turned against them (but now without Hegel's idealist base and with reference to ordinary individuals and everyday life rather than great events), Sartre shows how, often enough, human beings' need-satisfying intentions have unanticipated and radically self-destructive outcomes; in short, they become counterfinalized. The first extended illustration of this process that he invokes is that of the deforestation of China.

The facts are relatively well known. For several thousand years, it was the practice of Chinese peasants systematically to eliminate trees from the fields and mountainsides as the agricultural frontier advanced. The cumulative effect of all these individual actions has been to dislodge the topsoil and allow it to clog the great rivers, thus causing the massive periodic floods for which certain regions, especially the great plain of the north, are famous. As Sartre says:

> Thus the entire process of the terrible Chinese floods appears as a mechanism intentionally constructed. If some enemy of man had wanted to persecute the workers of the Great Plain, he would have charged mercenary troops with the task of systematically deforesting the mountains. The positive system of cultivation was transformed into an infernal machine. But the enemy who brought the loess, the river, the operation of gravity, the whole of hydrodynamics into this destructive apparatus is the peasant himself.[51]

And yet it never seemed that way to individual peasants clearing their individual patches of land over the millennia, at least until recent times when they began to be made aware of it.

Of course, as Sartre is well aware, this is a particularly simple example of the role of the ecosystem in human history. Further complexities could be introduced even in this example if one were to add an account of the *social* organization of traditional Chinese agriculture (but this would have involved introducing at this point elements from those later parts of Book 2 of the *Critique* in which he discusses institutions), and any comprehensive understanding of most ecological problems requires a strong awareness of the dominant mode of production that is involved. Sartre's next lengthy illustration of historical counterfinality in fact introduces some of these additional complexities: it is the fascinating process, well charted by the historian Braudel (to whose account Sartre is heavily indebted),[52] whereby the importation of precious metals from the Americas into Spain in the sixteenth and seventeenth centuries, conditioned as it was by the existing material techniques of mining, coining, and transporting them, eventually resulted in the impoverishment of that country in relation to much of the rest of the Mediterranean world and beyond. In the Chinese case under discussion, however, Sartre's principal concern is to insist on the element of human intentionality that underlies and ultimately explains ecological catastrophes, however deeply hidden that element may sometimes be. One theoretical implication of this is, obviously, to refuse to treat Nature as a fixed, closed entity at a distance, as a God might; the practical implication is to combat pessimism about past and present threats to the ecosystem, however grave and seemingly overwhelming they may be, and to suggest the possibility of working consciously to take these matters, so to speak, into our own hands—in which, whether we have been aware of it or not, they have always been. Sartre mentions in passing, for example, that a program of *re*forestation would have been needed to avert the consequences of the initial deforestation in China; nowadays, one is reminded of the ongoing deforestation of the Amazon region, with its even more global potential consequences, and of the possibility, if only the appropriate, nonexploitative socioeconomic structures were to be put in place, of beginning to reverse this process. This would of course entail setting aside both liberalism's and Marxism's traditional enthusiasm for the maximal exploitation of natural resources in the name of either private or social accumulation.

That to draw such inferences from Sartre's discussion is not a purely fanciful exercise on my part is well illustrated by a reference to the *Critique* made by one of Sartre's most original students and interpreters, André Gorz, in his book, *Ecologie et politique*.[53] Gorz clearly thinks of his own strong ecological activism as carrying out, rather than contravening, the spirit of Sartrism.[54]

Interest. Sartre's discussion of "interest" in the middle of Book 1 follows from his more general remarks concerning reification. Economists and some psychologists use the term, he says, to identify a certain kind of relationship of necessity between the human organism and its environment, a relationship that does not emerge automatically as long as one considers the human being merely abstractly, as free *praxis* characterized by needs and by projects designed to satisfy them. However, as soon as it is acknowledged that any concrete carrying out of projects must take place within a certain milieu that is external to the individual, interest in some form, however inchoate, necessarily comes into play.[55] This phenomenon therefore antedates capitalism and even private property, and it will not be totally eliminated with the advent of socialism.[56] Nevertheless, interest takes on special characteristics, first with the development of private property, and then in the bourgeois world of the nineteenth century. This topic thus furnishes the occasion for Sartre's first somewhat extended discussion of modern capitalism in the *Critique*.

The section of the text in which the discussion is offered is self-contained, and I shall not attempt to summarize it comprehensively. Sartre shows how workers, in a situation of subsistence wages imposed by their employers bent on maximizing profit, come to regard this interest of the employers as a kind of *destiny* for themselves, fatal and without appeal within the system, and thus are led to a collective (class) vision of their own future interest as consisting of the negation of that destiny. In a turn of thinking somewhat reminiscent of the analysis of the "we-subject" and the "us-object" in *Being and Nothingness*, he argues, convincingly to my mind, that the sense of class interest, of collective pride, arises as a secondary phenomenon among the bourgeoisie in response to the development of the workers' class consciousness. He goes on to suggest that certain aspects of capitalism's later (twentieth-century) evolution, in which, he implies, there may no longer be a *single* working-class interest, and new practices such as state intervention in the economy and the paying of higher wages to workers in order to augment consumption become salient, may be viewed as an effort to overcome the "destiny of capitalism itself, with all of its internal contradictions."[57]

While none of this, as Sartre readily admits, contravenes the gist of Marx's analyses in *Capital*, and while it suffers somewhat from the fact that Sartre has not yet entered into the detailed discussions of collectives and of groups that occupy later pages of the *Critique*, there is to be found here a subtle reorientation of perspectives away from that of Marx or at least of some of his interpreters, who tend to speak of the interest of the proletariat (or, conversely, of the interest of the bourgeoisie)[58] as if it were a univocal and unproblematic notion, in need of no further explanation. Sartre says that he finds it surprising that such Marxists find themselves in league with conservative thinkers who speak of the "conflict of interests" as if it were a given, natural law, without any further intelligibility.

If, however, Marxist writers sometimes treat the notion of "interest" in this unproblematic way, they are surely overwhelmed, in terms of the sheer weight of numbers, by writers in the broad liberal tradition with which British and American readers are much more familiar than Sartre was, and who often tend to treat it even more dogmatically. For some of our social scientists and ethicists, to identify some "conflict of interests" in a certain situation is to explain everything; nothing more needs to be said. But such a posture is extremely obscurantist. It is true that all human beings, whether as individuals or as members of groups, can accurately be said to have certain interests in certain given situations—often, in fact, in the form of clusters of interests, some of which may conflict with others. But it is equally true that any and all of these time-bound interests may change, that they are not nature-imposed destinies, and that, above all, they are not the primordial and fatalistic explanatory entities for human actions that they appear to be in so much of our philosophical and social scientific literature. Sartre succinctly summarizes his position as follows:

> As for conflicts of interest, in particular, we have discovered in our own investigation, as we are conducting it through this book, a means for removing the hedonistic and utilitarian mortgage that makes of interest an irrational mixture of subjective *conatus* and objective conditions. We must, in fact, choose: either "everyone follows his or her interest," which means that the division of men is *natural*—or it is the division of men, as a result of the mode of production, which makes interest (particular or general, of an individual or of a class) appear as a real moment of the relations among men.[59]

If Sartre's only contribution to contemporary political theory were to have been this radical questioning of the shibboleth of "interest," the whole enterprise would still have been eminently worthwhile.

Value. Even shorter and more completely self-contained than the sub-section on interest in Book 1 of the *Critique* is a footnote on value, "in the *ethical* sense of the word," which Sartre inserts as an aside in the midst of his first extended discussion of "class-being" as an initial (and initially inert, passive) form of collective existence.[60] It at once illustrates the increasing clarity of Sartre's thinking about the meaning of ethical values since the period of writing of the *Cahiers* and paves the way for the extensive, though not yet published, writings about ethics that occupied much of his time during the mid-1960s. It can be read with any number of different empha-ses: as an enrichment of the discussion of value in *Being and Nothingness* through the addition of considerations suggested by historical materialism; as a new gloss on the opposition between freedom and requirement *(ex-igence)* on which Sartre had elaborated at length in the *Cahiers;* as a signifi-cant though brief reflection on moralism in Soviet culture, connecting references made to this phenomenon in *The Communists and Peace* with aspects of the second volume of the *Critique;* and so on. Above all, perhaps, it can be taken as a brief exploration of the implications of conjoining a philosophical perspective "beyond good and evil" (though Nietzsche's name is never explicitly invoked) with the social theory being unfolded here in Book 1.

It is the ambiguous, double-edged character of values that Sartre wishes especially to stress. Whereas requirements appear to me as not belonging to me, values, however easily an observer might be able to demonstrate the fact of their having been imposed by virtue of existing social structures, are seen as my own.[61] They are ultimately, after all, the free creations of human *praxis*, however mystified. They both reflect existing patterns of dominance and subordination and point to the possible future transcendence of these patterns. Readers familiar with *Being and Nothingness* will recognize in this analysis more subtlety, more distinctions, and a much greater awareness of the relationship of value to sociopolitical oppression than was to be found in that book, but still a considerable continuity in Sartre's thinking about the issue. What is most novel in this footnote discussion, by comparison with Sartre's earlier thought, is his clear suggestion that, since values are always bound up with the "hell" that is the practico-inert field, so that they always themselves have a negative quality inasmuch as they point to the negation of its various oppressive structures, then

> if—a question that we shall examine in the moment of the progressive in-
> vestigation—there is to be a possible liquidation of these structures, values will
> disappear with them in order to rediscover *praxis* in its free development as the
> only ethical relationship of man with man.[62]

It is this remarkable speculation on the possible "liquidation" of the entire domain of the practico-inert, the subject matter of all of Book 1 of the *Critique*, and of the always Janus-faced (liberating/alienating) phenomenon of values along with it, that leads me to regard this footnote as the most "Nietzschean" point in the work, a momentary glimpse into a possible world beyond good and evil. It is what is left, perhaps, of the bold notion of a "radical conversion" of an entire society, of which we found such strong hints in the *Cahiers pour une morale*.

But it is only a fleeting glimpse. The footnote concludes with a reference to the atmosphere of thoroughgoing moralism that pervades Soviet society, an unfortunate development that Sartre attributes to a philosophical confusion, as it were, in its official "Marxist" ideology: namely, the erroneous conflation of ethics as a living system or systems of practices with ethics as the linguistic vocabulary in which intellectuals speak about such systems. This confusion is in turn, according to Sartre, connected with another one: the sharp dichotomizing of "base" and "superstructure" that we have already had occasion to see him criticize. Since ethics in the sense of intellectual values-talk was supposed to disappear, as a part of the superstructural baggage, with the coming of socialist society, and since nevertheless ethical conduct as patterns of daily activities in accordance with quite specific values continues to prevail in the postrevolutionary USSR, the failure to distinguish between the two different senses of "ethics" has assured, Sartre claims, the existence of an atmosphere of rampant moralizing, for there are no intellectual safeguards against it within the official ideology. He urges, however, that readers distinguish between this moralizing climate, on the one hand, and the ongoing construction of socialism in that country through all its numerous contradictions, on the other.

This distinction itself, however, strikes me as highly dubious. As we know, much of the "progressive moment" of his theoretical analysis that Sartre had always intended to constitute Volume 2 of the *Critique* is going to be taken up with developments over a few years in Soviet society. While there is no *extended* discussion of the phenomenon of moralism in that volume, it seems clear to me in terms of the comprehensive explanatory demands of Sartre's own theory that this phenomenon, with all of its puritanical and thought-restricting consequences, must be seen as an integral mechanism within the ongoing process of historical totalization called "building socialism" under Stalin, rather than as a separable aberration. Moreover, the very fact that, in the work that he undertook toward his "progressive investigation" before abandoning it entirely, Sartre was to feel compelled to concentrate so much on the Soviet Union's historical experience of freedom rechained shows just how thoroughly his intensified reflections on existing sociopolitical reality were to lead him to put into question his passing speculations on the possible future liquidation of the structures of the practico-inert field of the sort that I cited above.

On the other hand, I find considerable worth, once again, in the critical implications of this brief excursus of his for philosophizing about value issues in many traditions. In addition to pointing up the superficiality of so much that has been written on the topic of values and ethics within the "orthodox" Marxist tradition, he also, by exploring the simultaneously social and individual basis of moral values and their necessary, fundamental ambivalence and relativity, deflates the pretensions of stipulative axiologists of all stripes. In light of textual passages in the *Critique* such as this one and regardless of whatever new insights may be gleaned from Sartre's later writings on morality when they are eventually published, ethics as a subject of study needs to be seen in a very different, much more complex and skeptical, perspective from those that are adopted in the majority of our contemporary college ethics courses.

Collectives. The discussion of "serial" collectives, agglomerations of human beings engaged in some enterprise to which a common name can be given but which, far from unifying them, reinforces their isolation and practico-inert impotence, concludes Book 1. It paves the way for Sartre's treatment of the contrasting type of social structure, the "group" engaged in a genuinely common *praxis*, that dominates the opening of Book 2. And it contains a disproportionate share of the most memorable and interesting passages of the *Critique*, in which Sartre's clear-headed outrage against all kinds of so-called laws and other rules that are supposed to be iron, inevitable, and thing-like, and that are constantly invoked to block us from even thinking of acting for radical change, comes to the fore. While I fully share this outrage, it seems to me that a careful examination of the first and most famous of the phenomenological descriptions in which this section abounds, that of the bus queue at the Place Saint-Germain in Paris, goes far toward showing the ambiguities of Sartre's own stated goal of "liquidating the practico-inert field" (a notion to which he again refers with approval in this section),[63] as well as the overwhelming obstacles that lie in the way of attempting to do so.

At the bus stop in question, prospective passengers, as they arrive, take tickets indicating the order in which they will be entitled to board the buses—if not the first one, then the next. The emphasis of Sartre's description, established in the first paragraph,[64] is on the serial *isolation* of the individual commuters. True, he acknowledges that there are certain respects in which they do form a group, and not a pure "series": they have a common location, for instance, and in particular they have a common interest in "improvement of public transportation, freezing of fares, etc."[65] However, what is most important for Sartre is the individuals' interchangeability, their condition of alterity, their roles as ordinal units in a mathematical formula (one of which some bureaucrats in the transport authority are presumably aware), and so on. In short, Sartre's description captures the anonymity of this and similar features of modern life with great apparent cogency.

I would like to suggest at least three difficulties with this by now somewhat famous Sartrean illustration of serial collectivity. First, it is cogent as such an illustration only to the extent to which the existence of the system, in this case the Paris transport system, is taken for granted by its participants. A regime that is hostile to public transportation, such as the Reagan administration in the United States, could come to power and threaten to eliminate ("liquidate") the system; many riders would undoubtedly then organize themselves into action groups opposing such a move. The transition from the series to the group is, of course, the principal subject of the beginning of Book 2, the next section of the *Critique;* but the type of group that would be involved here would be a group organized to *preserve* an existing series. This point leads to my second objection, which is that in fact public transportation today, particularly in large urban centers, sometimes functions as a counterweight to the serial anonymity of modern life. Passengers sometimes derive satisfaction from aspects of the journey or from studying other riders (or future riders while still in the queue), and occasionally regular acquaintanceships develop among the commuters, especially in the type of daily routine situation conceived by Sartre (the 7:49 a.m. bus, in his example). The public transport vehicle, unlike the private automobile, has about it some of the communal aspects of the market places of ancient cities, and hence it is a mistake to regard it simply as an instance of stark seriality. Finally, I find enormous difficulty in trying to imagine a world in which all collectives similar to this one had been "liquidated." True, nuclear holocaust could eliminate Paris and all other major cities and their bus systems along with them. Moreover, real estate speculation has made the Left Bank and other older sections of Paris increasingly inhospitable to the sorts of ordinary, lower middle- or middle-class workers who have typically ridden the buses, thus perhaps ultimately threatening the transport system in a different way; there exist influential French city planners who look enviously to the sprawling, automobile-oriented, newer American cities as models of what they would like Paris to be. Then, too, many of the kinds of jobs that have hitherto required mass commuting to certain central locations are beginning to be accomplished by workers using sophisticated computers in the total isolation of their own homes; eventually, many of them may never have to meet their fellow-workers at all! But it is not at all obvious that Sartre would regard any such developments, of the sort whereby the particular form of serial collective that he has described could be dissolved, as progressive in the sense of changing the human multiplicity into a group praxis. On the contrary; the alternatives, other than annihilation, appear to be, if anything, even more serializing. In short, the difficulties, both practical and normative, involved in seriously pursuing the idea of "liquidating the practico-inert field" *entirely* are enormous, and it is just as well that this theme is played down and never becomes a dominant one in Sartre's political theory.[66]

Some of the other examples of seriality that Sartre provides in succeeding pages serve better as illustrations of his critical point or points. They show that we indeed live and act in a world in which we are often compelled simultaneously to participate in a number of different "serial" practices, the natures of which prevent us from taking common action with others to overcome the thing-like status to which they have reduced us, and which are reinforced in their supposed inevitability by the very language used to name them. Among the most salient of these examples are the "hit parade" of popular songs in the United States, a rank-ordering that is based on a kind of nationwide guessing as to which new albums will be most preferred by the greatest number of *other* people and that then conditions and intensifies others' preferences; the government-controlled media broadcast laying down an "official" policy line to millions of listeners who have no way of persuading the others either to agree or to disagree, or even of knowing what the others "really" think; and, above all, the so-called free market in which prices are determined by the supply/demand conception of human beings as impersonal forces. Sartre brilliantly shows the dehumanizing, practico-inert aspects of these and a number of other phenomena, present and past (e.g., the "Great Fear" that swept parts of France in 1789), that he selects. In short, he makes us vividly aware of our practico-inert chains. I find special value in this contribution of his in view of the recent recrudescence of propaganda supportive of "letting market forces operate," as if that were a superior human achievement.

Finally, Sartre shows the important connections between this analysis of serial collectives and his increasing rejection of conceptual, universalist thinking in favor of "dialectical nominalism" throughout the *Critique*, on the one hand, and his career-long preoccupation with racism, on the other. For example, he shows that "*the* Jew" is primarily a stereotypical serial unity imposed on Jewish people in a hostile, racist environment as an "Idea," a supposed essential reality that in fact has no such solidity.[67] Here, of course, he is returning (though without explicitly mentioning it) to the *leitmotif* of *Anti-Semite and Jew*, but now with the benefit of the more sophisticated theoretical framework generated in the *Critique*. Some pages further on, he discusses what he calls "the Idea-*exis*"[68]—thoroughly habituated thought that triggers automatic linguistic and practical responses from those who share it and that is therefore in fact not thought at all—and cites racism as a prime example of this. Here, he refers particularly to the form of racism with which, as we have seen, he and the French people in general had become deeply absorbed at this point, namely, colonialism. Colonialism, as he shows, leads otherwise intelligent people into practices of stupidity, using purely formulaic language ("The natives are lazy") that reflects a secret hope, paradigmatic of practico-inertness, "that thought is a stone" and hence that their unjustifiable way of life can be perpetuated indefinitely.

In short, so-called inexorable laws—of ethnicity, of politics, of economics, of language itself—are seen to surround human beings on all sides within this infernal practico-inert swamp, the exploration of which might be prolonged indefinitely. Throughout, the purpose of the exploration has been above all to describe the many ways in which human individuals, in their necessary involvements with their material environment, become thoroughly imbued with the inertness, the thing-like quality, that characterized nonhuman matter; but its underlying assumption has always been that none of these "laws" is *totally* inexorable, and hence that important sectors of the practico-inert field, if not that field as a whole, are in fact capable of being "liquidated." It is at this point that Sartre feels himself ready to move on to the moment of human freedom and of hope for alternative social (if not socialist, or at least proto-socialist) structures in the *Critique*, the moment that he calls "the group." This is the transition to something like the political, or at least the proto-political, region of human activity, and ultimately to the domain of history; I shall deal with these in the next chapter.

FIVE

Politics and History

Book 2, subsection A is the heart of Sartre's political theory. While it contains numerous themes worth exploring in their own right, just as Book 1 did, it is somewhat less diffuse and more clearly structured than the latter, in keeping with their respective subject matters: in Book 2 the generation of organization and, eventually, of *conscious* sociopolitical structures, in contrast with the diffuse realm of the practico-inert. I shall first summarize its main themes and then consider the perspectives that it offers on some of the traditional questions of political theory against which, sometimes almost despite Sartre's obvious desire to reconsider the entire political dimension of human life in an original way independent of past views, he is forced to brush in passing.

Book 2 begins with the analysis, central and climactic for Volume 1 of the *Critique* as a whole, of the group's formation, using as its historical model the group of "activists," as we would call them, who captured the Bastille in the event that we now retrospectively designate as the beginning of the French Revolution. As Sartre retells the story, the residents of an early working-class district of Paris, the Quartier Saint Antoine, had heard rumors that the King's troops might come to seal it off and proceed to massacre them, since there had been considerable unrest in Paris and this neighborhood was known to harbor actual or at least potential trouble-makers. Whether well founded or not, the rumors constituted an enormous menace in the minds of the residents: they saw themselves defined as *"excédentaires"* (superfluous) in the most literal and fatal sense. The fortress-prison of the Bastille was both the symbol and the practical basis of the government's dominance over the inhabitants: it towered over the neighborhood on that side of it that gave them access to the rest of the city, since the district was defined on its other sides by a bend in the River Seine. Small groups began to gather on streetcorners as the rumors gained strength, and eventually they began to merge and finally to move toward the fortress. It is not important who actually first uttered the words of the first person plural imperative that articulated the common goal of capturing it: *anyone* in the group could as easily have played this role of what Sartre calls "the regulative Third," articulating not a command, as in a structured military situation, but simply the common *praxis*.

This phenomenological description, whether entirely accurate or not (there may in fact have been a few outside agitators who helped to spur the evolution of the actual historical event), has a ring of plausibility to it, at least for anyone who has ever participated in, observed, or even empathized at a distance with spontaneous collective action. Sartre is of course not claiming that it must be replicated in all details in every such instance if it is to count as an instance of a "group-in-fusion,"[1] nor is he even maintaining that the sequence in which he sketches these and subsequent developments of groups is necessary or canonical. He is, however, asserting that a group is a radically different type of entity from any serial collective and that its genesis and structure must first be made intelligible before full sense can be made of the various "degraded"[2] groups, often closely resembling serial collectives, with which we are so familiar in history and in our own experience. The formation of a group is always a moment of "apocalypse"—the term that he had already applied to the notion of fundamental historical change in an important passage in the *Cahiers pour une morale*, and that he now uses to designate the group in fusion at its height.

My reference, following Sartre, to the "degradation" of groups after this moment of *crescendo* anticipates the path of his analysis throughout the rest of the portion of the *Critique* under discussion. The felt need for the group to perpetuate itself, to provide itself with more than a momentary existence, leads to its taking, in one form or another, an oath or "pledge": each member binds him/herself in fealty and solidarity to the others, these assurances being accompanied by more or less violent anticipatory self-denunciation lest the member should ever renege in the future, in a bivalent phenomenon that Sartre labels "fraternity-terror." Then comes a recognition of the need for *organization*, in the sense of apportioning tasks and functions; whereas the group in fusion was, strictly speaking, unorganized (though as close to total unity as any group that is by definition composed of separate individuals could ever be), there now arises the distancing that is well captured, as Sartre points out, in the linguistic ambivalence that allows us at once to criticize "the organization" (an entity from which we distinguish ourselves) as being lacking in one way or another and yet to identify it as "our organization," implying our own personal responsibility for it.[3] By this time in the course of his investigation, the allusions to French Revolutionary events such as the "Tennis Court Oath," the slogan of "Liberty—Equality—Fraternity" (although Sartre has very little to say about equality), and the Reign of Terror, which have served Sartre well as illustrations, begin to be set aside. From the topic of "organization" he moves on, after a methodological interlude concerning the historian's or other outside observer's task of reconstructing the sociopolitical dialectic and rendering it intelligible, to that of formal institutions such as the postal system, the political party, the Army, and ultimately the State and manipulative bureaucratic state apparatuses such as propaganda networks. Here, more contemporary examples, particularly allusions to the Communist Party and to the USSR, begin occasionally to surface. And it is here that Western political theory's traditional questions about sovereignty, authority, and legitimacy begin to find expression.

Before considering Sartre's perspectives on these issues in somewhat more detail, we need to ask a preliminary question: what should we regard as the principal aim(s) of this section, the core of his political theory? Most writers in the tradition, of whatever stripe, have been concerned to offer their readers both wisdom (Plato's knowledge of the essence of justice, Aristotle's understanding of the good life, Machiavelli's insights into the *"verità effettuale della cosa,"* Marx's critical comprehension of the capitalist system) and, in offering that wisdom, a guiding or regulative ideal. The latter element has generally consisted in proffering an allegedly ideal state of affairs that differs sharply from one writer to the next (the Republic for Plato, polity as Aristotle's "average best," a united Italy holding the promise of an ultimate revival of Republican Rome for Machiavelli, communist society for Marx).[4] This combination takes on a particularly interesting form in the case of Hegel, for whom philosophical wisdom or insight becomes possible only "when a form of life has grown old," i.e., *post festum,* and whose political guidance consists in reconciling readers to the *present* order by attempting to demonstrate that it is the best possible. Against this background, Sartre's *Critique of Dialectical Reason,* which in its very title invokes Hegel and Marx above all, must be seen as especially heavily weighted on the side of intelligibility, wisdom, and as offering nothing clear-cut by way of guidance—*certainly* not Hegel's counsel to find reconciliation in the present(!), but also no confident orotund statements about the future "society of associated producers" such as one occasionally finds even in Marx's later, to say nothing of his earlier, work. Sartre, in his almost obsessive quest for intelligibility, rejects the glibness and even superficiality of many of the stocks-in-trade of traditional political philosophy: the notion of the social contract is a good example, as I shall show. But this entails that, since he tries to be consistent, he must also eschew glibness about the ideal of socialism to which he is firmly committed. The result may be a strong impression on the part of readers that either his ideal consists in a perpetuation of the pure moment of "Apocalypse," of the group in fusion at its height, or he has left us without hope.

Since the former alternative, the perpetuation of the apocalypse, is quite untenable for any number of reasons (it has been defined by Sartre as virtually structureless and outside of ordinary time),[5] which are simply confirmed by the order of the discussion in later sections of the *Critique,* the inference of ultimate pessimism may appear compelling; it is this fact, I think, that accounts for the assiduousness with which a number of observers, including individuals both sympathetic and unsympathetic to his overall thought, have seized upon his last published dialogue with Benny Lévy, "L'Espoir, Maintenant," as evidence of Sartre's having taken a radical new turn on the eve, as it were, of his death. But this finding is unnecessary, since Sartre's attitude toward future political possibilities, as manifested both in the *Critique* itself and in numerous other interviews, was already one of a mild optimism tempered by an exceptionally profound and well-informed awareness of the dark, negative potentialities of every kind of social and political institution or development. It is true that there were moments in his life, as in everyone's, when either excessive enthusiasm (as after his first visit to the USSR) or near-despair (as at certain periods during the Algerian War, when he was composing the *Critique*) temporarily predominated over his better, more measured judgment. It is in certain respects unfortunate that reference to such personal psychological episodes should be made at all in the course of evaluating an author's political theory, but the nature both of his life and even of his theory makes it necessary to mention them in Sartre's case. On the whole, at any rate, he appears to have lived his life with a certain zest, as he himself asserted,[6] that it would be difficult (although not, I admit, inconceivable) to reconcile with the view that the thought about politics which loomed so large in this professional thinker's later years was as implacably gloomy as some critics have implied. (The relationship between his psychological disposition and the "pure" existentialist beliefs of his earlier years is another matter, which Sartre himself epitomized very well in *Les Mots:* "Fake to the marrow of my bones and hoodwinked, I joyfully wrote about our unhappy state. Dogmatic though I was, I doubted everything except that I was the elect of doubt . . . I was happy.")[7] Having cast serious doubt, at least, from a biographical perspective on the hypothesis that the normative outcome of Sartre's political theory should be construed as one of despair, we may return to a consideration of what the text itself of the *Critique* implies in this regard.

Three passages in particular, two from near the end of Book 1, just prior to Sartre's depiction of the group in fusion, the third from the concluding section of Volume 1, are probably the most directly pertinent to a consideration of the important issue that now concerns us. The first, from a footnote that begins with a contrast between medieval communities, in which "there is no trace of atomization," and the capitalist world and then goes on to argue that there was nevertheless considerable *alienation* in those communities, poses the question in a very straightforward way:

> The genuine problem—which we do not have to study here—concerns less the past, in which recurrence and alienation are found in every period, than the future: to what extent will a socialist society banish atomism *in all its forms?* To what extent will collective objects, signs of our alienation, be dissolved in a genuine intersubjective community in which the only real relations will be those of men among themselves?[8]

The footnote continues by suggesting strong systematic considerations (e.g., that *every* society must remain an ongoing, "detotalized totality" and that the elimination of capitalist forms of alienation does not entail the elimination of *all* forms of it) weighing against the optimistic hypothesis and concludes with a scholarly reference to Jean Hyppolyte's book on Marx and Hegel.

The second passage, which occurs two pages further on in the main text itself and is reminiscent, in its practical implications, of Sartre's view of the French proletariat's limited possibilities for practical action in *The Communists and Peace*, is very assertive; it reads as follows:

> The worker will only be saved from his or her destiny if the entire human multiplicity changes forever into group *praxis*. His or her only future is therefore at the second degree of sociality, in other words, in human relations insofar as they are formed within the unity of a group (and not in the disunity of the milieu-gathering).[9]

(It will be recalled, from my earlier discussion, that Sartre is using "destiny" as a quasi-technical term, as a contrast with "interest.") Finally, in the paragraph immediately following Sartre's declamation against "revolutionary pastorales about the group" that I cited earlier, he asks: "Is there not— as we grasp it in daily experience—a perpetual double movement of regrouping and petrification?" His answer: "Little matter to us: the essential thing was to establish the intelligibility of these possibilities; that we have done."[10]

We should not allow ourselves to become too mesmerized by a single text or two in a work the length of the *Critique*. It seems clear enough to me that the idea of changing the human race "pour toujours en *praxis* de groupe" (note that the language does not go so far as to imply a *single* group, since there is no indefinite article) is, on the basis of all of Sartre's later analyses, a purely utopian, unrealizable ideal of the sort that Sartre himself almost always avoids articulating. (For one thing, even if the entire world were somehow eventually to be filled with "genuine intersubjective communities," the *possibility* of their relapsing in the direction of renewed seriality could never be eliminated.) At any rate, as I have already strongly suggested, the entire direction of analysis in both Books 2 and 3 of the *Critique*—the former, now under discussion, with its tale of groups becoming "degraded" into, eventually, bureaucratic institutions, the latter dominated by the question of how an actual historical effort to construct a socialist society produced a new kind of "hell" in that very process—argues against any such ideal's plausibility.

And yet these comments do not, I would like to urge, imply a surrender of socialist ideals on Sartre's part, on the ground that there *must necessarily be* a "perpetual double movement of regrouping and petrification," ceaseless and ineluctable, like the movement of the tides in the oceans. Sartre's evasive retort, "Little matter to us," while it is made in the context of emphasizing *intelligibility*—or "wisdom," as I have put it in introducing this issue of Sartre's aim in writing the *Critique*—as his principal quest, should, I believe, be regarded as having another motivation as well:

namely, the implied attitude that passing speculations about ultimate, universal questions of the sort "Will a socialist society banish atomism *in all its forms?*" should not affect the process of working to overcome particular forms of atomism, particular cases of alienation within serial collectives, or, at another stage, within bureaucratic states in the here and now. (This interpretation becomes increasingly plausible when we recall the intense skepticism about universals that Sartre manifests throughout the *Critique*.) In other words, Sartre's fundamental political commitment to "socialism and freedom" entails striving to "liquidate the practico-inert" wherever this can be identified and dealt with in the present, without regard to the eventual form(s) that society could optimally take in a distant and in principle unknowable future. A commitment of this sort is not reducible to any formula, such as (to take an extreme example, probably not intended with complete seriousness even by its original formulator) Lenin's famous remark that communism consists of Soviet power plus electrification of the entire country, and it involves the risk of making major mistakes. (But what commitment does not?) Above all, this sort of commitment to "socialism and freedom" depends for whatever success it may have on a clear-headed, unblinking analysis of existing sociopolitical structures, undeterred by idealistic, wishful thinking about what we would like them to be or what they themselves claim to be; and such analysis depends, in its turn, on one's having developed some tentative fundamental framework of hypotheses about what, ultimately, sociopolitical structures *are*. That is why Sartre places such great stress in the *Critique* on achieving intelligibility above all else.

Having now briefly considered the issue of Sartre's principal purpose or purposes in writing this central text of his political theory, we may now turn to a review of his answers, as found especially in Book 2, to some of earlier political theory's traditional questions. I find it convenient to group them under three general, though obviously interrelated, headings: (1) the nature of proto-political and political association and freedom; (2) right and law; and (3) sovereignty, authority, legitimacy, and the State.

The Nature of Association and Freedom. It should already be quite obvious that Sartre's way of arranging his analyses militates strongly against sharply distinguishing between political and other sorts of institutions, which I have therefore labelled "proto- [or pre- or quasi-] political." By contrast, two of the best-known modern political theorists who have come to define very opposite approaches to the subject, Locke and Hegel, both agree in separating the level of "civil society" from that of the government (Locke) or of the State (Hegel). Such a separation allowed Locke to argue, among other things, that the dissolution of a government by a justifiable revolution does not necessarily entail the dissolution of civil society itself, since government should be regarded as a trustee for the interests of civil society, and a justifiable revolution therefore amounts to society's replacing a no longer trustworthy trustee with a new one. For Hegel, the *Trennung* between civil society and the State enabled him to depict the former as the domain of competing private interests, the world of the "free market," the lack of full rationality of which is compensated by the State's synthesizing and reconciling role "at a higher level"; it was precisely this Hegelian claim to having found in the modern State a higher synthesis rendering the existing sociopolitical order legitimate and just that Marx subjected to devastating internal criticism in his early *Critique of Hegel's Philosophy of Right*. The term "civil society," which has played some role even in twentieth-century Marxist thought, particularly in the writings of Antonio Gramsci and again recently in the wake of a Gramsci revival and of the rising animosities against the extremely strong *étatisme* of East European and Chinese Communist regimes, is to be found rarely in Sartre's *Critique*; and even "State" and government receive only a brief, passing treatment there—at least *eo nomine*. That is because Sartre has attempted to shift the ground, to undermine the traditional distinctions, images, and terminology.

As we have seen, Sartre has his own *Trennung*, his own sharp separation, but it is quite differently located: the dividing line between the series and the group. Sartrean groups are to be found in all sizes, shapes, and states of cohesiveness or dissolution, except that even the most cohesive groups never achieve the status of *totalized* totalities, the across-the-board "agreement of minds" that idealist political thought identifies as "the essential structure of communities."[11] There are no minds in the sense intended, any more than there are souls, Sartre asserts, and the ancient metaphor, revived by Hegel, of the political community as an *organism* is seriously misleading and untenable. A group is always constituted, never constitutive: the only constitutive organism in the sociopolitical world is the human individual. Between any pair of selected individuals within even a group in fusion at its height there remains, even at the moment at which it is closest to complete "fusion," at least an infinitesimal gap.

The theoretical framework which Sartre elaborates here in Book 2 of the *Critique* goes far toward destroying the often attractive but dangerous myths of perfect community that have dominated so much of that whole major portion of the Western political tradition, from Plato through Hegel and Western Marxism,[12] for which the "liberal" label is unsuitable. The reader of Book 2 is compelled to think, as Sartre himself obviously thought frequently, of the often profoundly disillusioned aftermaths—whether hours or days or years in coming—to those historic moments of widespread popular enthusiasm and unity that have greeted the successful overthrows of unpopular regimes—in 1790s France, in 1930s Russia, in 1960s Cuba, and so on. The initial moments of apparent revolutionary triumph came as close as any historical experience to embodying that "agreement of minds" (among vast numbers of people, though of course not among opponents of the takeovers!) by which the great organicist political theorists—most of them, in an interesting but psychologically comprehensible paradox, political conservatives at least in their later years—identified their political community ideals. But then slippage always seems to have occurred, with a virtual inevitability, as tasks began to be assigned, organizations to be constructed, and new hierarchies—in the final analysis no more rationally justifiable than the old ones—to be established. To have shown in detail why the organicist community model is unacceptable both as description and as norm is, then, one of Sartre's major achievements in this central part of his *Critique*.

But he is equally successful, I think, in pointing up the inadequacies of classical liberal individualist theory, with its baggage of social contract, voluntary association, and so on. What the contract theorists have conveniently forgotten—David Hume, though sharing the same general epistemological viewpoint as the majority of them, was astute enough to point this out long ago[13]—is the implausibility of their account of the origin of human associations, not only in terms of past history (as some social contract theorists have been willing to concede: historical societies, in other words, have seldom or never actually originated in accordance with their model), but also in terms of how human beings necessarily interact with one another. Elsewhere, Hume put the point rather crudely, in his famous dictum that reason is and of right ought to be the slave of the passions. With greater sophistication and complexity Sartre, in his account of the origin of groups in the *Critique*, shows the essential force of material circumstances and of external compulsions in the form of pressures, threats, or overt violence, as well as the comparatively small role of what we normally understand by "conscious decision," in the formation of groups. If he shares with contractarian liberalism a recognition that only the individual can be a constitutive unit in human community, his conceptions of what both the individual and the community are differ drastically from those of that tradition, with its images of calm, rational decision-makers contracting to erect neat constitutional structures of one sort or another. The typical contractarian, with an imaginary world of Robinson Crusoes still perhaps serving as his or her unconscious archetype for understanding the formation of community, finds it very difficult indeed even to begin to understand the nature of untidy human groups such as mobs, much less to describe their collective activities (except as being thoroughly irrational and incomprehensible), to attribute responsibility to them, etc.;[14] Sartre has no theoretical difficulty in dealing with such phenomena, while at the same time, aware as we have seen him to be of the degenerative tendencies lurking in every group formation, he tries to avoid composing or reciting "revolutionary pastorales."

One enormously important question, crucial in evaluating both the evolution of Sartre's thought and the nature of his political theory in the *Critique*, now needs to be asked: what has happened, in this analysis, to human freedom? Hegel, the quintessential organicist, claimed to find the fullest embodiment of freedom in citizenship in the modern state, but too many millions of citizens of modern states have reached opposite conclusions to leave such a claim plausible without undergoing infinite qualification. Freedom, though differently contoured than in Hegel's thought, is of equal importance for the contract tradition: it was in order to provide theoretical backing for the assertion that individuals in civil society living under governments could still retain all, or nearly all, of the personal autonomy which they would presumably have enjoyed in the imaginary presocietal "state of nature" that the device of the free contract became so popular with them. (In the words of that ever-fascinating borderline figure between the two traditions that I have been juxtaposing, Jean-Jacques Rousseau: " 'To find a form of association . . . by which each one, uniting with all, would however only obey himself, and would remain as free as before.' Such is the fundamental problem of which the *Social Contract* gives the solution."[15] Sartre was always known above all else as a champion of human freedom, and he was always profoundly critical of the bad-faith illusions and self-delusions concerning freedom in which the entire spectrum of political theory abounds. This accusation of bad faith certainly applies to most contractarians, who typically endorse the hypocritical view that every member of a contract society is equally free as long as he or she has a formally equal legal status, regardless of how disproportionate individuals' shares of power, wealth, etc., may be. But what kind of freedom is it that appears to find its fullest expression in the common *praxis* of a group? Moreover, what room is left for freedom even of group action, much less of individual choice, in a world so replete with material necessities and inevitabilities as that depicted by Sartre in the *Critique*?

A more adequate answer to this second question must await the examination of Sartre's philosophy of history, and especially his analysis of Stalinism, in the final section of the present chapter. However, it should already be very clear that by the time of the writing of the *Critique* Sartre had become much more aware of the role of necessity in history, without for a moment being tempted to think of these necessities as being *imposed* by any force or entity outside of ongoing historical totalizations themselves. But to infer from this that the role of freedom in the world has now "diminished" for Sartre, as though it were now to be seen as a smaller *quantity* than before, would be to misunderstand the nature of his intellectual evolution: in the *Critique* he has not repudiated either his earlier view that to be human is to be free and hence that we are always compelled to make choices, or his commitment to human liberation as a supreme and open-ended goal. What has altered greatly is his awareness, now vastly increased, of the innumerable ways in which the dialectic of human freedom in the worlds of society, politics, and history in which we all exist constantly results in freedom's contravening itself in its very efforts at expression.

A good example is his footnote discussion of the phenomenon of religious baptism. He used to find it almost incomprehensible, he says there, that nonbelieving Catholic parents who retain some ties with and feelings of respect for that religion would insist on having their children baptized. He now realizes that their reasoning is valid from the standpoint of the Catholic group; their contention is that this initiation in fact furnishes the child with a higher, more comprehensive standpoint and hence with more choices (including, of course, that of eventually rejecting the religion) than the child of thoroughly atheist parents will have. But neither his own early attitude nor that of these "lapsed" Catholics, he now feels, captures the truth, which is that

> it is necessary to decide, for the child and without being able to consult him, on the meaning of faith (i.e., of the History of the world, of humanity), and that he will bear, whatever one may do, whatever precaution one may take, the weight of that decision all his or her life. But it is also true that it can only mark him to the extent to which he will have freely interiorized it and to which it will become, not the inert limit that his father assigns to him, but the free self-limitation of his or her freedom.[16]

There are several fascinating aspects to this citation in addition to the principal point about freedom that it is making: an allusion to Sartre's own family background, the patriarchal assumptions (it is "the father" who chooses) and somewhat sexist language, the designation of a religious confession as a kind of "group" within Sartre's broad meaning of the term, the distinction between truth from the standpoint of the group and the observer's truth, etc. What is central for my purposes and his, however, is his making it very clear that he has conjoined, to his earlier and still strongly held view that free choice is always definitive of the human, the strong recognition that we always begin and live in a situation of having already been chosen for, by others.

To return to my first question about the sort of freedom it must be that appears to find its fullest expression in the common *praxis* of the group, I am inclined to think that Sartre's position concerning the assumption underlying this question remained ambivalent, but that the ambivalence may be as much that of the human condition as of Sartre. The freedom of the isolated individual, Aristotle's *idiōtēs*, is for the later Sartre a reality but as such an impotent one. (The same might be said about the totally uncommitted fictional antihero Roquentin, of the early Sartre, as well.) Effective action occurs within a group setting. (One is again reminded of Sartre's controversial assessment in *The Communists and Peace* of the situation in the 1950s of the French proletarian, whose chances for being effective for change were said to depend on Communist Party allegiance.) And yet, as the entirety of the analysis of this section of the *Critique* brings out so very well, the likelihood of one's freedom's becoming narrowed and subverted through adherence to a group's "truth" and to its values is overwhelming.

Sartre himself, as we have noted, committed himself to very few obviously political groups, except for short-term action groups designed for specific purposes such as protesting a particular policy or government action (e.g., the trial of Henri Martin). Two of the most notable counterexamples in his career, the RDR period already mentioned and the era of *"les Maos"* late in his life, were arguably quite unfortunate and counterproductive. Yet there is an important sense in which he also belonged, throughout his post-World War II life, to a team that importantly shaped and expressed his freedom: *"l'équipe"* of *Les Temps Modernes*, the regular meetings of which remained extremely important to Sartre even when he was becoming quite enfeebled. Hence, his discussion of teams, of which he takes as examples primarily sports teams but also a theater cast, as a form of organized group is quite revealing. The appearance of *alienation* of the individual, who on the team has become "the common individual," committed to a common objective, is misleading, he says. Even the "star" must fulfill certain assigned functions in order for the team's success to continue, and his own stardom along with it. It is rare in sports or in research teams, he continues, to find someone who is "lacking team spirit," but this is quite common among "great" actors. What happens in the actor's case, however, is not a genuine return to the solitude of serial existence, but rather "confiscation of power to the profit of a single person. . . . He becomes the unity in act of the group."[17] And Sartre adds that he will return to discuss this case at length.

Although there is in fact no such lengthy return to the case of the star actor later in the *Critique*, one may well regard that large part of the second volume that is devoted to a consideration of Stalin's elevation to the position of incarnation of the enveloping totalization of Soviet history as a more strictly political illustration of what can happen when individuals express their freedoms through groups. Sartre's position on the *Temps Modernes* team, in the years following Merleau-Ponty's resignation, had some structural resemblance to Stalin's within the Soviet Communist Party (although the role of some members of Sartre's editorial board, such as Simone de Beauvoir, was relatively much stronger). On the other hand, even though it is true that *Les Temps Modernes* and related Sartrean literary and philosophical enterprises strongly bore his mark, it is equally true that Sartre would never have been able to exert the influence that he did, indeed to "become known" at all, without the cooperation of the members of various more or less loosely organized groups in which he participated throughout his life, from his Ecole Normale Supérieure classmates through the staff of Gallimard publishers (who, after all, gave him his career "break") to his army companions and many other organizations, including *Les Temps Modernes*. In short, his individual freedom would have remained totally impotent apart from these groups. It may be remarked that this is just as true of anyone else's career as it is of Sartre's. But that is precisely his point! The group's potential to distort and subvert individual freedom is enormous, but freedom finds no effective expression at all, much less what I have called its "fullest expression," outside the orbit of some common *praxis*. The question then becomes one of deciding which groups will cause an expansion and which a retraction of human freedom; but Sartre does not pretend, any more than anyone else can reasonably pretend, to have a universal magic formula for making this decision on a theoretical level aside from examining individual cases.

Right and Law. "The oath" *(le serment)*, it will be remembered, is Sartre's way of designating a group's initial, fateful move in the direction of overcoming ephemerality and attempting to perpetuate itself. If, indeed, it is only through groups that the inhuman or antihuman condition of seriality can be transcended, then the oath must be regarded as "the beginning of humanity."[18] But, at the same time, it is taken against the background of the (actual or potential) violence that pervades our social world and in an atmosphere of fear—dramatic in momentous historical circumstances such as the Tennis Court Oath or the signing of the American *Declaration of Independence* (one recalls Benjamin Franklin's remark at the time about either hanging together or hanging separately), undramatic or even banal in cases of the formation of more garden-variety groups. (In such cases, the word chosen by the English translator of the *Critique* to render *"serment,"* pledge, would be more appropriate.) The oath, it will further be recalled, generates the dual phenomenon that Sartre calls "fraternity-terror": the solidarity that each member thereby pledges to all the others is accompanied by an implied condemnation of any member, whether another or oneself, who in the future might decide to renege. It should now be further noted that Sartre uses his overall theoretical framework of the *Critique* and in particular this same dramatic phenomenon of "the oath" to elucidate, in a clearer way than he was able to in the *Cahiers pour une morale*, the phenomena of law and right.

Here, as in the *Cahiers*, Sartre emphasizes the violent origin of law and right. Here, too, again as there, the English-language reader must contend with what will appear to her or him as the deep ambiguity associated with the fact that *"droit"* is the French word for both "right" and "law." Moreover, the text of the *Critique* at this point highlights yet another linguistic ambiguity by stressing the word *"statut,"* which is translatable into English as both "status" and "statute." I have concluded that it would be mistaken to insist on using the same English word to translate either one of these French words in every instance in which it occurs; one must consider the context.[19] If this judgment is warranted, then some philosophically interesting implications about the interpretation of texts can be drawn, although I shall not attempt to spell them out here. Sartre's point, at any rate, is that the taking of an oath to adhere to a group that has now definitively been "formed," recognized as a social entity, at the same time creates new structures, which at this initial stage are not clearly differentiated from one another, of reciprocal rights and duties and specific functions—in short, a statutory or legal apparatus.

Sartre insists that this account is not to be confused with one of a social contract, which he defines as the attempt to find some kind of (legitimizing) foundation for such and such a society, but rather that it is intended to explain the general necessity for any fusing group to transform itself, at some stage, into something more permanent.[20] Indeed, the classical social contract theories were designed to argue that citizens had an obligation to adhere to one or another particular form of political order—even the recent revival of the term in Great Britain a decade or two ago had a similar didactic and admonitory purpose[21]—whereas Sartre's more purely descriptive account has no such aim. The Sartrean formula has the value of offering explanations at once of the felt need for by-laws and constitutions in even the most unpretentious voluntary associations once they have become "established" (I am thinking, for example, of my own and others' experiences in the formation of the Sartre Society of North America!), and of what has pretentiously been called "the nature of law."[22] It also, as it were almost incidentally, takes account of the frequent and multiple connections that have been made historically between legal institutions and "the Sacred"—witnesses' sworn oaths in courts of law, for example—by showing how this element is employed, often but not always in strictly religious forms, to reinforce the "terror" aspect of the juridical order that has been put into place by the oath's fraternity-terror.[23] Sartre does not insist on this last point at any length, but the framework that he has provided could be of use in further explorations of the close relationship between law and religion that has always been an important theme, alike for supporters and for critics of religion's role, in the tradition of Western political thought.

In this tradition, the sanction of Divinity has often been invoked to legitimize the authority of a particular political order or indeed of political order in general. But since it is obvious from the entire thrust of his argument, to say nothing of all of his earlier thought, that Sartre regards any such invocation as a mere mystification, we need now to consider, in order to complete this discussion of the political and the sociopolitical in the *Critique*, what he has to say about authority, legitimacy, and related matters.

Sovereignty, Authority, Legitimacy, and the State. Whereas, for the tradition, these questions (as expressed, e.g., in such formulas as "the basis of political obligation") constitute the essence of political philosophy, Sartre gives all of them relatively short shrift, at least in Volume 1 of the *Critique*. He is, after all, attempting, as I have indicated, to undermine traditional distinctions and terminologies. Nevertheless, he does clearly indicate just how these questions fit within his highly iconoclastic framework, and he even places considerable weight, at one point, on the related notions of sovereignty and authority. As far as sovereignty is concerned, it is useful first to recall Sartre's *Cahiers* discussion, based in part on his readings about the role of the sovereignty of the chiefs in many African tribes, of a sovereignty as at once oppressive and yet incarnating the freedom of all who accept it. In Volume 2 of the *Critique,* the idea of Stalin as sovereign incarnation becomes absolutely central. But it is in Volume 1 that Sartre offers his theoretical account of sovereignty.

Sartre's account is not intended, as he quite explicitly maintains, to provide some legitimizing *basis* for sovereignty, for which, he says, so many writers have evinced a felt need: "Unfortunately, neither God nor the totalized group has a real existence. And if it were really necessary to find a basis for sovereignty, we could be looking for a long time: there is none."[24] The truth, he continues, is that the free individual human being alone is truly sovereign and that, outside of institutions—the resemblance of Sartre's thought on this point to Hobbes's conception of the state of nature is very obvious—the range of this sovereignty is limitless. What is created within institutions, then, as the second major transformation of groups after that of the oath, is strictly speaking a quasi sovereignty, whereby an individual (or several individuals with shared power, but the case of the single individual is clearest and permits us to imagine variations on it) is recognized by all the other members as the "regulative third party" who maintains their bonds with one another. At the earlier moment of the "group in fusion," it will be recalled, there was also said to be a "regulative third" who articulated the goal of all (e.g., "Let us capture the Bastille"), but who could have been anyone at all within the group. Now, within a juridically constituted order, a specific individual is designated in this role and thus functions as sovereign.

What seems to me capital in this account is Sartre's insistence that sovereignty of this sort, if it is to exist at all, must in some way be *accepted* by the group's members: that is why it is really only a *quasi* sovereignty, as contrasted with the genuine sovereignty that lies in the freedom of every individual. He points out that a king who commands the execution of, let us say, some captured enemy soldiers cannot truly be said to be exercising his sovereignty over them, because he is not treating them as human beings. But the king's own soldiers must *accept* his sovereign authority, whether gladly or grudgingly, in order for him to remain king. Such acceptance of sovereign authority, however, which carries so much coercive power with it, is by no means necessarily a positive act of consent; often, in fact *usually* when we reach the stage of analysis of concrete historical examples of sovereignty, the following is the case:

> Everyone obeys in seriality: not because he takes on his obedience directly, but because he is not certain that his neighbor hasn't objected to obeying. That does not prevent the order from being received as *legitimate*, quite the contrary: it prevents raising the question of its legitimacy.[25]

Thus the elevation of a particular individual to the position of "sovereign" completes the process of reserialization of a group, although the type of seriality involved here—modern political life, for example, under an unpopular but sullenly accepted dictator—is still different from that initially described by Sartre earlier in the *Critique*, precisely because it is imbued with the trappings of "authority."

What about the supreme "authority" in the modern world, the State? Is it to be accorded any legitimacy? In the last analysis no, according to Sartre, but his answer is a good deal more complicated. The group as such, he maintains, can claim legitimacy, "inasmuch as it realizes for itself and . . . manifests for all the action of freedom against necessity."[26] But modern societies consist of very complex amalgams of groups and serial collectives of all sorts, and the modern State can never be an expression of the totality, or indeed even of a majority, of the society's members; it can never be a group in his sense. He rejects as a mystification the idea of a "diffuse popular sovereignty that would incarnate itself in the sovereign," since the sovereignty of an individual is always quite well defined, never diffuse;[27] what Sartre is here dismissing as illusory is the notion, dear both to Hobbes and to modern "consensus" theorists, that a sovereign can ever "represent" his or her subjects adequately. On the other hand, the modern State, while it does not and cannot have the legitimacy of a group, except perhaps within the relatively small and frequently changing circle of individuals who really constitute it (what we might call the "inner circle of the government") at any given time, cannot be said to be illegitimate, either, according to Sartre: something remotely resembling acceptance of it does go on, most of the time, among the citizenry at large, but this amounts to an impotent recognition of my impotence to do anything but obey—a very passive acceptance. In short, the question, so dear to traditional political theory, of whether the State, or some given state, is legitimate or illegitimate is for Sartre a foolish one: it can be neither.

At this point, Sartre goes on in effect to take issue with the putative Marxist view, supported by some passages in Marx's own writings, that the State is nothing but the organ of the exploiting class. It is in fact important, he says, to realize that the modern State tends to play an integrating function, claiming, for example, to stand for *all* classes and hence for the Nation as a whole, and moreover that this is not *mere* mystification. Such State pronouncements tend to be seized upon by the oppressed classes as something of a guarantee for them against more extreme exploitation by the very powerful, and hence to reinforce their passive acceptance of the State as "legitimate" until such time as a revolutionary consciousness may begin to develop. With this declaration of distancing from an important tenet of "orthodox" Marxism,[28] Sartre completes his brief discussion of the State. He then devotes a final portion of Book 2, subsection A to the *praxis* of manipulation through propaganda, advertising, and similar devices of deception that is so often carried out by the modern State, for instance in the Nazi Party's official campaigns of anti-Semitism,[29] but that is also exemplified in the "other-directedness" promoted by many other groups that exercise power over the rest of us in modern society.

Sartre's concern throughout the long, central portion of the *Critique* that we have been considering has obviously been quite differently focused from the thought of those more conventional political philosophers who, to take a salient contemporary example, debate the relative merits of various theories of justice. The word "justice" may, for all I know, never once appear in all of these pages. For Sartre is profoundly skeptical—this is an understatement—of pronouncements about ideal patterns, or even ideal principles, of justice *überhaupt*, which would have to be made from the standpoint of a Totalizer; in his view, there is no such being. He has not even been concerned to discuss such traditional topics as alternative forms of government or even the related controversy within the Marxist tradition, to which he had alluded in his early essay on Yugoslavia and later in *The Communists and Peace*, about "spontaneity versus consciousness," i.e., the relative value of participatory democratic decision-making as opposed to Lenin's "democratic centralism" or even more authoritarian command structures; while such issues have an unquestionable political importance, he admits, he has been preoccupied above all with "the type of formal intelligibility and rationality" that is common to organized groups of both "top-down" and "bottom-up" varieties.[30]

This stance may be disconcerting to readers eager to see Sartre attack such contemporary debates with the moral passion characteristic of his occasional essays, and indeed I see no compelling, in principle, methodological reason for him not to have dealt with the question of forms of political organization at this point in Volume 1, as he ultimately needs to do when confronting the Stalinist form in Volume 2. But the *advantage* of his "deep structure" approach is to cast an insightful new light of intelligibility on the successive phases of group action and of seriality that come and go, with an often bewildering speed both in our own experience and in others', at a level different from that of specific institutional forms. (To take two disparate examples of what I mean, consider the radically different atmospheres of an American university campus during periods of apathy and periods of intense ferment around issues whether of internal administrative management or of national politics within a single generation; or consider the sequence of stances through which the typical older citizen of Beijing, China, has passed from the time of organized celebration of the new era initiated by the triumph of the Communist Party, through the Cultural Revolution, through the 1989 student uprising, and so on. Precise political forms—constitutional structures, whether in an American university or in the Chinese nation—while significant as background information and central to any discussion about what is to be done in times of ferment and potential fundamental change, are indeed of secondary importance in attempting to comprehend just how the restructuring of groups has actually come about in both instances.) That is why the *Critique* has generally been seen as prophetic of the great movements of the 1960s and beyond, for the comprehension of which the categories of more traditional political theories have been of only limited use.

If the positive achievement of Sartre's analysis is to cause readers to view the world of sociopolitical structures through new categories, new and different lenses from those provided by the mainstream political theory tradition, its critical or (to speak anachronistically but quite accurately) deconstructive achievement is to view with new skepticism all transcendent pronouncements about "the nature of legitimate (political) authority" or variants thereupon. In this limited sense, the outcome of Sartre's political theory is anarchistic, although he was never to be seen waving the Black Flag. His analysis, I believe, greatly enhances our ability to separate the recognition of the existence of authority-structures, which may be real enough even over a large, acquiescent population in a modern state, from claims of some sort of ultimate "legitimacy"—usually made today in terms of supposed "democratic" conformity with the imputed popular will—for *any* such "authority." This, as far as I am concerned, is all to the good, since recent years have witnessed too many instances of oppression by "democratic" movements and leaders, as well as by authoritarian ones.

But a serious difficulty remains. Sartre asserts, as we have seen, that group *praxis* is legitimate only inasmuch as it expresses the freedom of the human individual, who alone can claim "sovereignty" (i.e., who alone is the source of effective action), but who alone in the other sense of that word—that is, by her/himself, isolated—is ineffective. This general validation of groups as expressive of freedom leaves him open to the objection that while it certainly supports "socialism" against liberal individualism both in the broad sense that it emphasizes the necessary role of social groups in the political world and in the narrower sense that it sanctions the actions of oppressed groups against seriality and against other structures of dominance, and while it also both retains and elaborates upon Sartre's earlier philosophy of human freedom, it has somehow become disconnected from the original meaning of his commitment to *"Socialisme et Liberté"* because it is incapable of readily generating criteria for favoring those groups that enhance others' freedom in this "One World" of ours over those that, like the Nazis, diminish it. In the absence of such criteria, Sartre's theory will have to be regarded as *purely* descriptive, offering no political direction. If he can answer this objection at all satisfactorily, it will have to be from the perspective of a philosophy of history, the subject matter of the concluding portions of the *Critique*.

Philosophy of History. Is human history one gigantic "totalization in course"? It is because a hypothetical affirmative answer to this question, when properly understood and qualified, seemed plausible to Sartre that he undertook to write the second volume of the *Critique*. We can go still further and say that this possibility, first expressed at any length in Sartre's work when he was writing his *Cahiers*, underlay the *entire Critique*, not merely Volume 2. He is very explicit about this in Section B of Book 2, the last 150-odd pages of Volume 1, to which he pointedly gives a separate title: "Of the Dialectical Investigation [*Expérience*] as Totalization: The Level of the

Concrete, the Site [*Lieu*] of History,"[31] and which ends with a clear statement of the intellectual connection among *Search for a Method*, Volume 1, and Volume 2. Here are a few excerpts from these closing lines:

> History is intelligible if the different practices that one can discover and situate at a moment of historical temporalization appear in the end as partially totalizing and as rejoined and grounded, in their very oppositions and their diversities, by a totalization that is intelligible and without appeal. . . . We have, up to now, attempted to ascend back up to the elementary and formal structures and—by the same token—we have situated the dialectical bases of a structural anthropology. We must now let these structures live freely, oppose and compose with one another: the reflective investigation of this adventure, still a formal one, will constitute the object of our second volume. If truth must be *one* in its increasing internal diversification, then in replying to the ultimate question posed by the regressive investigation we shall discover the profound meaning of History and of dialectical rationality.[32]

It should be noted that Sartre is claiming here in Volume 1 to have answered the "question" of *Questions de méthode*, to wit, whether we have the means for constructing a structural anthropology, by doing it. Moreover, he equates the "regressive" part of the "regressive-progressive method," outlined in *Search for a Method*, with the contents of Volume 1, leaving for Volume 2 the "progressive" part. In a portion of this final paragraph that I have not directly cited, he further identifies Volume 1 with a synchronic approach and Volume 2 with a diachronic one, thus emphasizing the element of *time* (temporalization) that is fundamental to history. He also makes it clear in the paragraph immediately preceding this one that the question of the meaning of history cannot be separated from that of the role of the historical investigator, the historian, and finally that the section (B) of the book that he is concluding here, with its emphasis above all on interactions, especially *struggles*, between groups, is the crucial point of linkage between the two parts of his effort.

Is human history of such a nature as to be susceptible to such treatment, I began by asking. Part of what we need to consider in order to understand Sartre's response to this question, as reflected in the above citation and in the entire effort particularly of Volume 2 of the *Critique*, is the extreme ambiguity of this "is." Sartre is thoroughly consistent in maintaining that there is no Totalizer of history, no standpoint transcendent to the historical process itself, and this implies that neither he nor his readers nor anyone else is entitled to talk about the essence of history, what history "really" is, as a closed and fixed entity. Therefore, the investigation into the implications of seeing History as ultimately *one* must be founded on an hypothesis, not a demonstrated philosophical fact. (Sartre uses the capital letter to distinguish history in this general and ongoing sense from segments of past history, such as the history of the French Revolution—although this usage is apt to stir unwarranted but understandable fears that he is assuming Hegel's stance of "knowing the meaning of History.") The dialectical inquiry into history construed, hypothetically, as "a totalization that is intelligible and without appeal" must be self-validating, as in our earlier methodological discussion we saw that all of dialectical reason must be.

The alternative, as Sartre conceived the alternative, to maintaining this apparently daring hypothesis is more serious, more negative for human thought, than might at first appear to be the case. It makes sense, perhaps, to regard an isolated tribe in a very remote area, one with no contacts for many centuries with any other human tribe, and (let us suppose) with no memory of its origins and no collective interest even in orally transmitting a record of more recent achievements, as having no history in any interesting sense. If an outsider were somehow (but how?) to research the facts about the temporal evolution of that tribe over several generations, then his or her results might be said to be a purely "regional" history, one with no connection with the rest of the human race. (But of course, as soon as the outside historian's observations began to be transmitted to others, and indeed even before that as soon as she or he first encountered members of that tribe, its historical isolation would have ended.) Beyond this type of case, one that is purely imaginary at least in today's world (apart from an occasional possible counterinstance, having virtually no larger significance, in New Guinea or other remote jungle areas discovered up to a decade or two ago), interactions of all sorts among peoples from the most distant parts of the globe have become commonplace; in fact, the very sense of "distance," of remoteness, between any two points on the planet Earth has lost most of whatever edge it still had when I was a child. Sartre's point is that either we find a means, through dialectical reason, to comprehend this ongoing and increasingly interactive process, however difficult it may be to grasp it in all its complexity and recalcitrance to comprehension, or we give up intellectually and lapse into the strictly analytic habit of treating small segments of history as if they in fact had taken place and were continuing to take place in isolation from the other segments. But to do so would be conscious self-deception: we know that ours is, increasingly "One World," and the successive generations of what our Western conventions designate the twentieth century have become and are becoming increasingly clear on this point.

It is ironic, though psychologically understandable, that some strands of "postmodern" thought have made light of the very notion of a global—totalistic or "totalitarian" in the pre-ideological sense of this term—vision[33] at the very time when its basis in historical reality has become increasingly obvious in our everyday lives: in the news, in the goods that we purchase, and even in philosophical ideas that are transmitted instantaneously over thousands of miles. I myself, in reflecting on the reasoning that lies behind Sartre's brave hypothesis about (historical) truth's being *"one* in its increasing internal diversification," have become much more sympathetic to it than I was when I first read the conclusion of Volume 1 of the *Critique*. It is indeed only if we can at least begin to fill in our understanding of history up to now and of its immeasurably complex future possible directions (which is certainly not the same as *predicting* its actual future course!) along the lines of this unitary hypothesis that we can come to grips with the relativist challenge that I posed at the end of the previous subsection of this chapter. In other words, either we achieve some comprehension, however painfully tentative, of history—that ongoing temporal process of which we are all constantly evolving parts as long as we are alive—as an objective reality which is composed of the *praxeis* of billions of human beings, or there is no defensible standpoint from which to evaluate the relative merits of one group's projects over another's; we might as well give up conscientious thinking and become involved in the crack racket or the hostile takeover game or whatever other activity, engaged in by like-minded people, "turns us on."

But this is not to say that Sartre himself succeeded in achieving anything more than, at best, an extremely primitive comprehension of the sort that he sought; he did, after all, give up in his effort to push Volume 2 to completion. However he may have formulated, at various times, his reasons for having done so, it seems clear that he arrived at a point at which he decided that what he had done with it thus far was inadequate in relation to the project, and that he could not possibly increase its adequacy sufficiently, in the years remaining in his life, to make it worthwhile to continue. Therefore, it is more important for my purpose here to try to convey as clearly as possible the main lines of Sartre's philosophical reasoning about history, as an extension of his political theory, at the time of the writing of the *Critique* than to enter into most of the details of the central portion of Volume 2.

At first glance, a summary of the extant contents of Volume 2, when viewed in light of Sartre's overall plan of complementing his formal, synchronic account of underlying sociopolitical structures with a formal, diachronic account of the structures of history, will make them seem rather bizarre. First, we find a phenomenological analysis of boxing that begins on the third page of text and that continues, with some apparent divagations, for nearly fifty pages, followed soon thereafter by a reference to Merleau-Ponty's description, in *Humanism and Terror,* of "the climate of fraternity-terror" in which "all opposition . . . is treason."[34] This ushers in, as the reader immediately, or at least very soon, realizes, the discussion of the Stalinist era at its height (or depth, if one prefers) that will occupy more than 200 pages. This section, one half of the text, likewise includes some apparent digressions, such as a discussion of sexuality as a kind of incarnation, most of it presupposing though not condoning the alienated hierarchical standpoint of "the superiority of the male,"[35] and only marginally connected with Soviet life. The "Stalinist era" of Volume 2 itself comes to a close after a brief treatment of Stalin's anti-Semitism, with the following paragraph:

> With this last example, we have buckled the buckle, for we have seen the sovereign as totalization enveloped in his own sovereignty. We can therefore

bring together in a few pages the conclusions of our investigation of enveloping totality [*sic:* he means "totalization," as the editor notes] (in the case of a society with a *personal* sovereign).[36]

These "few pages" lead back into the discussion of methodological and ontological issues, occupying the final one hundred pages (more or less) of the text proper, to which I have already referred earlier in this chapter. Finally, the editor, Arlette Elkaïm-Sartre, has added as an appendix another fifty-odd pages of notes about a variety of topics (e.g., the history of Venice, progress, Verdi's career, Eskimo society, etc.) written by Sartre during roughly the same time period as the *Critique*, in an even more tentative and less finished state than the second volume of the *Critique* itself. As a whole, then, the book does not appear to hold a great deal of promise as a balanced philosophy of history.

Ronald Aronson has entitled one of the chapters of his book on the second volume of the *Critique* "Why Stalin?"[37] By this he means to refer to Sartre's effort to understand just why the members of Soviet society, in their efforts to "build socialism," took the deviational route that led to Stalinism. But one must also ask the "meta-" question, "Why 'Why Stalin?'?"—that is, why did Sartre devote so much space, in what was planned to have been his analysis of history, to this one brief recent epoch in a single country? The germ of the answer to this question, which I mentioned at the outset of my discussion of Sartre's methodology and ontology, is to be found near the beginning of Volume 1; it now needs to be recalled and considered more carefully. Since we are living in One World, and since the Soviet Union was the first major society to undertake a radical self-reconstruction with a recognition of the implications of this reality clearly in view, the fact that the Soviet experiment deviated so much, in a way that was so obvious throughout the world, from its projected path ("failed so dismally," if one prefers that locution) must be a matter of the deepest concern and interest for thoughtful persons in the second half of the twentieth century. However important Lenin and other pre-Stalin elements many have been in preparing the way for this result, there is some consensus that the complex phenomenon known as "Stalinism," some of the most extreme manifestations of which (e.g., the slaughter of untold numbers of independent peasants) took place during the 1930s, is the historical point upon which to focus if one is to understand what has happened. In trying to achieve this understanding of a series of events and phenomena that many have given up attempting to understand, often in horror and amazement, what must be avoided because it would be counterproductive is judgmental moralism, whether condemnatory of Stalin and all who supported him even passively, or exculpatory of him on the grounds that some eggs need to be broken in order to make omelettes, and some chefs are rougher than others.

In this entire Sartrean line of reasoning, there is one important assumption that holds it together but that I have refrained from articulating up to this point: it is that *socialism*, the building of which was supposed to be Soviet society's project after the October Revolution of 1917, is in some way a key, at least as a regulative ideal, to the historical totalization in which we are participating; were it not so regarded by Sartre, then the Stalinist *deviation* of socialism would not be such a serious development for him. "In a word," says Sartre at the end of a passage in which he attacks with vigor the idea that history can be conceived as a rigorous schema and insists on its uniqueness or singularity and on the importance of the role of the *accidental* in the realization by human *praxis* of its objectives, "Stalinism saved socialization by deviating socialism; there remain its successors who have received from it the means of correcting this deviation."[38] In other words, Sartre had not yet at that time given up hope for the future emergence of a socialist society in the USSR, transformed ("socialized") as it was during the Stalinist era into a modern industrialized nation.

Nevertheless, the historical deviation that Sartre studies in such depth in Volume 2 was indeed extreme. It was epitomized in Stalin's slogan, designed to deal with the unplanned situation of a Soviet Union surrounded by hostile capitalist neighbors, and used to justify all sorts of "emergency" measures within the USSR: "socialism in a single country." Sartre takes time to analyze the evolution of the meaning of the word "socialism" beginning with something more or less equivalent to "communism," to a state of affairs that has been designated as the necessary prelude to the full communist state of the distant future, and that therefore may include elements acknowledged to be very far removed from the ideal:

> Socialism, in this theoretical synthesis, is fundamentally *homogeneous* with communism to the extent to which the radical transformation of social and economic structures was carried out in the very first years of the Revolution; it is very simply the mediation between the abstract moment of *socialization* and the concrete moment of *common enjoyment*. This means that, in certain concrete historical circumstances, it can be synonymous with *hell*.[39]

This entire early segment of Sartre's discussion of Stalinism in Volume 2,[40] of which the above-cited sentences constitute the climax, is useful for the light that it sheds on Sartre's understanding of the socialist goal to which, as the context of the discussion makes clear, he remained committed as he wrote his often devastating (despite his refusal most of the time to be explicitly condemnatory) analysis of Stalinist practices. In addition to the interesting, protopostmodern formula of "common enjoyment" just cited, there is a passage on the preceding page in which Sartre is quite specific about what he understands socialism, the outcome of a radical transformation rather than of an evolutionary series of reforms, to be:

> What basically characterizes it is *neither* abundance *nor* the total liquidation of classes *nor* working-class sovereignty—although these characteristics are *indispensable*, at least as distant goals of the essential transformation. It's the sup-

pression of exploitation and of oppression, or, in positive terms, the collective appropriation of the means of production.[41]

If there is something surprising about these words, it is that they are so *un*surprising: they reflect, I think, a common understanding among many varieties of socialists about what "socialism" means. Although the expression "means of production" in its technical sense is most closely identified with Marx, the aim of shifting control of the basic building-blocks of modern economies from a comparative few who manipulate the rest, workers and consumers, for the profit of the former and at the severe cost of the latter, to the collectivity, however defined, is one that is widely shared even among socialists who disavow much of Marxist theory.

At the same time, by relegating to a position of secondary importance the three "distant goals" that he mentions and that at various times have been proposed as definitions of socialism as a state of affairs, Sartre avoids some major theoretical difficulties that his own philosophical investigations have brought out: the problem of defining the overcoming of scarcity that I noted in discussing *Search for a Method;* the ambiguity of the notion of "sovereignty" when used in a political sense that we have seen him treat in Volume 1 of the *Critique;* and the difficulty of defining "class" and "class struggle," to which I shall come shortly. All in all, these texts, although they were written with a view to making more explicit the basis and nature of Stalinism's "deviation" of socialism, constitute perhaps the clearest evidence in the entire *Critique* of Sartre's continued commitment to the "socialism" portion of the formula, "socialism and freedom," while at the same time they make it clear that Sartre's understanding of the word was not an eccentric one. The texts also serve to strengthen and complete my answer to the metaquestion, "Why 'Why Stalin?'?".

If this account of mine helps resolve one major puzzle about the outline of Sartre's truncated and unfinished effort at writing a philosophy of history, at least three further questions about it strike me as most salient. First, why boxing—in other words, why does Sartre spend his first fifty-odd pages of Volume 2 probing a sport that he insists is "a singular reality, a process that is totalizable but impossible to conceptualize"?[42] Second, just what are his findings here about history as the site at which, as most writers on the subject including Sartre tend in some sense to agree, the issue of freedom versus necessity seems to arise most dramatically? Finally, where might the rest of the book have gone if Sartre had persisted in working on it?

Boxing. In order to understand the role that his extended phenomenology of boxing is intended to play in Sartre's theoretical framework, we must first understand the rationale of the transitional section, B, of Volume 1. It is, in fact, relatively straightforward. The first portion of the *Critique* after the discussions of methodology, it will be recalled, began with individual *praxis* and described the domain of the practico-inert, the level at which human beings, through their own need-satisfying activities, took on the attributes of things. The second portion traced the formation of groups. From the outset, it was emphasized that human history has taken place thus far in a milieu of scarcity, which entails that it has also taken place in a milieu of violence. However, although the formation of groups was acknowledged to occur under conditions of external threat, more often than not involving already existing rival groups (e.g., the king's court and army based at Versailles), Sartre made no attempt throughout Book 2, Section A systematically to study interactions between groups—i.e., struggles. That is the task that he assigns himself in Section B, and in his subtitle for this section he calls this "the site [*lieu*] of history." Fundamentally, therefore, history is (has been) struggle, and it is important above all first to consider just what *kinds* of struggle have predominated. Sartre's leading hypothesis concerning the answer to this question is the Marxist one of *class* struggle, and so he needs to pay some attention to the nature of classes; in the course of doing this, he provides illustrations from the history of nineteenth-century French capitalism, with its peculiarly Malthusian tenor, a topic that he had already undertaken to treat in the last part of *The Communists and Peace*. Except for a few closing remarks to which I have already alluded, this ends Volume 1.

But Sartre then feels the need, having embarked on the overall subject of history conceived as struggle, to try to make more intelligible the fundamental paradox whereby two (or more) antagonists, each with opposite sets of goals and a commitment to defeat the other, are nevertheless both parts of a *single* "totalization" that the historian can describe. And so he proposes to begin with what is perhaps the simplest, most overt, and unambiguous instance of this known in the contemporary world, the boxing match, in which just two individuals publicly confront each other, each having the stated and agreed-upon purpose of knocking the other one out. (In feudal times, the joust had a similar function.) He thinks that if some meaning can be extracted from this relatively simple phenomenon of a boxing match, then it will become easier to grasp the far more complicated and ambiguous struggles that occupy center stage in history, such as the struggles, both internal and external to the Soviet Union, surrounding the phenomenon of Stalinism.

As far as class struggle as central to historical transformations is concerned, Sartre believes firmly in it, as did Marx. So did Aristotle, and so do I. One cannot, for example, look back at the process of industrialization throughout the nineteenth century without being forced to acknowledge the salience of class struggle; today, it seems obvious to me, although class struggle has not disappeared in the United States or other countries, it has taken on different forms, which in general have a more "international" or global flavor than those that predominated a century ago. In short, to recognize the centrality of class struggle to history should hardly be controversial. More interesting and debatable are two interrelated questions about the *meaning* of this recognition: is class struggle *uniquely* central, and what is to be understood by "class"? Sartre says nothing to anticipate the later, very important and illuminating debates over the uniqueness or non-uniqueness of the factor of class that have been generated particularly among feminist theorists and that still continue. But what he has to say about the *meaning* of class, as well as his brief comments about sexuality in Volume 2 of the *Critique* and his much longer discussions of it in earlier writings, suggests that he would at any rate not experience the same difficulty with assimilating gender antagonism into his explanatory framework as do "orthodox" Marxists.

For Sartre's entire tendency, in this section of the *Critique* as elsewhere, is to emphasize complexities. He insists from the outset of his discussion of classes, for example, that the working class as a whole never becomes an organized group;[43] on this basis one can begin to understand the phenomenon, itself very complicated, of labor unions. When he later focuses on the "Malthusian" practices of dominant segments of the late nineteenth-century French bourgeoisie (restraints on the commitment to the unlimited capital expansion that was characteristic, for example, of American industry during the same period; concentration primarily on the domestic market; consequent severe repression of workers' demands, leading to the perceived need for workers to refrain from having very many children, as reflected in declining birth-rates; and so on), he shows that emphasizing "class struggle" is only the beginning of historical explanation, not the end. He finds particular fault, in this context, with his old *bête noire*, Engels (and hence with the whole "orthodox Marxist" tradition that owed so much to Engels's formulas), arguing that the latter, while he makes fun of Dühring for writing too quickly about "oppression" rather than sufficiently analyzing the supposedly scientific basis of class struggle, is in fact guilty of a denial of the reality of class struggle itself.[44] Instead, what is to be found in Engels is "Economistic" talk of economic processes and emerging objective contradictions.

The more important word, for Sartre as against Engels, in the expression "class struggle," is *struggle*, rather than class as an abstract theoretical concept. To see the result, for instance, of French colonialist practice in Algeria, to which Sartre devotes an extended discussion toward the end of Volume 1, as some sort of process called "pauperization" [*clochardisation*], deemed inevitable for an agrarian society when it comes into contact with an advanced industrial society, is to hide the essential reality, the human violence involved, behind a thing-like veil:

In fact, *first* it must be said that the contact of the industrial society with the agrarian society was brought about by Bugeaud's soldiers, by the atrocious massacre of which they made themselves guilty; that the liquidation of forms of inheritance proper to Muslim tribes did not spring from some sort of idealistic interpenetration of two different legal systems, but from the fact that merchants encouraged by the State and supported by our armies imposed the [Napoleonic] Code on the Moslems *in order to rob them better.*[45]

The Western proletarian class, Sartre says, along with its counterparts among colonized peoples, has played a justifiably large role in the social thinking of bourgeois intellectuals like himself because the fact of its exploitation is living proof of the limitations and contradictions of bourgeois humanism, despite the latter's universalistic aspirations, and because its struggle against this exploitation points to the future possibility of overcoming those limitations and contradictions.[46] But the actual, concrete proletariat is by no means a homogeneous entity, reducible to the status of a theoretical concept, the object of intellectual contemplation. Rather, its reality comes from its being oppressed and from its *struggling*, never as a whole and seldom in a way that is simple either for itself or for any observer to grasp, against that oppression.

This brings us back to the boxers, whose struggle does seem somewhat simpler to grasp. But its very simplicity at first appears to render it suspect as a case study. We may concede Sartre's point that boxing is not to be taken as a mere symbol or metaphor for social reality, that there is *real* violence involved in a match and that the opponents are not just involved in an enterprise of the imagination, a stage play.[47] We may also be gratified and experience the feeling of returning to familiar territory when Sartre's lengthy analysis of boxing eventually situates prizefighters within a class society, from the more exploited portions of which most of them are drawn, although very few make it to the "big time" and many of the rest, including the champions, end up as physical and mental wrecks.[48] Nevertheless, the sport of boxing does not really occupy an extremely prominent position in today's "One World," not even in the global sports world. Moreover, in this age of still weak but improved women's sports competition, boxing is among the sports of least interest to women. These negative considerations may be somewhat mitigated by our recalling that Sartre himself had been an amateur boxer in his younger years, especially during the period of his first *lycée* teaching position, at Le Havre, when he and another instructor had organized an informal sort of boxing club involving some of their students, and by the fact that those younger years were the golden age of the sport of boxing in France. Such nostalgic and idiosyncratic biographical facts, however, are in themselves insufficient to justify according such pride of place in the *Critique* to the phenomenology of boxing.

It now seems to me, after considerable reflection on Sartre's choice of this phenomenon, that it is not nearly so eccentric as at first appears. On the one hand, it must be remembered that Sartre's increasing insistence, in his later work and especially in Volume 2 of the *Critique*, on dealing with "singular universals" rather than large, general concepts meant that he needed to focus on a particular "incarnation" of violence in the real world rather than on a topic such as "violent sports" in general. Since boxing was a central sport in his time (as the joust had been in feudal times) and had the additional advantage of not involving complex interactions among players, the roles of "stars," and so on in the way in which team sports do, it was not an unreasonable choice. Today, in American society, football would undoubtedly be a better, even though more complicated, case to choose, while in Europe and much of the rest of the world soccer would be.

Now, it is not irrelevant that these sports do attract enormous public interest, as boxing did in Sartre's day. (He mentions, during his central discussion of "enveloping totalizations" in Volume 2, the societal implications of the diminished crowds attending boxing matches or going to the movies at times of rising political tensions, such as the day of the *Anschluss:* events in one sector of social life directly affect others.)[49] One has only to take note of the huge crowds that filled the streets of Paris, in almost farcical recreation of 1968, when the French team defeated the Brazilians in the World Soccer Cup semifinal match in June, 1986; or the recent history of enormous violence, intertwined with both national and class hostilities, wrought by segments of the British soccer public; or the statistics of viewership for televised American football, culminating in the almost unbelievable intensity of interest in the annual Super Bowl, far greater than that in Presidential elections. Just as important, one must be aware of the extent to which both political contests and even international negotiations are described, at least here in the United States, in sports terms with overtones going beyond mere metaphor: "President Bush scored a big hit over Gorbachev," and so on.

If all of this is "bizarre," as of course from certain points of view it surely is, then the word "bizarre" loses all meaning, because we are talking about central phenomena of our world. The ultimate point of Sartre's concentration on boxing at the outset of Volume 2 is to show the intelligibility and explicability, through numerous layers of analysis and from numerous perspectives, of what at first must indeed appear very bizarre: two men, each with his own objectives incompatible with the other's, accepting certain regulations and hitting each other as hard as possible in an enclosed space. Or two teams repeatedly tackling each other, and so on; it is roughly the same idea, though more complicated in actuality. But this, Sartre is saying and I now agree, precisely *is* our historical world as we experience it. True, other types of interactions do not so frequently involve *physical* assaults—though they are numerous enough, and even, for example within the family, far more numerous than has been recognized at least until recently—but overt or latent violence, on the model of the boxing match or the football game, dominates our lives even in everyday occurrences, much less on the stage of world history. This is, after all, just what the defenders of our increasingly dominant economic system, private enterprise capitalism, tout as its glory: fierce competition, with winners and losers. To try to insist against this backdrop that it is really love that makes the world go 'round, or something of the sort, is at best to be muddled and at worst to attempt to deceive one's readers or listeners for the advancement of one's own ideological interest. I conclude that Sartre was very clever to start his quest for historical intelligibility with the microcosmic paradox of two individuals "slugging it out," themselves already parts of a large institutional system, with its own rules and structures, known as world boxing.

Freedom and Necessity. It has become virtually a cliché to say that freedom plays a more limited role in the *Critique* than in Sartre's earlier work,[50] and this cliché has usually been based on Volume 1. In Volume 2, where history is finally confronted directly as an object of study, this appears even more evident. But once we probe beneath the level of cliché, what does this mean? I have already shown, in discussing core notions of Volume 1, some of the senses in which it is simply untrue, in which Sartre is as much the asserter of human freedom in his later work as he was in his earlier work. On the other hand, the word "freedom" is no doubt found much less frequently in Volume 2 than in earlier Sartrean writings, and the question as to whether Stalinism was in some important sense inevitable, at least given the goal of "socialization" supposedly leading to socialism, remains a salient one throughout the middle portion of that book.

One textual passage in particular crystallizes the issue. In it, Sartre begins by asking whether Stalin's personal idiosyncrasies could be said to have been necessary and points out that a defender of Stalin would reply to suggestions that Trotsky—more cultured, more intelligent, an excellent organizer—would have been a preferable leader by saying that perhaps this would have been so on a personal level but that under Trotsky the Russian Revolution would have gone the way of the Paris Commune. Whether this is correct or not, Sartre says, cannot be known, but in any case the situation demanded *some* leader with personal idiosyncrasies: it is only in this way that any common *praxis*—which, it must be remembered even in the absence of the word itself, begins as an expression of human freedom—can be realized in the real world: "Consequently the idiosyncratic determination of the totalizing praxis—and of the regime through it—is *inevitable,* although it remains, at the beginning, indeterminate." Of course, he continues, if the process of planned development of Soviet society could have been directed by an angel, then there would have been no rough edges: no mistakes, no pigheadedness, no brutality:

> But, precisely for this reason, angels are not individuals: they are abstract models of virtue and wisdom: in situation, the genuine individual, ignorant, disquieted, fallible, undone by the immediate urgency of dangers, will react (according to his or her history) at first too softly, then, at the point of being overwhelmed, too brutally. Those jolts, those accelerations, those brakings, those hairpin turns on horseback, those violences that characterize Stalinism were not all necessitated by the objectives and requirements of socialization:

however, they were inevitable inasmuch as that socialization required, in its first phase, to be directed by an individual.

We have reduced the role of accident without eliminating it: we have noted that the necessities of integration rendered that accident, whatever it was, *necessary*. It remains the case that the content of the accident does not appear determined by the requirement.[51]

This passage brings together, in an interesting way, Sartre's life-long fascination with "contingency," his constant stress on the importance of the individual, his *Critique* theme of realizing freedom (in however ultimately distorted a fashion) through common *praxis*, and his unswerving quest in Volume 2 to make history intelligible as human activity, however unsavory and unpleasant the piece of history under examination may be. Of course Sartre does not endorse an Hegelian view of history as directed toward a goal that is given in advance, even if that goal is said to be the maximum realization of freedom itself. There is no brooding, transcendent destiny or fate—indeed, no transcendence at all. But, given certain large objectives, what we can say is that the free realization of those objectives (or the failure to realize them, as the case may turn out to be) lies in the hands of fallible and inevitably idiosyncratic individuals. And this may entail horrifying results. This summary of Sartre's view of the way history operates brings us, finally, to the larger issue: what about the "large objectives"—in this crucial case, socialization supposedly leading to socialism—themselves? Are they necessitated? Is there a necessary pattern to history as a whole?

We have seen, often enough in the course of this study, that Sartre speaks openly about seeing history as one vast "totalization in course" and buttresses the plausibility of this vision with his references to the "One World" that we are increasingly becoming today. It has been obvious that socialism, in some minimally specified sense, plays a very large role in Sartre's understanding of where history appears to be moving and should be moving. At the same time, however, it should by now have become equally evident that he makes no claims, of the sort that Marxists used frequently to make, concerning the inevitable triumph of any version of socialism itself at some future historical *kairos:* he simply cannot do so within his theoretical framework, and so in a number of passages in his writings he stops with a question about what the future might hold. People simply might, he is forced to admit, just abandon the socialist vision entirely, as millions have in fact done—in a large measure as a result of the long Stalinist legacy, and perhaps increasingly so since the time of Sartre's death. He would have regarded this as a mistake, but as a very intelligible, understandable one. Even this abandonment, however, is for Sartre a part of the ongoing, enveloping historical totalization in which we are all caught up even as we collectively concoct it. (It also has something to do with the differences of *generations,* as more and more time passes since the original historical *praxis* of, for example, the Russian Revolution or of nineteenth-century workers' movements—an important notion to which, here as in some earlier writings that we have discussed, Sartre alludes without considering it in much detail.) And so we historians and philosophers of history—which means most of us, at least in certain moods, and not just professional thinkers—also go on distilling the meaning of that totalization, but without being able to get outside of it to see it as a fixed whole (totality) even up to now, much less from an end-of-time standpoint.

To view history in this way is not, however, to deny it all meaning; Sartre never abandoned the assumption that it is intelligible and hence that Camus's question as to whether it *had* a meaning, which presupposes a transcendent vantage point of some sort, was a senseless question. In fact, Sartre believes very strongly in the objectivity of history, albeit in a very complex sense, well captured in the following passage:

> Shall we say that there are *meanings* of the synchronic totalization and by no means *a single one*? As you will; or, if you prefer, there are in fact *various* meanings—and very different one from another—according to levels and sectors; but in each one, precisely, . . . the unity of the total meaning is rediscovered as its basis and its product. . . .
>
> The same reality will be *enveloping totalization* insofar as it is produced by the temporalization of historical agents and *meaning* insofar as it is reactualized by the work of the situated historian. But it must not be concluded from this that this *meaning* is relative to the knowledge that the historian assumes about it. . . . In short, each phase of an historical adventure has its own *taste* which is, in everyone, the objective presence of the whole. And this taste . . . is the actuality of the meaning. Consequently, it is not that the historian *constitutes* it: he confines himself to making it explicit.[52]

Those readers who are familiar with *Being and Nothingness* will recall that Sartre there designated the past as one element of what he called *facticity,* the totality of objective realities which designate the given situation in which I am condemned to exercise my freedom. In his philosophy of history, having developed a much more detailed and concrete awareness of the ways in which past and present situations are determined, Sartre still clearly adheres to the distinction between fact and fantasy (imagination), and he places history in the former category. But this is in no way equivalent, of course, to maintaining either that history is a domain of necessity from which human freedom is lacking, or that every totalizing historical group movement is just as good as every other.

What Might Have Been. This way of expressing the final set of questions that I wish to consider with respect to the philosophy of history portion of Sartre's political theory itself suggests fantasy. Where would Sartre have taken these analyses, had he continued them? Near the end of the text of Volume 2, the editor has included a one-half page outline by Sartre that furnishes us with what is very nearly our only certain indication of the answer to this question. It contains, first, three numbered items:

(1) Retotalization in a dictatorial society. (Stalin)
(2) Retotalization in a non-dictatorial society. Unity and class struggle. Already, problems.
(3) Retotalization of several related histories. (History of Europe, etc.—the proletariats and the proletariat): pure questioning as long as we don't know what History is.[53]

This is followed by cryptic mentions of several philosophical issues about history, notably the idea of infinity as its contrary, the importance of *death* as an historical constant, without which history would either be very different or not exist, and finally the question of the effect of human consciousness on historical *praxis*, ranging from the consciousness of a great thinker, such as Marx, to that of a premodern consciousness clouded by unscientific myths and superstitions.

Elsewhere in Volume 2, Sartre makes anticipatory references to the second part of his outline, having to do with how historical totalization takes place in a liberal democracy, as counterpart to a Stalinist-type society. Since, as we have seen, he refuses to generalize about "types" and instead insists on studying a "singular universal" instance, he would presumably have had to analyze the evolution of a particular liberal democracy during a particular historical period. This would have been *most* interesting, from the standpoint of political theory. It would also have been extremely arduous if it had been carried out, as one must assume it would have been, with the same rigor and attention to detail that Sartre devoted to his analysis of Stalin's regime during the 1930s. The latter, in a sense, was much easier, because sovereignty there was incarnated in a single human being; in the former, as Sartre noted, it would have been a question of studying "diffuse sovereignty," variously incarnated in a number of individuals.

As for the third part of the outline, which refers to the projected task of relating different but parallel national histories, with different and unevenly developed class structures, etc., we have very few clues indeed as to how Sartre would have undertaken it, other than a schematic outline, several pages long, of a projected history of Venice. Since this includes references going back as early as the fifth century A.D.,[54] and since Venice is only one of many national entities in European history, one that had lost virtually all larger historical importance by the early nineteenth century, we have some sense of the enormity of the prospect that Sartre found himself facing. Moreover (as if these considerations were not already enough to doom the project as hopeless!), Sartre was obviously beginning, by the time of writing of the *Critique,* to have a very strong sense of the importance of non-Western nations for history, especially, it goes without saying, for the history of today's "One World." A full implementation of his dialectical analysis would have entailed paying considerable attention to the increasing interrelationship of these nations with European history. (The latter presumably includes the Americas, North and South, although here we are confronted with the important issue of the Native American tribes, their conquest and genocide, etc., as an additional complexity.) Sartre was not aiming at writing a new "universal history," it is true, but the project of focusing in some detail on selected "singular universal" societies by way of contributing to the intelligibility of the totalization of history as an ongoing whole amounts to something that is even more ambitious than universal history writing as it has more conventionally been understood—e.g., in Toynbee's work.

Already in his middle age, engaged as he was in many other literary and political commitments, even Sartre, with his phenomenal energy and almost limitless capacity for writing, was not equal to the task that he had set himself. It would have entailed a great deal of research prior to the actual writing, as the study of Stalinism had already done. Rather than needing to ponder very long the question as to why he left the second volume of the *Critique* unfinished, we might rather feel some amazement that he carried it out as far as he did, particularly in his analysis of Stalinism. It is probably not altogether irrelevant that one of the themes mentioned by Sartre in the outline that I have cited is that of the phenomenon of death as related to history. Indeed, there is a very interesting, somewhat detached short discussion of "Death, experience of the Nothing-in-itself as shedding light on Being-in-itself: History with holes" in Volume 2; here, death, especially violent death, is seen as the clearest case of an historical totalization's turning into pure, inert Being-in-itself.[55] Here, too, one finds one of the most explicit linkages made by Sartre in all of his later writings to the theoretical framework of *Being and Nothingness,* and one also finds a very rare positive reference to the thought of Sartre's erstwhile intellectual comrade and later opponent, Raymond Aron. One need not be a professional psychoanalyst to remark that taking up the theme of death here evoked certain old associations in Sartre's thinking.

More to the point for our present purposes, attention to the theme of death no doubt helped Sartre to realize that his own finitude rendered highly improbable, if not totally impossible, any completion of his master-work of political theory, inextricably intertwined as he had demonstrated it to be with a philosophy of history, along the lines that he had laid down for himself. The result was that he turned to other projects, some complete but very brief (e.g., the preface to Fanon's *Les Damnés de la terre*), one incomplete but published and even lengthier than all that we have of the *Critique* (i.e., *The Family Idiot*), others lengthy but even now unpublished— many of them of some interest for filling out aspects of his political theory, but none of them of the same importance for that theory as the *Critique of Dialectical Reason.*

SIX

The Last Two Decades

In a certain sense, the 1960s constituted the Sartrean decade par excellence. The French war against Algeria, which had been such a central factor in the sense of depression under which Sartre had labored while furiously composing the *Critique,* and which was classical colonialism's (as distinguished from neocolonialism's) last great stand under the auspices of a major Western nation,[1] was resolved in favor of the Algerian natives. Both the Civil Rights movement in the United States in the early years of the decade and the wave of protests, usually based in student groups, against oppressive governmental policies and in favor of liberalization of various sorts the world over during the later 1960s can be seen as instantiations of the Sartrean description in the *Critique* of group formations overcoming seriality; their relative open-endedness and amorphousness seemed to vindicate his approach by comparison with the simplistic, unrealistic visions of clear-cut, surgical uprisings by the masses against the powerful few that had been encouraged by "orthodox" Marxist imagery. In fall 1963, *Les Temps Modernes* published in two installments what is arguably his greatest work from a literary point of view, *Les Mots.* (The book version appeared the following year.) In fall 1964, Sartre was named winner of the Nobel Prize for Literature, an honor that he declined on the ground that acceptance of what he saw as an increasingly politicized award might be interpreted as an act of complicity on his part. And so forth. In short, there was much that seemed to be going his way—in a certain sense.

In other senses, however, this first of the two decades between the publication of Volume 1 of the *Critique* (April 1960) and Sartre's death (April 1980) can just as easily be regarded as anticipating the more obvious phenomenon of decline, characterized by loss of eyesight and frequent incidents of other physical and even mental destablization that have been documented by de Beauvoir and others, of the 1970s. His living quarters were twice bombed by supporters of "Algérie Française" prior to the cessation of the hostilities. Charles De Gaulle, through whose wily duplicity (appearing as champion of these French "ultras," then negotiating with the Algerians) the war's end was effected, held a position of virtually dictatorial power in France until 1969; Sartre despised him. The Cuban Revolution, which had seemed to Sartre to hold so much promise, gradually degenerated into a repressive regime dominated by the Soviet model. The Soviet Union settled into the greyness and stagnation of the Brezhnev Era, perhaps the "highlight" of which was its crushing of the reform movement in Czechoslovakia in 1968. Meanwhile, the United States government had launched its ignominious and seemingly interminable military "escalation" in Vietnam. The 1968 demonstrations in Paris failed to fulfill their admittedly vague promise, in part because of the refusal of the declining but still-powerful French Communist Party to give them any support. In terms of intellectual fashion, the political theory of the *Critique* never achieved the popularity of Sartre's earlier existentialism, and versions of "structuralism," especially the "neo-Stalinist structuralism" (a label that I use as a reasonably accurate shorthand, but that the author himself would never accept) of Louis Althusser, became the rage for a relatively short time. (This ended, more or less, with the tumultuous events of '68, during which Althusser himself stood by the Party line.) In fact, the political and intellectual landscape especially after 1968 can be said to reflect Sartre's accounts of complex and degenerating social structures after the Apocalyptic moment of the "group in fusion," and ironically the Sartrean enterprise itself in its literary and other manifestations can be seen as an obvious part of this "degeneration."

This last, very impressionistic and "hindsight"-based remark should not be taken to imply that Sartre's writing abilities or intellectual acuity had already begun to diminish significantly before the onset of his most severe health problems in the early 1970s, nor that he had nothing more of importance to say. He was involved, perhaps more than ever before, in what might be called "celebrity globe-trotting," activities that are entirely understandable in light of his enormous fame and that at times resulted in significant lectures, such as the "Plaidoyer pour les intellectuels" that he presented in Japan. He devoted hundreds of pages to notes and a lesser but still significant amount of space to more polished analyses of issues in ethics, to which I shall give some attention here despite the tenuousness of what is as yet publicly known about them. Above all, in terms of his expenditure of writing time, he composed the three volumes and wrote notes towards a fourth volume of *The Family Idiot*, his last *magnum opus*, which was published in 1971 (Volumes 1 and 2) and 1972 (Volume 3).

Meanwhile, beginning in the late 1960s and in the aftermath of Sartre's and others' final and irreconcilable loss of all hope that the Communist movement could ever reverse its historical betrayal of the ideals of "socialism and freedom"—in other words, could ever return from the path of "deviation" depicted in the second volume of the *Critique*—he joined forces with some of the small Left groupings that were known as the "Maos." While he may legitimately be regarded as having shown courage in deciding to accept a couple of newspaper editorships for them as a way of blocking, by virtue of his personal prestige, French government moves to shut them down, as well as in "putting his body on the line" by distributing newspaper copies and participating in some demonstrations, the theoretical products of this last period of Sartre's active life are meagre both in quantity and, on the whole, in quality. Finally, prevented by his physical condition from venturing forth on his own in public, he began the taped collaboration with Benny Lévy (one of the former students and then "Mao" leaders) that was to be called *Pouvoir et liberté*, of which we at present have only the relatively brief pages that were published in *Le Nouvel Observateur* just before Sartre's death. It is with this mass of disparate and uneven material, as far as it has a bearing on Sartre's political theory, that I intend to come to grips in this last chapter.

Two brief articles testify to Sartre's increased interest, at least during the early part of the period now under discussion, in problems of the so-called Third World. They are his still rather famous preface to Frantz Fanon's *Les Damnés de la terre* (*The Wretched of the Earth*, the audience addressed in the first line of the anthem, the *Internationale*) and his less well remembered preface to a collection of speeches by the recently (1961) "executed" Congolese leader, Patrice Lumumba. The emphasis of the first,[2] in keeping with the emphasis of Fanon's book itself, is on the role of violence in both the maintenance of colonialism and its extirpation. Fanon was a psychiatrist, born in Martinique but living in Algeria and serving as a member of the provisional Algerian government during these last months of its successful revolution. He was therefore personally familiar with the practices of French colonialism on two continents and with its effects on the psyches of the colonized. Those who now criticize Sartre's acceptance in this essay of violence as (in the Engelsian phrase that he recalls) "the midwife of history" ought to reread the chronicles of the Algerian War as it was carried out both in Algeria (widespread practices of torture by the French Army) and in metropolitan France (the open campaign of terror, of which Sartre was one victim, carried on by the "Organisation de l'Armée Sécrète" against those relatively few who publicly opposed the French government's position)[3] in order to see whether such criticism makes any sense in light of the context. It was not a situation in which the techniques of nonviolent resistance, as they were then being preached by Martin Luther King in the American South, stood any chance of success. Sartre's concluding remarks about the "racist humanism" of both Europe and the United States seem to me simply to capture, with his usual bluntness, the existing situation— lofty, egalitarian rhetoric versus brutally oppressive reality—that was evident to all of us who witnessed it on both sides of the Atlantic.

"Lumumba and Neo-Colonialism," the preface to *The Political Thought of Patrice Lumumba*,[4] is interesting both as an expansion on the general theme of *neo*colonialism, already mentioned in the Fanon essay, and as a fairly detailed analysis of the situation and fate of that early leader of the Congo, just liberated from Belgian political domination, whose aspirations to guide this huge country in a direction away from continued Western economic control and exploitation ran afoul of many entrenched interests, including those of some of the new African petite bourgeoisie as well as those of the Belgian mine owners in Katanga. The book of speeches to which this serves as a preface was published in the series Présence Africaine, an important cultural outlet for forward-looking thinkers from the various former French-speaking African colonies. Sartre's treatment of Lumumba is more dispassionate than hagiographic, as he compares his predicament to that of Robespierre in attempting to create a national unity and consensus amid complicated circumstances following a major upheaval, and being frustrated and ultimately removed from the scene and killed. Sartre also compares Lumumba's attempts to centralize control of his country with the more successful efforts of Fidel Castro in Cuba, suggesting that an identification between national unity and the common interest is feasible only in the aftermath of a socialist revolution,[5] which the Congolese uprising against Belgian rule had not been. Essentially, this piece of Sartre's is more an examination of failed strategies than a highly theoretical work; its interest for us here lies primarily in the demonstrated awareness, on Sartre's part, of the fact that the One World of the future will no longer be Eurocentric, with all that this may imply for rethinking sociopolitical theory itself. Unfortunately, Sartre was not to follow up on this thinking in any significant or extensive way, even if "his heart was in the right place."[6]

Instead, one of Sartre's more important initiatives during the early 1960s was his involvement with some of the leading intellectuals of the Italian Communist Party, open as they were, in contrast to their French counterparts, to less "orthodox" variants of Marxist thinking and hence to Sartre's philosophy. Sartre and de Beauvoir were already frequent visitors, as tourists, to Italy and especially Rome, and Sartre apparently had a reasonably good comprehension of spoken Italian. In late 1961 he gave a brief talk on the problem of subjectivity within Marxist thought at the Istituto Gramsci in Rome and stayed to participate in a three-day seminar there, speaking French himself and responding to the Italian of his hosts, who by and large appear to have understood him. They found intriguing comparisons between his insistence that there is always a subjective moment, that is, a way in which an individual, with all his or her personal history, interiorizes and lives objective reality, and the early insistence of Antonio Gramsci himself on the role of specific cultural factors in accounting for the way in which hegemony is exercised in a particular place at a particular time. The group achieved agreement, after some initial skepticism about Sartre on the part of some, in totally rejecting deterministic interpretations of Marxism. Meanwhile, Sartre alluded at several points to the need, as he perceived it, for a Marxian ethics or even "axiology" (including, for example, a theory about aesthetic values), owing nothing to Kant's idealism but focused on the idea, which finds its most famous formulation in Kant, that "ought implies can."[7]

The theme of subjectivity is again prominent, but this time less *eo nomine*, in a rather sympathetic lecture given by Sartre in April 1964 concerning one of Western philosophy's greatest proponents of subjectivity, Soren Kierkegaard. The occasion was a UNESCO-sponsored conference on

Kierkegaard. Sartre entitled his talk "L'Universel singulier" and proceeded to dismiss as irrelevant the reductionist sort of Marxist treatment of Kierkegaard that would focus on such points as his wealthy family background, his approval of the Danish monarchy, and so on. None of this, he says, captures Kierkegaard as an unique individual, who was also "the first, perhaps," to have "shown that the universal enters as singular into History, to the extent to which the singular establishes itself there as universal."[8] This piece thus enunciates in clear terms the most central theme of *The Family Idiot*, namely, the sense in which no amount of universalistic labeling can capture the uniqueness of any individual, such as Flaubert, even though neither Kierkegaard nor Flaubert nor Sartre can be understood in abstraction from his particular historical circumstances. By the same token, however, through its thematic deflection of focus away from Kierkegaard's own obsessive insistence on "the subject" toward the formula of "the singular universal," it points to the part played by Sartre in the so-called death of the subject that was to become such a familiar topic of philosophic and literary discussion a decade or two later.

There is something of a paradox involved here, but Sartre and probably even Kierkegaard himself would trace the paradoxicality to the nature of human existence. From his earliest writings on, certainly including *Being and Nothingness*, Sartre consistently refused to treat any human "subject" as substantially, permanently identifiable as a fixed "personality" or ego. On the other hand, he has rightly been considered a leading proponent of the indispensable importance of the human individual, hence of the "subjective moment," in society and history. In a 1965 interview with Pierre Verstraeten, he went so far as to say: "But you know, I use the notion of subjectivity rarely except in order to set limits, to say 'this is only subjective,' 'I have no element sufficient to . . . ,' etc., but for me subjectivity doesn't exist, there is only interiorization and exteriority."[9] While one must somewhat discount an offhand remark in an interview, and while explicit references to "subjectivity" are not exactly "rare" (depending on one's measure of "rarity") in certain Sartrean texts, the kernel of truth in this comment should not be overlooked. The notion of the singular universal was to become Sartre's preferred formula for preserving the role of the individual against all sorts of scientific, Marxist, and (later) structuralist reductionisms preaching gospels of pure objectivity, while at the same time avoiding the undesirable and philosophically indefensible ontological conceptions of "the subject" that have pervaded so much of modern Western thought.

But Sartre apparently continued to be tempted, at least as I read him primarily at secondhand, by another of the shibboleths of modern Western philosophy, the belief in the possibility of a systematic ethics. We saw this temptation surface at points in his *Cahiers pour une morale*. In his 1961 appearance in Rome, he actually lamented the lack of a Marxist "axiology." And even in his spring 1964 presentation of the outline of what is often called his "dialectical ethics" back at the Gramsci Institute in Rome, he again, according to Professors Stone and Bowman, called for the generation of a socialist value theory. However, the actual outcome of what he wrote for that occasion as well as for his eventually aborted Cornell University lectures that were to have been given a little less than a year later does not apparently amount to anything approaching an axiology, or constellation of allegedly supreme values; indeed, it seems to reinforce the impression that any such enterprise, if literally understood, would be quixotic and doomed to irrelevance, at least in the form in which he would have undertaken it.

The opening sentence of this "lecture" of more than 100 pages (through all of which, according to eyewitnesses, Sartre actually ran in some way, turning over many pages and omitting many subsections en route in order to stay within a reasonable time frame) is cited by Stone and Bowman. It is interesting and suggestive: "Our meeting proves that the historical moment has arrived for socialism to rediscover its ethical structure, or, rather, to remove its veils from it."[10] This sentence calls attention to the context, a meeting sponsored by the Italian Communist Party, which will help to account especially for the unusual attention paid by Sartre in the fourth and final section to questions of party discipline, of the limited conditions under which terrorist actions may be permissible, and of deficiencies of a system in which self-criticism is confined to the leadership alone. It also suggests a certain megalomania, absent both from the *Critique* before it and from the many interviews given by Sartre in later years, in Sartre's stance of the time: he is about to reveal the hitherto hidden ethical core of socialism, which underlay the spirit of the revolutionaries of 1848, albeit in an idealistic form, as he goes on to say, but which has lain dormant and "gone on vacation" under the maleficent influence of Stalinism. Finally, there is the allusion to the *structure* of socialist ethics, a term sufficiently close to "axiology" to rekindle alarm about the possibility that Sartre may be planning to produce a new list of ethical commandments. (I shall say nothing about the possible sexism involved in the metaphor of removing veils.)

By contrast with the Promethean tone of the brief opening section of this lecture, the next section exhibits the paradigmatic Sartrean insistence, to which I have called attention on a number of previous occasions, on seeking to begin with lived experience—in this case, the experience of ethical norms and of ethics in general. (This will also, as we shall see, be a salient part of the unpublished Cornell lectures, in which Sartre actually refers to this move to ethical experience as a phenomenological one.) Part of this second section of the Rome lecture was actually published some years ago, under the limp title of "Determinism and Freedom," as one of the appendices to Contat and Rybalka's bibliography. It begins, oddly but less grandiosely, as follows:

What is ethical experience? Let us begin by eliminating the *imperative moralities* (Kant, Nietzsche, etc.): they all tend to explain moral experience, to unify the empirical prescriptions of their time, to rearrange the "tables of values" or the imperatives, by objectifying subjective and basic impulses in a moral (and by that token universal) form.

(The oddness, in my view, lies in Sartre's categorizing Nietzsche in this way.) Instead we must, he continues, deal with human beings as social, in their everyday work situations.[11] The first example that he takes is from a survey of students at a French girls' high school which showed that the vast majority (95%) agreed that one must not lie, but that 50 percent of them said that they themselves lied frequently, and only 10 percent said that they never did. This shows that ethical norms are generally perceived as unconditional, but also that they are far removed from the daily life practices of vast numbers of people.

Sartre does much more with another example, which is omitted from the Contat and Rybalka volume but with which Stone and Bowman deal extensively.[12] It is taken from a then-recent news story about a group of mothers in Liège, Belgium, who had while pregnant taken a prescription drug (thalidomide, under the brand name of Softénon) that turned out to produce severe deformities in their infants. The mothers then made the decision to commit infanticide. It is through analyzing various aspects of this story—the clash with traditional moral values, the middle-class backgrounds of most of the mothers, the problem of failed medical technologies, etc.—that Sartre develops the single central theme of this lecture, which Stone and Bowman characterize as "making the human," that is, acting now in such a way as to move toward a possible "human" future in which we (or future generations) shall be freed from structures of dominance and subordination and able freely to control our own lives, to "be our own products."

This lofty ethical goal incorporates, for Sartre, several corollary notions. Most central among them, in the Stone/Bowman account, are the conjoined values of autonomy and need satisfaction—the first reminiscent, of course, of the Kantian ethic as well as of Sartre's career-long emphasis on freedom, the second crucial in the Marxist understanding of human beings as material entities. At the same time, it is understood that the realization of this conjuncture is a sociohistorical task—that is, an attainable goal only through a common effort of many individuals across time. It is for this reason that the Rome lectures, while they are ostensibly about ethics, must also be regarded as providing an important perspective on Sartre's evolving political theory. Their tone, it is evident, is far more optimistic, in the superficial sense of displaying a belief in the real possibility of radical transformation toward a more "human" society in the future, than is the *Critique*, especially its second volume. Toward the end of his Rome talk, Sartre admits that there will always remain some practico-inert elements in any socialist society and contrasts such a society, in terms reminiscent of the most utopian strains of the early Marx, with a communist society in which there would be some sort of total autonomy. Although in general I am supportive of Sartre's explorations of "limiting case" situations such as this Marxian notion of an ultimate communist society, in this particular instance I find it unhelpful because too brief and, it would appear, too vague. In fact it must necessarily remain vague, because Sartre continues to stress as much here as elsewhere in his writings that the future can only be constructed by free human *praxis* and is therefore in no sense determined or predictable.

More satisfactory to my mind than such traces of dizzying speculation about a distant and indefinite future is the third and longest section of the Rome lecture notes, in which Sartre takes the evolution of the Algerian Revolution as a case study of a particular society's process of self-humanization. Here he identifies three historical stages from the time of definitive French conquest in the nineteenth century to the point of French defeat in the twentieth. They are, as Stone and Bowman reconstruct them, first blind revolt against dispossession of lands, next efforts at assimilation with a view to obtaining the colonizers' approval, and finally "the dialectic of the impossible," which eventually leads to emancipation despite the realistic recognition, at the beginning of this stage, of the overwhelming odds against success.[13] At the end of this final stage, however, Sartre shows a frank awareness of the problems that remain for the successful revolutionaries in Algeria, beginning with the tensions between the demands of their radically new situation and traditionalist calls to return to the past through such practices as (for women) wearing a veil and so forth. In short, far from offering a ready-made axiology to his Rome audience, Sartre presented it with useful insights into ethico-political complexities and dilemmas, with special reference to the case of a recently successful revolution that had broad popularity.

As Sartre was presumably working, later in that same year of 1964, on the lectures that he had agreed to give at Cornell, he submitted to an interview, most interesting in light of future events, that was published in *Le Nouvel Observateur* and later reprinted in *Situations* VIII under the title "The Alibi."[14] The issue, as posed by the interviewer, was the strong feeling of "depoliticization" in France at the time, especially among the young. Sartre's responses are generally judicious and commonsensical (after all, he replies, the intensity of the Algerian conflict is only two years behind us, and in any case the degree of depoliticization now is not at all comparable to the extremely depoliticized climate that prevailed among us just prior to World War II, etc.), but a contemporary reader is likely to be surprised by this report of what the intellectual atmosphere was like just before the dramatic escalation of U.S. military activity in Vietnam and only three and a half years before the intensely political period of spring 1968.

The Cornell notes continue a number of the themes raised in the Rome lecture, according to Stone and Bowman, even to the point of elaborating at greater length on one of the case studies broached there, that of the survey of high school girls concerning lying. The Cornell material is, however, more obviously fragmentary and also not quite so optimistic in tone—in keeping, Stone and Bowman speculate, with the differences between the two intended audiences.[15] It is in any case surely not unrelated to the identity of his planned audience that Sartre wrote, as part of these notes, a substantial analysis of the West Virginia Democratic Party Presidential primary contest of 1960 between Hubert Humphrey and John Kennedy. This segment has been translated by Elizabeth Bowman. I shall not attempt here to reproduce the Stone/Bowman summary of these lectures as a whole, the only such summary available to the public, except to cite their report of Sartre's planned outline. I find this outline exceptionally interesting, particularly because of the additional light that it sheds on Sartre's methodological approach to ethics in late 1964, and suggestive:

> In the case of *Morality and History* [the title that Stone and Bowman have given to these notes, on the basis of a newspaper reference to *Morale et histoire* as the proposed title of the Cornell lectures on the occasion of their cancellation] Sartre sets himself five tasks regarding moral phenomena: (1) to describe and fix ethical conducts and structures with their specific characteristics; (2) to ascertain, really as an extension of (1), whether ethics possesses its own efficacity in the evolution of a practical ensemble; (3) to elucidate the foundations of ethical conducts and their internal laws; (4) to effect, through rigorous mediations, a progressive synthesis of the various foundational structures in an enriched account of the contemporary practical agent; and (5) to grasp the moral problem as it is manifested to this agent.[16]

The first two tasks, they say, are phenomenological preliminaries, the third is the "regressive" part of the analysis strictly speaking, and the last two are the "progressive" parts. The notes contain little or nothing, it would seem, of this last part. On the other hand, they contain some interesting analyses of ethical phenomena, such as imperatives in everyday life (on signs, in newspapers, etc.) and an important extended case study of the ethical situation of persons undergoing torture.

The Kennedy-Humphrey primary analysis is presented, very significantly in terms of Sartre's overall political theory, as a clear refutation of the "orthodox" Marxist view of ethics as merely superstructural, having no real influence on historical events. The outcome, on the other hand—a Kennedy victory, which in fact was pivotal in his successful campaign to become President—also seems to Sartre to prove that a purely ethical posture, divorced from sociopolitical considerations, has only very limited efficacy. The situation, as he very plausibly analyzes it, was that West Virginia (Sartre apparently refers to it as "Wisconsin" in his notes, but there is no doubt that this is simply a slip and that he *means* West Virginia) was an overwhelmingly Protestant state in which the primary elections happened to fall at a time at which the fact of Kennedy's being a Catholic had become a central issue. Kennedy of course maintained that that should make no difference to voters, but there were those who insisted that no committed Catholic could possibly uphold, as President, the Constitutional separation of Church from state.[17] Kennedy therefore pitched his appeal to the moral virtue of tolerance, in effect making the election a referendum on West Virginians' morality in this regard. Humphrey, who did not wish to capitalize on intolerance, was effectively neutralized. Whether or not this amounted to a clever, manipulative maneuver on the part of the Kennedy camp, Sartre argues, is beside the point. The unconditional norm of tolerance—which, as he points out, may prevail in a stable society like the American one, but may in other historical situations be inappropriate or irrelevant—exerted historical efficacy here. One by-product of this concentration on the purely ethical, however, was that the very pressing needs of the people of one of the country's poorest and most depressed states received virtually no attention, either during the campaign or after the Presidential election. Moreover, as Sartre remarks presciently near the end, Kennedy turned out to be a man of his class, dedicated to continuing postwar American imperialist policies, as illustrated by his attempted invasion of Cuba and his getting "the United States bogged down in its *colonialist* politics in South Vietnam."[18] Thus the serious limitations of "pure ethics" in separation from politics are richly exemplified in this case.

In February 1965, shortly before Sartre was to have completed the preparation of these lectures and flown to the United States, the U.S. government initiated its dramatic military escalation by bombing North Vietnamese territory in response to a successful new antigovernment military initiative in the South. (The Gulf of Tonkin episode of the previous summer had been the prelude to this, eliciting a *carte blanche* from the Congress that enabled President Johnson to proceed with impunity, but nothing of great significance had taken place during the intervening half year.) Sartre made the decision to cancel his trip, much to his would-be hosts' dismay. There was widespread disappointment. His judgment was debatable; did he not have some obligation—as a member of the Cornell lecture committee, Professor Grossvogel, who happened to be in Paris at the time and wrote an open letter to Sartre on the subject, maintained—to recognize and appear in solidarity with the then-minority of American academic personnel and others who were opposed to this escalation? Instead, according to Grossvogel, Sartre had chosen, illegitimately, to "remain pure."[19] Neither Sartre's prior explanation, in an interview in *Le Nouvel Observateur* that concludes by pointing out that the United States is not the center of the world and that the Third World must be considered and respected,[20] nor his very perfunctory open reply to Grossvogel is, in my view, very satisfactory. This does not mean, however, that I am convinced that his decision was wrong—merely that he did not defend it well. The fact is, from my vantage point as one who foresaw much of what was to come by way of future escalation when I joined in protesting the government's action during the February week in question, that the majority of

Americans even at the universities did not recognize the significance of their government's decision in initiating the chain of cataclysmic events— this language is not excessive—that were to follow. Some dramatic gestures and outcries that would attract media attention were needed to call the attention of larger numbers of people to the impending menace, and Sartre's gesture was one such. On the other hand, one must still wonder, in retrospect, whether it could have taken some other form that would not have involved breaking his agreement to appear and depriving the American audience of his reflections on (what irony!) the paradoxes of morality in a sociopolitical context.

This episode sets the background for Sartre's subsequent involvement in protesting against the American military actions in Vietnam, which culminated in his participation in the "war crimes tribunal" organized by the nonagenarian British philosopher, Bertrand Russell, in 1967. The tribunal unanimously found the American side guilty of gross violations of international law and achieved at least some success by serving as the occasion, through the large amount of evidence that it elicited, for the Pentagon to admit publicly for the first time that it was indeed employing antipersonnel bombs. On the whole, however, it would seem that its accomplishments in changing people's minds were probably not enormous, given the private nature of the organization of the tribunal and the fact that, although in interviews of the time Sartre stressed both their initial openness to a verdict of not guilty and the initial differences among them especially on procedural questions, the members of the jury had been rather carefully selected to exclude defenders of the American government's posture. To the opponents of that posture, and in particular to those increasing numbers of individuals who had recently switched from support to opposition, the Russell Tribunal proceedings amounted to preaching to the converted. Nevertheless, from the standpoint of our interest in Sartre's political theory, the literature surrounding his participation in that jury, though meager, offers several valuable insights.

In response to a number of contemporary criticisms to the effect that this enterprise is putting too much emphasis on legalisms, a typically petit-bourgeois perspective, Sartre straightforwardly acknowledges that it is the petite bourgeoisie—that is, in more modern language, ordinary middle class citizens—whom the tribunal intends above all to address and, if possible, to convince. Moreover, he remarks, in the present conjuncture it happens that *international* law, unlike typical petit bourgeois legislation, serves popular needs.[21] We are reminded here both of Sartre's earliest published essay on theories of international law, a topic on which he had not focused in print for about forty years, and of the generally inhibitory role that he assigns to *Droit* in most of those subsequent writings in which he mentions it. Here, however, in his commentary on the Russell Tribunal, he lauds the expression of what he regards as the will of the working classes to support a *jus contra bellum* as a victory for *popular* Law or Right against the manipulation of more ordinary national laws by dominant interests with a view to continuing the conflict.[22]

A blatant example of such manipulation, of which Sartre had already seen a great deal in the course of the Algerian struggle and was to see considerably more in the course of the French government's gradual suppression of "Mao" activities through arrests and litigation in the post-1968 period, was the action taken by President De Gaulle to ban the holding of a second Russell Tribunal session in France. (The Swedish government had allowed the first, and subsequently permitted the second, to be held in Stockholm.) One of the members of the jury, Vladimir Dedijer of Yugoslavia, had applied to the French consulate in London for a longer-term visa in preparation for the anticipated session. The French government responded by canceling even his transit visa. Apparently somewhat shocked by this, Sartre wrote a very "correct" appeal to De Gaulle to reverse this action. De Gaulle himself responded quite negatively, showing clearly that, despite his publicly-expressed disapproval of the United States government's conduct of the war, he deferred to that government's assumed military prerogatives and loathed the notion of a private tribunal's attempting to "meddle" in such matters. Although it was De Gaulle's quaint, at once slightly deferential and slightly mocking, epistolary salutation, "Mon cher Maître," and Sartre's tart comment that no one but café waiters who knew of his fame as a writer ever called him "maître" (master) that attracted the greatest attention in this exchange, what is much more interesting about it is its way of clearly drawing the lines between quintessential Gaullism and Sartrean philosophy.

One sentence in De Gaulle's letter, characterized as it is by his usual orotund, ultra-paternalistic and slightly old-style prose, captures this divide: "It is not to you," he writes, "that I shall teach that all justice, both in its principle and in its execution, belongs only to the State."[23] Needless to say, Sartre rejected this proposition in his reply, remarking, in the philosophically unsubtle, more popular language that is suited to interviews and public exchanges but that can be misleading when taken to be of equivalent importance with his written texts, that true justice is derived at once from the State and from the masses, as was the case at the time of the French Revolution.[24] (As we shall see, Sartre was to take this sentence of De Gaulle's as the key "text" for his 1972 lecture, "Justice et état.") In his published statements concerning the activity of the Russell Tribunal itself, Sartre more than once cloaks its activities in the conceptual mantle, so very dear to President De Gaulle himself, of *legitimacy*, implicitly invoking a supposedly fundamental distinction between (in this case, revolutionary) legitimacy and (petit-bourgeois) legality that has been employed by political theorists of very different persuasions.[25] Against De Gaulle's insistence on arrogating all legitimacy to the State, Sartre's counterassertion of the "legitimacy" of the Russell Tribunal makes considerable sense as a slogan; but serious philosophical questioning of the very notion of legitimacy is necessarily absent from this exchange.

A final, salient feature of Sartre's writings and interviews concerning the Vietnam War is the extent to which the intertwining of ethical with political values becomes increasingly evident to him: morality and politics are virtually (but never, of course, for reasons suggested in the analysis of the West Virginia primary, entirely and absolutely) one. During the same period other forums, notably the series of invited lectures in Japan that is entitled "Plea for Intellectuals" (fall 1965), produced clarifications of Sartre's political vision for the future as well as a reaffirmation of his belief that true intellectuals must have a commitment to revolutionary change. In these lectures, which begin by tracing the rise of intellectuals as a discernible group in Europe and go on to consider their social function and then the specific case of the writer as an intellectual, a major distinction is drawn, in light of the notion of the singular universal, between complicitous ("false") intellectuals who claim that we already live in the era of universality and the "true" ones who oppose all monopolies of power in the name of an *effort of universalization* directed toward the as yet unachieved One World. At the end of the second of these three lectures, which is probably the most important, Sartre places special insistence on the role of the true intellectual, by virtue of his or her contradictory status of being privileged and solitary and yet in solidarity with the exploited, as

> guardian of *democracy:* he challenges the abstract character of the rights of bourgeois "democracy" not in that he might want to suppress them but because he wants to complete them with the concrete rights of socialist democracy by conserving, in all democracy, the *functional* truth of freedom.[26]

In other words, the liberal distinction, as Rawls was to draw it a few years later, between freedom and the function or "worth" of freedom[27] is virtually meaningless, inasmuch as abstract freedom that cannot be utilized concretely is without practical significance; but this does not entail disregarding or discarding liberal rights. This is one of Sartre's simplest and clearest pronouncements on this set of issues.

The year 1968 was, as I have already indicated, a turning-point—probably the last significant turning-point except for the onset of his lengthy final period of illness and nearly total blindness—in Sartre's life, as it was in so many others' lives as well. There is, to my mind as to Sartre's, an important distinction between the student-dominated uprising in Paris and the somewhat broader-based upheaval in Czechoslovakia, even though one can also find a number of connections between them. (The much smaller student uprising in Yugoslavia, which like the others brought repression by the authorities in its wake, strikes me as an interesting intermediate phenomenon between these two, but Sartre only mentions it in passing.) Although geography dictated that it would be the French events that would involve Sartre personally, not only at the time but also in their aftermath by virtue of his activities with the "Mao" groups that were formed then, I find this relatively brief analysis of the Czech events, written as a preface to a collection of testimonials by Czech intellectuals that was published in 1970, more interesting and significant from the standpoint of his political theory than all of his comments about the implications of the Paris May. I shall therefore discuss this analysis first.

"The Socialism That Came from the Cold," the title of this essay, refers to the Soviet style of socialism, derived from the peculiar circumstances of a successful socialist revolution in a backward, peasant country, that was blindly imposed on the relatively advanced and industrialized Czech economy in 1948. Nowhere is Sartre's ultimate judgment about "the system," the rigid and deviated socialism practiced in the USSR and the countries within its orbit, expressed more mordantly than in this essay. He recalls reassurances given by Soviet acquaintances at the beginning of the decade of the 1960s to the effect that improvements would take time but that the process of lifting that system out of its dark ages was "irreversible": "I sometimes have the feeling," he says, "that nothing was irreversible except the implacable and continual deterioration of Soviet socialism."[28] He praises the thirteen witnesses cited in the volume, including Milan Kundera and Vaclav Havel, whose sense of realism as a result of their experiences put them in a very different place in 1968 from persons in the West, preoccupied as we are with our neuroses rather than with problems of material well-being.[29] The Czechs, he says, have "had it" both with Marxism, given the kind of Marxism that has been served to them, and with humanism, given the regime of lies and failed promises in which they have been living.

Yet what was the envisaged goal of the "Prague Spring," Sartre asks, as reflected in the statements of these writers? It was not, he says, "the return of bourgeois liberalism but, since truth is revolutionary, to vindicate the revolutionary right to speak the truth."[30] They were not, of course, clear concerning all the details of the future Czech society as they wished it to be, and there were various tendencies among them. The Yugoslav example showed that self-management would remain a dead-letter idea as long as political control remained concentrated in the hands of a privileged minority. "But," Sartre adds, "one cannot doubt, either, that they were attempting to *realize socialism* by liquidating the system and establishing new relations of production."[31] Unfortunately, as we all know, they were crushed by counterrevolution, just as *Pravda* claimed, but with one small qualification: it was the Soviet leaders, not the Czechs, who were the counterrevolutionaries. He concludes by speculating bitterly on the possibility of a Western imperialist alliance with the USSR to "maintain order everywhere" and laments that he and others sign protest after protest and will no doubt continue to do so, but it does not make any difference.

It is for me an extreme, and extremely gratifying, irony that the days (in late November 1989) during which I have been reflecting on this very significant little essay—significant not just for understanding Sartre's thought, but for understanding a great deal about the general evolution of

French and European consciousness over the past two decades—and writing the above paragraphs have been precisely the days of revolutionary upheaval in Czechoslovakia. The Soviet leader, Gorbachev, has very deliberately recalled the slogan of the Prague Spring, "socialism with a human face," which appears to have influenced his own thinking over the years, and Vaclav Havel has reappeared as spokesperson for the successful popular opposition to the hapless heirs of the August 1968 repression. Alexander Dubček, who was deposed as prime minister at that time, has reappeared in the public forum and has suggested that his vision of socialism still has merit; Havel, on the other hand, had demurred at even employing the word "socialism" because of the terrible abuses that it has been used to justify during the intervening time. One wonders how Sartre himself, who, as I have pointed out in discussing *Search for a Method*, was to give up identifying his worldview with "Marxism" in part for reasons similar to Havel's in the case of "socialism," would have responded to the widespread loss of confidence in the value of the latter term that Havel's remark reflects. At any rate, as we shall see, Sartre certainly did not suffer such a loss of confidence with respect to socialism during the period immediately preceding his physical decline, and indeed was to use this word more frequently in his long dialogues of the early 1970s than in any of his earlier writings or published remarks. If still alive today he would not, I am convinced, have endorsed a restoration of bourgeois liberalism, a development that appears to enjoy wide support among the new leadership in Poland and Hungary, if not elsewhere in Eastern Europe and the Soviet Union. But his feelings of total despair about "the socialism that came from the cold," Soviet socialism, as revealed in this essay are a *cri de coeur* that in retrospect speaks volumes about the highly volatile state of current political thinking at all levels, from technical (as is to be found, for example, in the *Critique*) to popular.

One of the changes in Sartre's own approach to political thinking that the crucial year of 1968 brought about, as we turn now from the aftermath of the Czech events to the effect on Sartre of events in Paris, was, as I analyze it, a noticeable loss of respect for the value of what I have just called more "technical," or "professional," writing—with the salient exception, to which his new "Maoist" friends frequently alluded with some disdain, of his work on Flaubert. Sartre, by no means unique in this respect, underwent a lifestyle change, dressing less formally than in the past and apparently finding great enjoyment in the company of these much younger people, mostly men, well read but often with only what might at most be called (I say this without intending to be pejorative, but simply as a statement of fact) the equivalent of a good undergraduate education, whom he addressed by the familiar second person singular pronoun, "tu", rather than the more traditional "vous." His looser, less complex way of dealing with questions of political theory is in large measure a reflection of this new milieu and of its members' attitudes.

In one of the recorded and later published conversations with Pierre Victor (the pseudonym of Benny Lévy) and Philippe Gavi that have the collective title *On a raison de se révolter* ("People Are Right to Revolt") Sartre reflects with what seems to be great candor and openness on an event during this period that proved to be very significant for him. It was a special meeting of students and some Sorbonne faculty members that had been called in response to certain repressive measures on the government's part; he was invited to speak at it. This was an action meeting where specific measures were to be decided, rather than the pure protest type of gathering with which he was familiar, and as he began he was handed a note saying "Sartre, be brief" in the familiar (and therefore, given the traditional hierarchical assumptions of French language usage, highly impolite) imperative. "It's beginning badly," he said to himself. Later (we may omit the other details), he began to reflect on the experience and came— only gradually, as he recounts it in December 1972—to realize just what had been wrong. First, he had had no real business there: he was neither a student nor a professor, and he was not involved in the proposed actions. He had been invited simply as a "star," because of his name recognition, and his talk had been about general universal "problems of youth," of no interest to the audience. In short, he had acted there like the "classical intellectual," for whom in the new, proto-revolutionary situation, as he now understood it, there was really no place.[32]

The contrast between the classical and the revolutionary intellectual is one of several themes that are repeated often in the publications of Sartre (other than the work on Flaubert), most though not all originating in the form of interviews or conversations, that date from the period between 1968 and 1974. They do not represent a *sharp* break with his past thinking about political topics, except, of course, as far as the possible future role of the Communist Party is concerned, and yet the context has changed radically as a result of '68. In these texts, Sartre frequently employs some of the technical terminology and ideas of the *Critique,* such as "seriality" and "groups," the sovereignty of the individual, the critical analysis of bureaucratic stagnation, and so on, but he usually does so in order to apply them simply and straightforwardly to the existing historical situation. For example, in one of the earliest of these interviews (June 1968), he speaks of having felt himself more "sovereign" when addressing a group of students (on a different occasion from the notorious one that I mentioned earlier) on terms of equality than he had ever felt as an all-powerful and (at least initially) feared high school instructor, exercising "rightful" authority over his pupils, in his earlier years.[33] (In the context and specifically in response to the interviewer's next question, this leads him to reflect on the possible desirability of combining studies with manual labor, as was said to be the practice in Cuba and China. This is one of the earliest indications of the attraction that the *notion* of the Chinese Cultural Revolution, so little understood then by Westerners, by contrast with its really brutal details that have since become universally known, was to exert on him and especially on his future "Maoist" friends.) He thus articulates what he now considers to be the practical implication of his past theoretical reflections on "sovereignty" as rooted in the individual: namely, to motivate working toward an egalitarian, radically anti-hierarchical, democratic society, of the type that he will later call "direct democracy,"[34] in which the problem of unequal *power*, now seen as more central and more serious than that of property, will become susceptible of resolution.[35] At the same time, this 1968 text also points to the rationale for the announced theme of the book *Pouvoir et liberté* that Sartre and Lévy were to attempt to coauthor some years later, after the onset of Sartre's blindness.

One of the latest of the published dialogues with Lévy ("Victor") and Gavi provides considerable insight into the direction that this book would no doubt have taken. A recurrent theme in Sartre's remarks throughout these dialogues is that in these last years he has come back more strongly than ever to his early insistence on freedom, though now it must of course be understood in a group context. In the dialogue entitled "La liberté retrouvée" ("Freedom Rediscovered"), Lévy asks Sartre, quite reasonably, to clarify the distinction between the freedom that he posits as social goal, on the one hand, and the "free" exercise of coercion over others by those who have power, on the other. The latter, Sartre says, is not freedom, because by eliminating others' freedom one makes oneself unfree; freedom, on the other hand, does give one power, but precisely *not* the power of coercion.[36] This exchange leads immediately, as so often happens in these dialogues, to a discussion of socialism. Here, in a remarkable passage, Sartre says:

> Socialism really only has meaning as the dreamed-of but in fact poorly conceived state in which man will be free, and what people who want socialism are looking for, whether or not they say so, is that state of freedom. Consequently, the revolutionary man of whom we were speaking is a man who conceives freedom as the genuine reality of a future, socialist society.[37]

He then goes on to distinguish between this state of freedom and a society, such as that of the USSR, in which everyone does what he or she is told and there is no freedom, no socialism, only alienation on a vast scale.

Sartre's renewed emphasis on alienation and the need to overcome it is another theme that finds frequent expression during this period. In a 1969 interview with the Italian Communist newspaper, *Il Manifesto*, he speaks of his increasing perception, which we have already noted in his remarks on the contrast between Czechs' principal concerns and those of Western Europeans, that basic *needs* and their satisfaction are no longer always the principal problem, since need-satisfaction can now sometimes be benignly integrated within an advanced capitalist system; rather, the focus of concern in such a system must be on alienation.[38] Moreover, he continues, he does not share the views of those who think that advanced capitalism is at bay. It is interesting to contrast his remarks in this interview with his lecture on Marxism and ethics, presented in the same city, Rome, only five years earlier, in which he had invoked the satisfaction of needs as a starting-point.

But if this readjustment away from needs, at least those of a material sort, as a focal point constitutes a certain change of direction in Sartre's thinking about the more affluent societies,³⁹ the literature of the 1968–74 period, in particular *On a raison de se révolter*, shows him becoming even more insistent than he already was in 1964 on the importance of a moral or ethical dimension in political thought. He now makes a clear distinction between mere moral systems, which we, like "the Marxists" (note this move of distancing on his part), may rightly regard as parts of a society's superstructure, and its "living morality," which is "at the level of production" and hence in no sense illusory.⁴⁰ At one point he even traces a rather facile, three-stage "itinerary" of his thinking about ethics (somewhat reminiscent of some of his fleeting self-analyses that we found in his wartime *Cahiers* from many years earlier), according to which he has moved from an idealistic unrealism at age 18 to an amoralist realism at age 45 (i.e., in 1950, when he was beginning his period of closest collaboration with the Communist Party), to "a materialist and moralistic realism" in his old age.⁴¹ It seems obvious to me that he is here oversimplifying both his philosophical view about ethics and his practical relationships with the French Communist Party during the middle period, but that is a matter of secondary importance by comparison with his strong new emphasis on "living morality," the morality of everyday experience.

The example of "living morality" that he most frequently cites is the popular sense of *justice,* a notion that we have already found foreshadowed in his comments about popular *Droit* and legitimacy in connection with his opposition to the Vietnam War. This notion takes center stage in the interesting lecture, originally presented by invitation to an association of young lawyers in Brussels in early 1972, entitled "Justice and State" *("Justice et état").* Starting, as I have already mentioned, with a reference to former President De Gaulle's outrageous remark to him concerning the State's supposed monopoly on "all justice," Sartre proceeds to explain some of the intricacies of the legal situation in which he found himself at the time as a result of his involvement with "Maoist" organizations that the French government was endeavoring, with its characteristic combination (recalling the cases of Jacques Duclos and Henri Martin from the 1950s) of strict legalism in some respects and flagrant flouting of constitutional guarantees in other respects, to repress. His principal message in this lecture, however, is the vindication of *"justice sauvage"* (wild justice), sometimes illegal, sometimes violent, against the "bureaucratic justice" of the State. The ultimate aim of wild justice, he asserts, is not "license," but, on the contrary, "sovereignty for each worker and responsibility."⁴²

It is this little lecture/essay, obviously more self-contained, polished, and self-directed than the many interviews and dialogues from the same period, that perhaps best captures the quintessential "late Sartre" (aside from *The Family Idiot* and prior to "the Last Words"): less restrained than ever before with respect to governmental authorities and yet very sensitive to the background and interests of a particular audience (in this case, young lawyers); concerned with complex matters of detail (in this case, the exact charges preferred against him and others) and yet always thinking in terms of the great questions of justice, power, sovereignty, and freedom; capable of scholarly references even to matters found probably nowhere else in his writings (here, to cite two examples, Montesquieu's doctrine of the separation of powers and the history of the French judiciary) and yet eager above all to present political ideals in a straightforward, nontechnical language. In short, we see Sartre striving to be the new, activist, nonclassical sort of intellectual that had become his beau ideal in the aftermath of 1968.

The "late Sartre" of this period, whose principal political notions I have been summarizing, emerges as both less and more ambiguous than the Sartre of the *Critique* and of earlier periods. He is less ambiguous in obvious ways. The reader no longer needs to take my proposal, articulated very early in our retracing of his intellectual itinerary, that "socialism and freedom" should be seen as the leitmotifs of that itinerary, as just a working hypothesis for understanding his complex texts: on page after page of the late publications, Sartre fairly shouts out this theme, over and over again. Whereas readers of the *Critique* had cause to wonder just how seriously Sartre might be regarding the possibility of a definitive, Apocalyptic movement that would bring the progressive development of history's totalization into clear focus once and for all, Sartre's remarks of this late period of his life make it perfectly evident that he regards such a notion as a fairy tale. What he has to say and write is certainly not unintelligent, and the main points can be reconstructed very quickly, as I have just done.

On the other hand, this new style brings with it new uncertainties of interpretation. Take, for example, a passage in which Sartre is discussing with Lévy and Gavi the implications of an important industrial action in France at the time, the workers' takeover of the Lip factory, that is their preoccupation in several of the dialogues in *On a raison de se révolter*. Sartre remarks: "Impossible to conceive of the Lip movement without thinking, I repeat to you, of freedom, that is to say without seeing that behind socialism there is perhaps a still more important value, which is just freedom."[43] While in one sense this is just a simple articulation of the common belief of that huge majority of politically-oriented people, whether or not they consider themselves socialists, who have repudiated what current shorthand calls "the Stalinist model," a belief that vindicates Sartre's life-long concern to uphold the claims of freedom, in another sense this remark reopens all the old questions, beginning with those of what we are to understand by either "freedom" or "socialism," to which earlier writings may be seen as painstaking efforts to formulate careful, though tentative, answers. Of course, that is precisely what Sartre intends throughout these dialogues and in many of his other publications of the period. As he says in a sort of "preface" to the dialogues,

> One must not take any page whatever with the idea that it's a page that says what it says for eternity. It's a page that says what it says, but which may be refuted on page 150 or page 200; one must really read it as a time-bound affair [*une temporanéité*].44

As for socialism, it can have many different meanings, as Sartre points out in a brief essay of the same period concerning the implications of a recent political trial (in Spain) of Basque separatists, whose insistence on the "singular universality" of their ethnic nationalism he strongly supports: the Basques, he says, have demonstrated to us French, with our Jacobin revolutionary traditions, "*another* socialism, decentralizing and concrete."45 Polyvalence of meanings, extreme tentativeness except with respect to the ultimate, simultaneously libertarian and communitarian revolutionary goals: the Sartre of the last active years is in many respects *un homme postmoderne*.

What are we, concerned as we have been above all here with Sartre's political theory, to make of all this? In keeping with the spirit that I have just been delineating, I must strongly insist on finally leaving any such judgment to the individual reader. However, I shall allow myself a few personal reflections. In the introduction to this book, I wrote about the importance of Sartre's work in the evolution of my own ideas and career. The period of his life that we have just been considering, however, which is still relatively recent and hence corresponds to my earlier professional years, was of much less interest or importance to me at the time. It is not that I turned away from the core insights of his existentialist Marxism to the structuralism of Althusser or to any particular one of the succeeding waves of postexistentialist thought, as many others did. It is rather that I at once found the theoretical and even the lifestyle evolution of the late Sartre to be "nothing new" (more or less), very much what I would have expected, and his practical political alliances and choices of that period to be unproductive.

As for his theoretical evolution, if one had followed the odyssey of his political theory up to 1960 or so, then the very blatant crossing of t's and dotting of i's that we find in his post-1968 publications should have come as no shock. Seen from one perspective, the latter are simply manifestations of a very mature and at last fully self-confident thinker, no longer needing to mask his own uncertainties with either endless academic qualifications or seemingly dogmatic bluster. His "lifestyle" changes reflect the same process of mature self-unmasking: we see him, particularly in his dialogues with Lévy and Gavi, attempting finally to act fully in keeping with the deep, and to me deeply attractive, antihierarchical impulses that had been intellectually supported by his lifelong philosophical concern for human freedom, but that had been contravened, at the height of his career, by the objective situation of the *"vedettariat"* ("stardom" or "starhood," a coined word that was at one time important in the vocabulary of the "Maoists") in which he found himself. (It is understandable resentment at the searing memory of that situation that accounts, more than any other single factor, for the principled disregard shown to Sartre by so many younger French philosophers.) When he comments, at several points in these dialogues, about just how *good* he feels *"dans sa peau"* (in his skin) in his relationship with his young interlocutors (often in the context of his recollections of years of tense, difficult, "correct" relationships with French Communist Party nabobs), I believe him; it makes sense to me, as it did when I heard about these remarks at the time of their publication.

At the same time, while I fully sympathized then with Sartre's felt need, in light of his newly clarified insights into himself and the rest of society, to become more of an activist and to rub shoulders with the ordinary workers about whom he had written for so many years and with the young would-be revolutionaries who at the time seemed to him to have these workers' interests closest to heart, I felt that he was making a strategic mistake in many of his activities as reported by the press at the time. They were, I thought, a *gaspillage,* a waste, of his ever more limited time and energy. I still think this, but I am now not sure of what he could or ought to have done instead, or if indeed there was a serious alternative to what he did. He did not and could not *choose* the individuals who, after the initial defeat of the student-led revolt of 1968, tried to reignite its spark in the high schools, in the factories, and wherever else they thought they could during subsequent years. Lévy and the other "Maoists" were those individuals, and it was therefore they with whom, for better or worse, Sartre had to work and fraternize if he was to remain faithful to his own conception of the "new intellectual" as political activist in the time and place in which he was living. Thus, his own situation exemplified the constraints on freedom about which Sartre had so often ruminated throughout his career. There was something pathetic and tragic about it, as it seemed to many at the time, and it is likely to seem even more so in retrospect, in light of the general withering away to nothingness of the "Maoist" movement and of the vastly different pursuits in which its survivors, notably Lévy, are now engaged. But these retrospective appearances are not in consonance with Sartre's own frequently recorded perceptions of his life experiences during this period.

The "Maos'" initial recourse to Sartre had in large measure been, as is freely admitted in the dialogues, opportunistic, based on their need for him to protect their publishing and other activities by virtue of his reputation. Later, after the serious decline in Sartre's health, Lévy's monopolization of much of Sartre's time while serving in the role (shared with Simone de Beauvoir and other female friends) of a sick old man's companion appeared to many as an even more blatant case of opportunism. But was it so? And indeed, what is the exact force of this charge? We shall shortly have to reconsider these matters one last time, at least to the extent to which they bear on the understanding of Sartre's final recorded thinking about politics and political theory. But we must first pause to examine briefly a few of the implications for political theory of Sartre's last and longest work as a "classical intellectual," completed even as his "Maoist" associations were intensifying, *The Family Idiot*.

The theoretical *aim* of this work is extremely clear and designates it in a very obvious sense as the culmination of all of Sartre's political theory. It is such a culmination in principle at least, but the actual execution of the project leaves me rather dubious about its relative value, by comparison especially with the *Critique*, in enhancing our theoretical understanding. A simple, overly simple, way of characterizing the basis of these doubts is to say that *The Family Idiot* is just too long: nearly 3000 pages, more if the planned fourth volume had been written, just in order to analyze the career trajectory of one famous French author of the nineteenth century. In fact the deeper reason for my comparative lack of enthusiasm for this work—or, to put it in another context, the reason why I shall devote less space to discussing its importance for understanding Sartre's political theory than I have devoted even to some considerably shorter works—is rather less banal and more interesting: it has to do with the very nature of Sartre's project in writing it.

The Family Idiot, as Sartre asserts in the first sentence of his preface, is intended as the sequel to *Search for a Method*;[46] in other words, it is an application or instantiation of ideas that were developed in the latter work concerning the need to understand an individual in terms at once of his or her psychological development—with special emphasis, in accordance with Freud's insights (as distinguished from his unacceptable implicit metaphysics), on childhood and adolescence—and of the social milieu of his or her place and time. This Sartrean conception of adequate social explanation was a product, as I have pointed out in discussing *Search for a Method*, of dissatisfaction with the dominant social science reductionisms of our century—Marxist, Freudian, and American behavioralist—and seems to me to be clearly correct and to be applauded. Now, such a conception of social explanation, if it is to be carried out rigorously, entails considerable attention to detail and the eschewing of all glib generalizations. In the case of *The Family Idiot*, the details of Flaubert's early personal life occupy, roughly and with some excursuses into the lives of others and events of those times, the first 2,100-odd pages, the analysis of the general French cultural and social climate of the times occupies the next 400-odd, and the synthesis of these two analyses in order to present a comprehensive picture of Flaubert within his times consumes 200 pages more. (We also have a final 150 pages of rough and diverse notes toward what would have been the fourth volume.) At the end, we have been presented with a rather exhaustive but of course contestable account of just what it was that "made Flaubert tick." It may be conceded (although there are many critics who would refuse such a concession) that we now have the most comprehensive and profound—though not necessarily the "truest," whatever that may mean—explanation ever written or ever likely to be written of Gustave Flaubert as both a private individual and a social being. But that *is* our principal acquisition. Of course, there are some marvelous insights about the "objective spirit" of the mid-nineteenth century in France and about numerous other matters along the way. However, the "narrative" remains essentially a "local" one, to use terminology that Lyotard and other spokespersons of postmodernism favor, and its usefulness in illuminating *other* narratives is perforce very limited, as Sartre himself would have been forced to agree.

In answer to the often-asked question, "Why Flaubert?", Sartre offered a number of not inconsistent reasons—for example, the fascination that Sartre had about trying to understand someone whose personality was so different from his in so many ways, the totally opposite view that Flaubert held concerning the function of literature vis-à-vis the sociopolitical world, the availability of an enormous mass of material that Flaubert wrote about himself from childhood on, their shared interest in the imagination, and so on.[47] Sartre obviously found nineteenth-century French history, with its alternate periods and styles of extreme reaction and revolution, of brutality and opulent *joie de vivre*, of artistic brilliance and incredible stupidity within the successive political leaderships, endlessly intriguing, and his knowledge of it was quite wide-ranging. Any questions that might have been raised as to whether Sartre was capable of sustained scholarly study must be put to rest by his proficiency in conjuring up citations, not so much from the secondary literature on Flaubert as from Flaubert's own writings, including thirteen 600-page extant volumes of correspondence. (One could argue that, with this much material at his disposal for dealing only with certain aspects, generally the more personal and less social ones, of his overall topic, Sartre's decision to limit his own work to a mere 3000 pages showed considerable restraint.) But what of all this remains of contemporary, much less "permanent," value for the nonspecialist? To pose this question is to highlight the paradoxicality of attempting to write philosophy, or theory in general, with its traditional emphasis on universality, while at the same time regarding universal transtemporal concepts with extreme suspicion and focusing on the "singular universal." For it is in this light that Sartre's project in *The Family Idiot* must be seen.

The overall scheme of *The Family Idiot* may be summarized as follows. The first two volumes, the pages of which are numbered consecutively, are divided into three parts. The first, entitled "Constitution," deals with Flaubert's make-up as determined by his family structure: his successful provincial doctor-father; his mother with aristocratic pretensions, an attitude of total devotion to her husband, and a sense of disappointment with her life especially by virtue of her having to live for years at the Rouen hospital and having borne Gustave instead of a girl; and his considerably older brother, the heir-apparent to the elder Flaubert's medical practice. Although a younger sister, Caroline, was born after Gustave, Sartre focuses in the first, or "regressive," half of his study of Flaubert's constitution primarily on the father-son relationship, a negative one that Sartre imagines to have reached a climax when the father came to realize that Gustave was a slow learner and presumably expressed his anger and disappointment at this "family idiot." These factors led, from Gustave's very early years on, to an attitude of great passivity—Flaubert was *not* a man of *praxis* in Sartre's sense—a lack of positive vision, and a cosmic rancor toward the world that clearly appear through an in-depth reading of his juvenilia: at age 13, Gustave was already asserting that "The world is hell."[48] In the succeeding, "progressive" part of this first section, then, Sartre catalogues some of the principal components of this youthful world-outlook, components that were to condition Flaubert for the rest of his life: vassality, insufficiency, inferiority, submissiveness, resentment, envy. Finally, Sartre summarizes Flaubert's constitution in light of the two conflicting "ideologies" of Flaubert's parents: his mother's unassertive and unintellectual religious faith and his father's agnostic "scientism," or science boosterism. (Sartre uses the word "ideologies" here in an even less technical, less Marxian sense than in the opening section of *Search for a Method*, where he contrasted "ideologies" with "philosophies.")[49] These two worldviews played themselves out in Flaubert, according to Sartre, in such a way as to lead him to reject both and to adopt a stance of principled "stupidity," whereby he regarded all human ceremonies and conventional language as universally ridiculous and themselves stupid.

The second and longest part of Volumes 1 and 2 of *The Family Idiot* is entitled "Personalization" and analyzes Flaubert's development from early childhood through his prep school (*"collège"*) days and his brief subsequent period, after his expulsion for challenging the authorities, of private reading in Paris for law examinations that he took and failed. Sartre traces Flaubert's childhood abandonment of dreams of being an actor in favor of literature and shows that at the same time Gustave never gave up role-playing as central to his personality. His "constitutional" attitude of resentment permitted him to develop a stance of scornful laughter toward the world at large, which eventuated in a vulgar, mythical, larger-than-life character (he himself was a very large man) of his creation that he called *"le Garçon"* and that he played out, along with his closest acquaintances at school, in extreme ways that often made them uncomfortable. There is a consensus among commentators that Sartre's abbreviated but incisive discussion, in this portion of the book, of laughter as a "recourse against pity" that necessarily involves an appeal to a serial collectivity[50] is among the most interesting and valuable excursuses of *The Family Idiot*.[51] When Sartre begins to set Flaubert in the context of his school—the same school that his older brother had attended, with great distinction, earlier, and on the advisory board of which his father served for some time—he furnishes us with a useful account of its recent history (prior to Gustave's admission), which included an "apocalyptic" period in the early 1830s during which a student revolt was suppressed by a strategy of temporarily closing the school and persuading parents to reprimand their sons for protests that the latter had believed to be in the very spirit of liberalism and progress that their parents professed. These events were connected, as Sartre analyzes them, with the larger events in France in 1830: the accession to power of Louis-Philippe, the "citizen-king," whose regime disappointed many of its initial supporters by encouraging the most conservative forces, particularly the Church, to strengthen their dominance over French institutions. (The protest at the *collège* of Rouen was sparked by a student's refusal to submit to mandatory confession to the school's chaplain.) At this oppressive institution, which Gustave Flaubert entered only a few years after the student uprising and subsequent events, a universal atmosphere of *ressentiment* had set in, Sartre shows: the students were alienated from the older generation of their parents, encouraged to pursue a demoralizing competition with one another, and effectively rendered incapable (by virtue of their age and of the institutional structures themselves) of seeing that the source of their mutual distrust and fear was these liberal institutions themselves rather than some eternal essence of man.[52] Gustave, who apparently enjoyed greater popularity among some of his fellows than his later reminiscences about those days imply, absorbed and embodied this poisonous atmosphere; as Sartre concludes, the invention of *le Garçon* can be seen as a final step in acquiescence to this regime, and even the note of remonstrance written by a few students when Gustave was expelled shows how thoroughly bourgeois they had all become.[53]

"Elbenhon or the Final Spiral" is the subtitle of the last section of the first two volumes. The reference to "Elbenhon" is an allusion, esoteric for a nonspecialist in French literature, to a character in one of Mallarmé's works and is, moreover, misspelled, as Hazel Barnes has pointed out in her study of *The Family Idiot*.[54] The metaphor of the spiral, however, is of some real importance: it indicates Sartre's conception of the evolution of an individual's life as a spiral movement, involving movements of reaction against previous phases which do not involve *simply* negating the latter and which continue to carry within themselves, though in greatly changed forms, earlier themes and attitudes. The central event of this section is the psychosomatic crisis to which all Flaubert biographers must perforce accord primary importance: a dramatic seizure of some sort that Gustave experienced while driving back with his older brother from a visit to the country house that his family was having built and that would eventually become his home. This "fall," as Sartre called it, put an end to all pretensions concerning a legal career for the young Flaubert and effectively determined

him as the neurotic proponent and practitioner of art for art's sake that he
was to be for the rest of his life. Important and in principle unresolvable
questions of diagnosis lurk behind this event; as I know from my own
interest and readings in current neurological literature, fundamental issues
about the nature of a wide variety of such neurophysiological phenomena
remain fuzzy and debatable even today, and in 1844 the most advanced
medicine (it will be recalled that Flaubert's father and brother were distinguished physicians) lacked even many of the labels (e.g., "temporal lobe
syndrome," which *may* help locate Gustave's problem) that now exist.

This situation presents a major challenge to Sartre's whole lifelong
philosophy of freedom, as well as a specific challenge to the complex
"method" that he intends his study of Flaubert to instantiate: can it not be
said that Flaubert became the mature author Flaubert, as known in the
history of literature, by virtue of a mere unfortunate physiological accident?
Sartre is masterful, I think, in showing that, regardless of the exact somatic
events that brought about the seizure at that particular time, Flaubert had
engaged in relevant preneurotic behaviors prior to it and that his neurotic
response to it, from which he was able personally to profit in such a way as
to become the celebrated writer that he eventually became, illustrates the
perennial theme of much of Sartre's theatre, "Loser wins."[55] To put it in
earlier Sartrean terminology that occasionally reappears here, Flaubert's
neurophysiological condition may be considered as a "coefficient of adversity" in response to which he freely chose the complex future course of
action with which today's historians of nineteenth-century French literature are so very familiar.

What relevance has all of this to social theory, however? From the
outset, in keeping with the position that was so forcefully expressed in
What Is Literature? and contrary to Flaubert's own point of view, Sartre
insists that literature is an important part of the objective spirit of a given
place and time.[56] Volume 3 of *The Family Idiot* deals with the objective spirit
of Flaubert's place and time, labeling it "the objective neurosis" (the title of
the first half of the volume), and goes on to discuss the close "fit" between
Flaubert's personal neurosis and the atmosphere of the Second Empire
period of Louis Napoleon, during which Flaubert's career flourished. Sartre
defends the notion of "objective spirit," showing that this Hegelian expression is a useful and valid way of understanding the dominant ideological currents of a given epoch—its culture regarded as "practico-inert"—that
need not include in its connotations any of the machinery of Hegel's idealist
ontology.[57] He wishes strongly to insist that not every epochal ideology is
neurotic, but that that of the Second Empire (roughly from the time of
Napoleon's acquisition of the title of "emperor" in 1850, following the
revolution and massacres of 1848, until his surrender to the Prussians in
1870) really was so. The central symptom of this neurosis as far as its
literary manifestations are concerned was, according to Sartre, the reduction of writing to mere role-playing:[58] the dominant writers, members of

the petite bourgeoisie, cultivated the aesthetic and pseudoaristocratic attitude of art for art's sake, expressing a contempt and even hatred for
humanity and especially for the contemporary middle class which constituted their readership, glorifying Nothingness, and archetypically (i.e.,
in Flaubert's *Madame Bovary*) employing a pseudoscientific style, supposedly founded in experience and misleadingly labeled "realist" by the
critics, in order to promulgate this "black humanism" of theirs.

Flaubert, in Sartre's interpretation, had already experienced his private
equivalent of the political events of 1848–50 (in which he took no personal
part) in the form of his "fall" of January 1844 and its aftermath. The national
mood in France during the 1850s and 1860s was both venomous and
bizarre. (I remember being amazed when I first saw a heroic statue of the
Emperor Napoleon that had been erected, with a fulsome dedication, by
the business community of Lille during that period, which at the time of my
viewing was less than a century earlier; it seemed unreal to think that the
heirs of the French Revolution would have erected such a *kitschisch*, syco-
phantic, and blatantly class-biased monument in such relatively recent
times.) Those Second Empire times were Flaubert's days of glory. Sartre's
analysis in Volume 3 is designed to show how Flaubert's constitution and
neurotic adult personality coincided with those neurotic times in such a
way as to make him a popular success. On the other hand, as Sartre shows,
Napoleon's capitulation at Sedan in 1870 was a mortal blow to Flaubert,
rendering him and his generation nothing but, in his own word, "fossils"
thenceforth; the severe personal financial reversal that followed at best only
hastened his premature death in 1880.

Thus, the central lesson of *The Family Idiot* is to show in exquisite detail
just how a human being, while not being a mere mechanism determined
by events, is inevitably a "product of his or her times," including the
sociopolitical institutions of those times, as well as a product of a particular
family milieu. To cite a Sartrean aphorism from Volume 3, "A man—
whatever he may be—totalizes his epoch to the exact extent to which he is
totalized by it."[59] As I have already noted, the question of whether particular points in Sartre's interpretation (e.g., his long digression on the
reasons why the ex-socialist-turned-reactionary writer, Lecomte de Lisle,
did not experience great popular success during the very period in which
the studiedly apolitical Flaubert did) are debatable or clearly valid is of
relatively minor importance, at least from our point of view here. I think
that the work as a whole does vindicate Sartre's "method" of understanding
a human being within the context of his or her time, although it goes
without saying that future practitioners of this method should learn to be
more concise than Sartre was. (I suspect, for example, that the often
megalithic sentences in Volume 3 are longer on the average than in any
other writing of his—a self-indulgence that may be attributable in part to
his increasing age.) The more satisfactory nature of Sartre's treatment of
Flaubert by comparison with, for example, his *Saint Genet* is due above all,

as he remarked in an interview and as I agree, precisely to his inclusion of the social dimension—the institutions, the times—in *The Family Idiot;* "none of all that," as he said, "was specified in *Saint Genet.*"[60] If an individual, such as Flaubert, has bequeathed to posterity enough documentation about himself or herself, then one really can grasp his/her "singular universality" rather fully and well: *The Family Idiot,* in my opinion, proves this. In doing so, it restates with an almost infinite attention to detail the glib utterance of Sartre's early years, "There is no human nature." As he now says, "society in general . . . does not exist at all, nor does man;" what we have instead, in the case of the period of Flaubert's adolescence, is the image of "French society under Louis-Philippe or rather of the triumphant bourgeoisie at the stage of primitive accumulation."[61] Just as Flaubert was neurotic in a certain unique and specifiable way, but not everyone is neurotic, so the Second Empire society of Flaubert's adulthood exhibited an objective neurosis of a certain type, but not every social ideology is neurotic.[62] We must examine each individual instance in detail.

Thus, the singular has become for Sartre decisively more important than the universal in this final major work. Yet many general themes from earlier writings perdure and play very important roles here—for example, just among those few that I have mentioned in my brief summary, totalization, the practico-inert, coefficients of adversity, the relationship of literature to politics, and so on. Stupidity, which Sartre began to discuss in some brief but suggestive pages of the *Cahiers* to which I have referred, is of course a very important *motif* in *The Family Idiot:* Flaubert was considered stupid by his father when he was a young child and later ranted endlessly about the stupidity of his bourgeois society and of human beings in general, while Sartre, more faithful to Descartes's dictum that good sense is the best distributed of human endowments than to any other aspect of that philosophy, argues forcefully and at length that "stupidity" is a function of oppression.[63] *Property* and its accompanying alienation is another old and here recurrent Sartrean theme, particularly in light of the very strong property-orientation of the dominant class of Flaubert's time and of the adult Flaubert himself. As Sartre remarks at one point, the cliché, "take life seriously," in this context translates into the imperative of bourgeois alienation: "Always act in such a way as to sacrifice the man within you to the property-owner, that is, to the thing possessed."[64] Yet another important notion from Sartre's earlier reflections on history, the problem of different and overlapping generations, comes to the fore in *The Family Idiot,* with reference both to the gap between Gustave's generation and his father's and to the "fossilization" of his own generation with which Gustave became so impressed in the aftermath of the emperor's surrender at Sedan. In this context we find Sartre, interestingly enough, still promising, in a footnote to the third volume, to take up the generations question in detail in Volume 2 of the *Critique.*[65] There must no doubt have been a moment of self-reflection when Sartre, as a man in his middle sixties with increasing health problems, was writing this; but one can find, I think, no trace of Flaubertian self-pity in Sartre's own text. He seems to have felt neither alienated from nor fettered by his earlier books and ideas, using many of them freely but also not insisting on a strict adherence to any of their structures or formulations—the very attitude that I showed him articulating in my introduction.

What finally has now become of the two interrelated ideas that I have identified as most central to Sartre's political theory over all of the years, socialism and freedom? Sartre certainly believed that they were still present and central in *The Family Idiot*. In *On a raison de se révolter*, in the course of defending his scholarly preoccupation with Flaubert, he insists that *The Family Idiot* is "a socialist work."[66] And in the notes toward Volume 4 that have been included at the end of the new edition of Volume 3, he begins a sketch entitled "Reading of *Madame Bovary*" by discussing the importance of breaking with the ideology of one's own time in order truly to understand a classic of this sort, and then writes: "My point of view: Marxism and freedom."[67] This expression of adherence to Marxism, which from all the evidence previously considered here must have been one of his last such, clearly has to do above all with certain obvious terminological and methodological affinities—in other words, with Marxism as an approach to social critique—while Sartre's socialist vision has now been refined and tempered by his realization that any socialist society would also have to be a singular universal, not an absolute. In a very important text, in which the heavy use of the future conditional tense reinforces the sense of uncertainty that Sartre always and increasingly had about the real possibility of a future socialist society, he combines his youthful obsession over the problem of "contingency" with his mature views about the "singular universal" in the following way:

> In fact, when human society would have overcome its divisions and achieved a socialism of abundance, it would still be the case, at the heart of its internal necessity, that it has been constituted on the basis of original contingency, not by eliminating it but by integrating it into its own order. Even so, it would only be a singular universal, that is, it would draw out of its own history a radical idiosyncrasy which would be the interiorization of its facticity, in other words of its contingency grasped as necessity.[68]

In other words, given the singularity of "the human adventure," there can never be socialism as such or *überhaupt*.

As for freedom, in an interview concerning *The Family Idiot* Sartre produced a definition of it, after having expressed amazement at some of the formulations of it that he had encountered when rereading earlier writings of his, that well captures its role in his biography of Flaubert. Freedom is, he says, "that small movement which makes, out of a totally conditioned social being, a person who does not give back the entirety of what he or she has received from his or her conditioning; which makes of

Genet a poet, for example, even though he had been rigorously conditioned to be a thief."[69] This recognition of freedom's extreme limitations, however, does not dethrone it as supreme Sartrean value, just as the recognition of socialism's necessary singularity renders socialism no less of an ideal, or perhaps we should say no less of a useful shorthand for a number of ideals that are interrelated with each other and that undergird the vision of a free society, than it was before.

Even if I am correct about Sartre's outlook at the time of publication of *The Family Idiot*, however, can the same claim of continuity of fundamental social projects be made in regard to the last "text" that we need to consider here, Sartre's so-called Last Words? In contrast to *The Family Idiot*, this "text" is very short, and in fact it is merely a transcript of a tape-recording that Sartre was unable, given his physical condition, to "review" in the literal sense, although presumably he was aware of its contents. (He could not have argued, as he is known to have done, with Simone de Beauvoir over its being sent for publication if he had not had this awareness.) First of all, we must recognize that Sartre's own self-interpretation, as recorded in the transcript, favors the hypothesis of continuity. In fact, he asserts that this is one point on which he is "in conflict" with his interlocutor, Benny Lévy, in that the latter regards certain contradictions in Sartre's thinking as of far greater importance than Sartre himself does: "I myself," Sartre says, "think that my contradictions mattered little, that despite everything I have always remained on a continuous line."[70] That this was Sartre's belief does not of itself prove that he was correct, of course, but it is important to remember when analyzing this very curious document.

The circumstances of publication need to be recalled. *Le Nouvel Observateur* presented the dialogue in three weekly segments, on March 10, 17, and 24, 1980, the first of these being the newspaper's eight hundredth issue. By way of introduction, the editors commented that Sartre was still neither in retreat nor retired ("n'a rien d'un homme en retrait ou en retraite") and reproduced, at the top, the first page of the short interview with Sartre entitled "The Alibi," which had appeared in its very first issue in 1964.[71] Sartre was forced to enter the hospital on March 20. Benny Lévy, who had publicly abandoned his long-standing pseudonym of Pierre Victor and reassumed his original name for the first time in this publication, was called back from a trip to Cairo, his birthplace, in early April as a result of Sartre's worsening condition. Sartre died on April 15. The aftermath of the funeral, which turned out to be a mass demonstration of curiosity and mourning, was one of enormous bitterness among various factions of Sartre's former associates, particularly between Simone de Beauvoir, who had been so strongly opposed to publishing the dialogue, and some other *Temps Modernes* collaborators, on the one hand, and Benny Lévy and, for other reasons not closely associated with the newspaper piece, Arlette Elkaïm on the other. But this later history must not be of central concern to us here. What is important to remember, and what has given these internally fragmentary dialogues the historical significance that they possess, is that they represented one of the few sustained public pronouncements made by Sartre in years, and they were the last. (Presumably the unfinished book *Pouvoir et liberté*, which Sartre and Lévy were in the process of composing over a period of months, and to which Sartre alludes at one point in the transcript as a future occasion for him to express reservations about a Lévyan analysis of "violence" that he agrees to accept without reservations for the moment,[72] may contain some more or less contemporaneous thoughts. But this document may not be published for years, if ever. I had occasion to observe it, in the form of a large collection of audio tapes on some high shelves in Benny Lévy's Strasbourg apartment in 1987, and its owner seemed quite uncertain about its likely fate.)

Although the text of the dialogue is fairly evenly divided between the two speakers, with Sartre's portion being somewhat greater, there is a clear sense in which it is Lévy, more than Sartre, who calls the tune. In particular, it is Lévy who decides on the topics to be discussed, who usually (but not always) determines the thought transitions, and who on occasion peremptorily asserts the opposite of what Sartre has just maintained, before moving on. (The best example of this is a point midway through the dialogue at which Lévy says that "the schema of radicalization, of stand-up sovereignty, of direct democracy [as] opposed to an unfaithful, representative sovereignty" has turned out to be a false solution and is "finished."[73] Sartre has just been *insisting*, on the contrary, on the importance of retaining the idea of being radical, while admitting that in practice it leads to an impasse. So, says Lévy, let us go on to consider the more underlying problem, which is that of *democracy*.) Lévy's tone is frequently very accusatory towards Sartre: he sees the latter, with whose works he has a considerable familiarity, as having been fundamentally wrong on a number of points, and he tries to get Sartre to admit this. Sartre, on the other hand, is generally compliant and conciliatory, apparently trying to concede as much as he honestly thinks he can, and on some points making no comment when this would have been in order, while still maintaining throughout that there are issues on which they simply disagree.

Does this contrast in stances, between an intellectually aggressive young discussion leader and a physically very feeble old man who is constantly being called upon either to renounce, modify, or defend previous positions, amount to a malicious manipulation, as some have claimed? Not necessarily. Sartre accepted this situation and, as we know, insisted on publication. He enjoyed at least some of the verbal sparring, appreciated what Lévy had given him by way of, for example, a greatly heightened understanding of Judaism, and made it clear that he regarded himself as an old man only because that was the way others labeled him. In their dialogues, Lévy did not treat him with the deference and special respect usually accorded to much older persons. (This had already been true in *On a raison de se révolter,* recorded years earlier and at a different time in the intellectual evolutions of both, especially of Lévy; but Gavi had served as a moderating influence in those dialogues.) But Sartre, egalitarian to the end, seems not to have demanded or even wished such deference and respect, at least in this one relationship. While one might personally disapprove of Lévy's manner of dealing with Sartre in this dialogue, the charge of malicious manipulation seems fully sustainable only if we assume that Sartre was really "not in his right mind" during the recording periods. I admit to having once thought this myself, to having reacted with the standard, morally unacceptable ageist language of "senility" when I under-took a first, superficial reading of the dialogue.[74] But reconsideration has long since convinced me that, while Sartre was at times slower here to challenge his interlocutor's assertions than he would once have been and hence makes errors of judgment in letting certain claims pass with which he is clearly uncomfortable, on the whole he was at that time still fully capable of serious reflective thinking even if many of his other faculties had deserted him, and hence merits being taken seriously in what he has to say.

The most central theme of the dialogue, with which it begins and ends, is what attitude to take toward the future. *On a raison de se révolter* had terminated with an amusing but desultory Sartrean self-analysis con-cerning his congenital "pessimism," in which he had distinguished be-tween the "easy" pessimism that sees everything as going badly, and his kind, which involves just "not being completely with the movement which one is for."[75] Sartre had added there that pessimism can be a mistake, but that radical optimism always is. Now, in "L'Espoir, maintenant," Sartre begins by saying that he has always believed having hope to be part of being human, to which Lévy replies that Sartre used to hold that every-thing failed. "You exaggerate," retorts Sartre, quite justifiably, but he then goes on to concede that he often wrote about despair and anguish in his early years because they were fashionable, and suggests that failure (*"échec,"* a word that occurs frequently in his psychoanalyses of Flaubert, though the latter are not mentioned here) would have been a more accurate word to employ. At any rate, he adds, since 1945 he has believed in hope, although there is admittedly a deep contradiction between this belief and his recognition of the inevitability of failure in human affairs. Soon there-after, he acknowledges that he has not always said quite what he has meant to say, particularly in support of the now-foundering Left, and that this points to the failure in his own work. On the other hand, he has always retained an admittedly naive belief in progress, so that he continues to anticipate some perhaps distant future time when what he has written will be able to be seen to fall into place within a larger general historical pattern. Finally, at the very end of the dialogue, he expresses discouragement over the dominance of Rightist tendencies everywhere—in the Soviet Union, in the United States, and even in Sweden, where the conservative party had just won an election—, over wars (especially that in Afghanistan) and rumors of wars, and generally over the ugliness of "the world of today, which is horrible."[76] Since 1975, before which he had still been a "sixty-eighter," imbued with the ideas of that banner year of hope, he says that he has been strongly tempted for the second time in his life to fall into deep despair. (The first time was the period of the German Occupation.) This would be easy to do, he adds, for someone who will die in five or ten years at most. However, he still wishes to construct a basis for hope after all, since "hope has always been one of the dominant forces of revolutions and of insurrections," and to explain "how I still feel hope as my conception of the future."

Before turning to other aspects of this dialogue, I think it important to comment on this pervasive theme of hope. Hope is first and foremost, it seems to me, a mental attitude and not a philosophical position. It can enter into philosophical discourse in various ways, such as through theology or alternatively through a secular "theology" that asserts some historical inevitability or other.[77] Just prior to the dialogue's conclusion, for instance, Sartre expresses admiration for Jewish Messianism and says that non-Jews like himself would like to appropriate it for other purposes, in particular in support of a certain idea of revolution. But since it is above all an *attitude* that we are considering, my philosophical instincts are not at all disturbed by Sartre's obvious wavering, even within this one dialogue, over whether to be optimistic or pessimistic, for this is normal in a very thoughtful person and does not represent a genuine philosophical contradiction. Nor is there anything in Sartre's remarks about hope that should be found shocking by his public, at least by those who are familiar with the outlines of the evolution of his political theory as we have followed them in this book, despite Lévy's suggestion at the outset that it *is* astonishing. After all, as some of Sartre's own comments in the dialogue remind us, it would have made no sense for someone with an outlook of complete hopelessness or despair to have taken many of the political stances that he did over the years.

Among the specific past actions and assertions for which Lévy, employing his superior mnemonic abilities, castigates Sartre are his period of "fellow traveling" with the Communist Party—an old issue between them, as we have seen in reviewing *On a raison de se révolter*—his insistence on the combination of terror with fraternity in the *Critique*, his recognition of the necessity of violence on the Algerian side in his preface to Fanon's *Les Damnés de la terre*, and his characterization of elections as a "trap for fools" in the short essay bearing that title.[78] Sartre resists the label of "Stalinism" that Lévy uses at one point, remarking with accuracy that people now apply it indiscriminately.[79] He admits to having erred in some of his more extreme statements about violence in the Algerian context, but in partial defense tries to recall the superheated atmosphere of the time and the exceptionally difficult situation in which any French person who opposed the government's actions there was placed; at the same time, he acknowledges still being somewhat unclear about the precise relationship between fraternity and violence.[80] As for Lévy's assertion, in the form of a rhetorical question, that Sartre's attitude toward elections had been a serious mistake, since elections have some value even if not an ultimate one, Sartre seems to ignore this direct attack by reflecting somewhat more deeply on the meaning of the vote as an expression of a set of human relationships which preexist any such event.[81] (He might well have raised questions about Lévy's own earlier attitudes toward elections during the latter's "Maoist" phase, but he did not do so.)

It is with respect to this domain of the nature of human relationships, rather than to such sensational but essentially unserious and ultimately unanswerable questions as those of whether Sartre ever personally experienced deep *Angst* and just how optimistic or pessimistic he "really" was in the final analysis, that this dialogue has the most interest for understanding his theoretical outlook at the end of his life. Already in an interview conducted by Michel Sicard in 1978, Sartre had claimed that the new ethical theory that he was in the process of working out with Lévy differed from his earlier ones at an ontological level (to the point where it "requires regarding the ontology that I have developed up to now as incomplete and false"),[82] in that he now accepted the reality of an interpenetration of consciousness, in fact of a human community that is more integrated than the terminology of a confrontation of "consciousnesses" implies. He had contrasted this conception of what might be called internal relations among human beings with a more external perspective that he had attributed to Marx. But he had then proceeded to turn the interview in a new direction by observing that the matter was quite complicated and that it would need to be explained at great length.[83] Here, in his dialogue with Lévy, he picks up on the latter's suggestion, made in response to Sartre's lament that the trouble with the vanishing political Left is that it never clearly spelled out its fundamental principles, that there is just such a principle, a broadly applicable one, to be found in the history of Leftist movements, namely, fraternity. Sartre then proceeds to reflect on just what fraternity might mean. These sparse reflections, interconnected as they are with other remarks in the dialogue concerning the importance of ethics, constitute, in my view, its core philosophical interest.

In "running with" Lévy's suggestion about fraternity, Sartre exhibits such enthusiasm that Lévy eventually feels obliged to caution him against falling into myth, comparable to Socrates' "Founding Myth" about the three types of citizens, all offspring of the common mother, earth, in the *Republic*. For Sartre goes on to say that Marx's theory of superstructures completely falsified the nature of human society by overlooking the importance of fraternity, that he himself had begun to work on the notion of fraternity in the *Critique* but had not gotten very far with it, that in fact fraternity is the first human relationship, and that he likes to think of every man he sees as sharing with him a common mother.[84] Although he cautions that this principle of "fraternity" should not be taken in a biologically literal way, he nevertheless allows his excitement about it to lead him into exceedingly mythical formulations, including one about totemism that envisages all "brothers" as having a single, nonindividualized mother who "can as well be a totemic bird."[85] (The reader is reminded of Aristotle's letter from exile near the end of his life, where he says that he has begun again to read and to be attracted by the ancient myths.) But with the help of Lévy's sharp questioning concerning the literal, nonmythical point of all this, Sartre finally arrives at a formulation of fraternity as a future possible experience, the realization of "the end that all men have in themselves, Man."[86] And this can only be achieved in a regime beyond scarcity, through Ethics. Earlier in the dialogue, Sartre has conceded that he would once have laughed at the emphasis that he and Lévy are now placing on the need for ethics; his notion of being-for-another in *Being and Nothingness* was a good start, he says there, but it needed development, since it still left consciousness too autonomous.[87] The close connection between the idea of fraternity and the demand for a revolutionary morality, the latter already prominent in the *Cahiers* of the 1940s, in the Gramsci Institute lecture of the 1960s, and in the discussions of the early 1970s, now becomes fully clear.

This entire, frustratingly brief text can be regarded as a kind of Rorschach Test concerning Sartre's final philosophical position. Read in one way, especially in conjunction with the lines from the Sicard interview that I have cited, it amounts to a thoroughgoing repudiation of past positions. Read in another way, in light of its circumstances, it should be seen as an instance, if not of manipulation, then at least of *"complaisance"* towards Lévy on Sartre's part: that is, of giving Lévy the answers, at least within certain bounds of credibility, that Sartre anticipates (not always accurately) that Lévy will want to hear. Read in yet another way, it is merely a final (not logically or conceptually final, but temporally so) expression of a long, continuous evolution in Sartre's thinking about the "we," about community, that began with the widespread dissatisfaction, evinced by critics and even by de Beauvoir (in *The Ethics of Ambiguity*) and eventually felt by Sartre himself as shown in the *Cahiers* and in the *Critique*, over the excessively individualistic description of almost exclusively conflictual human relationships to be found in *Being and Nothingness*. (The passage in the *Cahiers* in which the earlier work is said to have confined itself to the hell of the passions and hence not to have dealt with all possible human relations, must be recalled here.) Read in yet a fourth way, in light of Sartre's "laid-back" attitude concerning his own work and his insouciance, especially in later years, about criteria of consistency from one work to another, it is an affair of no great moment, to which some critics have, for the most diverse reasons, attached much more importance than it deserves.

There is surely some merit to all of these interpretations and no doubt to others that I have not articulated here. In "strictly ontological terms"—if, as I rather doubt, this phrase has a univocal meaning—there is obviously a sharp contrast between the confrontational "beings-for-another" of *Being and Nothingness* and the interpenetrating, fraternal consciousnesses of the Sicard interview and the Lévy dialogue. But on the other hand, the exploration of the phenomenon of the group in fusion in the *Critique* should be seen precisely as Sartre's careful, detailed way of bridging the gulf between these two maps of human community. Both, after all, are based in the lived experiences of virtually everyone. By the same token, there is an apparent absolute opposition between the earlier Sartrean proposition that conflict is at the heart of human relationships and his statement in this dialogue that fraternity is a first principle; but in fact, to the sensitive, dialectical mind, they may both be equally true simultaneously, as the old line of Latin verse, "*Odi et amo,*" reminds us with classic simplicity. In the remark that I have cited from the dialogue concerning "the end that all men have in themselves, Man," Sartre does indeed seem to be embracing an idealistic conception of a universal human nature, as well as an implicit Aristotelian philosophy of potentiality and final causality, that is strongly at odds with much of his intellectual evolution, culminating in the emphasis on the "singular universal" in *The Family Idiot,* as I have depicted it. But the rapid-fire structure of the relatively brief interchange permits him no time to reflect upon this formulation or to qualify it, and so it would be a mistake to take it too seriously as a full-blown new worldview in Sartre's intellectual life. Indeed, within the terms of the dialogue as we have it, this remark has the force of above all expressing in the simplest, most straightforward language a deep Sartrean longing that I have noted throughout this book in isolated but significant earlier passages—in references, for example, to a "radical conversion" within a sociohistorical context in the *Cahiers,* to the possibility of "group *praxis* forever" in the *Critique,* and, less rhetorically, to our emerging "One World" in several writings.

It was, in fact, this longing, this conviction that somehow all men are at least in principle somehow "brothers," despite the overwhelming predominance of conflict in this world of scarcity, that underlay Sartre's commitment over three and a half decades to the political ideals of socialism and freedom. "Socialism" is, as far as I can ascertain, never mentioned as such, and freedom as a philosophical concept receives no special emphasis, in the dialogue with Lévy, and yet these ideas inform the entire discussion. Even Lévy, who has obviously come to see great value in more traditional institutions, such as elections and religion, that meant little or nothing positive to him at an earlier time in his life, continues to feel a solidarity of opposition to the triumphant political Right, which he characterizes as "*salope*" (filthy) when early in the dialogue Sartre refers to it as "miserable."[88] For Sartre at the end of his life, then, the goal of a community of free human beings, freely entered into and maintained, remains *the* goal, even though the means for reaching it appear less clear than ever and even the very names with which it was once labeled, including now even that of "socialism," have come under suspicion by virtue of our shared historical experiences.

While not hesitating throughout this book to criticize certain of Sartre's formulations and tendencies, including aspects of the very tendency to Apocalyptic thinking that, unsurprisingly, reappears in force in this final discussion of the chances for hope amid the apparent hopelessness of the then-current world situation, I have at the same time not concealed my general agreement with his implicit ideals of human interrelationship. These ideals find expression within his writings primarily, and in my opinion rightly so, in his trenchant criticisms of past and existing sociopolitical institutions and practices, rather than in positive, utopian formulations. There is one very salient aspect of any conception of ideal human community about which Sartre failed fundamentally to write much that was helpful or even satisfactory, and that is the relationship between men and women; the one-sidedness of the language about community ("fraternity," "brothers," "Man," a "common mother," etc.) that is so blatant in the dialogue with Lévy reflects a lifetime of theoretical inadequacy on Sartre's part in this domain. (This theoretical inadequacy was no doubt reflected also in Sartre's mind-bogglingly complex personal relationships with women, a subject about which I wish to say nothing more here.) However, I am convinced, as Simone de Beauvoir was, that this enormous flaw was not fatal to his entire thought, which in fact could be utilized, as it was by her, for radically critiquing existing male/female relationships of dominance and subordination. With this very important exception, then, Sartre's efforts to comprehend and explain the sociopolitical world have, especially since the appearance of *Search for a Method* and the *Critique of Dialectical Reason*, appeared to me as superior to those of any of his contemporaries who have undertaken comparably extensive philosophical accounts.

As we have had occasion to recall throughout this book, Sartre's theoretical explanations were always self-consciously and proudly *situated*, a favorite word of his, within his own time and place or alternatively, as notably in the case of his study of Flaubert, within some other very clearly specified time and place; in certain respects skeptical of transtemporal universals and universal claims from the very beginning of his philosophical career, he became increasingly so as time went on, while never completely denying himself the possibility of generalizing, tentatively, concerning overall trends and tendencies—"totalizations in process." Thus, all of Sartre's work is quite time-bound, having the significance of a "singular universal." In coming to terms in detail here with the long evolution of Sartre's political theory, I have in fact become more comfortable than I was at the outset of my study, and even more comfortable than Sartre himself sometimes seemed to be, with recognizing that the differences between his most formal philosophical texts and his most occasional political essays were not total differences in kind.[89] So it is and so it *must* be with all thinkers, however much they may wish that it were otherwise and try to conceal their time-boundedness—as Sartre's own biographical work demonstrates convincingly.

Given this, one may justifiably raise once more the question mentioned in my introduction concerning Sartre's continuing relevance for the last decade of the twentieth century and beyond, as postmodernist intellectual currents swirl and the very idea of "socialism," to say nothing of Marxism, seems to have fallen widely into disrepute. A recurrent theme particularly in this chapter concerning the last two decades of Sartre's life has been to show the extremely important senses in which he anticipated this present atmosphere and no doubt, given his importance, even helped to stimulate thinking along lines that have led to it. I remain convinced of the truth of this claim, *even though* it is rapidly becoming more fashionable to make it. But even if there were little or no truth to it, I would still argue for the enormous value of considering and reconsidering Sartre's political theory for the penetrating explanatory light that it sheds on most of the major historical, cultural (including philosophical), and political developments of, roughly, the middle fifty years of this century of ours that we are now preparing to exit. For *explanation* was his greatest talent. If I have managed to expose, critically but sympathetically, some of the main lines of explanation that he advanced especially in the areas of politics, society, and history, showing their continuing usefulness and their deliberate open-endedness, and have done so in some detail without implying a belief that I have myself effected closure in these matters, then I have fulfilled my initial intentions.

Notes

INTRODUCTION

1. For a somewhat detailed chronological account of these years, see Simone de Beauvoir, *La Cérémonie des adieux, suivi de Entretiens avec Jean-Paul Sartre* (Paris: Gallimard, 1981); *Adieux: A Farewell to Sartre*, trans. P. O'Brian (New York: Pantheon, 1984). The second half of this volume consists of transcripts of an interview dialogue conducted by de Beauvoir, to which references will be made later in this chapter and elsewhere.

2. Annie Cohen-Solal, *Sartre* (Paris: Gallimard, 1985); *Sartre: A Life* (New York: Pantheon, 1987).

3. Ibid., p. 651.

4. *Le Nouvel Observateur*, Mar. 10, 1980, p. 19; Mar. 17, 1980, p. 52; Mar. 24, 1980, p. 55. The text is reprinted, almost in its entirety, in *Dissent*, Fall 1980, pp. 397–422, trans. A. Foulke. It is noteworthy that *Dissent*'s editor, Irving Howe, in his introductory note, presents this text as perhaps "moving in a direction closer to our own" (p. 397).

5. *Le Nom de l'homme* (Lagrasse: Editions Verdier, 1984). Here, Lévy often criticizes Sartre, notably for his belief in what Lévy now regards as the *myth* of Socialism (p. 130), and never suggests that Sartre had revised his views with respect to socialism at the end of his life to the satisfaction of his partner in dialogue.

6. Olivier Todd, a conservative journalist and erstwhile Cambridge University philosophy student who has written an ambiguous, bittersweet memorial of his relationships with Sartre over the years, *Un Fils rebelle* (Paris: Bernard Grasset, 1981), writes about the Sartre-Lévy text somewhat in this vein: "J'accuse Victor [the pseudonymous surname by which Lévy was known for some years] d'abus de confiance intellectuelle, d'un détournement d'un vieillard" (pp. 14–15).

7. Cohen-Solal, *Sartre*, pp. 652–53; *Sartre: A Life*, pp. 514–15.

8. Sartre, *Lettres au Castor et à quelques autres 1926–1939*, (Paris: Gallimard, 1983), p. 518 (Dec. 31, 1939). Fifteen days later, returning to the theme of his new theory of nothingness and at the same time attempting to justify the large amount of time that he is devoting to his philosophy, he says: "It has a role in my life, which is to protect me against the melancholies, morosenesses, and sadnesses of the war, and moreover at this time I am not attempting to protect my life after the fact by my philosophy, which is dirty, nor to conform my life to my philosophy, which is pedantic, but truly life and philosophy make only one" (trans. mine, as with all subsequent references to both volumes of *Lettres*). *Lettres au Castor et à quelques autres 1940–1963*, p. 39 (Jan. 15, 1940).

9. Sartre, *Cahiers pour une morale* (Paris: Gallimard, 1983), p. 61.

10. "As soon as there will exist *for everyone* a margin of *real* freedom beyond the production of life, Marxism will have lived out its span; a philosophy of freedom will take its place." Sartre, *Search for a Method*, trans. H. Barnes (New York: Alfred A. Knopf, 1963), p. 34; *Critique de la raison dialectique*, vol. 1, 1st ed. (Paris: Gallimard, 1960), p. 32; 2d ed. (Paris: Gallimard, 1985), p. 39.

11. Sartre, *Les Mots* (Paris: Gallimard, 1964), p. 210; *The Words*, trans. B. Frechtman (New York: Fawcett, 1966), p. 158.

12. *Adieux*, p. 415; *La Cérémonie*, p. 522. One already finds the same theme years earlier, in Sartre's *Carnets de la drôle de guerre* (Paris: Gallimard, 1983), in the following remarks in which Sartre is reflecting on a quarrel that he has just had with one of his fellow soldiers, during which he said that he had made a mistake when he joined the meterological service in 1929 and that he should not be held accountable

ten years later for that mistake: "It is my pride that makes me speak, my sense of progress and that manner I have of distancing myself from what I was the day before. Every time someone seems struck by the permanence of my self, I am overcome with uneasiness." (p. 19). (I have utilized my own translation here, because I disapprove of certain key words in the published English translation of this passage. See Sartre, *The War Diaries*, trans. Q. Hoare [New York: Pantheon, 1984], p. 8. In subsequent references to this work, I shall sometimes use Hoare's translation and sometimes my own, as noted.)

13. Sartre, *Search for a Method*, p. xxxiv; *Critique de la raison dialectique*, vol. 1, 1st ed., p. 8; 2d ed., p. 14.

14. Sartre, *The Family Idiot: Gustave Flaubert, 1821–1857*, vol. 1, trans. C. Cosman (Chicago and London: University of Chicago Press, 1981), p. ix; *L'Idiot de la famille: Gustave Flaubert de 1821 à 1857*, vol. 1 (Paris: Gallimard, 1971), p. 7.

15. This is the implication that Wilfrid Desan draws in the second sentence of his early study, *The Marxism of Jean-Paul Sartre* (Garden City: Doubleday, 1965), p. v. For a book-length attempt to defend the value of both *Being and Nothingness* and the *Critique* for professional sociologists, see Ian Craib, *Existentialism and Sociology: A Study of Jean-Paul Sartre* (Cambridge: Cambridge University Press, 1976).

16. Sartre, *Being and Nothingness*, trans. H. Barnes (New York: Philosophical Library, 1956), p. 628; *L'Être et le néant* (Paris: Gallimard, 1943), p. 722. There are also various Washington Square Press paperbound editions of the English translation, with two different paginations (there is a difference of 30 pages between them throughout), both different in pagination from the hardbound original, which I am treating as the standard.

17. *Cahiers pour une morale*, p. 435.

18. de Beauvoir, *La Force des choses* (Paris: Gallimard, 1963), p. 218 (my translation); *The Force of Circumstance*, trans. R. Howard (New York: Putnam, 1965), p. 199.

19. There exist numerous allusions to these manuscripts, which will no doubt be published some day. In the conversation with de Beauvoir, for example, Sartre mentions "a work on ethics I prepared for that American university which invited me. I began by writing four or five lectures that I was to deliver over there and then I went on for myself. I have piles of notes." *Adieux*, p. 182; *La Cérémonie*, p. 235. He goes on to say that he does not know what has become of these notes, but that they must be somewhere in his apartment. He then goes on to agree with de Beauvoir when she suggests that this material dealt with the relationship between ethics and politics and that it was "completely different" from his earlier work on ethics. Moreover, Benny Lévy, in *Le Nom de l'homme*, makes several allusions to "un texte essentiel de 1964" (p. 108), a text of lectures that Sartre presented at the Gramsci Institute in Rome, and that remain unedited. Robert Stone and Elizabeth Bowman, two of several possessors of typescripts of these manuscripts, have clarified some of the details concerning them. There are three of them altogether—the projected American lectures, the Gramsci Institute lectures along with some subsequent additions, and the mass of notes proper—and they run to 776 typescript pages. The "American university" to which Sartre alluded was Cornell: he had accepted an invitation to speak there, but eventually rescinded his acceptance in protest against the United States government's escalation of its military involvement in Vietnam. Among the topics to which Sartre devotes detailed analyses in these manuscripts are the American primary election contest between Robert Kennedy and Hubert Humphrey in West Virginia (erroneously identified by Sartre as "Wisconsin") in 1964, and the decision of some mothers in Belgium who had taken the drug thalidomide, before it became known that it caused severe birth defects in progeny, to commit infanticide when the tragic facts began to emerge. The theoretical focus of the Gramsci Institute lectures, as both Stone/Bowman and Lévy agree, is the

concept of *need*, a significant expansion of a theme that is already to be found in the *Critique*. See Robert Stone and Elizabeth Bowman, " 'Making the Human' in Sartre's Unpublished Dialectical Ethics," in *The Future of Continental Philosophy and the Politics of Difference*, ed. H. Silverman (Albany: SUNY Press, 1990); "Sartre's *Morality and History:* A First Look at the Notes for the Unpublished 1965 Cornell Lectures," in *Sartre Alive*, ed. R. Aronson and A. van den Hoven (Detroit: Wayne State University Press, 1990); and "Dialectical Ethics: A First Look at Sartre's Unpublished 1964 Rome Lecture Notes," *Social Text* 13–14, Winter/Spring 1986, pp. 195–215. As of this writing, the literary executor of Sartre's estate, Arlette Elkaïm-Sartre, his adopted daughter, who by French law has ultimate jurisdiction over permissions to publish or even to cite unpublished writings of Sartre's (note Simone de Beauvoir's oblique reference to this jurisdiction in her one-page introduction to the *Lettres au Castor*, p. 7), has not yet authorized the publication of these manuscripts (except for a fragment, translated by E. Bowman, that appears in *Sartre Alive* and another fragment that was printed before Sartre's death). What can be publicly said about these manuscripts will be discussed in greater detail in chapter 6. In any event, their present status constitutes yet another argument in favor of adopting an open-ended stance toward Sartre's political theory and indeed all other significant aspects of his thought. But even the eventual publication of these manuscripts will not eliminate this argument, for there remains yet other unedited material—e.g., certain letters. There remains even the theoretical possibility that some of the lost *Carnets de la drôle de guerre*, left on a train by a colleague to whom Sartre had entrusted them during those hectic wartime days, may survive and be recognized for what they are some day.

20. *Cahiers pour une morale*, p. 487. The initial heading, "Plan d'une morale ontologique," appears on p. 484.

21. Aristotle, *Nicomachean Ethics* 1, 2.

22. Sartre, *L'Existentialisme est un humanisme* (Paris: Nagel, 1965), p. 83 (my translation). There is no separately published English translation of this book in print at present. One readily-available translation, by Philip Mairet, is to be found in Walter Kaufmann, ed., *Existentialism from Dostoevsky to Sartre*, revised edition (New York: New American Library, 1985), pp. 345–64. It has the virtue of correctly reproducing the French title in English, "Existentialism Is a Humanism," rather than, as some other editions have made it, "Existentialism and Humanism" or simply "Existentialism."

23. Even Anna Boschetti, whose *Sartre et 'Les Temps Modernes'* (Paris: Editions de Minuit, 1985) is often viciously reductionistic, flaunting a disdain of attention or fidelity to texts in the name of a preconceived notion of the subject's "real" role within his "intellectual field," places great emphasis on the assimilation of literature and philosophy as Sartre's fundamental life project, beginning with his college years at the Ecole Normale Supérieure. As she expresses it: "It is a question of appropriating for oneself the models of one genre, philosophical literature, which seeks to articulate the universal in accordance with philosophy's finality, in the form of the singular instance, as literature does; to preserve within the proceedings of philosophy, which abstracts, generalizes, the charm of a concrete and unique experience . . ." (my trans.) (p. 43). This book has been translated by Richard McCleary under the title *The Intellectual Enterprise: Sartre and Les Temps Modernes* (Evanston: Northwestern University Press, 1988).

24. *Adieux*, p. 174; *La Cérémonie*, p. 221.

25. *Adieux*, p. 172; *La Cérémonie*, p. 223.

26. *Adieux*, pp. 168–69; *La Cérémonie*, p. 219.

27. *Adieux*, p. 374; *La Cérémonie*, p. 473.

28. Maurice Merleau-Ponty, *Adventures of the Dialectic*, trans. J. Bien (Evanston:

Northwestern University Press, 1973, pp. 95–201, esp. p. 200; *Les Aventures de la dialectique* (Paris: Gallimard, 1955), pp. 131–271, esp. top of p. 270.

29. There are those, such as Robert Cumming in his essay "To Understand a Man" (in Paul Schilpp, ed., *The Philosophy of Jean-Paul Sartre* [LaSalle: Open Court, 1981], pp. 55–85), who have maintained that Sartre was a dialectician from his early years; in the interview in which Sartre attempted to respond to verbal questions based on the critical essays in the Schilpp volume, Sartre denies this (p. 9), contending that he became consciously dialectical in his approach only after the publication of *Being and Nothingness*.

30. "R. [Michel Rybalka] And today you no longer consider yourself a Marxist? . . . Sartre No. I think, by the way, that we are witnessing the end of Marxism . . ." Schilpp, ed., *The Philosophy*, p. 20. The principal basis, within the Schilpp volume's critical essays, of this set of questions appears to be my essay on "Sartre and Marxism", pp. 605–30.

31. *Social Theory at a Crossroads* (Pittsburgh: Duquesne University Press, 1980), chapter on "Sartre's Contribution to Social Theory: A Retrospective Glance," pp. 41–80. The book is a revision of lectures delivered at Duquesne in Fall 1977.

32. *Being and Nothingness*, p. 627; *L'Être et le néant*, p. 721. Of course, this appears within a larger context, but that context only exacerbates, if anything, the apolitical implications of this sentence.

33. Sartre's commemorative essay on Nizan, written as a preface to a new edition of the latter's *Aden, Arabie*, is very moving and revealing. It is also published in *Situations*, 4 (Paris: Gallimard, 1964), pp. 130–88.

34. The first essay in the second series of the influential collection *Philosophy, Politics and Society*, edited by P. Laslett and W. C. Runciman (Oxford: Basil Blackwell, 1964), is by Isaiah Berlin and well reflects, at least in its title, the period of Anglo-American analytic philosophy that I am recalling. Originally published (ironically, in the *Revue Française de Science Politique*) in 1961, it is entitled "Does Political Theory Still Exist?" (pp. 1–33).

ONE. BEGINNINGS

1. Sartre, *Search for a Method*, p. 62; *Critique de la raison dialectique*, vol. 1, 1st ed., p. 47; 2d ed., p. 57.

2. See Michel Contat and Michel Rybalka, *Les Ecrits de Sartre* (Paris: Gallimard, 1970), p. 380; *The Writings of Jean-Paul Sartre*, trans. R. McCleary, vol. 1 (Evanston: Northwestern University Press, 1974), p. 398, on this subject. Sartre began writing the book in 1954, when he felt more self-critical about his career as a writer than he later came to feel.

3. Rousseau's *Confessions* is the historical work that perhaps best sets this modern tone. As the example of Rousseau proves, this is an area of literature in which the threat of self-deception is omnipresent, and the likelihood of falling into it repeatedly is overwhelming.

4. "We well know that this distinction between private life and public life does not exist in fact, that it is a pure illusion, a mystification." Sartre, *Situations*, 10 (Paris: Gallimard, 1976), p. 176 ("Autoportrait à soixante-dix ans," interview with Michel Contat, my translation); *Life/Situations*, trans. P. Auster and L. Davis (New York: Pantheon, 1977), p. 44.

5. See, however, a short but very interesting interview, conducted by Lucien Malson, with Sartre on this topic, in *Le Monde*, July 28, 1977, pp. 10–11. It includes a discussion of the *political* implications of music, which Sartre claims may exist (e.g., the use of certain music to promote a particular regime) but are always "borrowed" and never profound or intrinsically very exact. Sartre's commitment to music is

indicated by his comment that this extraordinarily prolific writer never tries to write seriously and to listen to music simultaneously. There is also a discussion of Sartre's interest in music in his interview with Contat. See *Life/Situations*, pp. 37–41; *Situations*, 10, pp. 167–72.

6. Cohen-Solal, *Sartre*, p. 352.

7. Typical, and very amusing, are the letters that Sartre wrote to de Beauvoir while on a cruise with his parents along the Norwegian coast, July 24–27, 1935. See *Lettres . . . 1926–1939*, pp. 57–62. The last sentence of the last of these letters, before the complimentary closing, reads: "Parents are wedged like a knife in their children's skulls, and they cut all their thoughts in two."

8. *Adieux*, p. 148; *La Cérémonie*, p. 193.

9. "Conflict is the original meaning of being-for-others." *Being and Nothingness*, p. 364; *L'Être et le néant*, p. 431.

10. As Martin Heidegger says in reply to critics' charges that "the lecture ['What Is Metaphysics?'] raises an isolated and, what is more, a morbid mood, namely dread, to the status of the one key-mood," what interests him is dread as a way of ingress into the most fundamental of philosophical realities, not dread as a mere mood or feeling: "Our lecture neither puts forward a 'Philosophy of Dread' nor seeks to give the false impression of being an 'heroic' philosophy." Postscript to "What Is Metaphysics?" trans. R. F. C. Hull and A. Crick, in Walter Kaufmann, ed., *Existentialism from Dostoevsky to Sartre*, rev. ed. (New York: New American Library, 1975), pp. 259, 261.

It is ironic that Sartre is quoted in his "final" interview, with Lévy, as saying: "I have never known anguish. That is a key philosophical notion of the '30s. It came principally from Heidegger. It's one of the notions people were making use of, but to me it meant nothing." *Dissent*, Fall 1980, p. 398. It is probably this remark more than any other in the interview that, rightly or wrongly, has lent some credence to the suspicion that Sartre experienced moments of genuine senility in his last years.

11. Unfortunately from the standpoint of his own credibility as a theorist, Eric Werner seems somehow to wish to deny this, at least to the extent of imputing to Sartre a "totalitarian," even "Stalinist," conclusion similar to Hobbes's, as a result of supposedly similar "mistaken" views about the nature of society, in *De la violence au totalitarisme: Essai sur la pensée de Camus et de Sartre* (Paris: Calmann-Lévy, 1972), esp. pp. 162–63.

12. Hobbes, *Leviathan*, part 2, Chap. 29. He begins: "Though nothing can be immortal, which mortals make; yet, if men had the use of reason they pretend to, their commonwealths might be secured, at least from perishing by internal diseases . . ." (Oxford: Basil Blackwell, 1960), p. 209.

13. Contat and Rybalka, *Les Ecrits de Sartre*, pp. 517–30; *The Writings of Jean-Paul Sartre*, trans. R. McCleary, vol. 2, *Selected Prose* (Evanston: Northwestern University Press, 1974), pp. 22–36. (Note: The French original is in one volume, the English translation in two volumes.)

14. "For example," he says in the introductory interview in Schilpp, ed., *The Philosophy*, "I took Husserl for a realist, which he is not; that is a philosophical error. He is much closer to Kant." (p. 25)

15. It is most interesting that this long essay, while it became available in English translation in 1947 and was frequently cited and even used as a text in ensuing years, as I can testify from personal experience, in explaining the evolution of Sartre's philosophy to American students, was not available in an accessible French version (i.e., to those who could not obtain a back issue of vol. 6 of *Recherches philosophiques*) until 1965! See Contat and Rybalka, *Les Ecrits de Sartre*, p. 56.

16. Sartre, *The Transcendence of the Ego*, trans. F. Williams and R. Kirkpatrick (New York: Farrar, Straus and Giroux, 1957), pp. 104–106; *La Transcendance de l'ego* (Paris: Librairie Philosophique J. Vrin, 1985), pp. 85–87.

17. See Edmund Husserl, *The Crisis of European Sciences and Transcendental Phenomenology*, trans. and ed. David Carr (Evanston: Northwestern University Press, 1970), p. xvi (Carr's introduction).

18. Sartre, *L'Imagination* (Paris: Librairie Félix Alcan, 1936); *Imagination: A Psychological Critique*, trans. F. Williams (Ann Arbor: University of Michigan Press, 1962).

19. Gerassi, "Using Sartre's Regressive-Progressive Method against Him: From Guilt to Commitment," *The French Review* 55, special issue #7, Summer 1982, pp. 101–108. Gerassi tells us that his father learned the news of Franco's action from Sartre when he went, his young child in tow, to an informal meeting that the two of them had arranged; the elder Gerassi was presumably so shocked and stirred to action by this news that he set off immediately to join in the combat, leaving Sartre to take the little boy back home to his mother!

20. *Sartre, Un film réalisé par* Alexandre Astruc et Michel Contat (Paris: Gallimard, 1977), p. 63.

21. Sartre, *The War Diaries*, p. 182; *Les Carnets*, p. 224.

22. "The person who will read [my little black notebook] after my death—for you will only publish it posthumously—will think that I was an ugly personality unless you accompany it with kindly and explanatory footnotes." *Lettres . . . 1926–1939*, p. 300.

23. Sartre, *Lettres . . . 1940–1963*, p. 285.

24. Ibid., p. 121.

25. Sartre, *Les Carnets*, pp. 355–56 (my translation); *The War Diaries*, p. 293.

26. Sartre, *Lettres . . . 1926–1939*, p. 378.

27. Sartre, *The War Diaries*, p. 301; *Les Carnets*, p. 366.

28. Sartre, *Lettres . . . 1940–1963*, p. 257.

29. Sartre, *The War Diaries*, p. 24; *Les Carnets*, p. 37. He speaks of this in the context of an awareness on his part of the tendency of those who have been mobilized to regard themselves as an elite by comparison with the civilian population. He says that his own *natural* membership, to which his political attitude is always opposed, is with the strong or favored group, and he lists three interesting examples of weaker parties with whom he is inclined to side: wives against husbands, children against parents, and students against professors. I find this a particularly attractive passage.

30. Sartre, *The War Diaries*, p. 172; *Les Carnets*, p. 212.

31. Sartre, *The War Diaries*, pp. 72ff.; *Les Carnets*, pp. 95ff.

32. That Sartre himself was somewhat aware of this is shown by his admission, in the midst of these reminiscences, that he had been thoroughly imbued with "what I shall call the biographical illusion, which consists in believing that a lived life can resemble a life in a story [*une vie racontée*]." *Les Carnets*, pp. 105–106 (my translation); *The War Diaries*, p. 81.

33. *The War Diaries*, p. 28; *Les Carnets*, p. 42.

34. Sartre, *Lettres . . . 1926–1939*, p. 470.

35. Sartre's *Auseinandersetzung* with humanism could easily be the topic of a complete study in itself. The major problem for any interpreter attempting to deal with it stems from the fact that one of Sartre's most popular and best-known works, the transcript of a brief lecture that he gave one evening at the height of his early popularity, is entitled "Existentialism Is a Humanism"—a seemingly clear-cut identification. The problem is only slightly lessened, as Sartre himself realized, by the fact that he later declared himself dissatisfied with the rather partial development of his ideas that this lecture displays; he had acceded to a publisher's request to print a small edition of the transcript, only to find that more than 100,000 copies were printed. (See *Sartre, Un film*, pp. 94–95.) But even in *Nausea* he had expressed,

through the fictional personage of Roquentin, a disgust for that sort of humanism that amounts to a saccharine admiration for "man" as such, and in another, early passage in *The War Diaries* (pp. 21–22; *Les Carnets*, p. 34) he clearly articulated the inadequacies of humanism as a substitute religion, based on a worship of the human *species*. Much later, in *The Family Idiot*, he would return to similar themes in a manner that is consistent with these early remarks but blatantly inconsistent, at least on the surface, with his best-known statement on the subject.

36. There is one isolated passage in the *Carnets* upon which unfriendly critics have seized in order to raise questions about Sartre's consistency with respect to conservative, and even ultra-conservative, thinking. In it he says that he recognizes in his own thought at the time a pinch *("un soupçon")* of fascism, even though he hates fascism. By way of explaining what he means, he enumerates the following elements: "historicity, being-in-the-world, all that binds man to his time, all that roots him in his land and his situation."—*The War Diaries*, p. 146; *Les Carnets*, p. 184. Any reasonable reading of the text must, it seems to me, lead to the conclusion that it demonstrates only that Sartre was still rather unclear with respect to the nature of his nascent social thought, for which, later on, these very elements were to be building-blocks of a thoroughgoing, radical antifascism and anticonservatism. It must also be recalled that Sartre was under a heavy debt to Heidegger at this time, as he was very well aware, and that he had at least some general sense of Heidegger's having flirted with Naziism.

37. *The War Diaries*, p. 95; *Les Carnets*, pp. 121–22.

38. The concept itself has its ancestry in Nietzsche's *der Geist der Schwere* in *Also Sprach Zarathustra*. The usual English translation of this, "the spirit of gravity," preserves Nietzsche's double meaning, whereas neither *"l'esprit de sérieux"* nor *"l'homme sérieux"* does so.

39. de Beauvoir, *Pour une morale de l'ambiguïté* (Paris: Gallimard, 1947), p. 70; *The Ethics of Ambiguity*, trans. B. Frechtman (New York: Citadel, 1970), p. 48.

40. Sartre, *The War Diaries*, p. 325; *Les Carnets*, p. 394.

41. Sartre, *Lettres . . . 1926–1939*, p. 510.

42. I have discussed a few of the ontological and ethical aspects of these matters, partly in response to George Schrader's accusation "that Sartre is 'too tense to enjoy the comedy of existence,'" in my section on "Play" in "Jean-Paul Sartre: Man, Freedom, and *Praxis*," in George Alfred Schrader, Jr., ed., *Existential Philosophers: Kierkegaard to Merleau-Ponty* (New York: McGraw-Hill, 1967), pp. 283–88.

43. Sartre, *The War Diaries*, pp. 239ff.; *Les Carnets*, pp. 292ff.

44. Sartre, *The War Diaries*, p. 243; *Les Carnets*, p. 296.

45. Sartre, *Les Carnets*, p. 294 (my translation); *The War Diaries*, p. 241.

46. See the interview in *Life/Situations*, p. 68; *Situations*, X, p. 201.

47. Sartre, *The War Diaries*, p. 249; *Les Carnets*, p. 303.

48. Sartre, *The War Diaries*, p. 251; *Les Carnets*, p. 306.

49. The Sartrean word in the *Carnets* that their translator and I would agree in designating as "pride" is *orgueil*. It signifies an intense pride. But there is another French word for more commonplace pride, *fierté*, the adjective of which *(fier)* would normally be used in a context in which one wishes to speak of being proud of something or other that one has done. This has some importance for trying to understand the total nature of Sartre's "metaphysical pride," because he draws a distinction between the two words in *Being and Nothingness*, in the English translation of which Hazel Barnes renders *"orgueil"* as "arrogance":

> In short there are two authentic attitudes: that by which I recognize the Other [*Autrui*] as the subject through whom I get my object-ness—this is shame [*la honte*]; and that by which I apprehend myself as the free object by which the Other gets his being-other [*vient à l'être-autrui*]—this is arrogance [*l'orgueil*] or

the affirmation of my freedom confronting the Other-as-object [*en face d'Autrui-objet*]. But pride [*la fierté*]—or vanity—is a feeling without equilibrium, and it is in bad faith. *Being and Nothingness*, p. 290; *L'Être et le néant*, p. 351.

Several observations suggest themselves. First, while "arrogance" is sometimes an appropriate translation of *"orgueil,"* the connotations of the English word are not exactly those of the French: "arrogance" conveys a sense of "putting down," even *oppressing*, others, a sense of evildoing, that Sartre did not mean to imply here. (Barnes's choice of the word "confronting" for *"en face de,"* while again not literally *incorrect*, reinforces this sense of *confrontation* which is not necessarily implied by Sartre's *orgueil*.) Second, Sartre's suggestion of "vanity" *(la vanité)* as an equivalent of *"fierté"* goes a long way toward explaining the subtle distinction that he is trying to make here: "vanity" does imply, in English as in French, an uneasy, unstable type of attitude—an effort to impress others, based on small details of one's behavior, dress, etc., that is always in danger of faltering; by contrast, a certain self-confident pride, in the sense of *"orgueil,"* may be more stable and more global, as was Sartre's *"orgueil métaphysique."* Third, this is philosophically important because the passage that I have just cited is the only one, I believe, in *Being and Nothingness* in which Sartre actually furnishes instances of supposedly *authentic* attitudes, and when they are rendered as "shame and arrogance," rather than "shame and pride," they make authenticity itself appear very unappealing, as many of my students have noted over the years. As we shall see when we consider *Anti-Semite and Jew* and the *Cahiers pour une morale*, Sartre did not mean that these were the only two possible stances of authenticity, and the notion itself, regarded as a key to morality, can be a very rich one.

50. This tension within Sartre's philosophical radicalism was a point I tried to illustrate by ordering my earlier summary of his thought in accordance with four "transcendental" categories of the *philosophia perennis:* truth, unity, goodness (value), and beauty *("la belle âme").* See my essay in Schrader, ed., *Existential Philosophers*, p. 326 and passim.

51. These terms, metaphysics and ontology, are often used interchangeably, as I am using them here. Heidegger, among others, drew a distinction between them, and Sartre adopts that distinction near the end of *Being and Nothingness*, where he contrasts the "ontological" enterprise of that work with a possible "metaphysical" inquiry, about the *origin* of being-for-itself ("In this sense metaphysics is to ontology as history is to sociology"), which he is not undertaking there. See *Being and Nothingness*, p. 619; *L'Être et le néant*, p. 713. But elsewhere he himself frequently uses "metaphysics" in the more general, less technical sense in which it is inter-changeable with "ontology."

52. *Search for a Method*, pp. 17–19; *Critique de la raison dialectique*, vol. 1, 1st ed., pp. 22–24; 2d ed., pp. 28–30. In the context, Sartre shows how the official attitudes of the institutions of higher learning of those days lent some support to Marx's assertion that the ideas of the ruling class are the ruling ideas.

53. Cohen-Solal, *Sartre*, esp. pp. 234ff.

54. Sartre, *Being and Nothingness*, pp. 586–97; *L'Être et le néant*, pp. 675–87.

55. Sartre, *Being and Nothingness*, p. 594; *L'Être et le néant*, p. 685.

56. Sartre, *Being and Nothingness*, p. 158; *L'Être et le néant*, p. 205.

57. One of the best shorter discussions is that of Dorothy Leland, "The Sartrean Cogito: A Journey between Versions", in *Research in Phenomenology* 5, 1975, pp. 129–41.

58. Sartre, *Being and Nothingness*, pp. 159–60; *L'Être et le néant*, pp. 206–207. The reference in this passage to the *psyche* should also be seen as a veiled allusion to an as yet unpublished manuscript of Sartre's by that name. If it is ever published, it should shed considerable new light on his earlier thought.

59. Sartre, *Being and Nothingness*, p. 556; *L'Etre et le néant*, p. 641. The entire subsection covers pp. 553–56 in the English translation, 638–42 in the French original.

60. Hazel Barnes's now-standard translation of this important expression, the title of a chapter of *Being and Nothingness*, "Concrete Relations with Others," is inadvertently misleading, because the use of the plural in English makes it sound as if Sartre's approach was already considerably less individualistic at this point in his development than it in fact was. The force of the French expression *"les relations avec autrui,"* with its impersonal singular pronoun, is, I believe, to make one think primarily of one-on-one relations, rather than of multiple interrelations with several or many others, as the paradigm.

61. Sartre, *Being and Nothingness*, pp. 415–23; *L'Être et le néant*, pp. 486–95.

62. Sartre, *Being and Nothingness*, p. 419; *L'Être et le néant*, p. 490.

63. Sartre, *Being and Nothingness* pp. 423–29; *L'Être et le néant*, pp. 495–502.

64. Sartre, *Being and Nothingness* pp. 244–50; *L'Être et le néant*, pp. 300–307.

65. Sartre, *Being and Nothingness*, p. 424; *L'Être et le néant*, p. 496.

66. Sartre, *Being and Nothingness*, p. 425; *L'Être et le néant*, p. 497.

67. Sartre, *Being and Nothingness*, p. 428; *L'Être et le néant*, p. 500.

68. Sartre, *Being and Nothingness*, p. 68–70; *L'Être et le néant*, pp. 108–11.

69. Sartre, *Being and Nothingness*, p. 580; *L'Être et le néant*, p. 669.

70. This is well demonstrated, against some recent expressions of skepticism concerning the intended function of this play and indeed concerning Sartre's entire stance vis-à-vis the Occupation and the Resistance, by Ingrid Galster, *Le Théâtre de Jean-Paul Sartre devant ses premiers critiques* (Paris: Editions Jean Michel Place, 1986).

TWO. FIRST ETHICS

1. *Adieux*, p. 180; *La Cérémonie*, p. 234.

2. While it is true that this essay includes, as I have noted in my introduction, an important early emphasis on the interdependence of one's own freedom with that of others, and that the central "case history" of an ethical dilemma that Sartre recounts here involves a choice between a young man's presumed family obligations (to his mother) and a political commitment (to join the Free French military forces), nevertheless its nearly exclusive focus is on individual choice without serious reference to sociopolitical structures. The highly "Kantian" tone of the essay, which was originally presented as a public lecture to a very large audience when existentialism as a cultural vogue was beginning to crest, has been noted by many commentators; it is a one-sided and somewhat too popularized expression of Sartre's thinking of that era. He himself overcame some personal reluctance in acceding to the request of a small publisher (Nagel) that it be printed in a supposedly "limited" edition, and he lived to regret this decision. As Contat and Rybalka note, "This is moreover, the only work Sartre has largely rejected," *The Writings of Jean-Paul Sartre*, vol. 1, p. 133; *Les Ecrits de Sartre*, p. 132.

3. Sartre, *Anti-Semite and Jew*, trans. G. Becker (New York: Shocken Books, 1968), p. 71; *Réflexions sur la question juive* (Paris: Gallimard, 1954), p. 86.

4. Sartre, *Anti-Semite and Jew*, p. 123; *Réflexions*, p. 153.

5. Sartre, *Réflexions*, p. 165 (my translation). The translation in *Anti-Semite and Jew* (p. 133) is misleading; it reads: "in the anxiety that moves us to a consideration of the condition of man . . . ," thus making anxiety a precondition rather than a consequence.

6. *Le Nouvel Observateur*, Mar. 10, 1980, p. 19; *Dissent*, Fall 1980, p. 398.

7. de Beauvoir, *The Second Sex*, trans. H. M. Parshley (New York: Vintage, 1974), p. 301; *Le Deuxième Sexe*, vol. 2, L'Expérience vécue (Paris: Gallimard, 1949), p. 13.

8. Contat and Rybalka, *The Writings of Jean-Paul Sartre*, vol. 1, pp. 143–44; *Les Écrits de Sartre*, p. 140.

9. This is the thrust of Ronald Hayman's interpretation in the final chapter of his *Sartre: A Life* (New York: Simon & Schuster, 1987), esp. p. 461.

10. Sartre, *Réflexions*, p. 137 (my translation); *Anti-Semite and Jew*, p. 170. (The latter, arbitrarily inaccurate once again, reads: "like any [sic] authentic man.")

11. Sartre, *Réflexions*, p. 60 (my translation); *Anti-Semite and Jew*, p. 72.

12. Sartre, *Réflexions*, pp. 34–35 (my translation); *Anti-Semite and Jew*, p. 41.

13. I am thinking above all of the dialectical method of Hegel and Marx, at which, as I have already noted (note 29, introduction), Sartre claims not to have been at all adept at the time of the writing of *Being and Nothingness*.

14. In *Anti-Semite and Jew*, Sartre at one point maintains that the anti-Semite tends to be playful and even to claim (*seriously*, I presume) a *right* to play (p. 20; *Réflexions*, p. 23).

15. Sartre, "Présentation des *Temps Modernes*" in *Situations*, 2 (Paris: Gallimard, 1948), p. 30.

16. Ibid., p. 17.

17. Ibid., p. 28.

18. Ibid., p. 21.

19. Ibid., p. 24.

20. Ibid., p. 16. The best discussion of the evolution of the notion of "materialism" in Sartre's thought that I know of is Hazel Barnes's chapter, "Sartre as Materialist," in Schilpp, ed., *The Philosophy*, pp. 661–84.

21. Sartre, "Présentation," p. 16.

22. Although Sartre in this essay is, as usual, very unsatisfactory as far as making detailed references to other texts is concerned, the original source of this theory is Lenin's *Materialism and Empiriocriticism*. The theory continued to be of importance within French Marxist circles by virtue of the fact that it was defended at length, albeit in a somewhat ambiguous and not fully enthusiastic way, in the doctoral thesis written by the leading Communist Party ideologue, Roger Garaudy, *Théorie matérialiste de la connaissance* (Paris: Presses Universitaires de France, 1953).

23. Sartre, "Matérialisme et Révolution," in *Situations*, 3 (Paris: Gallimard, 1949), p. 135. (The original *Temps Modernes* version of 1946 obviously does not include this footnote!) The English translation ("Materialism and Revolution," in *Literary and Philosophical Essays*, [New York: Collier Books, 1962], p. 198) erroneously reads "Neo-Stalinist Marxism" (Stalin was still alive in 1949, of course) instead of "Stalinist neo-Marxism"; Sartre has been badly served by many of his English-language translators.

24. Sartre, *Critique of Dialectical Reason*, trans. A. Sheridan Smith (London: NLB and Atlantic Highlands: Humanities Press, 1976), pp. 180–81; *Critique de la raison dialectique*, vol. 1, 1st ed., p. 248; 2d ed., p. 291.

25. Sartre, *Literary and Philosophical Essays*, pp. 214–15; *Situations*, 3, pp. 161–62.

26. Sartre, *Literary and Philosophical Essays*, p. 220; *Situations*, 3, p. 171.

27. Sartre's most famous portrayal of this attitude in the theatrical genre is *Les mains sales (Dirty Hands)*, first produced in 1948. This play came to be used and, as far as Sartre was concerned, abused so extensively in the cause of anti-Communist and often simply Right-Wing propaganda that for some years he refused to authorize performances of it.

28. Sartre indulges in some wicked fun at Garaudy's expense. Here is an example: "Our Garaudys are afraid. What they seek in communism is not liberation, but a re-enforcement of discipline; there is nothing they fear so much as freedom . . ." Then, reporting the shoulder-shrugging reaction, dismissive of Garaudy's importance, of some communist intellectuals to Sartre's account of a disturbing conversation between himself and Garaudy: "I admit . . . that M. Garaudy did not

seem to be a shining light, but after all, he writes a great deal and the communists do not disown him." *Literary and Philosophical Essays,* p. 249; *Situations,* 3, p. 215.

29. Sartre, *Literary and Philosophical Essays,* p. 237; *Situations,* 3, p. 196. The word "transcendence" has a long and complex history in Western thought and even, along with its corresponding adjectival and verb forms, in Sartre's own thought. In this passage, however, it has a rather simple and straightforward meaning, as a contrasting notion to that of a fixed natural order, allegedly characteristic of our human world, that would be impervious to radical or fundamental change. Readers familiar with de Beauvoir's *The Second Sex* will recall her pervasive use of the contrast between "transcendence" and "immanence." At any rate, Sartre's "transcendence" here is not meant to bear any other-worldly connotations.

30. Sartre, *Situations,* 3, p. 210 (my translation); *Literary and Philosophical Essays,* p. 246.

31. Sartre, *Situations,* 3, p. 225 (my translation); *Literary and Philosophical Essays,* p. 256.

32. This is the title of a movie screenplay by Sartre, first shown in 1947.

33. While "humanism" is not as central to "Materialism and Revolution" as are the other two notions mentioned, it remains, in continuity with *Existentialism Is a Humanism,* a key element in the revolutionary thought that Sartre is attempting to forge here as an alternative to orthodox Marxist materialism. But "humanism" can mean many different things, and it can also be a social and intellectual trap. Sartre's 1930s antihero Roquentin already shows this very well in a famous dialogue in *Nausea* with "the Self-Taught Man," in which he denounces the latter's vague, cosmic, and inefficacious "humanism," and Sartre will confront some of these issues once again, in a more sophisticated way, in *The Family Idiot.* (See note 35 of chap. 1.)

34. Sartre's new-found confidence here is most obvious with respect to his command of topics in political and social theory and of the contemporary scene. It is more ambiguous as far as the historical future is concerned. However, he is not the utter pessimist with respect to the latter that is implied by the back book-jacket blurb of the Collier edition of his *Literary and Philosophical Essays* from which I have been citing the English translation of "Materialism and Revolution": "[In] his final and most extended essay, . . . he . . . foresees a grim future for the revolutionary movement." To call this merely "fatuous" would be complimentary.

35. As Contat and Rybalka express it: "In spite of the rather large number of rough approximations and some actual errors of detail in its historical part, and in spite of the obvious rigidity of certain stands it takes, *What Is Literature?* is still one of the most stimulating books one can read, and it has been recognized for a long time now as a classic of criticism. The questions Sartre raises were topical in 1947; although the historical situation has changed considerably, they are just as topical today." *The Writings of Jean-Paul Sartre,* vol. 1, pp. 168–69; *Les Ecrits de Sartre,* p. 161.

36. Although Sartre does not mention specific essays by name at this point, he is clearly referring to the advocacy line that he took both in the "Presentation" of *Les Temps Modernes* and in an article of lesser importance, "The Nationalization of Literature" ("La Nationalisation de la littérature"), which appeared in the second number of that journal and was reprinted, along with it and *What Is Literature?,* as the total content of *Situations,* 2.

37. "Qu'est-ce que la littérature?" in *Situations,* 2, p. 58 (my translation); *What Is Literature?* trans. B. Frechtman (New York: Washington Square Press, 1966), p. vii. (There are several different editions of this English-language translation; I shall therefore always reference the French *Situations,* 2, version first).

38. Sartre, *Situations,* 2, p. 263; *What Is Literature?,* p. 16.

39. *Situations,* 2, p. 176 (my translation); *What Is Literature?,* p. 90. Sartre's contrast here between the "rebel" and the "revolutionary" was later to become

central in Albert Camus's *The Rebel (L'Homme révolté)*, but Camus found the rebel much more to his liking.

40. *Situations*, 2, p. 265 (my translation); *What Is Literature?* p. 165. Even at this point, *"exis"* is printed without the aspirate (') in Sartre's text; in English, the word is sometimes printed as *"hexis"* in order to convey the proper pronunciation.

41. *Situations*, 2, p. 86 (my translation); *What Is Literature?*, p. 10. (The published English translation reads ". . . nor ever quite subjective," instead of ". . . nor ever completely subjective," a substantial difference in meaning.)

42. *Situations*, 2, p. 197; *What Is Literature?*, p. 108.

43. *Situations*, 2, p. 130; *What Is Literature?*, p. 53.

44. *Situations*, 2, p. 265; *What Is Literature?*, pp. 165–66.

45. *Le Problème moral et la pensée de Sartre* (Paris: Editions du Myrte). A new edition was published by Editions du Seuil years later, in 1965; it includes an important new chapter, written as a postscript. There is an excellent English translation (*Sartre and the Problem of Morality*, as mentioned in the text) by Robert Stone, who also provides good background information in his introduction about the history of this book and of some of Sartre's subsequent relations with Jeanson (Bloomington: Indiana University Press, 1980). See also my review of this translation in *Canadian Philosophical Reviews* 1, 6 (Dec. 1981), pp. 263–66.

46. *Situations*, 2, pp. 245–48; *What Is Literature?*, pp. 148–51. These pages contain the gist of the ideas noted here, as well as the language of finding the (moral) absolute within (historical) relativity itself. But the phrase within quotation marks is taken directly from a passage near the end of de Beauvoir's interview with Sartre in *Adieux* (p. 439; *La Cérémonie*, p. 552), in which his fundamental attitude concerning relativism and moral Good and Evil is under discussion. The juxtaposition of these two texts published one third of a century apart is, to me, striking.

48. *Situations*, 2, p. 111; *What Is Literature?*, p. 40.

49. *Situations*, 2, pp. 251–52 (my translation); *What Is Literature?*, p. 154.

50. Sartre, *Cahiers pour une morale*, p. 573. All translations from these *Cahiers* are my own. Some of the issues that I shall be discussing in subsequent pages are also touched upon in my article "The Evolution of Sartre's Conception of Morals," *Phenomenological Inquiry*, Oct. 1987, pp. 24–44.

51. Sartre, *Cahiers pour une morale*, p. 46.

52. Included are running commentaries on certain famous passages in the *Phenomenology* (as well as many references to Alexandre Kojève's treatments of them), such as Virtue and the Course of the World, Lordship and Bondage (of course!), and *"die Sache selbst."*

53. *Cahiers pour une morale*, p. 285.

54. Ibid., pp. 484–87.

55. Since many critics used to contend, on the basis of their readings of *Being and Nothingness*, that Sartre could not even conceive of the possibility of authentic love, it may be useful, although it is not of enormous importance for our consideration of Sartre's political theory, directly to cite a line on the subject from this text: "Here we are able to understand what *loving* means in its sense of authenticity." Ibid., p. 516.

56. Ibid., pp. 490ff.

57. Ibid., p. 495.

58. Ibid., p. 496.

59. Ibid., pp. 514–15.

60. Ibid., p. 129. Many pages later (p. 529), Sartre characterizes as productive and creative even the housewife's action in moving pieces of furniture around a room in order to improve the appearance.

61. Ibid., p. 137.

62. Sartre's elevation of generosity to a position of such outstanding importance in the ethical schema of the *Cahiers* recalls Descartes's attribution of a similar place to

generosity among the "passions of the soul" in his much-neglected treatise of that name. As Sonia Kruks has pointed out, generosity is also central in Simone de Beauvoir's earlier essay, *Pyrrhus et Cineas*, published in 1944.

63. *Cahiers pour une morale*, p. 138.

64. Ibid., p. 139, Sartre gives two alternative French translations: *"la Cause ou Chose même."* My own preferred translation of what Hegel means here is the colloquialism, "one's own thing." This implies, of course, an individualistic and somewhat solitary approach to whatever one does in life; Hegel's dialectical point, on which Sartre places his own further gloss by associating the phenomenological analysis of *"die Sache selbst"* with the level of impersonal common action (the *"on," "das Man"*), is of course that it is an *illusion* to believe that this doing of "one's own thing" is an authentic expression of one's own isolated individuality.

65. Marcel Mauss, *The Gift*, trans. I. Cunnison (New York and London: W. W. Norton, 1967). More recently, Jean Baudrillard has been strongly influenced by this same small classic.

66. *Cahiers pour une morale*, pp. 382ff.

67. Ibid., pp. 300–301.

68. Ibid., p. 555. By "the original project" Sartre means, as he did in *Being and Nothingness*, the project of a single individual, but now understood as being carried out in a milieu in which there are many individuals with diverse projects.

69. *Cahiers pour une morale*, p. 178.

70. Ibid., p. 194.

71. Ibid., p. 179. At this point in the passage, Sartre begins to play on yet another meaning of "law" to illustrate the contrast between force in conformity with a natural "legality," as in the uncorking of a bottle, and destructive violence "exterior to [such] legality," as in breaking the bottle at the neck.

72. Ibid., p. 150.

73. Ibid.

74. Ibid., p. 185

75. Ibid., p. 244.

76. Ibid., p. 275.

77. One of the most ambitious recent such attempts is that of Carol Gould. In Chapter 7 of her *Rethinking Democracy* (Cambridge University Press, 1988), she announces her intention to provide an enumeration of "the human rights" and proceeds to do so. Among the most prominent issues discussed in the recent literature is the status of so-called subsistence rights (to jobs, health care, etc.) as distinct from more traditionally liberal rights against "interference" from one's cocitizens and from government, and the question of whether freedom itself should be regarded as a right. Henry Shue, now joined by a number of other writers, has become particularly well known for arguing for the reality of subsistence rights; Gould claims to go beyond his "minimalist" position in this regard (p. 201). Ronald Dworkin is probably in a minority in denying the existence of a right to liberty as such. (See *Taking Rights Seriously* (Cambridge, Mass.: Harvard University Press, 1977), chap. 12). What I am suggesting here is that Sartre's reflections in this section of the *Cahiers* raise fundamental questions about the assumptions underlying the entire enterprise of specifying a precise list of rights, to which this whole body of literature attempts to contribute.

78. For two discussions of different aspects of this point, which is rather complex, see my "Marxism and Human Rights," in *Infinity, Proceedings of the American Catholic Philosophical Association* 55, 1981, pp. 260–67, and "Rights and the Marxian Tradition," *Praxis International*, 4, 1 (Apr. 1984), pp. 57–74. The crucial point is that this *suspiciousness* on Marx's part, for which I see ample warrant from both historical and conceptual standpoints, is not reducible, as some have asserted, to the claim that he either rejected rights or denigrated law *tout court* and in every respect.

79. Despite the good intentions of the source of the dictum "Let reverence for

the law become the political religion of the nation," Abraham Lincoln, it is highly problematic. See my article, "The Fetishism of Illegality and the Mystifications of 'Authority' and 'Legitimacy'," in *Georgia Law Review* 18, 4 (1984), pp. 863–90. Indeed, this entire issue of this journal is devoted to discussing the alleged "Duty to Obey the Law."

80. *Cahiers pour une morale,* pp. 50–51.

81. Ibid., p. 279.

82. The word "subject" runs the risk of being misleading when used in this context, since it more often refers, in both Hegel and Sartre, to the human "subject," the source of action, in contrast to its "object." Here, of course, the word is being used in its more ordinary sense in legal and political theory: the sovereign's "subjects," loyal or disloyal as the case may be, or the "subjects of the legal system."

83. *Cahiers pour une morale,* p. 280.

84. This is precisely the obstacle posed by Kant in his work in legal philosophy, *The Metaphysical Elements of Justice,* when he categorically denies that there can ever be a *"right to revolution,"* for that would be a self-contradictory notion.

85. *Cahiers pour une morale,* p. 282. In using this little turn of phrase, Sartre is confronting the entire dominant social contract theory of modern Western political thought.

86. Ibid., p. 283.

87. Ibid.

88. The source of the modern sense of the notion is usually said to be Jean Bodin, although Sartre makes no mention of him.

89. At this point in his text, Sartre quotes at length from an article by Lacan in the *Encyclopédie française* concerning the beginnings of "narcissistic intuition," and hence of an initial alienation, in early infancy. This is said to be characteristic of all societies. Sartre does not challenge Lacan's observations. *Cahiers pour une morale,* p. 380.

90. *Cahiers pour une morale,* p. 381.

91. Ibid., p. 67.

92. Ibid., p. 396.

93. Ibid., p. 338.

94. Ibid., pp. 197ff.

95. Ibid., p. 189.

96. Ibid., p. 222.

97. Ibid., p. 315.

98. Ibid., p. 393.

99. Ibid., p. 312.

100. Ibid., pp. 316–317.

101. Ibid., p. 337.

102. Ibid., p. 338.

103. Ibid., p. 67. I have cited a little more of this passage than is needed just in order to show Sartre's attitude toward Marx and Marxism at the time, because of its enormous intrinsic interest.

104. Ibid., p. 87.

105. Ibid., p. 88.

106. Ibid., p. 129.

107. Ibid., p. 469.

108. Ibid., pp. 440–42. A few pages later (pp. 464–65), Sartre resumes this attack on traditional ontology along similar lines by focusing on Hegel's assertion that "the absolute is *subjects.*" Being, he says, has no preordained meaning, and it is human consciousnesses that have the absolute power of deciding upon its meaning for them.

109. Ibid., pp. 358–60.

110. Ibid., p. 482.

111. I try to show the usefulness, particularly with respect to the meaning of morality, of the distinction between the broad Marxist and the Marxian traditions (the latter referring to Karl Marx's own fundamental worldview or conceptual framework) in "Rights and the Marxian Tradition," p. 59.

112. An excellent example of an unsophisticated remark is Sartre's unpardonably careless account, if that is what it can be called, of Marx's way of dealing with the obvious real-world discrepancies between the actual prices of goods and their exchange-values as calculable within his economic theory:

> Exchange-value: entity, Platonism. There is only the use-value and the price, without this mediation which mediates nothing, because *on the one hand* Marx admits, in a small aside, that exchange-value is nothing without use-value. Labor could not confer exchange-value if it is undertaken on an object without use-value. And on the other hand he makes considerations foreign to exchange-value (History, myths, etc.) intervene in the setting of prices, in such a way that the exchange-value is expressed as mixed up, unrecognizable in the price, like the Platonic Eidos in the sensible domain: crushed between the use-value and the price, the exchange-value bursts apart. *Cahiers pour une morale,* pp. 124–25.

It is simply a caricature to reduce the careful analyses of Part 2 of Volume 3 of *Capital,* in which Marx tries (whether successfully or not is not the issue here) to show how exchange-values can be converted into prices by means of the notion of the average rate of profit, to "foreign considerations," such as History, myths, etc. Unfortunately, such cavalier dismissals of Marx's thought are, if I am not mistaken, very much à la mode once again these days. By contrast, many of the passages that might be cited from the *Cahiers* concerning Hegel's writings, especially the *Phenomenology of Spirit,* and concerning Kojève's interpretation of Hegel show a satisfactorily high level of attention on Sartre's part to what the texts actually say.

113. One could, of course, regard Sartre's line of thought during the overlapping periods of his greatest involvement in political theory and his greatest involvement in politics as the deviation, as measured both against his earlier, more individualistic existentialism and perhaps against the thrust of his last published remarks in *"L'Espoir, maintenant."* This is, essentially, the position taken by Jeannette Colombel in her two-volume work, *Sartre* (Paris: Librairie Générale Française, 1986), esp. vol. 2, part 4, chap. 2, "Sartre serait-il devenu marxiste?" It was also the position that she took in her thus far unpublished paper, "Morale et création," presented at the first meeting of the (North American) Sartre Society, at the New School, New York, October 6, 1985. See the remarks critical of this position made by Sonia Kruks, "Sartre's *Cahiers pour une morale:* Failed Attempt or New Trajectory in Ethics?", *Social Text* 13/14, Winter/Spring 1986, pp. 184–94, originally prepared in response to Colombel's New York paper. I am in fundamental agreement with Professor Kruks's remarks. In the discussion following the presentation of my own unpublished paper, "La Théorie politique de Sartre d'après les oeuvres posthumes," to the Groupe d'Etudes Sartriennes, Paris, June 21, 1987, Professor Colombel graciously conceded that I had shown certain aspects of her more individualistic interpretation of the *Cahiers* to have been somewhat exaggerated.

114. Sartre, *Search for a Method,* pp. 33–34; *Critique de la raison dialectique,* vol. 1, 1st ed., p. 31; 2d ed., p. 39.

115. The accusation that Sartre departs from Marx on this point and consequently represents a regression to Hegel is perhaps the most central critical claim of Pietro Chiodi's *Sartre and Marxism,* trans. K. Soper (Atlantic Highlands: Humanities Press, 1976).

116. *Cahiers pour une morale,* p. 72.

117. The unjustifiability of any certainty, within the logic of Marx's thought, that history will inevitably work out in the way that he would consider optimal is the central contention of Chapter 6 of my book *The Philosophy of Marx* (London: Hutchinson, 1977).

118. *Cahiers pour une morale*, p. 31.

119. Ibid., p. 353.

120. Ibid., p. 421.

121. Ibid., p. 429. In the *Critique*, this terminology of "Apocalypse" will be attributed by Sartre to Malraux, who used it in his novel, *L'Espoir*. I explore, half-seriously and half-humorously, some of the implications of taking it literally and to an extreme in Part 3, Chapter 6, "Totalization," of my book *Fundamental Change in Law and Society* (The Hague: Mouton, 1970).

122. Sartre, *Cahiers pour une morale*, pp. 47–50.

123. The continuity of this theme between *Being and Nothingness* and the *Critique* is the central point of James Sheridan's *Sartre: The Radical Conversion* (Athens: Ohio University Press, 1969). Sheridan, of course, did not have access to the *Cahiers* at the time of writing this.

124. *Cahiers pour une morale*, p. 20.

125. Ibid., p. 95.

126. Ibid., p. 109.

127. Ibid., p. 421.

128. Ibid., p. 99.

129. See note 54 of this chapter.

130. See note 18 of the introduction.

THREE. THE MASTERFUL THOUGH UNFINISHED
CRITIQUE

1. To be precise, Contat and Rybalka contend that Volume 1 was composed in its entirety between late 1957 and the beginning of 1960, with an interruption in the fall of 1958 as a result of Sartre's first serious health crisis, itself the product of his overwork, his concern over the political situation in France (and Algeria), and his excessive intake of over-the-counter drugs (see *Les Ecrits de Sartre*, p. 338; *The Writings of Jean-Paul Sartre*, p. 370). And Arlette Elkaïm-Sartre claims, simply, that Volume 2 was composed in 1958, although Sartre reread it in 1962 with a view to the never-realized possibility of continuing it. *Critique de la raison dialectique*, vol. 2 (Paris: Gallimard, 1985), p. 7. Sartre does refer to 1958 as the current year, on p. 196 of that book. He claimed still to be working on it, however, in the course of a three-day symposium in which he participated at the Gramsci Institute in Rome in late 1961.

2. *L'Affaire Henri Martin*, commentaire de Jean-Paul Sartre (Paris: Gallimard, 1953), p. 193.

3. *The Writings of Jean-Paul Sartre*, vol. 1, p. 214; *Les Ecrits de Sartre*, p. 203.

4. Cohen-Solal, *Sartre*, p. 401; *Sartre: A Life*, p. 307.

5. I make this point in my *Fundamental Change in Law and Society*, p. 130, and it is also an important theme in Ronald Aronson's *Sartre's Second Critique* (Chicago and London: University of Chicago Press, 1987).

6. This is what he claimed in his interview with Madeleine Chapsal, in *Les Ecrivains en personne* (Paris: René Juillard, 1960), p. 206.

7. Sartre, *Situations*, 6 (Paris: Gallimard, 1964), pp. 23–68. The book *Le Communisme yougoslave depuis la rupture avec Moscou* with Sartre's preface was published in July 1950. More precisely, "lièvres" means "hares."

8. Sartre, *Situations*, 6, p. 51.

9. Ibid., p. 28.

10. Ibid., p. 40.

11. Georg Lukács, *Existentialisme ou Marxisme?* trans. E. Kelemen (Paris: Nagel, 1948). I refer to this work in my article "Reification Re-Examined," in T. Rockmore, ed., *Lukács Today,* vol. 51 of *Sovietica* (Dordrecht: D. Reidel, 1988), p. 110.

12. He refers specifically, in this context, to Kardelj.

13. *Situations,* 6, p. 24.

14. Hayman, in discussing Sartre's response to the Soviet invasion of Hungary six and a half years later, refers to "Stalinism" as a "new word" then! *Sartre: A Life,* p. 327. But it was obviously already very much in currency in 1950.

15. *Situations,* 6, p. 38.

16. Ibid., pp. 23 and 25.

17. Ibid., p. 66. Sartre continued to take an interest in Yugoslavia in later years. There exists, notably, a filmed interview made with him in Dubrovnik in 1969 by Eleonora Prohić, on the topic of the then-current state of Marxism.

18. *The Nation,* Dec. 30, 1950, p. 696.

19. "Merleau-Ponty Vivant" in Sartre, *Situations,* 6 (Paris: Gallimard, 1964), p. 212. Translations from this essay are my own. See "Merleau-Ponty Alive," trans. Benita Eisler, in *Situations* (New York: George Braziller, 1965), p. 250.

20. Duclos's automobile, when he was arrested, contained a couple of pigeons that he insisted he had been taking to his wife to be cooked for dinner. The police regarded the pigeons as evidence that Duclos was using carrier pigeons to transport secret messages to and from Moscow. The birds had, in fact, been destined to be used for dinner.

21. *Situations,* 4, pp. 248–49; *Situations,* pp. 287–88.

22. *Situations,* 6, p. 238. Translations from this essay are my own. See *The Communists and Peace, with a Reply to Claude Lefort,* trans. Martha Fletcher (New York: George Braziller, 1968), p. 120.

23. *Situations,* 6, p. 251; *The Communists and Peace,* p. 131. (The translator substitutes "idle" for "Byzantine.")

24. This term, "spontaneity," has a somewhat technical meaning in the Marxist-Leninist tradition, having been used by Lenin to designate the notion, roughly, that initiatives for political action should come from "below," from the "masses," in contrast to his own preferred policy of "consciousness": instigation by the wise Party leadership.

25. *Situations,* 6, p. 112; *The Communists and Peace,* p. 26.

26. Claude Lefort, "Le Marxisme et Sartre," *Les Temps Modernes* 89 (April 1953), pp. 1541–70.

27. In his Merleau-Ponty memorial essay, Sartre even claims to have toned down his polemic somewhat before publishing it! He was, clearly, extremely tense at the time.

28. The adjective "Trotskyite" or "Trotskyist" has by now come to bear so many different, vague meanings and emotive connotations that my eyes tend to glaze over when I read it. Nevertheless, in this historical context it was still somewhat meaningful.

29. *Situations,* 6, p. 222; *The Communists and Peace,* p. 108. Here, as so often, the translation simply does not say the same thing as the original.

30. Sartre, "Réponse à Claude Lefort," in *Situations,* 7 (Paris: Librairie Gallimard, 1965), p. 52; *The Communists and Peace,* p. 267.

31. *Situations,* 7, p. 76; *The Communists and Peace,* p. 284.

32. *Situations,* 7, pp. 15 and 38; *The Communists and Peace,* pp. 240 and 257.

33. *Situations,* 6, p. 118; *The Communists and Peace,* pp. 30–31.

34. *Situations,* 6, pp. 250–51; *The Communists and Peace,* pp. 130–31.

35. *L'Affaire Henri Martin,* p. 198.

36. Ibid., p. 213.
37. Ibid., p. 206.
38. *Situations,* 6, p. 258; *The Communists and Peace,* p. 136.
39. *Situations,* 6, p. 343; *The Communists and Peace,* p. 200.
40. *Situations,* 4, p. 108; *Situations,* p. 88.
41. *Situations,* 4, p. 125; *Situations,* p. 104.
42. *Situations,* 7, p. 101.
43. Ibid., p. 110.
44. Ibid., p. 130.
45. There is a slight discrepancy in accounts of just when this invitation was extended. Hayman (*Sartre: A Life,* p. 331) says that it was in November 1956—in other words, very soon after Budapest—when Sartre met the editor of *Twórczość,* Jerzy Lisowski, at the Polish embassy in Paris. Contat and Rybalka (*Les Ecrits de Sartre,* p. 310; *The Writings of Sartre,* vol. 1, p. 338) say that it took place when Sartre was traveling in Poland, and that would place it in January 1957.
46. Sartre, "Le Fantôme de Staline," *Les Temps Modernes* 129–31 (Nov.-Dec. 1956—Jan. 1957), pp. 577–697; reprinted in *Situations,* 7; *The Ghost of Stalin,* trans. Martha Fletcher (New York: George Braziller, 1968); *The Spectre of Stalin,* trans. Irene Clephane (London: Hamish Hamilton, 1969).
47. *Search for a Method,* p. 8; *Critique de la raison dialectique,* vol. 1, 1st ed., pp. 17–18; 2d ed., p. 22.
48. *Search for Method,* pp. 91ff.; *CRD,* vol. 1, 1st ed., pp. 63ff.; 2d ed., pp. 76ff. I shall retain this shorthand ("*CRD*") for the remainder of the footnotes alluding to the French editions of Volume 1 in this and subsequent chapters.
49. The contrast is first introduced, as far as I have discovered, on p. 78 of *Search for a Method* (*CRD,* vol. 1, 1st ed., p. 56; 2d ed., p. 67), but it becomes pervasive in the text of the *Critique* proper.
50. This becomes a focal point of discussion, as I shall note later, in Claude Lévi-Strauss's critique of Sartre's *Critique* in *La Pensée Sauvage* (Paris: Plon, 1962), pp. 324–57.
51. Sartre takes it for granted, however, that such societies lack a fully developed sense of history. Thus, his attitude toward them retains something of a conventional, patronizing tone, despite his considerable interest in studying anthropologists' reports about them.
52. *Search for a Method,* p. 90; *CRD,* vol. 1, 1st ed., p. 63; 2d ed., pp. 75–76.
53. At the very end of Volume 1, Sartre poses the problem of history, to be dealt with in the next volume, as that of "totalization without a totalizer." *CRD,* vol. 1, 1st ed., p. 754; 2d ed., pp. 893–94; *Critique of Dialectical Reason,* p. 817.
54. *Search for a Method,* p. 26; *CRD,* vol. 1, 1st ed., p. 27; 2d ed., p. 33.
55. *Search for a Method,* p. 23; *CRD,* vol. 1, 1st ed., p. 26; 2d ed., p. 32.
56. *Search for a Method,* p. 30; *CRD,* vol. 1, 1st ed., p. 29; 2d ed., p. 36.
57. *Search for a Method,* p. 34; *CRD,* vol. 1, 1st ed., p. 32; 2d ed., p. 39.
58. This overview of Marxism as a philosophy is developed in detail in my book *The Philosophy of Marx* (London: Hutchinson; New York: St. Martins, 1977).
59. Schilpp, ed., *The Philosophy,* pp. 21 and 30. Another particularly interesting but quite differently focused explanation is to be found in his long interview with Michel Sicard (*Obliques,* 1979, my translation), p. 15. Here he discusses his work-in-process with Benny Lévy (Pierre Victor) as pointing to a new ontology of consciousness "which will be obliged to leave nothing standing from *Being and Nothingness* and from *Critique of Dialectical Reason*"; when Sicard presses him on the exact difference, if there is any, between his supposedly new insistence on the "we" and the Marxist dialectic with which he found common ground at the time of the *Critique,* Sartre replies, somewhat arcanely: "Because they are integrated [in Marxism] as *men,* individuals belonging to a community, but not as *consciousness* [*sic*—it

should read 'consciousnesses'] having common points with another consciousness. For Marx, it is outside that the relationship of agents is made. For us, it is made first of all within. But it is very complicated, it would be necessary to speak at length . . ." I shall revert to these matters when discussing the question of the significance of Sartre's "last words."

60. On the resurgent role of this text in some relatively recent scholarship on Marx, see my review essay, "Tendencies in Marxology and Tendencies in History," *Ethics* 92 (Jan. 1982), pp. 316–26.

61. *Search for a Method*, p. 92; *CRD*, vol. 1, 1st ed., p. 64; 2d ed., p. 77.

62. Sartre makes this translation explicit in a very important footnote in *CRD*, vol. 1, 1st ed., p. 286; 2d ed., pp. 336–37; *Critique of Dialectical Reason*, p. 227.

63. *CRD*, vol. 1, 1st ed. pp. 85–86; 2d ed., p. 102, my translation. The Barnes translation (*Search for a Method*, pp. 132–33) fails to capture the obviously Marxian flavor of the original, especially in the rendering of *"marchandises"* as "merchandise" instead of the classical Marxian term, "commodities."

64. *CRD*, vol. 1, 1st ed., p. 220; 2d ed., p. 258, my translation; *Critique of Dialectical Reason*, p. 147.

65. In Schilpp, ed., *The Philosophy*, "Sartre and Marxism," pp. 605–30. It is no accident, I think, that some of the issues that I raised in this article figured particularly prominently in the dialogue between Sartre and his three interlocutors that opens this volume: these were among the issues that were of greatest concern to him at this late stage of his career.

66. Ibid., p. 30.

67. Ibid., p. 32.

68. *CRD*, vol. 1, 1st ed., p. 9; 2d ed., p. 14, my translation; *Search for a Method*, p. xxxiv.

69. *CRD*, vol. 1, 1st ed., p. 754; 2d ed., p. 894; *Critique of Dialectical Reason*, p. 818.

70. *Search for a Method*, p. 62; *CRD*, vol. 1, 1st ed., p. 47; 2d ed., p. 57.

71. See note 82, below.

72. See note 14 to introduction.

73. *CRD*, vol. 1, 1st ed., p. 145; 2d ed., p. 171; *Critique of Dialectical Reason*, p. 55.

74. "Perspectives de sociologie rurale," in *Cahiers de sociologie*, 1953.

75. *CRD*, vol. 1, 1st ed., p. 42; 2d ed., pp. 50–51, my translation; *Search for a Method*, pp. 51–52.

76. There is a certain amount of "turning the other cheek" on Sartre's part here: Lefebvre's 1946 Communist "potboiler," *L'Existentialisme* (Paris: Editions du Sagittaire), was a scathing denunciation of Sartre, accusing him of lack of rigor, dishonesty, irrationalism, and so on. But by 1957 this distinguished thinker, certainly (in my opinion) the most interesting French philosopher still holding membership in the C.P. at the time, was on his way out. John Gerassi retains very strongly negative feelings about Lefebvre's role in C.P. attacks on Sartre and even more on Paul Nizan. In his last reference to him in his recent Sartre biography, Gerassi says: "That . . . intellectuals still speak reverently of such *salauds* as Henri Lefebvre, explains why so many French intellectuals have so often betrayed their ideals—and their friends." *Jean-Paul Sartre: Hated Conscience of His Century* (Chicago: University of Chicago Press, 1989), p. 154.

77. *Search for a Method*, p. 133; *CRD*, vol. 1, 1st ed., p. 86; 2d ed., p. 103.

78. It is important to recall Marx's own distinction, made in the Afterword to the Second German Edition of *Capital*, between his method of presentation, which appears in the work itself and may, he fears, seem somewhat artificial and contrived, and his antecedent method of inquiry. For a discussion of this, in which the latter is identified as the phenomenological moment in Marx's philosophy, see my article "Marxism and Phenomenology," in *Journal of the British Society for Phenomenology* (JBSP) 6, (Jan. 1975), pp. 13–22.

79. Sartre, "Nous sommes tous des assassins," in *Situations*, 5 (Paris: Gallimard, 1964), pp. 68–71.

80. Sartre, "Les Grenouilles qui demandent un roi," ibid., pp. 113–44.

81. Examples are "Des Rats et des hommes," the preface to *Le Traître* by André Gorz (Paris: Éditions du Seuil, 1958), printed in translation ("Of Rats and Men") in *Situations*, pp. 327–71; and the preface to Nizan's *Aden Arabie*, previously mentioned.

82. Sartre, *Le Scénario Freud* (Paris: Gallimard, 1984); *The Freud Scenario*, trans. Q. Hoare (Chicago: University of Chicago Press, 1985).

83. The publication in 1986 of the French text and Portuguese translation of a conference given by Sartre at the University of Araraquara during his tour (with Simone de Beauvoir) of Brazil is of considerable interest. See *Sartre no Brasil: A Conferência de Araraquara*, trans. L. R. Salinas Fortes (Rio de Janeiro: Paz e Terra; Sâo Paulo: UNESP, 1986). For one thing, it puts into a somewhat unusual perspective the phenomenon of delays in planned publications: Salinas Fortes says (p. 18) that he actually undertook the translation of this 1960 conference in 1963, 23 years before it eventually appeared. For another thing, more important for Sartre scholarship, it brings out the very well integrated character of Sartre's conception of his life-work in the period immediately following the appearance of the *Critique* and his trip to Cuba. He summarizes several of the themes of *Search for a Method*, notably the importance of Marxism and of a kind of sociohistorical wisdom (*compréhension*) that is different from, and superior to, mere intellection (p. 72). If there is one point on which he particularly takes issue with Marx in this conference, it is the latter's notion of the "realization of philosophy," of a kind of terminal-point of history, with which the text begins and which Sartre characterizes as "a little optimistic and more Hegelian than Marxist" (p. 26, my translation). To me, this shows the extent to which Sartre had already, in his own mind, qualified the assertion about the possibility of reaching a time at which History would have a single meaning, about which he had written in *Search for a Method*.

In addition, Sartre speaks readily in this conference about the relationship—a relationship of continuity, as he sees it—between *Being and Nothingness* and the *Critique*, saying that, while the direction of the two is essentially the same, the manner of formulating problems is different, the earlier work dealing at a formal level with truths that are "undeniable, but almost empty [*nulles*]," the latter attempting to reconstitute "an ontology, or at least a dialectical anthropology" (p. 92). Finally, there is one theme that Sartre emphasizes here much more, in my opinion, than in any of his later writings, the theme of "the Cartesian *cogito*" as a still indispensable basis for social theory (p. 86), although he does make a remark, interesting in light of later French philosophy's assault on the whole notion of "the subject" and subjectivity, to the effect that "man-subject" is an improper expression, for which the term "man-questioner" (p. 70) would better be substituted. By reverting so strongly to this last mentioned theme, which played perhaps even more central a role in his philosophical writings of the 1930s than in *Being and Nothingness*, much less in later works, Sartre is taking a more unitary view of his philosophical career up to that time than even I, who am in general supportive of such a view, would care to. It seems to me that the connotations of the notion of "*praxis*" which dominates the *Critique* take us a considerable distance away from the "*cogito*" especially from, to use Sartre's term, "the Cartesian *cogito*."

84. See Wilfrid Desan, *The Marxism of Jean-Paul Sartre* (Garden City: Doubleday Anchor, 1965); Joseph Catalano, *A Commentary on Jean-Paul Sartre's* Critique of Dialectical Reason, Volume 1, *Theory of Practical Ensembles* (Chicago: University of Chicago Press, 1986); and R. D. Laing and D. G. Cooper, *Reason and Violence* (New York: Pantheon, 1971), which is primarily but not entirely a summary of Volume 1.

85. See note 5 of this chapter, above.

86. The second half of my book *Fundamental Change in Law and Society* is a case in point. Two useful bibliographies, although they are of course not up to date, are Robert Wilcocks, *Sartre: A Bibliography of International Criticism* (Edmonton: University of Alberta Press, 1975), and François Lapointe, *Jean-Paul Sartre and His Critics: An International Bibliography (1938–1980)*, 2d ed. (Bowling Green, Ohio: Philosophy Documentation Center, 1981).

87. Alan Sheridan-Smith, the English translator of the *Critique*, also rightly renders *"expérience"* as "investigation" when he thinks it appropriate.

FOUR. THE *CRITIQUE*

1. *Critique de la raison dialectique*, vol. 2, p. 313.

2. *CRD*, vol. 1, 1st ed., p. 115; 2d ed., p. 135, my translation (as will be the case for all subsequent translations from this volume); *Critique of Dialectical Reason*, p. 15. A more detailed discussion of dialectical methodology as it is to be understood within a Sartrean context is found in the chapter "Dialectics" in my *Fundamental Change in Law and Society*, pp. 152–63.

3. *CRD*, vol. 1, 1st ed., p. 135; 2d ed., p. 159; *Critique of Dialectical Reason*, p. 41.

4. *CRD*, vol. 1, 1st ed., p. 140; 2d ed., p. 165; *Critique of Dialectical Reason*, p. 48.

5. *CRD*, vol. 1, 1st ed., pp. 141–42; 2d ed., p. 166; *Critique of Dialectical Reason*, p. 50.

6. *Critique de la raison dialectique*, vol. 2, pp. 196–97.

7. See note 50 of chap. 3, above.

8. *CRD*, vol. 1, 1st ed., p. 120; 2d ed., p. 141; *Critique of Dialectical Reason*, p. 21.

9. *CRD*, vol. 1, 1st ed., p. 117; 2d ed., p. 137; *Critique of Dialectical Reason*, p. 17.

10. *CRD*, vol. 1, 1st ed., pp. 130–31; 2d ed., p. 153; *Critique of Dialectical Reason*, p. 35.

11. *Critique de la raison dialectique*, vol. 2, p. 317.

12. *CRD*, vol. 1, 1st ed., p. 123; 2d ed., p. 144; *Critique of Dialectical Reason*, p. 25. It should be noted that in this text Sartre evinces a certain ambivalence about the question of just where *Marx*, as distinguished from Engels, stood on these issues— an ambivalence that I share.

13. See Schilpp, *The Philosophy*, p. 629 (note 33 to my article) and pp. 28–29 (in Sartre's interview with his interlocutors).

14. *Critique de la raison dialectique*, vol. 2, p. 393.

15. Ibid., p. 394. Interestingly, something like this goal, survival, came to be of central importance to Wilfrid Desan, whose work has been so important for Sartre scholarship in the United States, in his essay of original philosophy, *The Planetary Man*, vol. 1 (New York: Macmillan, 1972, 2d ed.), published (in 1961) long before Volume 2 of the *Critique* appeared.

16. *CRD*, vol. 1, 1st ed., p. 132; 2d ed., p. 156; *Critique of Dialectical Reason*, p. 37. Catalano, *A Commentary*, p. 75 and passim, places special emphasis on this notion. See my review of this book in *Canadian Philosophical Reviews* 8 (Nov. 1988), pp. 430–32.

17. *CRD*, vol. 1, 1st ed., p. 146; 2d ed., p. 172; *Critique of Dialectical Reason*, p. 56.

18. *Critique de la raison dialectique*, vol. 2, p. 359.

19. It will be recalled that the latter forms of reciprocity are the subject of the earlier essay by Sartre that has been published as an appendix to the *Cahiers pour une morale*.

20. See my essay, "Sartre and the Phenomenology of Social Violence," in *New Essays in Phenomenology*, ed. James Edie (Chicago: Quandrangle, 1969), pp. 290–313.

21. *Critique de la raison dialectique*, vol. 2, p. 38.

22. Wilfrid Desan begins *The Marxism of Jean-Paul Sartre* by contrasting the "speculative philosophy" of *Being and Nothingness* with the *Critique*, which he says

tells us what Sartre thinks "in the realm of sociology" (p. v). I have contested the latter label in an otherwise generally positive review of this book in *Man and World* 2, Fall 1969, pp. 613–25.

23. *Critique de la raison dialectique,* vol. 2, p. 311.

24. Sartre's tendency to use the word "Being" in this pejorative, anti-Heideg-gerean and antitraditional fashion is already to be found in *Being and Nothingness,* where "being" *tout court* is sometimes used as shorthand for "being-in-itself." However, since that entire book was designed as an ontological study, that is, a study of the various "regions" of being, consistency required Sartre to designate the second region as "being-for-itself" and the third as "being-for-others" (or, as I have explained, "being-for-another"). The replacement of *être-pour-soi* by *praxis* in the *Critique* permits Sartre now to use "being," often capitalized, in a more straightfor-wardly negative way, except in a few isolated instances such as the one to which I am calling attention.

25. *Critique de la raison dialectique,* vol. 2, pp. 330–31.

26. Ibid., p. 335.

27. "The reductionist would regard Sartre's view as anthropocentric, but, for Sartre, there is nothing wrong with being anthropocentric where humans are concerned." Catalano, *A Commentary,* p. 50.

28. *CRD,* vol. 1, 1st ed., p. 200; 2d ed., p. 235; *Critique of Dialectical Reason,* p. 123.

29. *CRD,* vol. 1, 1st ed., p. 208; 2d ed., p. 243; *Critique of Dialectical Reason,* p. 132.

30. *CRD,* vol. 1, 1st ed., p. 358; 2d ed., p. 424; *Critique of Dialectical Reason,* p. 318.

31. Jean-Jacques Rousseau, *Du Contrat Social I,* 1 (Paris: Garnier, 1954), p. 235.

32. Karl Marx, *Capital,* vol. 1, trans. S. Moore and E. Aveling (Moscow: Foreign Languages Publishing, 1961), p. 77.

33. The "chains" of seriality, for Sartre, are self-forged. As for the slogan about being "born free," Sartre will now insist, as we shall see, that although free *praxis* is indeed, as it were, the definition of what it means to be human and hence charac-terizes us from birth, so does alienation. In one of his rare explicit criticisms of his earlier work, he says in a footnote: "Fundamental alienation does not stem, as *Being and Nothingness* might wrongly make one believe, from a prenatal choice: it stems from the univocal relationship of interiority which unites man as practical organism with his environment." *CRD,* vol. 1, 1st ed., p. 286; 2d ed., p. 337; *Critique of Dialectical Reason,* p. 228.

34. For a discussion of this idea of "legitimacy" as it is found in, inter alios, Sartre, Rousseau, some contemporary philosophers of law, and Habermas, see my essay, previously cited, "The Fetishism of Illegality and the Mystifications of 'Au-thority' and 'Legitimacy.' "

35. *CRD,* vol. 1, 1st ed., p. 179; 2d ed., p. 209; *Critique of Dialectical Reason,* p. 95.

36. *CRD,* vol. 1, 1st ed., pp. 642–43; 2d ed., pp. 759–60; *Critique of Dialectical Reason,* pp. 677–78.

37. *CRD,* vol. 1, 1st ed., p. 205; 2d ed., p. 240; *Critique of Dialectical Reason,* p. 129.

38. Sartre, *La Nausée* (Paris: Gallimard, 1938), p. 186.

39. *CRD,* vol. 1, 1st ed., p. 170; 2d ed., p. 199; *Critique of Dialectical Reason,* p. 85.

40. *CRD,* vol. 1, 1st ed., pp. 182ff.; 2d ed., pp. 213ff.; *Critique of Dialectical Reason,* pp. 100ff.

41. *CRD,* vol. 1, 1st ed., p. 219; 2d ed., p. 256; *Critique of Dialectical Reason,* p. 145.

42. *CRD,* vol. 1, 1st ed., p. 213; 2d ed., p. 250; *Critique of Dialectical Reason,* pp. 138–39.

43. This has been the subject, of course, of a vast amount of discussion within the so-called socialist countries themselves. A simple but classical article on this topic is "Socialism and the Problem of Alienation" by Predrag Vranicki, trans. W. Hannaker, in Erich Fromm, ed., *Socialist Humanism* (Garden City: Doubleday, 1965), pp. 299–313.

44. For my earlier discussion of this, see note 11 of chap. 3, above.

45. *"Praxeis"* is the correct plural form in Greek, although Sartre himself and, following him, most commentators misspell it as *"praxes."* An exception is Thomas Flynn, who, in his review essay of the English translation of the *Critique*, says that this translation leaves "the impression that this Greek word is of Latin origin." "Another Sartrean Torso," *Social Theory and Practice* 6, 1 (Spring 1980), p. 92. Flynn's own book, *Sartre and Marxist Existentialism: The Test Case of Collective Responsibility* (Chicago: University of Chicago Press, 1984), is among the best recent studies.

46. He speaks of "the structure, properly so called, of alienation insofar as it is linked to capitalist exploitation." *CRD*, vol. 1, 1st ed., p. 252; 2d ed., p. 296; *Critique of Dialectical Reason*, p. 186.

47. Sartre, in fact, having repeated the distinction between alienation in the Marxist sense and alienation in the more general sense, asks himself the question, "Would we be returning to Hegel, who makes of alienation a constant characteristic of objectification, whatever it may be?" His answer is "Yes and no." *CRD*, vol. 1, 1st ed., p. 285; 2d ed., p. 336; *Critique of Dialectical Reason*, p. 227. This passage serves as particularly good grist for the mill of Pietro Chiodi, *Sartre and Marxism*.

48. *CRD*, vol. 1, 1st ed., p. 239; 2d ed., p. 280; *Critique of Dialectical Reason*, p. 170. Although the word "reification" does not occur in this particular passage, I cite it because I find it significant that Sartre here places scare quotes around the word "superstructures." See also my review discussion of Cohen, cited in note 60 to ch. 3, above, and written in the same skeptical spirit.

49. *CRD*, vol. 1, 1st ed., pp. 243–44; 2d ed., p. 286; *Critique of Dialectical Reason*, p. 176.

50. *CRD*, vol. 1, 1st ed., pp. 224–25; 2d ed., pp. 263–64; *Critique of Dialectical Reason*, pp. 152–53.

51. *CRD*, vol. 1, 1st ed., pp. 232–33; 2d ed., p. 273; *Critique of Dialectical Reason*, p. 162.

52. F. Braudel, *The Mediterranean and the Mediterranean World in the Age of Philip II*, trans. S. Reynolds (New York: Harper & Row, 1972).

53. André Gorz, *Ecologie et politique* (Paris: Galilée, 1975); *Ecology as Politics*, trans. P. Vigderman and J. Cloud (Boston: South End Press, 1980).

54. I have dealt with this issue in my paper "Sartre and Problems in the Philosophy of Ecology," in preparation for publication, as part of conference proceedings, by the University of Lodz, Poland.

55. *CRD*, vol. 1, 1st ed., pp. 26off.; 2d ed., pp. 307ff.; *Critique of Dialectical Reason*, pp. 197ff.

56. *CRD*, vol. 1, 1st ed., p. 272; 2d ed., p. 320; *Critique of Dialectical Reason*, p. 210.

57. *CRD*, vol. 1, 1st ed., pp. 275–76; 2d ed., pp. 324–25; *Critique of Dialectical Reason*, p. 215.

58. Consider, for instance, the famous passage in the Preface to the First German Edition of *Capital*, in which Marx says that "their own most important interests dictate to the classes that are for the nonce the ruling ones, the removal of all legally removable hindrances to the free development of the working class" (p. 9).

59. *CRD*, vol. 1, 1st ed., p. 277; 2d ed., p. 326; *Critique of Dialectical Reason*, p. 216.

60. *CRD*, vol. 1, 1st ed., pp. 301–303; 2d ed., pp. 355–58; *Critique of Dialectical Reason*, pp. 247–50.

61. *CRD*, vol. 1, 1st ed., p. 302; 2d ed., p. 356; *Critique of Dialectical Reason*, p. 248. A serious translator's error in this passage would have Sartre writing that, in the case of a *requirement* (here translated as "exigency") as distinguished from a *value*, the *praxis* of the other "is not *mine*: it is myself as nothing." What Sartre actually wrote is that the other's *praxis* is not mine, but instead I am its.

62. *CRD*, vol. 1, 1st ed., p. 302; 2d ed., p. 357; *Critique of Dialectical Reason*, pp. 248–49.

63. *CRD*, vol. 1, 1st ed., p. 348; 2d ed., p. 412; *Critique of Dialectical Reason*, p. 305.

The sentence from which this important phrase is taken is treated differently in the three texts: as a subfootnote to a very long footnote in the first edition; as a separate footnote to the rest of the material, which is now treated as part of the main text, in the revised edition; and as a parenthetical sentence within a lengthy footnote in the translation. The second French edition contains, in effect, no substantive changes, but it does make a number of formal alterations of this type.

64. *CRD*, vol. 1, 1st ed., pp. 308–10; 2d ed., pp. 364–66; *Critique of Dialectical Reason*, pp. 256–58.

65. *CRD*, vol. 1, 1st ed., p. 310; 2d ed., p. 366; *Critique of Dialectical Reason*, p. 259.

66. The material in this paragraph is to be found, in a slightly altered form, in my article "Sartre and Lived Experience," *Research in Phenomenology* 11 (1981), p. 85.

67. *CRD*, vol. 1, 1st ed., pp. 317–18; 2d ed., p. 375; *Critique of Dialectical Reason*, p. 267.

68. *CRD*, vol. 1, 1st ed., pp. 344ff.; second ed., pp. 406ff.; *Critique of Dialectical Reason*, pp. 300ff.

FIVE. POLITICS AND HISTORY

1. The English translation of this key phrase is "fused group." This, as scholars have been virtually unanimous in pointing out, is a very bad rendering of *"groupe en fusion,"* since the past participle makes it sound like a *fait accompli*, whereas Sartre wished to emphasize it as an ongoing phenomenon—a becoming, not a "being." Anthony DeCorso, in his unpublished doctoral dissertion, "Jean-Paul Sartre's Fusing Group and Its Relation to Marxism" (Purdue University, 1980), proposed, and consistently uses, "fusing group."

2. "'To degrade,' here, does not, of course, bear any reference to a system of values whatsoever." *CRD*, vol. 1, 1st ed., p. 574; 2d ed., p. 678; *Critique of Dialectical Reason*, p. 591.

3. *CRD*, vol. 1, 1st ed., p. 460; 2d ed., p. 543; *Critique of Dialectical Reason*, p. 445.

4. Robert Nozick's sweeping criticism, in *Anarchy, State and Utopia* (New York: Basic Books, 1974), of "end-state" (or "end-result") principles of justice, immediately occasioned by John Rawls's theory of justice, has been seen by some as vitiating large portions of this "ideal state of affairs" element in social and political philosophy generally. But the criticism is damaging, as even Nozick himself appears to suggest (pp. 154–55), only if a fixed, frozen "end-state" is considered as epitomizing the philosophy in question (including Rawls's) in complete, artificial abstraction from all its other, diachronic features.

5. See my book, *Fundamental Change in Law and Society*, esp. pp. 180–81.

6. "[Contat:] In sum, until now, life has been good for you? [Sartre:] Overall, yes. I don't see what I could reproach it for. It has given me what I wanted, and, at the same time, it has made me realize that it wasn't a big deal. But what can you do?" "Autoportrait à soixante-dix ans," *Situations*, 10, my translation, p. 226; *Life/ Situations*, p. 92.

7. *The Words*, p. 252; *Les Mots*, p. 210.

8. *CRD*, vol. 1, 1st ed., p. 349; 2d ed., p. 413; *Critique of Dialectical Reason*, pp. 306–307.

9. *CRD*, vol. 1, 1st ed., p. 351; 2d ed., pp. 415–16; *Critique of Dialectical Reason*, p. 309.

10. *CRD*, vol. 1, 1st ed., p. 643; 2d ed., p. 760; *Critique of Dialectical Reason*, p. 678.

11. *CRD*, vol. 1, 1st ed., p. 527; 2d ed., p. 631; *Critique of Dialectical Reason*, p. 623.

12. I am thinking above all of Lukács in this context.

13. See "Of the Original Contract," in *Hume's Moral and Political Philosophy*, ed. H. Aiken (New York: Hafner, 1948), pp. 356–72.

14. An important book aimed at correcting this deficiency in contemporary

mainstream thinking about politics and society, employing insights gleaned from Sartre's *Critique*, is *The Morality of Groups* by my colleague Larry May (Notre Dame: Notre Dame University Press, 1987).

15. Rousseau, *Du Contrat Social I*, p. 243 (my translation).

16. *CRD*, vol. 1, 1st ed., p. 492; 2d ed., p. 581; *Critique of Dialectical Reason*, pp. 485–86.

17. *CRD*, vol. 1, 1st ed., p. 471; 2d ed., p. 557; *Critique of Dialectical Reason*, p. 460.

18. *CRD*, vol. 1, 1st ed., p. 453; 2d ed., p. 535; *Critique of Dialectical Reason*, p. 436.

19. On this question of meaning and translation, Joseph Catalano defends, against critics, the English translator's decision always to render *"statut"* as "statute." *A Commentary*, p. 17.

20. *CRD*, vol. 1, 1st ed., p. 439; 2d ed., p. 519; *Critique of Dialectical Reason*, p. 420.

21. This point is made well by Carole Pateman in *The Sexual Contract* (Stanford: Stanford University Press, 1988), pp. 12–13. She also mentions revivals of social contract terminology in Australia and, during the Reagan Era, in the United States.

22. I now feel that I was too harsh in my judgment in the chapter on "Law" in *Fundamental Change in Law and Society* (pp. 199–205) that Sartre had simply neglected the phenomenon of law. Moreover, the more recent publication of the *Cahiers* furnishes new evidence, not available then, of the extent to which he did reflect on it, as I have indicated in chapter 2.

23. *CRD*, vol. 1, 1st ed., pp. 457–58; 2d ed., pp. 540–41; *Critique of Dialectical Reason*, pp. 441–43.

24. *CRD*, vol. 1, 1st ed., p. 588; 2d ed., p. 695; *Critique of Dialectical Reason*, p. 610.

25. *CRD*, vol. 1, 1st ed., p. 604; 2d ed., p. 714; *Critique of Dialectical Reason*, p. 630.

26. *CRD*, vol. 1, 1st ed., p. 607; 2d ed., p. 718; *Critique of Dialectical Reason*, p. 634.

27. *CRD*, vol. 1, 1st ed., p. 609; 2d ed., p. 720; *Critique of Dialectical Reason*, p. 636.

28. Perhaps the most detailed recent Marxist analysis of the contemporary State, written from a neo-Althusserian, structuralist perspective that is closer to "orthodoxy" than Sartre's but also comes to grips with the State's quasiautonomy and integrating function, is Nicos Poulantzas's *Political Power and Social Classes*, trans. O'Hagan et al. (Atlantic Highlands: Humanities Press, 1973). See my review of this and two other volumes by Poulantzas in *Society* 14, 4 (May-June 1977), pp. 84–88.

29. He wishes to distinguish such State racist *praxis* from simpler forms of racism at the level of seriality, previously discussed.

30. *CRD*, vol. 1, 1st ed., p. 518; 2d ed., p. 613; *Critique of Dialectical Reason*, p. 520.

31. The majority of subtitles in both the second French edition and the English translation were added by the editor and translator, respectively, and in fact the index and chapter divisions of the translation are misleading in not indicating the significant transition of topics that Sartre intended here.

32. *CRD*, vol. 1, 1st ed., p. 754–55; 2d ed., pp. 893–94; *Critique of Dialectical Reason*, pp. 817–18.

33. Wilfrid Desan's *The Planetary Man*, combined vols. 1 and 2, *op. cit.*, together with vol. 3, *Let the Future Come* (Washington: Georgetown University Press, 1987), is a significant exception to this trend.

34. *Critique de la raison dialectique*, vol. 2, p. 72.

35. Ibid., p. 269.

36. Ibid., p. 282.

37. Aronson, *Sartre's Second Critique*, pp. 150–83.

38. *Critique de la raison dialectique*, vol. 2, p. 238.

39. Ibid., p. 128.

40. This segment is the only part of the *Critique*, vol. 2, to have been published in English translation thus far. It is entitled "Socialism in One Country" and was part of the one hundredth number of the *New Left Review* (Nov. 1976–Jan. 1977).

41. *Critique de la raison dialectique,* vol. 2, p. 127.
42. Ibid., p. 54.
43. *CRD,* vol. 1, 1st ed., p. 644; 2d ed., p. 762; *Critique of Dialectical Reason,* p. 679.
44. *CRD,* vol. 1, 1st ed., p. 669; 2d ed., pp. 791–92; *Critique of Dialectical Reason,* p. 711.
45. *CRD,* vol. 1, 1st ed., p. 674; 2d ed., p. 797; *Critique of Dialectical Reason,* p. 717.
46. *CRD,* vol. 1, 1st ed., p. 741; 2d ed., p. 878; *Critique of Dialectical Reason,* p. 801.
47. *Critique de la raison dialectique,* vol. 2, p. 34.
48. Ibid., p. 51.
49. Ibid., p. 199.
50. Ibid., pp. 219–20.
51. Ibid., p. 308.
52. Ibid., p. 208.
53. Ibid., p. 437.
54. Ibid., p. 450.
55. Ibid., pp. 320–26.

SIX. THE LAST TWO DECADES

1. I have chosen my wording carefully here. *Neo*colonialism, not involving claims of *direct* political control, has of course precipitated numerous wars since then, including those in Vietnam and, arguably, in Afghanistan. Moreover, Portugal, not a major Western nation, was still waging fierce rearguard colonial wars in Africa years later. Of course, one could seriously question whether France itself was still a "major" nation at the time of the Algerian conflict.

2. In Fanon, *Les Damnés de la terre* (Paris: Maspero, 1961), pp. 9–26; reprinted in Sartre, *Situations,* 5, (Paris: Gallimard, 1964), pp. 167–93; English translation of *The Wretched of the Earth* by C. Farrington (New York: Grove Press, 1965).

3. That the enforced public attitude of silence and (presumed) passive support of the government policy did not reflect actual opinion was driven home forcefully to me one evening in an English conversation course that I conducted during the 1959–60 academic year at the U.S. Consulate (long since closed) in Lille. Somehow, the topic turned to the war, even though we were all aware of potential penalties risked by French citizens in criticizing the government policy. It turned out that everyone in this small, mixed-age group of upper middle class Lillois was firmly opposed! No one, of course, would have expected a working-class group to be supportive of it.

4. In Jean Van Lierde, ed., *La Pensée politique de Patrice Lumumba* (Paris: Editions Présence africaine, 1963), pp. i–xlvi; reprinted in *Situations,* 5, pp. 194–253.

5. *Situations,* 5, p. 238.

6. It is to Professor Dismas Masolo of the University of Nairobi that I owe my full realization of the extremely limited, even if historically not unimportant, extent of Sartre's contribution to thinking about political theory from an African perspective.

7. This account is based primarily on unpublished and unverified, but presumably reasonably accurate, transcripts of small portions of the tape-recorded sessions in the safekeeping of the Istituto Gramsci, to copies of which I have graciously been given access by Robert Stone and Elizabeth Bowman.

8. Sartre, "L'Universel singulier," *Situations,* 9 (Paris: Gallimard, 1972), p. 181 (my translation, as will be the case for all subsequent citations from Sartre and from his interviewers in this chapter).

9. "L'Écrivain et sa langue," in *Situations,* 9, p. 51. Similarly, in 1970: "Today, in any case, the notions of 'subjectivity' and of 'objectivity' appear totally useless to me. It may no doubt occur to me to use the expression 'objectivity,' but only in

order to emphasize that everything is objective. The individual interiorizes his or her social determinations . . . , then he re-exteriorizes all that in acts and choices which necessarily refer us back to all that has been interiorized." "Sartre par Sartre," interview with *The New Left Review,* reprinted in *Le Nouvel Observateur,* Jan. 26, 1970, in *Situations,* 9, pp. 102–103.

10. Cited by Elizabeth Bowman and Robert Stone in their article, "Ethique dialectique: un premier regard aux notes de la conférence de Rome 1964 inédite de Sartre" in *Annales de l'Institut de Philosophie et de Sciences morales* 1987 (Brussels), *Sur les écrits posthumes de Sartre,* p. 11.

11. Sartre, "Détermination et liberté," in Contat and Rybalka, *Les Ecrits de Sartre,* p. 735; "Determination and Freedom," *The Writings of Jean-Paul Sartre,* vol. 2, p. 241.

12. See both their " 'Making the Human' in Sartre's Unpublished Dialectical Ethics" and "Dialectical Ethics: A First Look at Sartre's Unpublished 1964 Rome Lecture Notes," cited in note 19 to the introduction.

13. Bowman and Stone, "Ethique dialectique," pp. 23–27.

14. Sartre, "L'Alibi," *Situations,* 8 (Paris: Gallimard, 1972), pp. 127–45.

15. See Stone and Bowman, "Sartre's *Morality and History:* A First Look at the Notes for the Unpublished 1965 Cornell Lectures," cited in note 19 to introduction.

16. Cited in Stone and Bowman, "Sartre's *Morality and History,*" prepublication manuscript, p. 7.

17. Although Kennedy's success and subsequent practices while in office seemed to lay this issue to rest at the time, some more recent developments connected with the controversy about abortion, in particular the view of some Catholic Church authorities that even to advocate maintaining abortion rights for those who do not share the Church's belief about the impermissibility of abortion is totally unacceptable and forbidden, have raised it anew. Since official Catholic moral doctrine also treats the practice of contraception as a serious sin, the logical next step would seem to be to forbid Catholic politicians from endorsing the continued legalization of contraceptive devices, as well. Elizabeth A. Bowman's translation of this analysis, "Kennedy and the West Virginia Primary of 1960," is to appear in *Sartre Alive* (Wayne State University Press, 1990) along with the explanatory essay to which I have just been referring.

18. Ibid., prepublication manuscript of translation, p. 19.

19. Sartre, "Sartre répond," in *Situations,* 8, p. 28.

20. Sartre, "Il n'y a plus de dialogue possible," ibid., pp. 18–19.

21. Sartre, "De Nuremberg à Stockholm," ibid., pp. 94–95.

22. Ibid., p. 97.

23. Charles De Gaulle, "Réponse du Président de la République," ibid., p. 44.

24. Sartre, "Sartre à De Gaulle," ibid., p. 51.

25. An example of this is A. P. d'Entrèves, *The Notion of the State* (Oxford: Clarendon Press, 1967), esp. pp. 141–50. D'Entrèves admits to having been stimulated to reconsider this theme of "legitimacy" by De Gaulle's pronouncements thereupon.

26. Sartre, "Plaidoyer pour les intellectuels," in *Situations,* 8, p. 430.

27. "The inability to take advantage of one's rights and opportunities as a result of poverty and ignorance, and a lack of means generally, is sometimes counted among the constraints definitive of liberty. I shall not, however, say this, but rather I shall think of these things as affecting the worth of liberty, the value to individuals of the rights that the . . . principle [of liberty] defines. . . . The worth of liberty is not the same for everyone. Some have greater authority and wealth, and therefore greater means to achieve their aims." John Rawls, *A Theory of Justice* (Cambridge: Harvard University Press, 1971), p. 204.

28. Sartre, "Le Socialisme qui venait du froid," in *Situations,* 9, p. 227.

29. Ibid., p. 260.

2

38 *Notes for pages 186–200*

30. Ibid., p. 267.
31. Ibid., p. 273.
32. P. Gavi, J.-P. Sartre, and P. Victor, *On a raison de se révolter* (Paris: Gallimard, 1974), pp. 65–66.
33. Sartre, "L'Idée neuve de mai 1968," in *Situations*, 8, p. 197.
34. The contrast between indirect and direct democracy is particularly emphasized in Sartre's essay, "Elections, piège à cons," in *Situations*, 10, pp. 75–87; *Life/Situations*, pp. 198–210.
35. *Situations*, 8, p. 203.
36. Sartre et al., *On a raison de se révolter*, p. 345.
37. Ibid., p. 347.
38. Sartre, "Masses, spontanéité, parti," in *Situations*, 8, p. 272.
39. None of these changes of emphasis entailed, however, an abandonment on Sartre's part of what might be called "the Marxist problematic"—that is, the set of issues and the terminology with which we have seen him working for a number of years. This is evident, for instance, in his long televised interview of 1969, "Zan Pol Sartr," voice-over in Serbo-Croatian, with Eleonora Prohíc in Dubrovnik.
40. *On a raison de se révolter*, p. 118.
41. Ibid., p. 79.
42. Sartre, "Justice et état," in *Situations*, 10, p. 55; "Justice and the State," in *Life/Situations*, p. 179.
43. *On a raison de se révolter*, p. 252.
44. Ibid., p. 20.
45. Sartre, "Le Procès de Burgos," in *Situations*, 10, p. 35; "The Burgos Trial," in *Life/Situations*, p. 160. (The English translation here is very inexact.)
46. *L'Idiot de la famille*, vol. 1, p. 8; *The Family Idiot*, vol. 1, p. ix.
47. "Sartre par Sartre," in *Situations*, 9, pp. 115–16.
48. *L'Idiot de la famille*, vol. 1, p. 328; *The Family Idiot*, vol. 1, p. 317.
49. Sartre, *L'Idiot de la famille*, vol. 3, 2d ed. (Paris: Gallimard, 1988), p. 210; 1st ed. (Paris: Gallimard, 1972), p. 212.
50. *L'Idiot de la famille*, vol. 1, pp. 811ff.; *The Family Idiot*, vol. 2, trans. C. Cosman (Chicago: University of Chicago Press, 1987), pp. 155ff. (It should be remembered that the volumes of the English translation, which is still in process, will not correspond exactly to the three volumes of the French original.)
51. See, for example, Hazel Barnes, *Sartre & Flaubert* (Chicago: University of Chicago Press, 1981), pp. 109–16, and Peter Caws, *Sartre* (London: Routledge and Kegan Paul, 1979), p. 195.
52. Sartre, *L'Idiot de la famille*, vol. 2 (Paris: Gallimard, 1971), p. 1149. (As I have noted in the text, the pagination between the first and second French volumes, though not between the second and third, is consecutive.)
53. Ibid., p. 1459.
54. Barnes, *Sartre & Flaubert*, p. 426.
55. This is a central theme of the excellent recent study by Linda Bell, *Sartre's Ethics of Authenticity* (Tuscaloosa: University of Alabama Press, 1989).
56. *L'Idiot de la famille*, vol. 1, p. 975; *The Family Idiot*, vol. 2, p. 312.
57. *L'Idiot de la famille*, vol. 3, 2d ed., p. 43; 1st ed., p. 44.
58. *L'Idiot de la famille*, vol. 3, 2d ed., p. 153; 1st ed., p. 155.
59. *L'Idiot de la famille*, vol. 3, 2d ed., p. 423; 1st ed., p. 426.
60. "Sartre par Sartre," *Situations*, 9, p. 114.
61. *L'Idiot de la famille*, vol. 2, p. 1121.
62. I question this claim, suggesting that every age has its illusions that could be called "neurotic" and that Sartre is overly confident about the possibility of rigorously distinguishing healthy from neurotic behavior, in my article, "Method and Madness in *The Family Idiot*," in D. Ihde and H. J. Silverman, eds., *Descriptions* (Albany: State University of New York Press, 1985), pp. 156–58.

63. *L'Idiot de la famille*, vol. 1, pp. 116–17; *The Family Idiot*, vol. 1, pp. 108–109. The translator's inaccurate rendering of Sartre's paraphrase of Descartes as "Good sense is the best thing shared" (p. 108) does not inspire confidence.

64. *L'Idiot de la famille*, vol. 2, p. 1350.

65. *L'Idiot de la famille*, vol. 3, 2d ed., p. 433; 1st ed., p. 436.

66. *On a raison de se révolter*, p. 73.

67. *L'Idiot de la famille*, vol. 3, 2d ed., p. 769.

68. *L'Idiot de la famille*, vol. 3, 2d ed., p. 187; 1st ed., p. 189.

69. "Sartre par Sartre", *Situations*, 9, pp. 101–102. This segment of the interview is also to be found, in translation, in R. Solomon, ed., *Phenomenology and Existentialism* (New York: Harper & Row, 1972), p. 513.

70. *Le Nouvel Observateur*, March 10, 1980, p. 92; *Dissent*, Fall 1980, p. 399.

71. *Le Nouvel Observateur*, March 10, 1980, p. 26.

72. *Le Nouvel Observateur*, Mar. 24, 1980, p. 115; *Dissent*, p. 417. (A sentence about his reservations is omitted in this translation.)

73. *Le Nouvel Observateur*, Mar. 17, 1980, p. 119; *Dissent*, p. 410.

74. A marvelous antidote for ageist tendencies is, precisely, Simone de Beauvoir's work, *La Vieillesse* (Paris: Gallimard, 1970); *The Coming of Age*, trans. by P. O'Brian (New York: Warner Library, 1973).

75. *On a raison de se révolter*, p. 374.

76. *Le Nouvel Observateur*, Mar. 24, 1980, p. 139; *Dissent*, p. 422.

77. A serious recent philosophical treatment of hope is Bernard Dauenhauer's *The Politics of Hope* (New York: Routledge and Kegan Paul, 1986). Dauenhauer takes Sartre's "last words" to be grist for his mill. But Joseph Walsh expresses some useful reservations concerning both Dauenhauer's specific uses of Sartre and his general approach to grounding hope in fundamental human relatedness in his review of the book in *Man and World* 21, 3 (July 1988), pp. 357–60.

78. Sartre, "Elections, piège á cons," in *Situations*, 10, pp. 75–87; *Life/Situations*, pp. 198–210.

79. *Le Nouvel Observateur*, Mar. 10, 1980, p. 94; *Dissent*, p. 402.

80. *Le Nouvel Observateur*, Mar. 17, 1980, p. 130; *Dissent*, p. 415.

81. *Le Nouvel Observateur*, Mar. 17, 1980, p. 121; *Dissent*, p. 411.

82. Michel Sicard/Jean-Paul Sartre, interview, p. 15. His additional remark, cited earlier in chapter 3 of this book, that this new philosophical treatise "will be obliged to leave nothing standing from *Being and Nothingness* and from *Critique of Dialectical Reason*" can only be dismissed as unfortunate "hype," gross exaggeration, if only because being "incomplete" is not identical to being worthless. Moreover, other parts of this very interview, to say nothing of the probably more significant later dialogue with Lévy, assume many continuities with earlier works, particularly the *Critique*.

83. Michel Sicard/Jean-Paul Sartre, interview, p. 15.

84. *Le Nouvel Observateur*, Mar. 17, 1980, pp. 121, 124, and 127; *Dissent*, pp. 411–12.

85. *Le Nouvel Observateur*, Mar. 17, 1980, p. 127; *Dissent*, p. 413.

86. Ibid.

87. *Le Nouvel Observateur*, Mar. 10, 1980, p. 101; *Dissent*, p. 404–405.

88. *Le Nouvel Observateur*, Mar. 10, 1980, p. 93; *Dissent*, p. 400.

89. I argue for this in "The Case of Sartre", *Social Research* 56, 4 (Winter 1989), on pp. 862–68.

Index

Action. See *Praxis*
Adieux, 7
Adversity, coefficient of, 198, 200
Aesthetics, 65
L'Affaire Henri Martin, 86, 91, 94, 99. See also Martin, Henri
The Age of Reason, 28, 33
Algerian War of Independence. See War: Algerian
"The Alibi," 180, 202
Alienation, 83, 123, 200; in capitalism, 144, 189–90; and duty, 62; and history, 80; and Marxism, 63, 77, 130, 233n47; and oppression, 71; origin of, 122; Soviet, 189; and the state, 69; and the team, 151
Althusser, Louis, 103, 174, 192
Analysis, spirit of, 46, 50–51, 52
Anarchism, 10, 21, 32, 66, 157
Anguish, 1, 48, 215n10
Anthropology, 4, 111, 158
Anti-Communism, 86, 90–91, 93
Anti-Semite and Jew, 44, 45–51, 52, 57, 140
Anti-Semitism, 46–47, 49, 50–51, 155, 220n14
Apocalypse, 80, 83, 191, 226n121; and group in fusion, 142, 143, 174
Appropriation, 34, 36, 38–39, 64
Aristocracy, 66
Aristotle, 12, 121, 143, 207, 208; and class struggle, 164; and ethics, 5, 83; and *exis*, 73; and freedom, 150
Aron, Raymond, 9, 39, 51, 172
Aronson, Ronald, 10, 161
Arrogance, 217n49
Art, 31, 51, 58, 64–65
Assimilation, 46–47
Association, 146–52
Atom bomb, 12, 75, 77
Atomism, 144, 146
Authenticity, 6, 18, 63–64, 218n49; and Heidegger, 27; and Jews, 49–50; and love, 222n55
Authority, 153–57. See also Sovereignty
Autonomy, 23, 179
Axiology, 176, 177, 178, 180

Bad faith, 3, 6, 41, 43, 149
Baptism, 149–50
Barnes, Hazel, 41, 197
Bastille, 112, 141–42
Beauvoir, Simone de, 18, 24, 176, 193–94; and *Adieux*, 7; and "L'Espoir maintenant" (Hope, now), 1–2, 202; and ethics, 45, 83, 212n19; letters to, 3, 27, 28–29; on seriousness, 33; and *Les Temps Modernes*, 151;

and violence, 19; *An Ethics of Ambiguity*, 4, 33, 207; *The Prime of Life*, 25–26; *The Second Sex*, 48, 73, 221n29
Being, 37, 124, 125, 129, 232n24. See also Being-in-itself; For-itself
Being and Nothingness, 3, 6, 12, 28, 29, 62, 87; and alienation, 77; and appropriation, 38–39; and authenticity, 49–50, 63–64; and being-for-others, 10, 207, 208; and conflict, 19, 20, 207; and creation, 64–65; and ethics, 32, 33, 60, 63; and facticity, 170; and freedom, 18, 53, 108; and historicity, 39–42; and "in situation," 50; and Marx, 129; on need, 128; as ontology, 4, 124; political theory in, 36–37, 43–44; and property, 34, 35; and radical conversion, 81; and the subject, 177; value in, 135, 136
Being-for-another, 10, 65, 207, 208
Being-in-itself, 38, 39, 172. See also In-itself
Being-in-the-world, 29, 35, 217n36
Being-with (*Mitsein*), 42, 64, 65–66
Bergson, Henri, 23
Bodin, Jean, 224n88
Bomb. See Atom bomb
Boschetti, Anna, 213n23
Bost, Jacques, 25
Bourgeoisie, 79, 134; African, 175; hatred of, 93; humanism of, 166; and law, 183; and oppression, 42; and seriousness, 33, 43; spirit of, 51; and the writer, 57–58
Boxing, 123, 160, 163–68
Braudel, Fernand, 133
Brezhnev, Leonid, 173
Bureaucracy, 28–29, 145
Burnham, James, 99

Cahiers pour une morale, 45, 60–63; and apocalypse, 142; and authenticity, 6, 49–50, 63–64; and class struggle, 78–79; and conversion, 40, 81–82, 98; and creativity, 64–65; and ethics, 44, 177; and generosity, 39; and history, 3, 79–80, 80–83; and Marxism, 74–78; and oppression, 71–74; and progress, 80–81; and right, 66–69; and socialism, 74; and violence, 66–69
Camus, Albert, 12, 51, 91; death of, 113; and history, 101, 104–105, 170; *The Rebel*, 87, 222n39
Capitalism, 28, 107, 134; and alienation, 130, 189–90; French, 100
Les Carnets de la drôle de guerre, Novembre 1939–Mars 1940, 27–28; and appropriation, 38–39; and ethics, 31, 32; and property, 34–36; and seriousness, 33

240

WILLIAM L. MCBRIDE is Professor of Philosophy at Purdue University. His publications include *Fundamental Change in Law and Society: Hart and Sartre on Revolution*, *The Philosophy of Marx*, and *Social Theory at a Crossroads*. He was cofounder and first Executive Committee Chairperson of the Sartre Society of North America.